AMERICAN WRITERS
Classics

VOLUME II

ISSN 1541-4507

AMERICAN WRITERS
Classics

VOLUME II

EDITED BY JAY PARINI

CHARLES SCRIBNER'S SONS®

THOMSON
GALE™

New York • Detroit • San Diego • San Francisco • Cleveland • New Haven, Conn. • Waterville, Maine • London • Munich

THOMSON
GALE

American Writers Classics, Volume II

Jay Parini, Editor in Chief

For more information, contact
Charles Scribner's Sons
An imprint of The Gale Group
300 Park Avenue South, 9th Floor
New York, NY 10010
Or you can visit our Internet site at
http://www.gale.com

ISBN 0-684-31268-9 (volume 2)
ISSN 1541-4507

Printed in the United States of America
10 9 8 7 6 5 4 3 2 1

List of Subjects

Introduction

It was Ralph Waldo Emerson who warned that "The path you must take, none but you must know. The critic can never tell you." What Emerson meant, perhaps, was that critics can only suggest a direction for reading, but that the actual work of reading involves the fierce application of the reader's mind to the text at hand. That application will, in each case, be highly individual. A critic's take on a book is just that: a single take, although one backed up by careful analysis, study, and reflection.

This is the second volume in a series that should prove immensely useful to students of literature who wish to benefit from the careful reflection on a single text by someone who has thought long and hard about that text. The series itself represents a further development of *American Writers,* which had its origin in a sequence of monographs called *The Minnesota Pamphlets on American Writers.* These biographical and critical monographs were incisively written and informative, treating ninety-seven American writers in a format and style that attracted a devoted following. It proved invaluable to a generation of students and teachers, who could depend on the reliable and interesting critiques of major figures that were offered in those pages.

The idea of reprinting the Minnesota pamphlets occurred to Charles Scribner Jr. Soon four volumes entitled *American Writers: A Collection of Literary Biographies* (1974) appeared, and it was widely acclaimed by students, teachers, and librarians. The series continues, with volumes added yearly as supplements and retrospectives. The articles in these collections all consider the whole career of an important writer, supplying biographical and cultural context as well as taking careful look at the shape of the individual achievement.

This new series provides substantial articles that focus on a single masterwork of American literature, whether it be a novel, a volume of stories, a play, a long poem or sequence of poems, or a major work of autobiography or nonfiction. The idea behind the series is simple: to provide close readings of landmark works. These readings, written by well-known authors and professors of literature, in each case examine the text itself, explaining its internal dynamics, and consider the cultural, biographical, and historical dimensions of the work, thus placing it within a tradition—or several traditions. Some effort is made to place the work within the author's overall career, though the main focus in each essay will be the text at hand.

In the past twenty-five years or so, since the advent of post-structuralism, the emphasis in most critical writing has been largely theoretical. What was called "close reading" during the days of the so-called New Criticism—a movement that had its origins in formalist criticism of the 1920s and 1930s, and which reigned supreme in university English departments for several decades—was often immensely useful to students and teachers, who wanted careful and detailed analyses of individual texts. Every effort has been made in these articles to provide useful and patient readings of important works without sacrificing theoretical sophistication.

This second volume of *American Classics* is largely concerned with novels. We take up a fair number of novels that must be considered central to the American tradition of literary fiction. The novels discussed are *All the King's Men, An American Tragedy, The Big Sleep, Ethan Frome, The Great Gatsby, Herzog, Invisible Man, McTeague, The Member of the Wedding, Mona in the Promised Land, The Naked and the Dead, Sophie's Choice, Tender Is the Night,* and *White Noise.* We also consider *Winesburg, Ohio* and *The Country of the Pointed Firs,* which are ingeniously integrated collections of short fiction. Each of these must be considered a touchstone of American fiction. As anyone will see, the range of works discussed is broad, though each text can lay claim to cultural significance. Each of these books has also managed to attract a wide audience—another factor in their inclusion here.

Two other classic texts under discussion here are Robert Lowell's influential book of poems, *Life Studies*—a key text in the Confessional School of poets—and the bizarre, unlikely *The Autobiography of Alice B. Toklas* by Gertrude Stein, a book that defies categorization but remains a landmark volume in American literature, and one that seems always to attract a new generation of serious readers.

Our hope is that these essays will encourage readers to return to the texts, thoughtfully, better informed than they were before. As Emerson noted, only the reader can forge a path, an individual way through a text, into knowledge and experience. But these essays provide a starting point, an encouragement to further consultation and reading. That is, after all, one of the traditional functions of criticism. My own sense is that we have achieved a good deal in this volume, and that readers will go away pleased and edified, encouraged along their own distinct paths.

—JAY PARINI

1946	*All the King's Men.* Wins Pulitzer Prize and National Book Award.
1948	Stage version of *All the King's Men* at President Theater in New York.
1949	Movie version of *All the King's Men* wins three Academy Awards.
1950	Leaves University of Minnesota to become professor of playwrighting at Yale. *World Enough and Time.*
1951	Divorces Emma Brescia Warren.
1952	Marries Eleanor Clark.
1953	Publishes book-length poem, *Brother to Dragons.* Daughter, Rosanna Phelps Warren, born.
1955	*Band of Angels.* Son, Gabriel Penn Warren, born.
1956	*Segregation: The Inner Conflict in the South.* Leaves Yale.
1957	*Promises: Poems 1954–1956.* Wins both the National Book Award and the Pulitzer Prize.
1958	*Selected Essays.*
1959	*The Cave.* Elected to the American Academy of Arts and Letters.
1960	*You, Emperors, and Others: Poems 1957–1960* and *All the King's Men: A Play.*
1961	Publishes seventh novel, *Wilderness: A Tale of the Civil War,* and *The Legacy of the Civil War.* Returns to Yale as professor of English.
1964	*Flood: A Romance of Our Time.*
1965	*Who Speaks for the Negro?*
1966	*Selected Poems: New and Old 1923–1966,* which wins Bollingen Prize the following year.
1968	*Incarnations: Poems 1966–1968.*
1969	Publishes short book-length poem, *Audubon: A Vision.*
1970	Receives National Medal in Literature.
1971	*Meet Me in the Green Glen.*
1973	Retires from Yale.
1974	*Or Else—Poem / Poems 1968–1974.*
1975	Delivers prestigious Jefferson Lecture ("Democracy and Poetry").
1976	*Selected Poems: 1923–1975.*
1977	Publishes tenth and final novel, *A Place to Come To.*
1978	*Now and Then: Poems 1976–1978.* Wins third Pulitzer Prize.
1979	*Brother to Dragons: A New Version.*
1980	*Being Here: Poetry 1977–1980.* Awarded Presidential Medal of Freedom.
1981	*Rumor Verified: Poems 1979–1980.* Receives fellowship from the MacArthur Foundation. Carlisle Floyd's opera *Willie Stark* premieres.
1983	Publishes book-length poem *Chief Joseph of the Nez Perce.*
1985	*New and Selected Poems: 1923–1985.*
1986	Selected America's first Poet Laureate.
1989	Dies of cancer on September 15.

informally on alternate Saturday nights to socialize and discuss philosophy. When Ransom began writing verse, he steered the bimonthly discussions to poetry. Soon members of the group started bringing their poems in progress for criticism and analysis. After a brief hiatus for the war, the meetings resumed in 1920. Older members, such as Ransom and Davidson, were joined by talented newcomers, such as Tate. Warren joined the group in 1923, the year it decided to publish *The Fugitive: A Magazine of Poetry.* Warren won a contest sponsored by the magazine late that year and was listed as one of the editors of the *Fugitive* by February 1924.

Although the magazine stopped publication in 1925 (the year of his graduation), Warren maintained close contact with his fellow Fugitives, even as he pursued graduate work at the University of California. After finishing his M.A., Warren entered the Ph.D. program at Yale in the fall of 1927. The following year, he won a Rhodes Scholarship and began a two-year program of study at Oxford University, which led to a B.Litt. degree in 1930. (In 1929 he was joined by poet Cleanth Brooks, whom he had known as an undergraduate at Vanderbilt.) It was while he was at Oxford that Warren became imaginatively engaged with the culture of the

American South. He published his first book, *John Brown: The Making of a Martyr,* in 1929, even as he and several former Fugitives were joining with other like-minded southerners in planning a symposium on the future of their home region. That symposium was published in November 1930 under the title *I'll Take My Stand: The South and the Agrarian Tradition.*

When Warren returned to the United States in 1930, he began living with Emma Brescia, to whom he was already secretly married. Having to decide whether to pursue a safe career as a scholar or to take his chances with fiction and poetry, Warren turned down a fellowship to resume doctoral studies at Yale and accepted a one-year position teaching English at Southwestern College in Memphis. The following year, he assumed a temporary assistant professorship at Vanderbilt. When the department's autocratic and myopic chairman, Edwin Mims, refused to renew his contract at the end of the 1933–1934 school year, Warren was rescued by Charles W. Pipkin, Dean of the Graduate School at Louisiana State University. Pipkin had already found Cleanth Brooks a position in the English department in 1932 and was more than eager to bring Warren in to join him.

Although Huey Long probably never heard the names of Cleanth Brooks and Robert Penn Warren, the Kingfish created an unorthodox free-spending atmosphere on campus that made it possible for a maverick administrator such as Pipkin to hire almost at will. By the spring of 1935, Brooks, Warren, and Pipkin were launching a literary quarterly called the *Southern Review.* Then, on Labor Day weekend, Huey Long was shot in the Louisiana capitol and died three days later in the hospital. Witnesses at the capitol reported that Long was gunned down by a physician, Dr. Carl Weiss, who belonged to a rival political family and who was then shot numerous times by Long's bodyguards.

Robert Penn Warren never knew Huey Long, but he knew what it was like to live in a world that Long had created. Years later, he recalled that the only time Long's

> presence was ever felt in my classroom was when, in my Shakespeare course, I gave my little annual lecture on the political background of *Julius Caesar;* and then for the two weeks we spent on the play, backs grew straighter, eyes grew brighter, notes were taken, and the girls stopped knitting in class, or repairing their faces.

Warren needed the distance of Oxford to start writing about the South, and he apparently needed to be removed in both time and place from Long's Louisiana to write *All the King's Men.* Although he wrote an earlier dramatic version of this story (the play *Proud Flesh*) in Mussolini's Italy in 1939–1940, Warren did not begin the novel itself until a year after he left Louisiana and did not finish it until 1946, nine years after Long's death. During that period, Warren published two other novels, two volumes of poetry, and two textbooks while teaching for four years at the University of Minnesota.

INTRODUCTION TO THE NOVEL

All the King's Men begins in medias res, as Governor Willie Stark's Cadillac is speeding down the road in an unnamed southern state. Readers are introduced to the governor; his fawning bodyguard, Sugar-Boy; his loyal secretary, Sadie Burke; his feckless lieutenant governor, Tiny Duffy; his long-suffering wife, Lucy; and the narrator, Jack Burden. Jack is a kind of southern-fried Philip Marlow, a tough-talking aide to Governor Stark who specializes in digging up dirt on Stark's political adversaries. After mesmerizing a crowd of supporters in his backwoods hometown of Mason City, Stark goes to Jack's aristocratic hometown of Burden's Landing to visit Judge Irwin, Jack's childhood mentor, who has just thrown his considerable political support to Stark's enemies. After he is instructed to dig up some dirt on Irwin, Jack gives readers a flashback to Stark's beginnings in politics and Jack's own rather aimless past.

Jack was raised the son of a scholarly attorney named Ellis Burden and the beautiful young wife Ellis had brought back to Burden's Landing with him from a trip to Arkansas. When Jack was a child, Ellis Burden inexplicably walked out on the family, only to end up as a kind of freelance missionary in the urban slums. Jack's best childhood friends were Adam and Anne Stanton, whose father was a former bourbon governor. Adam Stanton eventually becomes a successful physician with no personal life. After a failed romance with Jack, Anne Stanton drifts into spinsterhood devoted to good deeds. Meanwhile, Jack drops out of graduate school without ever finishing the dissertation for his Ph.D. in history and suffers through a bad marriage to a shallow hedonist. While working as a newspaper reporter, he meets Willie Stark, the idealistic young treasurer of Mason County. When he is played for a fool by a faction of professional politicians, Stark wises up and beats the old pols at their own game. After winning a landslide election for governor, he summons Jack to his staff. Having nothing better to do with his life, Jack decides to indulge his fascination with the phenomenon that is Willie Stark.

The choice of Jack Burden as narrator enables Warren to depict a politician obviously based on Huey Long without having to become the character. Although its roots go back at least to the nineteenth century, this narrative technique was used with increasing frequency after the dawn of modernism. Jack is what critics Robert Scholes and Robert Kellogg call the "typical Conradian" narrator, a compromise between third-person-omniscient and first-person-protagonist narration. Such a narrator—Joseph Conrad's Marlow, F. Scott Fitzgerald's Nick Carraway, Herman Melville's Ishmael—is an eyewitness who tells another person's story.

Contending that "this has been a very fruitful device in modern fiction," Scholes and Kellogg note that "the story of the protagonist becomes the outward sign or symbol of the inward story of the narrator, who learns from his imaginative participation in the other's experience." What this leads to is the sort of metafiction in which "the factual or empirical aspect of the protagonist's life becomes subordinated to the narrator's understanding of it." Thus, "not what really happened but the meaning of what the narrator believes to have happened becomes the central preoccupation." By dividing the narrator from his protagonist, the author obviates the "problem of presenting a character with enough crudeness of *hybris* and *hamartia* but enough sensitivity for ultimate discovery and self-understanding." If Willie Stark is Huey Long, Jack Burden is Robert Penn Warren imagining Huey Long.

Unfortunately, the initial reviewers of *All the King's Men* were so mesmerized by Stark's similarity to the Kingfish that this similarity was all they wanted to talk about. They failed to realize that Warren's relationship to history, even current history, was not as a political partisan. In the foreword to his book-length poem *Brother to Dragons* (1953), Warren writes, "Historical sense and poetic sense should not, in the end, be contradictory, for if poetry is the little myth we make, history is the big myth we live, and in our living, constantly remake." As a champion of agrarianism, Warren would have been philosophically more comfortable with the Tory benevolence of a Judge Irwin than with the acquisitive populism of a Willie Stark or Huey Long. But like Jack Burden and Anne Stanton, he is also fascinated by the myth of the strong leader. If Stark's assassin finally resembles Brutus striking down Julius Caesar, Warren's surrogate Jack Burden is more akin to Hamlet contemplating the vitality of Fortinbras. The problem is that Fortinbras is always stealing the show.

A year after the publication of *All the King's Men,* Robert B. Heilman wrote a scathing rebuke of those readers who could not see beyond the superficial topicality of the novel. Generally speaking, reviewers for national magazines and large circulation newspapers are liberal intellectuals, people who would instinctively regard Huey Long as the incarnation of evil. Long may have seemed a plausible savior in the 1930s, but a nation that had just defeated Hitler and Mussolini and now faced a protracted conflict with Stalin could not afford to romanticize a domestic strong man. The only way that Warren could be allowed to write about a character like Huey Long was to make him the villain of a cautionary parable about the threat of demagoguery to American democratic institutions. When he failed to do so, Robert Gorham Davis wrote a breathtakingly fatuous critique in the *New York Times Book Review,* accusing Warren of being a flak for the Kingfish simply because he taught at Louisiana State University and edited the *Southern Review.*

Davis and like-minded reviewers would have been pleased with the 1949 film version of *All the King's Men,* which turned out to be the politically correct melodrama that Warren had refused to write. No longer a complex and ambiguous figure, Willie Stark simply becomes another idealist corrupted by power. (In this regard, it is essentially the same story that the film industry would produce two years later in *Viva Zapata!*) Also, by depriving the audience of Jack Burden's brooding narration, the movie limits the audience's perspective on Stark; he is seen only for what he does and what other people say about him. Unsophisticated readers who do not confuse Willie Stark with Huey Long might well mistake him for Broderick Crawford, the actor who played him in the movie.

Perhaps because the film version of *All the King's Men* was made before negative images of the Deep South became a cliché of American popular culture, director Robert Rossen does not depict Stark as a stereotypical southern demagogue. Instead, the tale is removed from its southern setting to a small town in California. Almost all the characters speak a bland middle-American dialect. (The only obviously ethnic character is Stark's Irish-American secretary, Sadie Burke.) Moreover, the story is told in a strict chronological order, thus focusing attention on Stark's rise, corruption, and fall. But moviegoers (Warren included) finally accepted this vulgarization of *All the King's Men* for its sheer melodramatic power.

Because of his ability to appropriate the genres of popular literature for high thematic purposes, Warren could simultaneously appeal to literary intellectuals and a mass audience. Strip away the intellectual trappings, and there remains a story capable of entertaining anyone. Such crossover appeal has become exceedingly rare since the rise of modernism. The kind of baroque excess that was Warren's stock in trade reminds one more of opera than of the well made literary artifact. It is therefore not surprising that, in 1981, one of America's foremost composers, Carlisle Floyd, turned *All the King's Men* into a highly successful opera.

After the more commercial reviewers and the Hollywood dream merchants had their say, academic scholars and critics minimized the importance of Willie Stark in order to focus on the tortured psyche of Jack Burden. If anything, they learned their lesson too well. Almost all of Warren's novels feature a character like Jack Burden, but Willie Stark is one of a kind. Huey Long was a kind of "found metaphor" who embodied the clash between idealism and pragmatism. If the fictional Stark is less brutal and crude than the real-life Long, it is because Warren wanted to focus on that clash, not because he wanted to whitewash Long. In the opinion of Joyce Carol Oates, however, Warren's theme would actually have been enriched by greater fidelity to the historical record. "Set beside Huey Long," Oates writes, "Warren's Willie Stark, while far more than a caricature, is a generic creation manipulated by the author in the service of a plot that becomes anticlimactic after his death." The real Long was killed because of his slanders against members of his assassin's family. Stark is gunned down for an improbable romantic affair, which had no basis in Long's own life.

The most significant scholarly debate in Warren studies during the early years of the new dog and the calico cat, had eaten each other up. It is at this point that Jack Burden steps out of his role as peripheral narrator and takes center stage. Through his involvement in the deaths of his father and his two best friends he finally comes to know himself and to accept his complicity in a world that is all too real. Having experienced the psychological equivalent of a religious conversion, he assumes responsibility for the care of his first father figure, the saintly ascetic Warren calls the "Scholarly Attorney."

The old man, who spends much of his time writing and distributing religious tracts, dictates the following to Jack:

> The creation of man whom God in His foreknowledge knew doomed to sin was the awful index of God's omnipotence. For it would have been a thing of trifling and contemptible ease for Perfection to create mere perfection. To do so would, to speak truth, be not creation but extension. Separateness is identity and the only way for God to create, truly create, man was to make him separate from God Himself, and to be separate from God is to be sinful. The creation of evil is therefore the index of God's glory and His power. That had to be so that the creation of good might be the index of man's glory and power. But by God's help. By His help and in His wisdom.

Taken as pure theology, this statement is no doubt heretical. Man's separateness from God is a function of the Fall, not of the Creation. And, Willie Stark notwithstanding, man is singularly incapable of *creating* good. Nevertheless, the existence of evil—precisely because it necessitates so great a redemption—may well be the index of God's glory and power.

Those readers who find Judge Irwin to be a more appealing character than Ellis Burden should remember that, by the end of the novel, Jack tries to reject the judge's patrimony (land and money) and is on the verge of accepting what Ellis Burden offers him (moral insight). Of course, in his willingness to enter the "convulsion of the world" rather than retreat from it as Ellis Burden has done, Jack proves to be his own man. (It would seem that, in acknowledging the necessity of evil as part of the pattern of salvation, Ellis Burden has moved beyond his earlier pathological refusal to "touch the world of foulness again.") Nevertheless, Jack is finally more the son of his foster father than of his real one. The fact that he can understand the story of Cass Mastern (who is Ellis Burden's ancestor) is a strong indication that Jack knows more of Heaven and Earth than is dreamt of in Judge Irwin's philosophy.

James Ruoff has noted that "the conclusion to *All the King's Men* is reminiscent of the ending of another great tragedy as Jack Burden and Anne Stanton, like Adam and Eve departing from the Garden after the Fall, prepare to leave Burden's Landing forever." Although Jack and Anne are not fortified by the vision of the Second Coming that the Archangel Michael vouchsafed to Adam in Milton's *Paradise Lost,* Warren still seems to find the possibility of happiness to be grounded in eternal verities. And, if his statement of those verities is neither as specific nor as orthodox as some might like, the message is clear enough—beyond the stink of the didie and the stench of the shroud, it is possible to find a sort of redemption.

Select Bibliography

EDITIONS

All the King's Men. New York: Harcourt, Brace, 1946. (The first edition of Warren's classic novel. All quotations taken from this text.)

All the King's Men. New York: Modern Library, 1953. (Warren's introduction discusses the influence of William James, Machiavelli, and others on *All the King's Men.*)

All the King's Men. (Established by Noel Polk from Robert Penn Warren's typescripts at the Beinecke Library at Yale University.) New York: Harcourt, 2001. (An alternative, restored edition of *All the King's Men* based on an analysis of Warren's typescript.)

OTHER WORKS BY WARREN

"Knowledge and the Image of Man." *Sewanee Review* 62 (spring 1955): 182–192. (A philosophical meditation that serves as a gloss for *All the King's Men* and other imaginative works by Warren.)

"*All the King's Men* and the Matrix of Experience." *Yale Review* 53 (winter 1964): 161–167. (Warren's account of the process of writing *All the King's Men.*)

Foreword to *Brother to Dragons: A New Version.* New York: Random House, 1979. (Contains valuable insights into Warren's views regarding the historical imagination.)

SECONDARY WORKS

All the King's Men: A Symposium. Carnegie Series in English, no. 3. Pittsburgh: Carnegie Press, 1957.

Baumbach, Jonathan. "The Metaphysics of Demagoguery." In his *The Landscape of Nightmare: Studies in the Contemporary American Novel.* New York: New York University Press, 1965. Pp. 16–34. (Focuses on *All the King's Men* as primarily the story of Jack Burden's spiritual journey.)

Beebe, Maurice, and Leslie A. Field, eds. *Robert Penn Warren's* All the King's Men: *A Critical Handbook.* Belmont, Calif.: Wadsworth, 1966.

Blotner, Joseph. *Robert Penn Warren: A Biography.* New York: Random House, 1997. (The definitive biography of Warren, thoroughly researched and lucidly written.)

Bohner, Charles. *Robert Penn Warren.* Rev. ed. Boston: Twayne, 1981. (An excellent general introduction to Warren's work through 1980. Devotes fifteen pages to *All the King's Men.*)

Carter, Everett. "The 'Little Myth' of Robert Penn Warren." *Modern Fiction Studies* 6 (spring 1960): 3–12. (Argues that Warren sees Americans as "neither exclusively a band of angels or brothers to dragons.")

Casper, Leonard W. *Robert Penn Warren: The Dark and Bloody Ground.* Seattle: University of Washington Press, 1960. (The first book-length study of Warren. Contains only scattered references to *All the King's Men.*)

Chambers, Robert H., ed. *Twentieth-Century Interpretations of* All the King's Men. Englewood Cliffs, N.J.: Prentice-Hall, 1977.

Clark, William Bedford. *The American Vision of Robert Penn Warren.* Lexington: University Press of Kentucky, 1991.

———, ed. *Critical Essays on Robert Penn Warren.* Boston: G. K. Hall, 1981.

Davis, Joe. "Robert Penn Warren and the Journey to the West." *Modern Fiction Studies* 6 (spring 1960): 73–82. (Discusses the significance of the journey west in several of Warren's major narratives, both fictional and poetic.)

Fiedler, Leslie A. "Robert Penn Warren: A Final Word." *South Carolina Review* 23 (fall 1990): 9–16. (A meditation on Warren's ability to appeal to both sophisticated and popular audiences.)

Guttenburg, Barnett. *Web of Being: The Novels of Robert Penn Warren.* Nashville, Tenn.: Vanderbilt University Press, 1975. (Treats Warren as a philosophical novelist. Discusses *All the King's Men* in light of Coleridge and Heidegger.)

Justus, James H. *The Achievement of Robert Penn Warren.* Baton Rouge: Louisiana State University Press, 1981. (The best single book on the greater body of Warren's work.)

———. "Burden's Willie." *South Carolina Review* 23 (fall 1990): 29–35. (A consideration of the theme of fathers and sons in *All the King's Men.*)

Light, James F., ed. *The Merrill Studies in* All the King's Men. Columbus, Ohio: Charles E. Merrill, 1971.

Meckier, Jerome. "Burden's Complaint: The Disintegrated Personality as Theme and Style in Robert Penn Warren's *All the King's Men.*" *Studies in the Novel* 2 (spring 1970): 7–21. (An analysis of Jack Burden as divided personality.)

Oates, Joyce Carol. "'All the King's Men'—A Case of Misreading?" *New York Review of Books,* March 28, 2002, pp. 43–47. (A long, mostly negative, evaluation of *All the King's Men* occasioned by the publication of Noel Polk's "restored edition" of the novel.)

O'Connor, Flannery. "Introduction to *A Memoir of Mary Ann.*" In her *Mystery and Manners: Occasional Prose.* Selected and edited by Sally and Robert Fitzgerald. New York: Farrar, Straus and Giroux, 1962. Pp. 213–228. (This essay about a young girl who died of cancer includes a discussion of Hawthorne's Aylmer—a possible precursor to Warren's Adam Stanton.)

Rubin, Louis D., Jr. "Burden's Landing: *All the King's Men* and the Modern South." In his *The Faraway Country: Writers of the Modern South.* Seattle: University of Washington Press, 1963. Pp. 105–130. (Considers *All the King's Men* in terms of the social structure of the modern South.)

Runyon, Randolph Paul. *The Taciturn Text: The Fiction of Robert Penn Warren.* Columbus: Ohio State University Press, 1990. (A Freudian interpretation of Warren's fiction. Discusses the importance of winks and other gestures in *All the King's Men.*)

Ruoff, James. "Humpty Dumpty and *All the King's Men: A Note on Robert Penn Warren's Teleology.*" *Twentieth Century Literature* 3 (October 1957): 128–134. (A seminal analysis of the theological implications of *All the King's Men.*)

Scholes, Robert, and Robert Kellogg. *The Nature of Narrative.* New York: Oxford University Press, 1966. (A theoretical discussion of narrative techniques in fiction. Comments on the "Conradian" narrator are particularly relevant to *All the King's Men.*)

Snipes, Katherine. *Robert Penn Warren.* New York: Frederick Ungar, 1983. (A brief but useful introduction to Warren's work.)

Walling, William. "In Which Humpty Dumpty Becomes King." In *The Modern American Novel and the Movies.* Edited by G. Peary and R. Shatzkin. New York: Frederick Ungar, 1978. Pp. 168–177. (A consideration of the differences between the novel and movie versions of *All the King's Men.*)

Wilcox, Earl J. "The 'Good old Boy' King: Carlisle Floyd's *Willie Stark.*" *South Carolina Review* 22 (spring 1990): 106–115. (The fullest account yet of the operatic version of *All the King's Men.*)

Williams, T. Harry. *Huey Long.* New York: Knopf, 1969. (Still the definitive biography of the Louisiana Kingfish, at once magisterial and engrossing.)

Wilson, Deborah. "Medusa, the Movies, and the King's Men." In *The Legacy of Robert Penn Warren.* Edited by David Madden. Baton Rouge: Louisiana State University Press, 2000. Pp. 70–83. (An essentially feminist interpretation of the film version of *All the King's Men* with some passing references to film noir.)

Winchell, Mark Royden. "Renaissance Men: Shakespeare's Influence on Robert Penn Warren." In *Shakespeare and Southern Writers: A Study in Influence.* Edited by Philip C. Kolin. Jackson: University Press of Mississippi, 1985. Pp. 137–158. (Includes a discussion of Jack Burden as an American version of Hamlet.)

Woodell, Harold. *All the King's Men: The Search for a Usable Past.* New York: Twayne, 1993. (The only single-author book devoted exclusively to *All the King's Men.* An excellent introduction for university undergraduates and general readers alike.)

Theodore Dreiser's An American Tragedy

ROBERT NIEMI

IN TERMS OF overall unity of effect and sociopolitical significance, *An American Tragedy* (1925) stands unequivocally as Theodore Dreiser's masterpiece and is widely recognized as one of the great American novels of the twentieth century. The enduring importance of *An American Tragedy* rests in its theme and object of critique: the American culture's exclusive worship of what William James termed "the bitch-goddess, success," which can be defined as achievement measured by money, possessions, and social status rather than wisdom, learning, moral virtue, or spiritual striving. Dreiser's *An American Tragedy* remains part of the literary canon because the book tells a fundamental and ugly truth about an entire civilization. It is essential reading for anyone who wishes to understand the root psychology of American culture and the ideology of the so-called American Dream.

THE AUTHOR

The received, smug, and somewhat misconceived "wisdom" on Theodore Dreiser is that he was an embarrassingly inept prose stylist and leftist naysayer who wrote big, ponderous, pessimistic novels attacking American capitalism. Dreiser's political sympathies were, indeed, with the radical Left and his writing was often excessively wordy and sometimes clumsy, but it is nowhere near as awful as his detractors claim. The iconic figure in the literary naturalist tradition, Dreiser remains one of the greatest of twentieth-century American writers; not for his sometimes fitful prose mastery but as his nation's most trenchant critic of the American success ethos.

Dreiser was born August 27, 1871, in Terre Haute, Indiana, the ninth of his family's ten surviving children. Unlike most writers of his time, who were of venerable Anglo-Saxon Protestant heritage, Dreiser's parents were poor, devout German Catholic immigrants. His father, John Paul Dreiser Sr., had established a woolen mill in the 1860s, but the mill went out of business around 1870 due to a variety of factors, plunging the family into long-term poverty. Under the stern leadership of their somewhat demented and God-obsessed patriarch, the Dreiser family moved constantly in a ceaseless effort to avoid poverty and starvation. In 1879 John Paul Dreiser and his wife, Sarah, faced the realization that they could not provide for so large a family; father and mother were forced to separate, and the children were divided between them. In the years that followed, the family was repeatedly reconstituted, dissolved, and reconstituted again in a variety of midwestern cities and towns.

Not surprisingly, Dreiser's schooling was erratic at best. In 1887, at the age of sixteen, he fled his miserable, emotionally suffocating family and struck out on his own, surviving by working a series of menial jobs. With financial help from a former high-school teacher, Dreiser entered Indiana University in 1889. Although he dropped out of college after a year, Dreiser, an instinctive autodidact and voracious reader, continued to learn and to grow intellectually. In 1892 he started working as a journalist for the *Chicago Globe,* soon moving on to a better position at the *St. Louis Globe-Democrat,* but Dreiser's stint as a journalist was brief. In 1894 he moved to New York City and began a career in publishing, eventually working his way up to the presidency of Butterick Publications, a publisher of women's magazines.

In 1898 Dreiser married Sara White (nicknamed "Jug"), a schoolteacher he had met on a trip to the 1893 Chicago World's Fair. Though his passion for Sara White had faded years before they were wed, Dreiser married her out of a sense of duty. The union proved to be a disastrous mistake. A conventional sort of woman, Sara wanted nothing more than a respectable bourgeois marriage while Dreiser—mercurial, artistically ambitious, intensely libidinous, and freedom loving—was temperamentally unsuited to the lifestyle his wife desired. They lived apart after 1909 but never divorced. (Sara Dreiser died in 1942.) An adherent of the dictum that sex is the most powerful of human drives, Dreiser indulged his erotic appetites with numerous affairs and made sexual passion a salient feature of almost all his novels.

In 1900 Dreiser brought out his first novel, *Sister Carrie,* the story of a midwestern farm girl

CHRONOLOGY

1871	Herman Theodore Dreiser born August 27, in Terre Haute, Indiana.
1879	Family disintegrates; Dreiser accompanies his mother to Vincennes, Sullivan, and Evansville, Indiana.
1889–1890	Attends Indiana University.
1892–1893	Works as a reporter in Chicago and St. Louis.
1894	Moves to New York City and becomes an editor.
1898	Marries Sara White.
1900	*Sister Carrie.*
1901–1903	The failure of *Sister Carrie* and marital problems plunge Dreiser into a deep and prolonged depression.
1907	*Sister Carrie* republished; Dreiser becomes an editor for Butterick Publications.
1910	Dreiser is fired from Butterick after having an affair with the daughter of a female employee.
1911	*Jennie Gerhardt* published to critical and popular acclaim.
1912	Publishes *The Financier,* first volume in the Cowperwood Trilogy.
1913	*A Traveler at Forty,* autobiography.
1914	Harper's rejects *The Titan,* second volume of the Cowperwood Trilogy; John Lane publishes it.
1915	*The "Genius"* is published, subsequently attacked as obscene, and ultimately withdrawn from publication.
1916	*A Hoosier Holiday,* Dreiser's second autobiography.
1919	Meets the actress Helen Richardson; they begin a liaison that lasts for the rest of Dreiser's life.
1920	Starts writing *An American Tragedy.*
1922	*A Book about Myself,* another autobiography.
1923	*The "Genius."*
1925	*An American Tragedy;* becomes a critically acclaimed best-seller.

1926	*An American Tragedy* is a finalist for the Pulitzer Prize for fiction but loses to Sinclair Lewis' *Arrowsmith.*
1927	Visits the Soviet Union.
1930	Dreiser is nominated for the Nobel Prize for Literature but loses to Sinclair Lewis, the first American writer to be so honored.
1932–1934	Works as a contributing editor to the *American Spectator.*
1944	American Academy of Arts and Letters honors Dreiser with the Award of Merit; marries Helen Richardson.
1945	Becomes a member of the Communist Party; dies on December 28, at the age of seventy-four, in the Los Angeles area.
1946	*The Bulwark.*
1947	*The Stoic,* last volume of the Cowperwood Trilogy.

who achieves success as a wealthy man's mistress and, later, as an actress. Though Frank Norris (author of *McTeague* and other well-received novels) touted the book, the wife of Dreiser's publisher, Frank Doubleday, found the novel immoral and pressured her husband to suppress it. Doubleday published *Sister Carrie* only because Dreiser forced the company to honor its contract with him. Released without publicity, the book sold poorly and was duly attacked by critics for its scandalous subject matter. The debacle of *Sister Carrie* and Dreiser's failing marriage precipitated a nervous breakdown and near suicide. Deeply demoralized as a creative writer, Dreiser retreated to journalism and gradually regained his equilibrium after his brother Paul sponsored a hiatus at a health camp in Westchester, New York.

When a second edition of *Sister Carrie* was published in 1907, the national zeitgeist was ready for it. A modest popular and critical success, *Sister Carrie* began to establish Dreiser as an acute observer of the American class structure and a breaker of Victorian sexual taboos. Dreiser's second novel, *Jennie Gerhardt* (1911), was another story about a young woman who flouts her society's sexual mores. Despite its risqué subject matter, *Jennie Gerhardt* was well received by critics and the reading public. Thereafter, Dreiser was able to devote himself to fiction on a full-time basis.

Inspirited by the reception of *Jennie Gerhardt,* Dreiser commenced on the most prolific period of his career. With his third novel, *The Financier* (1912), Dreiser traced the early career of Frank Algernon Cowperwood, a fanatically ambitious and sexually promiscuous industrialist based on the infamously ruthless Chicago streetcar magnate, Charles Tyson Yerkes (1837–1905). Further installments in Cowperwood's story—*The Titan* (1914) and *The Stoic* (published posthumously in 1947)—eventually formed what Dreiser dubbed *A Trilogy of Desire,* a sprawling portrait of the rise and fall of an archetypal robber baron and a minutely detailed history of Gilded Age finance.

Dreiser based his fourth novel, *The "Genius"* (1915), on his own life. Much like Dreiser, the book's protagonist, Eugene Witla, comes out of poverty, moves to Chicago and later New York, and rises from proletarian to renowned artist and publishing executive—until a scandalous extramarital affair causes him to lose his job. Intended as a meditation on the travails of the artist in American society, *The "Genius"* is also Dreiser's attempt to explain his social views and justify, or at least rationalize, his emotional volatility, his sexual excesses, and the tumultuous private life that frequently threatened to swamp his literary career. Frank for its day in matters of sex, *The "Genius"* caused a firestorm of controversy when it was published. The New York Society for the Suppression of Vice banned the book as obscene, and its publisher, John Lane, was forced to suspend publication for eight years.

With the triumphant exception of *An American Tragedy,* Dreiser published no more novels during his lifetime. (*The Bulwark* and *The Stoic* appeared after his death.) In the last three decades of his life, Dreiser wrote articles, poetry, short fiction, travel books, memoirs, and political and philosophical treatises. Primed by his upbringing and early manhood to identify with the underdog of the capitalist system, Dreiser moved further to the Left of the political spectrum as he got older. Shortly before his death, he joined the Communist Party. Dreiser died of a heart attack on December 28, 1945, in the Los Angeles area.

GENESIS OF THE NOVEL

In his youth Dreiser was particularly taken with pulp-magazine stories that featured a poor young man rising dramatically in social class by marrying a wealthy young woman (sometimes the gender categories were reversed). Such stories expressed the widely held fantasy of a quick and easy shortcut through the craggy terrain of the American class structure. When he was a young reporter in St. Louis in the early 1890s, Dreiser began to notice that a certain kind of murder occurred on a fairly frequent basis. A poor young man hoping to marry into money kills his equally poor and pregnant girlfriend because she inadvertently stands in the way of his lofty social ambitions. As the years went on, well-publicized cases continued to accumulate. They strengthened Dreiser's intuition that the success-by-marriage myth was a particularly emblematic—and sometimes deadly—aspect of the American Dream. Dreiser later claimed that one crime of this type took place every year between 1895 and 1935.

In the winter of 1914–1915 Dreiser began to research his first attempt at a socially symbolic novel based on an actual murder case. For his model, Dreiser chose the notorious Roland Molineux case. When another man took an interest in the woman he was courting, Molineux, a chemist from a prominent Long Island family, surreptitiously poisoned his rival with cyanide—in minute quantities, a slow-acting toxin that imitates the symptoms of diphtheria. His first murder undetected, Molineux later tried to poison Harry Cornish, manager of the Knickerbocker Club, who had become involved with Molineux's love interest. Molineux mixed the cyanide in Bromo-Seltzer, and it was accidentally ingested by Katherine J. Adams, Cornish's aunt. Unbeknownst to Molineux, cyanide reacts with bromide to form a much more potent and fast-acting toxin; Mrs. Adams died a swift and horrible death. This time, Molineux's crime was discovered, and in 1899 he was sentenced to die in the electric chair at Sing Sing Prison. Three years later, however, Molineux was acquitted by reason of insanity and spent the rest of his life in and out of insane asylums.

In 1915 Dreiser wrote the first six chapters of *The Rake,* a novel loosely based on the Molineux case. He abandoned the project before going any further, however—most likely because its particulars clashed with the social paradigm that Dreiser wanted to illustrate. Roland Molineux came from an affluent background; his motive for both murders was not riches but insane jealousy. Dreiser attempted to turn Ausley Bellinger, his fictive version of Molineux, into an impoverished social climber but could not make the narrative work. Dreiser found it impossible to empathize with Molineux, and there were too many contradictions between the source material and the story he was trying to formulate.

There were two more false starts in the years immediately following World War I. Dreiser almost finished "Her Boy," a long story about Eddie Meagher, an Irish-American bank robber from the slums who dies in the electric chair, roughly based on a Philadelphia career criminal. Dreiser lacked knowledge of Irish ghetto life, however, and the actual story lacked the all-important success-marriage motif; it proved to be a dead end.

Much closer to what Dreiser had in mind was the Clarence Richeson–Avis Linnell case. Richeson was a Virginian who came to Mas-

In *The Novels of Theodore Dreiser: A Critical Study* (1976) Donald Pizer notes that "Dreiser's method in Book One was first to establish the impact upon Clyde of two irreconcilable worlds—one of dreary poverty and loneliness and a formalized religion of duty, the other of beauty, excitement, and wonder and therefore of a personal religious fulfillment." In the final analysis, though, these two worlds are reflections of one another; nihilistic hedonism is an overreaction to repressive religious superstition (which was and is a primitive overreaction to life's chaos). Both worlds fail Clyde, the former because it is too austere, smug, and life-denying, the latter because it is callously self-absorbed and venal. Having rejected religion as a dead letter, Clyde is betrayed by the empty promise of modern paganism. As quoted in *Theodore Dreiser's "An American Tragedy,"* edited by Harold Bloom (1988), Philip Fisher notes that "throughout the novel Clyde is in motion towards or away from worlds he does not merge with." Born an outsider, Clyde will remain one all his life, despite his every effort to fit in.

BOOK TWO

For a year and a half following the accident, Clyde drifts from "one small job to another, in St. Louis, Peoria, Chicago, Milwaukee—dish-washing in a restaurant, soda clerking in a small outlying drug-store, attempting to learn to be a shoe clerk, a grocer's clerk, and what not; and being discharged and laid off and quitting because he did not like it." In Chicago, he chances to meet Tom Ratterer, one of the other fugitives, who is working at the Union League, a swank men's club. Ratterer soon manages to get Clyde a job as a bellhop at the Union League, and Clyde finds himself in surroundings even more impressive than the Green-Davidson, where he observes the comings and goings of "the self-integrated and self-centered" captains of industry, finance, and government. Possessed of an extraordinarily weak and wavering sense of self—"a soul that was destined not to grow up," as Dreiser puts it—Clyde reflexively absorbs the sedate atmosphere of the club and assumes "a most gentlemanly and reserved air." Dreiser's point by now is clear: Clyde Griffiths is not really an autonomous individual striving to direct his own fate but is rather a kind of cipher, a floating nonentity whose only survival skill seems to be a chameleon-like ability to blend into his present social environment without actually becoming a part of it—and to escape when circumstances dictate.

Another chance meeting sends Clyde on a new life trajectory. Clyde's wealthy uncle, Samuel Griffiths, happens to be staying at the Union League while in Chicago on business. Clyde introduces himself and asks his uncle (whom he has never met) for a job at his shirt-collar factory in Lycurgus, New York. Samuel obliges and Clyde travels by train to Lycurgus, takes a room at a boardinghouse, and starts work in his uncle's factory. Though he begins at the bottom, in the aptly named shrinking room, Clyde entertains hopes of parlaying his status as a Griffiths into social and career advancement. He quickly works his way up to the stamping room at the factory but soon learns that he has placed himself in a strangely anomalous position. The Lycurgus Griffiths condescend to invite him to their house, where he meets and is smitten with the beautiful Sondra Finchley, but the family will have little to do with him thereafter. Nonetheless, Clyde—former lackey to the bourgeoisie—persists in thinking himself superior to his fellow factory workers. For their part, the workers categorically distrust him because he is related to the owner. A proletarian with blood ties to the capitalists, Clyde is effectively neither worker nor owner. The class-status dissonance he experienced in Kansas City between the surroundings of his family's mission and the hotel where he worked is not only reiterated in Lycurgus, it is brought into starker relief. In the highly stratified and rigid American caste system, Clyde's uncertain position in the class structure carries the potential danger that he will eventually fit into no class at all.

Socially rebuffed by the Griffiths, a lonely Clyde turns his attentions toward Roberta Alden, one of the workers he supervises in the stamping department—even though he has been warned against fraternizing with the help. The pretty but shy and naive daughter of an impoverished local farmer, Roberta soon succumbs to Clyde's blandishments and romance blooms. She falls in love with him but not vice versa; Clyde would much rather have Sondra Finchley, the very embodiment of wealth, beauty, and high social status. Clyde's interest in Roberta being purely sexual, he pressures her for intimacy. Although she is deeply infatuated with him, Roberta is reluctant to sleep with Clyde unless and until he proposes marriage. In a reversal of the position he was in with Hortense Briggs three years earlier, Clyde plays the sophisticated schemer and, as Samuel Griffiths' nephew, he enjoys the superior social position. Eventually, Clyde succeeds in seducing Roberta, and they become lovers—until another chance encounter upsets the delicate equilibrium of Clyde's life.

Driving at night on exclusive Wykeagy Avenue, Sondra Finchley mistakes a strolling Clyde for his look-alike cousin, Gilbert, offers him a ride, and so revives their acquaintance. To induce jealousy in Gilbert, who has been arrogant to her, Sondra pretends a romantic attraction to Clyde. She also encourages the Griffiths to let Clyde into their social set. Over time, Sondra's interest in Clyde goes from being feigned to quite real, and Clyde's ultimate fantasy seems to be coming true. Consequently, his private life splits into two very different and incompatible worlds, one involving clandestine bedroom nights with Roberta, the other revolving around parties and dances with the smart set of Lycurgus.

Clyde is able to sustain his precarious balancing act until Roberta discovers that she is pregnant. For Clyde, who thinks he has a genuine chance to marry Sondra, Roberta's disclosure is devastating news. Having no intention of marrying Roberta, Clyde obtains a useless chemical that will supposedly make her abort the baby. When that fails, he takes her to a Doctor Glenn in nearby Gloversville for an abortion. Glenn has, indeed, performed abortions for well-connected women of means but refuses Roberta, hypocritically citing legal and moral qualms. On the verge of showing her condition, Roberta leaves work at the factory and goes to her parents' farm to have the baby. There she writes Clyde a series of pathetic letters, begging him to marry her. The pressure steadily mounts on Clyde; he has no choice but to marry Roberta, but he desperately wants to hold on to his dream of marrying Sondra.

As if on cue from fate, an Albany newspaper story about an accidental double drowning fires Clyde's imagination. He begins to think the unthinkable: that he could solve all his problems by drowning Roberta and the baby and making it look like an accident. At the same time, Clyde is too horrified by the idea to fully admit it into his consciousness: "Never once did he honestly, or to put it more accurately, forthrightly and courageously or coldly face the thought of committing so grim a crime." Driven by the accelerating force of circumstances, Clyde's dark idea quickly develops into a desperate conviction, then into a detailed plan of action. The psychological effect of hatching such a plan is to make Clyde virtually schizophrenic; the gap between the seemingly benign persona he presents to the world and the homicidal impulse growing inside him is almost more than he can manage.

Though deeply conflicted about what he intends to do, Clyde nonetheless moves forward. He has no difficulty luring Roberta away from home; he tells her the trip they are taking is to get married and to have a honeymoon. After meeting, Clyde and Roberta take a train to Utica, stay overnight, and then continue on into Adirondack Park. Their first destination, Grass Lake, proves much more peopled with potential witnesses than Clyde anticipated. He opts to take Roberta to Big Bittern Lake, thirty miles to the south, the next day. After checking into Gun Lodge at Big Bittern, Clyde rents a boat and takes Roberta onto the lake. The serene beauty and absolute stillness of the landscape—except for the eerie, prophetic cry of the *wier-wier* bird—contrasts with the turmoil in Clyde's heart and mind. In an agonizingly protracted and masterfully realized scene, Clyde wrestles with his dark side while the unsuspecting Roberta cheerfully sings songs and glides her hand through the deep blue water.

Ultimately, the murder unfolds in an unexpected way and is almost as much an accident as a premeditated act. When Clyde steels himself to kill Roberta, his clenched body and the demented, trance-like look in his eyes unnerve her. As she moves toward him in the boat to comfort him, Clyde is filled with revulsion at himself over his failure to act and hatred of Roberta for having the power to thwart his dreams. He flails out at her to fend her off and accidentally strikes her in the face with the camera he is holding. She falls backward, the boat lurches, and she screams in fear and surprise. Rising to offer help and "to apologize for the unintended blow," Clyde inadvertently capsizes the boat, sending both he and Roberta into the water. Hit by the boat as it overturns, Roberta, a nonswimmer who is deathly afraid of the water, surfaces once and cries out to Clyde for help. The actual murder seems to occur at this moment, when Clyde's darker self reminds him this is what he wanted all along. Obeying his subconscious, Clyde hesitates for a brief moment, and in that moment Roberta goes under. Whether Clyde could have reached her if he acted immediately Dreiser leaves open to conjecture.

BOOK THREE

Using a narrative technique akin to cinematic crosscutting in the first seven chapters of Book Three, Dreiser devotes the first five chapters to the authorities' recovery of Roberta's body; the initial investigation into the circumstances of her death; the discovery of her pitiful letters to Clyde; the notification of her parents and their grief-stricken reaction; and the release of a warrant for Clyde's arrest. Also established are the political motivations and the psychological makeup of Cataraqui County District Attorney Orville W. Mason, the man who will prosecute Clyde. Son of a poor widow, Mason is a self-made man with an abiding resentment for what he considers privilege. Opportunistic in a more adept and sophisticated way than the hapless Clyde, Mason aspires to the Republican nomination for county judge. He knows full well that the Clyde Griffiths murder case will attract enormous publicity and that a successful prosecution on his part will undoubtedly advance his career. On a more personal level, Mason is predisposed to resent the handsome and seemingly popular Clyde. Facially disfigured as a teenager, Mason has what Dreiser luridly describes as "a psychic sex scar" and so is strongly motivated to achieve a sort of symbolic vengeance by convicting Clyde.

The events recounted in chapters 6 and 7 occur simultaneously with those described in the first five chapters. Dreiser shifts the focus back to Clyde and traces his movements in the aftermath of Roberta's death. Swimming to shore, Clyde hides his camera tripod and heads south through the woods. He is spotted by three hikers but is able to make his way to the nearby summer house of Sondra's friends the Cranstons by the next morning. Though he is "now compelled to suffer the most frightful fears and dreads," Clyde joins Sondra and her friends in the usual round of summer leisure activities—camping, boating, tennis, picnics—all while desperately hoping that he will somehow avoid detection.

In chapter 8 the two parallel narrative lines that follow pursuers and pursued converge: Clyde is arrested five days after the murder while camping with his friends near Bear Lake.

Interrogated by Orville Mason shortly after his arrest, Clyde denies everything. The next day he is indicted for murder before a local justice and then taken to the Cataraqui County jail in Bridgeburg to await trial. His first night in jail, Clyde is kept awake by a mob of some five hundred "noisy, jeering, threatening" citizens who would very much like to lynch him. Playing upon class resentment, the newspapers further fuel public hysteria by characterizing Clyde as a predatory society fop who murdered a poor working girl.

Approached by the Griffiths family, defense attorneys Alvin Belknap and Reuben Jephson agree to take Clyde's case, partly for its notoriety but mostly for partisan political reasons. As Democrats, they hope to defeat Mason at trial and therefore foil his bid for the county judgeship. Facing a mountain of incriminating circumstantial evidence against Clyde, Belknap and Jephson realize they must admit that he plotted to do away with Roberta. Their defense strategy is to concoct a none-too-plausible version of events on the lake that has Clyde experiencing a change of heart and agreeing to marry Roberta. In her joy, she upsets the boat and is accidentally drowned before a stunned Clyde can save her. As Donald Pizer notes in *The Novels of Theodore Dreiser,* "the trial is thus essentially a contest between rival sentimental myths—that of the city seducer versus that of the nobleman who had intended to expiate his seduction by marrying and elevating the poor and virtuous maiden because her qualities had at last impressed themselves on his heart." Unfortunately for Clyde, the jury has been predisposed against him from the outset on the grounds that he seduced and deflowered an innocent young girl; he is demonstrably guilty of that, so—by inference—he must be guilty of her murder as well. Ambivalent about his own guilt, Clyde does poorly on the stand, is convicted of murder in the first degree, and is sentenced to death in the electric chair. Clyde's fate was probably a foregone conclusion given the facts of the case and the political and cultural pressures brought to bear against him. As for Sondra Finchley, her family's money and connections keep her name out of the papers and free of scandal.

On death row, awaiting his execution, Clyde is visited by his mother. (In an exceedingly gauche display of journalistic opportunism, a Denver newspaper subsidizes Mrs. Griffith's trip from Colorado to New York in exchange for her exclusive dispatches on her son.) Elvira Griffiths tries to muster financial support from the religious community for a new trial for her son but meets with little success. Before she returns to Denver she leaves Clyde in the hands of the Reverend Duncan McMillan, who will act as his spiritual advisor in the waning months of his life. Like everyone else connected with the trial and its aftermath, McMillan has his own political agenda. He counsels Clyde to repent and accept the Lord—not so much to bring comfort to the condemned man as to restore ideological order by making sure that a notorious violator of the Christian-capitalist ethos is publicly brought back into the fold. Despite the fact that Clyde continues to be unsure about religion, his salvation, or even the possibility of an afterlife, he relents to McMillan. He composes a kind of surrender document in which he declares Jesus Christ as his "personal savior and unfailing friend" and advises young men across the country to "know the joy and pleasure of a Christian life." It does not matter whether Clyde really believes what he is saying; the important thing is that the declaration is made. A few days later, after his mother makes a final, futile plea to the governor, Clyde is executed.

In a brief coda to the novel, titled "Souvenir," Dreiser brings his saga full circle by depicting a missionary family, not unlike the Griffiths of Kansas City, who are preaching on the streets of San Francisco at dusk. Among the band is a small boy named Russell who asks his grandmother for a dime to buy an ice cream cone—another Clyde Griffiths in the making.

Mulligan, Roark. "The 'Realistic' Application of Irony: Structural and Thematic Considerations in *An American Tragedy.*" *Dreiser Studies* 25 (spring 1994): 3–11.

Murayama, Kiyohiko. "The Road to *An American Tragedy.*" *Hitotsubashi Journal of Arts and Sciences* 19 (November 1978): 40–51.

Orlov, Paul A. "The Subversion of the Self: Anti-Naturalistic Crux in *An American Tragedy.*" *Modern Fiction Studies* 23 (autumn 1977): 457–472.

———. "Plot as Parody: Dreiser's Attack on the Alger Theme in *An American Tragedy.*" *American Literary Realism* 15 (autumn 1982): 239–243.

———. "Technique as Theme in *An American Tragedy.*" *Journal of Narrative Technique* 14 (spring 1984): 75–93.

———. An American Tragedy: *Perils of the Self Seeking "Success."* Lewisburg, Pa.: Bucknell University Press, 1998.

Pizer, Donald. *The Novels of Theodore Dreiser: A Critical Study.* Minneapolis: University of Minnesota Press, 1976.

———. "Dreiser and the Naturalistic Drama of Consciousness." *Journal of Narrative Technique* 21 (spring 1991): 202–211.

Pizer, Donald, ed. *Critical Essays on Theodore Dreiser.* Boston: G. K. Hall, 1981.

Plank, Kathryn M. "Dreiser's Real American Tragedy." *Papers on Language and Literature* 27 (spring 1991): 268–287.

Riggio, Thomas P. "American Gothic: Poe and *An American Tragedy.*" *American Literature: A Journal of Literary History, Criticism, and Bibliography* 49 (January 1978): 515–532.

Rose, Alan Henry. "Dreiser's Satanic Mills: Religious Imagery in *An American Tragedy.*" *Dreiser Newsletter* 7 (spring 1976): 5–8.

Rosenman, Mona G. "*An American Tragedy:* Constitutional Violations." *Dreiser Newsletter* 9 (spring 1978): 11–19.

Saint Jean, Shawn. "Social Deconstruction and *An American Tragedy.*" *Dreiser Studies* 28 (spring 1997): 3–24.

Salzman, Jack, ed. *Theodore Dreiser: The Critical Reception.* New York: David Lewis, 1972.

Shapiro, Charles. *Theodore Dreiser: Our Bitter Patriot.* Carbondale: Southern Illinois University Press, 1962.

Spindler, Michael. "Youth, Class, and Consumerism in Dreiser's *An American Tragedy.*" *Journal of American Studies* 12 (April 1978): 63–79.

Town, Caren J. "Voicing the Tragedy: Narrative Conflict in Dreiser's *An American Tragedy.*" *Dreiser Studies* 26 (fall 1995): 12–29.

Trigg, Sally Day. "Theodore Dreiser and the Criminal Justice System in *An American Tragedy.*" *Studies in the Novel* 22 (winter 1990): 429–440.

Warren, Robert Penn. *Homage to Theodore Dreiser, August 27, 1871–December 28, 1945, on the Centennial of His Birth.* New York: Random House, 1971.

Wilson, Kenneth E. "A New Historicist Reading of Dreiser's Fiction: Money, Labor, and Ideals." *Dreiser Studies* 26 (spring 1995): 11–19.

Zasursky, Y. "Theodore Dreiser's *An American Tragedy.*" In *20th Century American Literature: A Soviet View.* Translated by Ronald Vroon. Moscow: Progress, 1976. Pp. 223–240.

Gertrude Stein's
The Autobiography of Alice B. Toklas

DINA RIPSMAN EYLON

PARIS IN THE early twentieth century was the hub of the avant-garde and modernist movements. Struggling young artists and writers from Europe and America flocked to the Left Bank of the Seine to establish themselves as innovators in art and literature. Readers today are lured by the self-indulgent hedonism and amazing intellectual fervor apparent in the works of writers such as Ernest Hemingway, Edith Wharton, F. Scott Fitzgerald, Colette, Ezra Pound, James Joyce, and Gertrude Stein.

In 1903 Gertrude Stein settled into her brother Leo's apartment at 27, rue de Fleurus. She lived the rest of her life as an American expatriate in Paris. Stein thrived in the hectic artistic and literary community of the Left Bank. However, only in 1932 did she embark on a fictional journey to document this fascinating era in cultural history: "And now I will tell you how two americans happened to be in the heart of an art movement of which the outside world at that time knew nothing." This simple and candid statement from *The Autobiography of Alice B. Toklas* (1933) captures the quintessence of that popular book. Apart from conveying personal stories from the lives of the "two americans," Gertrude Stein and her lifelong companion Alice Toklas, the *Autobiography* is an intricate novel that describes the development of cubism and modernism in Paris at the beginning of the twentieth century. The book became an international best-seller and made Gertrude Stein a literary icon known for defying conventional and traditional approaches to literature.

Cubism, considered the most influential art form of the first half of the twentieth century, began with the works of Spanish artist Pablo Picasso and French artist Georges Braque in 1907. The movement started as a reaction to nineteenth-century art by creating indistinct senses of space, an effect achieved by using simplified, flat geometric shapes, planes, fragments, and forms to overlie and diffuse each other to accomplish a new dimension in which both part and whole are introduced in a new light.

Traditionally, Picasso's *Les demoiselles d'Avignon* (1907, Museum of Modern Art, New York City) is regarded as the first cubist painting. The women portrayed in the painting are presented as a combination of fragmented, flattened figures, striking a chord with African art. Other art historians attribute the beginning of cubism to Paul Cézanne's *Mont Sainte-Victoire* (1902–1906, Metropolitan Museum of Art, New York City). Cubism is further divided into the analytical phase (1910–1912) and the synthetic phase (after 1912), in which Picasso, Braque, and others developed different stylistic methods, lasting through 1915. Not solely confined to visual art forms, cubism expanded into the literary world, headed by the French poet Guillaume Apollinaire, who frequented Stein's renowned Saturday-night literary salon.

Stein began to apply cubist literary techniques early in her writing career. In 1909 she published her first work of fiction, *Three Lives: Stories of Good Anna, Melanctha, and the Gentle Lena,* which critics claimed was influenced by cubism. Philip Heldrich observes that "the appeal both of a burgeoning cubism's fragmentation of the subject and of the short story presented in a cyclical form offered her just such freedom"—the creative freedom she was seeking incessantly. Moreover, in her 1946 "Transatlantic Interview" with Robert Haas, Stein illustrates how Cézanne's art affected her writing style in *Three Lives:* "Cézanne conceived the idea that in composition one thing was as important as another thing. Each part is as important as the whole, and that impressed me enormously, and it impressed me so much that I began to write *Three Lives* under this influence." If the relationship between part and whole forms the core principle of cubism, then Cézanne was the first painter who, with the use of light and color, introduced contrasts to his works, giving them multiple points of view. According to Wendy Steiner, Cézanne's modus operandi, which Stein adopted in her first published fiction, led critics to view the subject matter as "a function of time and memory."

CHRONOLOGY

1874	Born on February 3 in Allegheny, Pennsylvania, the youngest of Daniel and Amelia Keyser Stein's five children (two other children had died in infancy).
1875–1879	The Stein family moves throughout the United States and Europe.
1880	Family moves west and eventually settles in East Oakland, California.
1888	In July, Amelia Stein dies of cancer.
1891	In January, Daniel Stein dies unexpectedly. Michael Stein, the eldest son, becomes head of the family. They move to San Francisco.
1892	Family separates. Gertrude and Bertha move to Baltimore to live with their maternal aunt.
1893	Enters Radcliffe College (then called Harvard Annex).
1896	Stein's first publication, a research paper coauthored with Leon Solomons, appears in Harvard's *Psychological Review.* She visits Europe for the first time as an adult.
1897	Fails her Latin exam and does not earn her bachelor's degree. She enters Johns Hopkins School of Medicine.
1898	Belatedly earns her bachelor's degree from Radcliffe College.
1901	Fails four courses at Hopkins and spends the summer in Tangiers, Granada, and Paris.
1903	Begins to write *The Making of Americans* and *Q.E.D.* (later called *Things as They Are*). Settles in at 27, rue de Fleurus, in Paris.
1904	Joins her brother Leo in Italy, where they see Charles Loeser's collection of Cézannes and start their modern art collection.
1905	Begins *Three Lives.* She and Leo purchase Henri Matisse's *La femme au chapeau.* Meets Pablo Picasso.
1907	Meets Alice B. Toklas in Paris.
1909	*Three Lives.*

explains that Stein used the work of Daniel Defoe in lectures and essays to illustrate the sort of biographical narrative she admired. For Stein, the character—that is, his existence—rather than "what happens" should be the central interest of such a narrative. And the *Autobiography,* Meyers suggests, is Stein's accomplishment in narrating her own life as something that will have meaning to someone else.

Typically, as Meyer has observed, some of Stein's themes from the *Autobiography* resurface in her later writings. A couple of years after the publication of the *Autobiography,* Stein, in the third lecture included in *Narration* (1935), recaptures the subject of Defoe and his protagonist Robinson Crusoe:

> Think of Defoe, he tried to write Robinson Crusoe as if it were exactly what did happen and yet after all he is Robinson Crusoe and Robinson Crusoe is Defoe and therefore after all it is not what is happening it is what is happening to him to Robinson Crusoe that makes what is exciting to every one.

If Stein, the author, is interchangeable with Toklas, the narrator, as Daniel Defoe is with Robinson Crusoe, the narrative becomes increasingly "exciting" because Stein is exposed as the actual narrator of the book. Moreover, if the characters of Gertrude and Alice are interchangeable, they are also equal in terms of the roles they play in the book.

Catharine R. Stimpson in "Gertrude Stein and the Lesbian Lie" explains that Stein, the theorist, clearly believed in "the impossibility of autobiography if autobiography swears that it is the narrative of a unified self." Generally, says Phoebe Stein Davis, a work of autobiography implies that "the narrator and the subject of narration are the same person." An autobiographical narration suggests that the narrator, relying on her memory, is in control of the past as it actually happened. It may also suggest that facts outweigh fiction. Yet, Davis points out, the *Autobiography* conveys the same anecdotes repeatedly, using different sources or different points of view, like the sale of Matisse's *La femme au chapeau* and the account of the battle of the Marne in World War I.

Additionally, in many instances Toklas the narrator admits to losing her memory or vaguely recollecting the full details of certain events, such as Stein's sitting for Picasso: "It was only a very short time after this that Picasso began the portrait of Gertrude Stein, now so widely known, but just how that came about is a little vague in everybody's mind. I have heard Picasso and Gertrude Stein talk about it often and they neither of them can remember." On a different occasion Toklas could not conclude whether Stein's portrait lasted for eighty or ninety sittings:

> Spring was coming and the sittings were coming to an end. All of a sudden one day Picasso painted out the whole head. I can't see you any longer when I look, he said irritably. And so the picture was left like that.
>
> Nobody remembers being particularly disappointed or particularly annoyed at this ending to the long series of posings.

Even in a genre that focuses on remembering facts as they really happened, Stein reminds the reader of the frail quality of memory. Her manipulation of the life narrative in the *Autobiography* presents a case in which the author and the narrative voice become one entity, confounding existing literary norms while reconstructing language and style and obscuring the boundaries between the autobiographer and the autobiography. Still, claims Stimpson (1992), Stein's challenge "to the idea of a unified, coherent self is central to the *Autobiography.*"

THE GENRE OF AUTOBIOGRAPHY

The relationship between the autobiographer and the autobiography poses some pertinent questions as to the nature and ambiguity of the genre of autobiography. Timothy Dow Adams perceives all autobiographers as "unreliable narrators." In his opinion, the term "autobiography" "cannot really be defined." Adams notes the claim of William Spengemann and L. R. Lundquist, who suggest that "the modern autobiographer needs an especially flexible form, one that can always outrun attempts to define it." Robert Folkenflik, another scholar of the genre, defines autobiography as "self-biography" or "self life writing." However, for Adams "this form of writing . . . possesses a peculiar kind of truth through a narrative composed of the author's metaphors of self that attempt to reconcile the individual events of a lifetime by using a combination of *memory* and *imagination* [emphasis added]."

According to Sidonie Smith and Julia Watson, the term "autobiography" first appeared "in the preface to a collection of poems by the eighteenth-century English . . . writer Ann Yearsley." Some critics, however, consider "Robert Southey's anglicizing of the three Greek words [which make up the word autobiography] in 1809 as the first use of the term in English." Historically, prior to the first appearance of the term "autobiography," terms such as "memoir," "the life," "the book of my life," and "essays of myself" had been used to denote this relatively new genre.

Smith and Watson distinguish between three different terms in autobiography studies: "life writing," "life narrative," and "autobiography." They understand "life writing" as a broad term that includes the entire variety of writing about life "as its subject." "Life narrative" is a more restricted term that consists of "self-referential writing, including autobiography." In fact, they say, "life narrative . . . might best be approached as a moving target, a set of ever-shifting self-referential practices that engage the past in order to reflect on identity in the present." In these scholars' opinion, "autobiography" is a term used "for a particular practice of life narrative that emerged in the Enlightenment and has become canonical in the West." Ostensibly this third term has attracted controversy and dispute mainly because it epitomizes the entire field of life narrative, the most celebrated form of life story written or told by the self.

Readers may confuse life narratives with the literary form of the novel (when the narration of that novel is written in first person) due to the author's use in both of the pronoun "I." Some scholars of the newly instituted genre of autobiography presume that telling the truth is the fundamental principle underlying the relationship between autobiographers and their readers. Nevertheless this assumption is contradictory to the process of life writing due to its innate subjectivity. What the writer believes to be the truth might not be perceived as such by others who participated in the event. Furthermore, "if autobiographers," comments Jonathan Loesberg, "claim to be telling the truth about their past lives, they are not doing very well at it."

In the case of *The Autobiography of Alice B. Toklas,* the narrator retains the first-person voice throughout the work. The reader becomes familiar with the distinct style of Toklas' narration, her somewhat distant anecdotal approach, her humility and domesticity. Once the deceived reader realizes that Stein is the real narrator who has assumed Toklas' voice and role, it is too late for reconceptualization. The reader is then confronted with the question of the autobiographical boundaries: is it really an autobiography, the life of Alice B. Toklas, or is it merely a fictional account of the lives of Toklas and Stein? The straightforward answer would have to be that once Stein uses another narrative voice for her autobiography, she is entering the genre of fiction.

Stein never intended the *Autobiography* to conform to the genre of autobiography; she deliberately caused the boundaries between the life narrative and the novel to collapse by altering the narrator's voice and refusing to be "bound by historical time." Justifiably, George Wickes in *Americans in Paris* argues that Stein placed more importance on the myth of the modernist movement than on the actual facts of modernism. In fact Stein never presented the *Autobiography* as a historical or nonfictional work; she knowingly twisted actual facts in her continuous scheme of part and whole and purposely omitted the names of her family members (such as Leo, Michael, and Sarah Stein) who were instrumental to the development of modern painting.

THE RELATIONSHIP BETWEEN STEIN AND HEMINGWAY

Notably, Stein's account of Ernest Hemingway was written after "their relationship turned sour." Stein and Toklas first met him shortly after World War I when they returned to Paris. Equipped with "a letter of introduction from Sherwood Anderson," the young Hemingway presented himself at the couple's apartment. Hemingway, a journalist at the time, started to write short stories and some poetry. Gradually he became a regular visitor, and Stein, more than three decades his senior, "went over all the writing he had done up to that time." Although she liked his poems, finding them particularly "Kiplingesque," she found his novel "wanting," faulting it for having "a great deal of description," and "not particularly good description." During their friendship Stein mentored him into assuming his responsibilities as a writer and even as a young father. The Hemingways asked Stein and Toklas to be their baby's godmothers. Yet, according to the *Autobiography,* this was a sign of an ill-fated friendship:

> Writer or painter god-parents are notoriously unreliable. That is, there is certain before long to be a cooling of friendship. I know several cases of this, poor Paulot Picasso's god-parents have wandered out of sight and just as naturally it is a long time since any of us have seen or heard of our Hemingway god-child."

Gertrude Stein sullenly relates her disenchantment with Hemingway in the *Autobiography.* She was dismayed, for instance, by Hemingway's disrespect and betrayal of their friend Sherwood Anderson. According to the account in the *Autobiography,* Hemingway "repudiated Sherwood Anderson and all his works" in a letter he sent to the latter "in the name of american literature." Both Anderson and Stein accused Hemingway of being "yellow," a careerist and a hypocrite. Amusingly, they both admitted to having a "weakness" for Hemingway. As his mentors, they acknowledged an appreciation for the way he accepted "training," but agreed that his learning was merely superficial. Stein compared Hemingway to André Derain, the French painter, who in her opinion "look[ed] like a modern and . . . smell[ed] of the museums"—he was never a genuine modernist.

Hemingway's successful career grated on Stein (she believed she taught him everything he knew about literature), and she retaliated by criticizing him in the *Autobiography,* thereby "getting in the last word." However, Hemingway outlived Gertrude Stein and settled their dispute in his *A Moveable Feast* (1964), wherein Stein and Toklas are depicted in a different light. Hemingway recalls, "In the three or four years that we were good friends I cannot remember Gertrude Stein ever speaking well of any writer who had not written favorably about her work or done something to advance her career except for Ronald Firbank and, later, Scott Fitzgerald." Surprisingly, Ernest Hemingway admits to the fact that Stein did not like his early fiction, calling it "*inaccrochable.*" Worth noting, though, are the final words he has to say about Gertrude Stein and Alice Toklas:

> I said to my wife, "You know, Gertrude *is* nice, anyway."
>
> "Of course, Tatie."
>
> "But she does talk a lot of rot sometimes."

> "I never hear her," my wife said. "I'm a wife. It's her friend that talks to me."

Hemingway's version of their relationship might not resemble Stein's account in the *Autobiography;* yet, as Michael Hoffman has observed, it might be "just as well written a piece of fiction."

CRITICAL RECEPTION

A year after the publication of the *Autobiography,* the magazine *Transition* published a supplement titled, "Testimony against Gertrude Stein" in which Georges Braque, Henri Matisse, Tristan Tzara, and André Salmon disputed the factual truth of various anecdotes in the book. One such anecdote deals with the 1908 party that Picasso organized in his studio for his friend Henri Rousseau. Stein's account differs considerably from Fernande Olivier's in *Picasso and His Friends* (1964). The party, according to the *Autobiography*'s narrator, did not go well from the start. Guillaume Apollinaire and Henri Rousseau were late, and the waiting crowd had had too much to drink. Shortly after "the ceremonies began," André Salmon, "being completely drunk," started a fight. He had to be controlled by the other men in the party, and finally was "dragged . . . into the front atelier and locked . . . in."

This depiction of Rousseau's banquet, along with other anecdotes in the *Autobiography,* understandably enraged André Salmon. He called Stein's portrayal of the party "scandalous." "After all," he said, "we were all young at that time and had no thought of possible later echoes of our actions." Salmon insisted that Stein confused details of "dates, places and persons" in trying to reconstruct her memories of the art world in Paris. Of the particular spectacle during the party for Rousseau, he offered a totally different version:

> The spectacular features of [the banquet] were intentional and after the joke of drunkenness I simply went back to my own studio in order to make it seem more plausible. It is evident that Miss Stein understood little of the tendency that we all had, Apollinaire, Max Jacob, myself and the others, to frequently play a rather burlesque role.

He blamed the confusion and misunderstanding of this event on the fact that Stein and Toklas did not "understand very well the rather peculiar French we used to speak."

Furthermore, Salmon challenged Stein's comprehension of the cubist movement. He claimed that Picasso "was nothing of a doctrinaire," and "soon lost interest in it and left its further development to others." He called Stein's account of the formation of cubism "entirely false." Stein's depiction of Monsieur Princet, Germaine Pichot, and Jacques Vaillant was totally irresponsible and inaccurate and left the reader "astounded," he felt. In short, said Salmon, "What incomprehension of an epoch! Fortunately there are others who have described it better."

Georges Braque, in his response, did not contest the genuineness or correctness of Stein's anecdotes but rather questioned her grasp of the modern art world in general, and of cubism in particular. He ridiculed Stein's knowledge of the French language and argued that this lack of proficiency, a "barrier," made her see cubism "simply in terms of personalities." Braque added,

> In the early days of Cubism, Pablo Picasso and I were engaged in what we felt was a search for the anonymous personality. . . . Thus it often happened that amateurs mistook Picasso's painting for mine and mine for Picasso's. . . . Miss Stein obviously saw everything from the outside and never the real struggle we were engaged in."

Braque denied the report in the *Autobiography* that he and Marie Laurencin painted each other's portraits. He also recalled that during World War I, Stein and Toklas paid him a visit in Avignon. Upon their arrival, their strange outfits caused him a great deal of embarrassment and uneasiness. Offensively he dismissed Stein's reputation as a writer: "We in Paris always heard that Miss Stein was a writer, but I don't think any of us had read her work until *Transition* began to make her known in France. Now that we have seen her book, *nous sommes fixés* [our minds are settled]"

In *Picasso,* Gertrude Stein outlines the development of cubism. It is interesting to compare her account of the period with that of Georges Braque, one of its major players: "Once brought back with him some landscapes which were . . . the beginning of cubism. . . . It always amused me when every one protested against the fantasy of the pictures to make them look at the photographs which made them see that the pictures were almost exactly like the photographs." Stein, to whom Braque attributes the art appreciation of a tourist, maintains that cubism "began with landscapes." Later on, because Picasso was primarily interested in painting people, he engaged in "his long struggle to express heads faces and bodies of men and of women," which became his own unique "composition."

Despite their differences, Georges Braque and Gertrude Stein use similar words to describe the struggle of the first cubist artists. Stein writes about Picasso's ordeal of finding new ways of expression, new ways of painting portraits and still lifes. Although both write about conveying personalities on canvas, Braque is interested in the "anonymous personality," while Stein focuses on Picasso's subjects. Are Braque's "anonymous personality" and Picasso's portraits (the subjects of his paintings) one and the same thing? Highly unlikely. Neither Braque nor Stein mention Paul Cézanne's monumental art and the fact that many art historians deem him the real father of cubism and the modernist art movement. Even though Picasso has become its icon, cubism generally is not seen as his own invention or personal crusade but as a movement in which a considerable number of painters and sculptors recreated their unique artistic expression.

Stein was not oblivious to the strong opposition her friends, the *Autobiography*'s characters, voiced against her. After the initial excitement and shopping sprees that followed the monetary success of the book, Stein wrote, "In the first place Picasso and I are no longer friends. All the writers about whom I wrote wrote to me that they liked what I wrote but none of the painters. . . . They shuddered."

CRITICAL RESPONSE

Markedly, not all critics reproached the *Autobiography*'s authenticity. Many praised its gaiety, humor, and literary inimitability. In the *Saturday Review of Literature* (September 2, 1933) Stein's lifelong friend Bernard Faÿ commented, "Gertrude Stein has lived all the adventures of modern art as adventures, and she has built a very great work on them. . . . Now in this autobiography she offers the odyssey of the most intelligent American woman alive at present." In the *New York Herald-Tribune Books* (September 3, 1933), Stein's close friend Louis Bromfield called the book "fascinating," exclaiming that "more than any other book I ever read, I *lived* this book, page by page, sentence by sentence, through twenty-five years."

With the publication of the *Autobiography* and its astounding success, Stein discovered that she had suddenly gained an audience, as she recounts in "The Story of a Book":

> I write for myself and strangers, after these years to know that I have a public gives me what the French call a *coeur léger,* it makes me not light-hearted but it leaves me unburdened. . . . And so all this which has pleased and contented me will please and content [the readers].

A debilitating identity crisis followed this realization as she felt deeply and "completely lost," unable to write in the way she wrote before her leap to fame: "Well you see I did not know myself, I lost my personality. It has always been completely included in myself my personality as any personality naturally is, and here all of a sudden, I was not just I because so many people did know me." This identity crisis led to a writer's block that lasted for about three years. In 1935, just before embarking on a lecture tour in America, she recovered and resumed writing the way she used to write in *The Making of Americans.* Her writing became more introverted and insightful, regardless of anything that was "happening" outside of her. Apparently, becoming known to the outside world was a blessing for Stein, who then developed a deeper introspection as a writer.

STEIN'S LEGACY

As her peer Louis Bromfield noted, Stein's "influence upon American writing, so much greater than is known or conceded, has always been an intensely personal one. It has been achieved as much by Gertrude Stein the person as by Gertrude Stein the writer." The mark she left on the literary map of the twentieth century is irrefutable. Her groundbreaking undertakings in most literary genres have inspired generations of writers who followed in her footsteps to defy literary, linguistic, and cultural limitations.

In addition to her copious body of writings, Stein's legacy prevails in the "play form" she so adored, documented in films and plays worldwide. The first motion picture to commemorate Stein's life story, *Gertrude Stein: When This You See, Remember Me,* was produced and directed by Perry Miller Adato in 1970. Another film about her life, *Waiting for the Moon,* was released in 1987 and won first prize at the Sundance Film Festival and at the Houston Film Festival. Written by Mark Magill and directed by Jill Godmilow, the film is a "biographie imaginaire" of Stein and Toklas, who are challenged with Stein's fear that she is dying of an incurable disease. Though largely fictional, the film remains faithful in its portrayal of the dedicated relationship between the two women. Premiering in 1996, *Paris Was a Woman,* a documentary by Greta Schiller and Andrea Weiss, illuminates the history of the community of women who lived in Paris between World Wars I and II and were mentors to and promotors of emerging artists such as Picasso, Hemingway, and Joyce. In theater circles, worth noting is New York's Gertrude Stein Repertory Theatre (GSRT), founded in 1990 with the aim of promoting and supporting innovation in the performing arts; the GSRT's particular mission is to pioneer the application of new technologies to the process of creating live theater.

For decades Stein's inaccessible writing style kept her work on the margins of early twentieth-century literature. Often she had to resort to self-publishing her books, which steadily drained her financial resources. Even those critics who appreciated her literary innovation and abstract style were skeptical of her ability to write anything of a conventional nature. *The Autobiography of Alice B. Toklas* changed this criticism forever. Michael Hoffman calls the *Autobiography* "a masterful performance" and "the most important memoir of any Modernist figure." In his opinion, Stein has created a double myth: the myth of Paris as the center of modern art, and the myth of "Gertrude Stein," the mother of modernism. For the rest of her career, she struggled against the way that the success of the *Autobiography* and the persona it had made famous had the propensity to overshadow her other writings.

Nonetheless, Stein has been widely staged and well liked in academia, and her works attract new readership continuously. In "A Long Gay Book" (in *Matisse, Picasso, and Gertrude Stein,* 1933), she states, "Anyone being one is one." She was definitely not just "anyone." Gertrude Stein was someone extraordinary, an American literary icon.

Select Bibliography

EDITION

The Autobiography of Alice B. Toklas. New York: Harcourt, 1933. (First edition; this is the edition quoted in the text.)

OTHER WORKS BY STEIN

Three Lives: Stories of the Good Anna, Melanctha and the Gentle Lena. New York: Grafton, 1909.

The Making of Americans. Paris: Contact Editions, 1925.

Narration. Chicago: University of Chicago Press, 1935.

Everybody's Autobiography. New York: Random House, 1937.

Picasso. London: Batsford, 1938; New York: Scribners, 1938.

Paris France. London: Batsford, 1940; New York: Scribners, 1940.

Wars I Have Seen. London: Batsford, 1945; New York: Random House, 1945.

Gertrude Stein on Picasso. Edited by Edward Burns. New York: Liveright, 1970.

A Primer for the Gradual Understanding of Gertrude Stein. Edited by Robert Bartlett Haas. Los Angeles: Black Sparrow, 1973. (Excellent starting point to Stein's works. Features the famous "A Transatlantic Interview 1946.")

How Writing Is Written. Edited by Robert Bartlett Haas. Los Angeles: Black Sparrow, 1974. (Includes the essay "The Story of a Book," on the writing of *The Autobiography of Alice B. Toklas.*)

Baby Precious always Shines: Selected Love Notes between Gertrude Stein and Alice B. Toklas. Edited by Kay Turner. New York: St. Martin's, 1999.

SECONDARY WORKS

Adams, Timothy Dow. *Telling Lies in Modern American Autobiography.* Chapel Hill: University of North Carolina Press, 1990.

Benstock, Shari. *Women of the Left Bank: Paris, 1900–1940.* Austin: University of Texas Press, 1986. (Contains an indispensable analysis of Gertrude Stein's life and works.)

Berry, Ellen E. "On Reading Gertrude Stein." *Genders* 5 (July 1989): 1–20.

———. *Curved Thought and Textual Wandering: Gertrude Stein's Postmodernism.* Ann Arbor: University of Michigan Press, 1992.

Bloom, Harold, ed. *Gertrude Stein.* New York: Chelsea House, 1986. (Includes articles by Sherwood Anderson, Katherine Anne Porter, Thornton Wilder, and Catharine R. Stimpson.)

Braque, Georges, et al. "Testimony against Gertrude Stein." Supplement to *Transition* 23 (February 1935).

Bridgman, Richard. *Gertrude Stein in Pieces.* New York: Oxford University Press, 1970.

Chessman, Harriet Scott. "On Reading Gertrude Stein." In *Modern American Women Writers.* Edited by Elaine Showalter, et al. New York: Scribners, 1991. Pp. 485–498.

Copeland, Carolyn Faunce. *Language and Time and Gertrude Stein.* Iowa City: University of Iowa Press, 1975.

Curnutt, Kirk, ed. *The Critical Response to Gertrude Stein.* Westport, Conn.: Greenwood, 2000. (A collection of reviews and articles dated from 1909–1997, including reviews of the *Autobiography* by Louis Bromfield in the *New York Herald-Tribune* and Bernard Faÿ in *Saturday Review of Literature.*)

Davis, Phoebe Stein. "Subjectivity and the Aesthetics of National Identity in Gertrude Stein's *The Autobiography of Alice B. Toklas.*" *Twentieth Century Literature* 45 (spring 1999): 18–45.

Folkenflik, Robert. "Introduction: The Institution of Autobiography." In *The Culture of Autobiography: Constructions of Self-Representations.* Edited by Robert Folkenflik. Stanford, Calif.: Stanford University Press, 1993. Pp. 1–20.

Gygax, Franziska. *Gender and Genre in Gertrude Stein.* Westport, Conn.: Greenwood, 1998.

Heldrich, Philip. "Connecting Surfaces: Gertrude Stein's *Three Lives,* Cubism, and the Metonymy of the Short Story Cycle." *Studies in Short Fiction* 34 (fall 1997): 427–439.

Hemingway, Ernest. *A Moveable Feast.* New York: Scribners, 1964.

Hobhouse, Janet. *Everybody Who Was Anybody: A Biography of Gertrude Stein.* London: Weidenfeld and Nicolson, 1975; New York: Putnam, 1975.

Hoffman, Michael. *Gertrude Stein.* Boston: Twayne, 1976. (Superb analysis of Stein's works, arranged by genre.)

Loesberg, Jonathan. "Autobiography as Genre, Act of Consciousness, Text." *Prose Studies* 4 (September 1981): 169–185.

Lubar, Robert S. "Unmasking Pablo's Gertrude: Queer Desire and the Subject of Portraiture." *Art Bulletin* 79 (March 1997): 56–84.

Mailer, Norman. *Portrait of Picasso as a Young Man: An Interpretive Biography.* New York: Atlantic Monthly Press, 1995.

McCully, Marilyn, ed. *A Picasso Anthology: Documents, Criticism, Reminiscences.* Princeton, N.J.: Princeton University Press, 1981.

Mellow, James R. *The Charmed Circle: Gertrude Stein and Company.* New York: Praeger, 1973.

Meyer, Steven J. "Gertrude Stein Shipwrecked in Bohemia: Making Ends Meet in the *Autobiography* and After." *Southwest Review* 77 (winter 1992): 12–33.

Neuman, S. C. *Gertrude Stein: Autobiography and the Problem of Narration.* Victoria, B.C.: English Literary Studies Monograph Series, 1979.

Olivier, Fernande. *Picasso and His Friends.* Translated by Jane Miller. London: Heinemann, 1964.

Penrose, Sir Roland. *Portrait of Picasso.* London: Thames and Hudson, 1981.

Rogers, William Garland. *When This You See Remember Me: Gertrude Stein in Person.* New York: Rinehart, 1948.

Rose, Sir Francis Cyril. *Gertrude Stein and Painting.* London: Book Collecting and Library Monthly, 1968.

Rubery, Annette. "The Mother of Postmodernism? Gertrude Stein On-line." *Time-sense* 1, no. 1 (March 1998). (Electronic quarterly available at http:www.tenderbuttons.com/gsonline.)

Simon, Linda. *Gertrude Stein: A Composite Portrait.* New York: Avon, 1974.

———. *The Biography of Alice B. Toklas.* Garden City, N.Y.: Doubleday, 1977.

Smith, Sidonie, and Julia Watson. *Reading Autobiography: A Guide for Interpreting Life Narratives.* Minneapolis: University of Minnesota Press, 2001.

Souhami, Diana. *Gertrude and Alice.* London: Pandora, 1991.

Spengemann, William C., and L. R. Lundquist. "Autobiography and the American Myth." *American Quarterly* 17 (autumn 1965): 501–519.

Steiner, Wendy. *Exact Resemblance to Exact Resemblance: The Literary Portraiture of Gertrude Stein.* New Haven, Conn.: Yale University Press, 1978.

Stimpson, Catharine R. "Gertrice/Altrude: Stein, Toklas, and the Paradox of the Happy Marriage." In *Mothering the Mind: Twelve Studies of Writers and Their Silent Partners.* Edited by Ruth Perry and Martine Watson Brownley. New York: Holmes and Meier, 1984. Pp. 122–139.

———. "Gertrude Stein and the Lesbian Lie." In *American Women's Autobiography Fea(s)ts of Memory.* Edited by Margo Culley. Madison: University of Wisconsin Press, 1992. Pp. 152–166.

Toklas, Alice B. *What Is Remembered.* New York: Holt, Rinehart and Winston, 1963.

Weiss, Andrea. *Paris Was a Woman: Portraits from the Left Bank.* San Francisco: Harper-SanFrancisco, 1995.

Weininger, Otto. *Sex and Character.* London: Heinemann, 1906. (First published in German, in 1903.)

White, Ray Lewis. *Gertrude Stein and Alice B. Toklas: A Reference Guide.* Boston: G. K. Hall, 1984.

Wickes, George. *Americans in Paris.* Garden City, N.Y.: Doubleday, 1969.

———. "Who Really Wrote *The Autobiography of Alice B. Toklas*?" *Lost Generation Journal* 2, no. 1 (1974): 38–47.

Will, Barbara. *Gertrude Stein, Modernism, and the Problem of "Genius."* Edinburgh: Edinburgh University Press, 2000.

Wren, Celia. "Loving Repeating: Why Has Gertrude Stein Become a Recurrent Character on America's Stages?" *American Theatre* 18 (May–June 2001): 30–33, 76.

Raymond Chandler's The Big Sleep

MARY HADLEY

RAYMOND CHANDLER, AUTHOR of numerous short stories, novels, and screenplays, is important to the detective genre for having developed the hard-boiled private investigator from its beginnings, with Dashiell Hammett and other writers for *Black Mask,* one of the numerous pulp magazines that began in the 1920s. The early stories printed in the pulps reflected the American literary tradition of the adventure tales of such authors as James Fenimore Cooper. These stories were not all in the detective genre; they included westerns, love stories, and others. As LeRoy Lad Panek notes, "Although the pulps began as outlets for miscellaneous fiction, by the teens they developed into specialized magazines for particular audiences." The hard-boiled detective story arose out of the specialized detective pulp magazines and dime novels. Authors wrote several stories a year, aiming to please their immature, often poorly educated audience. Chandler was very different from many of the other hard-boiled writers: his own schooling, at a prestigious private boarding school in England, gave him a literary background that influenced his writing considerably.

Chandler found the British detective story boring, pretentious, and unrealistic, and thus, when he began to pen his own stories, he used fast-paced dialogue and true-to-life characters to mirror the world he saw around him in Los Angeles and the surrounding area. He was intrigued by the criminal element that existed below the surface of the lives of the rich and famous of the Golden State and determined to depict it realistically so that it would appeal to his readers, many of whom were intimately connected with the criminal fringe society. In his letter to Mrs. Robert Hogan in 1947, Chandler said of his writing in the pulp stories:

> I obeyed the formula because I honestly liked it, but I was always trying to stretch it, trying to get in bits of peripheral writing which were not necessary but which I felt would have a subconscious effect even on the semi-literate readers; I felt somehow that the thing to get in this kind of story was a kind of richness of texture.

This richness of texture is particularly evident when one compares Chandler's first novel, *The Big Sleep* (1939), with his last, *The Long Goodbye* (1953). *The Big Sleep* is fascinating in that it expands plots first introduced in Chandler's pulp offerings but cannot compare in its attention to detail and complexity of character development to *The Long Goodbye.*

Chandler is also interesting from a feminist standpoint because he was so influential to the first female hard-boiled writers of the 1980s, among them, Marcia Muller, Sue Grafton, and especially Sara Paretsky. All of these writers claim to have modeled their female private investigators on Hammett's Sam Spade and Chandler's Philip Marlowe. Like their male counterparts, the female detectives are single, take on more than one assignment at one time, and are prepared to use a gun if necessary. Chandler described numerous societal ills in the big city, but unlike the female hard-boiled novelists, his aim was not to change society, just to record it accurately. Another significant difference between the male and female hard-boiled writers lies in the way in which these women altered their narratives to include subject matters that reflect feminist concerns of everyday life and, in particular, relationships. While female detectives such as Grafton's Kinsey Millhone and Paretsky's V. I. Warshawski desperately try to have successful committed relationships and several friends or relatives are concerned about this aspect of their lives, Marlowe is always beset in his love interests and has almost no friends or family to support him. And although V. I. gains many of her assignments from her relatives, Marlowe gets his jobs strictly as business deals.

BACKGROUND TO *THE BIG SLEEP*

The early hard-boiled detective story grew out of a specific desire on the part of certain American male writers to write differently from the traditional novelists of the golden age writers to be found in Britain in the 1930s and 1940s. British writers favored villages and large country houses for many of their settings, whereas hard-boiled writers depicted the urban wilderness of New York and other big cities and the West Coast. Their detectives were professionals, and the police often were shown as corrupt. Above all, it was in the nature of the crimes committed that the differences were most noticeable. Both

CHRONOLOGY

1888	Raymond Thornton Chandler born on July 23 in Chicago.
1895	Chandler moves to London with his mother after his parents' divorce.
1900	Enters Dulwich College, a private boarding school south of London.
1905	Goes to France and later to Germany to study languages.
1912	Returns to America and settles in Los Angeles.
1917	Enlists in the Canadian army and goes to England.
1918	Joins the British Royal Air Force.
1919	Discharged from the service and returns to the West Coast of America.
1922	Takes a job with the Dabney oil syndicate and rises to vice president.
1924	Marries Pearl Eugenie ("Cissy") Hurlburt Porcher Pascal.
1932	Leaves Dabney Oil and begins writing regularly for *Black Mask*.
1939	*The Big Sleep,* Chandler's first novel, is published.
1940	*Farewell, My Lovely.*
1942	*The High Window.*
1943	*The Lady in the Lake.*
1942	*Double Indemnity* (screenplay with Billy Wilder, adapted from James M. Cain's novel of the same title) and *And Now Tomorrow* (screenplay with Frank Partos, adapted from Rachel Field's novel of the same name).
1945	*The Unseen* (screenplay with Hagar Wilde, adapted from Ethel Lina White's book *Her Heart in Her Throat*).
1946	*The Blue Dahlia* (screenplay).
1949	*The Little Sister.*
1951	*Strangers on a Train* (screenplay with Czenzi Ormonde and Whitfield Cook, adapted from Patricia Highsmith's novel of the same name).
1954	*The Long Goodbye* is published in the United States, a year after it appeared in London.
1958	*Playback.*

1959	Raymond Chandler dies in La Jolla, California, on March 26.

Hammett and Chandler depict criminals as sleazy individuals and the crimes as sordid. "The hard-boiled story . . . is full of dope-fiends, sex fiends, gamblers, grifters, corrupt politicians, and rotten millionaires," according to Panek. Compared with the British stately homes and aristocracy, both of which are quite appealing, the American rich and powerful are shown as unhappy individuals beset with a fearful number of problems and living in decadently opulent houses.

Indeed, it is not only the millionaires who are lonely and unhappy; so, too, is the hard-boiled detective. Inhabiting a precarious place midway between the criminal and the police, the detective is characterized as a loner. He has few friends and no close family, and when he finds himself falling in love or lust, the woman generally proves to be a villain. Unlike the classic detective, whose main task was to analyze clues and solve a mystery, the hard-boiled detective is a threat to criminals, who actively pursue him. Vivian Sternwood Regan describes Marlowe in *The Big Sleep* as "a killer at heart, like all cops. . . . One of those dark deadly quiet men who have no more feelings than a butcher has for slaughtered meat." Her harsh description is not entirely accurate: although Marlowe is prepared to use force when necessary, the only man he actually kills is the gunman Lash Canino, in *The Big Sleep.* Rather than being a man without feelings, Marlowe has too many. He often acts selflessly, but when he does, he can end up unappreciated or in jail, as in *The Long Goodbye.* In addition, as John G. Cawelti explains, the hard-boiled detective is very different in another way from the classic detective:

> The hard-boiled detective sets out to investigate a crime but invariably finds that he must go beyond the solution to some kind of personal choice or action. While the classical writer typically treats the actual apprehension of the criminal as a less significant matter than the explanation of the crime, the hard-boiled story usually ends with a confrontation between detective and criminal. Sometimes this is a violent encounter similar to the climactic shootdown of many westerns.

Because he is going to expose and judge societal problems as well as one particular criminal, the hard-boiled detective is often under pressure even by the police and threatened verbally and even physically by them.

Although the setting and the detective "type" mark the hard-boiled genre as very different from the detective stories coming out of Britain at the same time, realism is perhaps their greatest strength. Unlike British readers, who wanted a puzzle formula and minimal viciousness, American readers were keen to read about violent criminals in familiar, tough cities and see a criticism of clearly defined societal ills. This realistic element in the works of all the hard-boiled writers makes their writing appear harsh after the gentility of many of the British female golden age writers, in particular.

Another major difference in this new genre was its style. Clearly, if the plot is concerned with numerous murders or violent crimes and the lives of several hardened criminals are described, the dialogue will not be genteel. As Panek puts it, "Hard-boiled style consists of six elements: direct, uncluttered, active description; jokes and wisecracks; slang and street talk; purposely ungrammatical dialogue; clipped descriptions of events which have serious implications; and metaphors that vividly apprehend the everyday experience of the common man." It is a racy, vivid style, which allows the reader—even today's reader—to become actively involved in a multifaceted world.

RAYMOND CHANDLER: THE VOICE OF THE WRITER

Chandler is a more complex writer than the earlier detective writer Dashiell Hammett, yet he does not feature as much violence in his work as does the later novelist Mickey Spillane. In his letters and in the essay "The Simple Art of Murder," Chandler gives the reader a wealth of information about his hero, himself, and his attitude to the craft of writing. His analysis of his work leaves no doubt as to his intentions. He describes himself in a letter to Hamish Hamilton, his British publisher, in 1950 thus: "As a mystery writer, I think I am a bit of an anomaly, since most mystery writers of the American school are only semi-literate; and I am not only literate but intellectual, much as I dislike the term." When discussing his style with Mrs. Robert Hogan in 1947, he said:

> A good story cannot be devised; it has to be distilled. . . . The writer who puts his individual mark on the way he writes will always pay off. He can't do it by trying, because the kind of style I am thinking about is a projection of personality and you have to have a personality before you can project it.

While the letters give a great insight into many aspects of Chandler's personality and work, perhaps it is the oft-quoted essay "The Simple Art of Murder" that best describes Chandler's views on what makes good detective fiction. There he states, "The good novel is not at all the same kind of book as the bad novel. It is about entirely different things. But the good detective story and the bad detective story are about exactly the same things."

In this essay, too, he criticizes in some detail *The Red House Mystery*, by the British writer A. A. Milne (the children's writer better known for his stories about Winnie the Pooh), which had been critiqued by Alexander Woollcott, a literary critic, former journalist for the *New York Times,* and founding member of the Algonquin Round Table, as "one of the three best mystery stories of all times." Chandler took umbrage both at this fulsome praise and the lack of logic and deduction throughout the story. He was bothered, in particular, by novels like Agatha Christie's *Murder on the Orient Express,* where the solution is impossible to guess because, as he puts it, it "is guaranteed to knock the keenest mind for a loop." He continues to damn many of the puzzle-formula British stories, saying, "The English may not always be the best writers in the world, but they are incomparably the best dull writers." And he adds: "There is a very simple statement to be made about all these stories: they do not really come off intellectually as problems, and they do not come off artistically as fiction. They are too contrived, and too little aware of what goes on in the world."

Comparing the contrived and unrealistic (in his view) British novel of the golden age to those of Dashiell Hammett, Chandler says:

> I doubt that Hammett had any deliberate artistic aims whatever; he was trying to make a living by writing something he had first hand information about. He made some of it up; all writers do; but it had a basis in fact; it was made up out of real things. The only reality the English detection writers knew was the conversational accent of Surbiton and Bognor Regis.

This idea of a sense of "reality" is the key to the differences between the hard-boiled fiction of the United States and British detective stories and is linked to the audience to which the writers were appealing. Dashiell Hammett was writing "for people with a sharp, aggressive attitude to life . . . [who] were not afraid of the seamy side of things; they lived there. Violence did not dismay them; it was right down their street." In contrast, the audience of the female golden age writers usually was middle class, puzzle loving, and female. Marilis Hornidge makes an interesting distinction between the British writers of the 1930s and 1940s whom Chandler damns, differentiating between the "traditional" writers and those who wrote about a professional detective or policeman. Defining "traditional mystery" is difficult, and Hornidge characterizes it more by what the mystery is not. It is not the professional detective or "the espionage tale or the political twister." She maintains that the "traditional" mysteries of the golden age appealed to female readers, whereas the male writers wrote a detective novel with "stalwart" heroes. Clearly, it is those "traditional" mysteries that Chandler despises when he attacks Dorothy Sayers (famed for her Lord Peter Wimsey novels):

> I think what was really gnawing at Miss Sayer's mind was the slow realization that her kind of detective story was an arid formula which could not even satisfy its own implications. It was second-grade literature because it was not about the things that could make first-grade literature. If it started out to be about real people (and she could write about them—her minor characters show that), they must very soon do unreal things in order to form the artificial pattern required by the plot.

Thus, Chandler finds the British mystery story of his own period lacking in verisimilitude. It is perhaps the case, though, that much of Britain was made up of quiet and peaceful villages, dominated by the manor house and rather empty-headed upper-middle-class people—places filled with genteel old ladies like Agatha Christie's Miss Marple, where nothing very seamy happened and few crimes were committed. When they were, the perpetrator usually was caught because he was an aberrant personality. It was a very far cry from gangsters, gambling, murder, and mayhem. Boring the British mysteries might be, but it is not entirely accurate to say that they depict an unrealistic world. It is, however, fair to say that such writers as Christie did not aim to redress societal ills; indeed, Christie rarely even mentions the Great Depression or other topical events in her novels.

PHILIP MARLOWE AS HERO

Philip Marlowe, the protagonist of *The Big Sleep,* is a complex individual who is as fascinating to today's readers as he was to those of the 1930s and 1940s. The opening of *The Big Sleep* has Marlow arriving at the house of the Sternwoods. In the hallway he notices a stained glass panel depicting a knight who is attempting to free a naked lady tied to a tree. Marlowe remarks: "I stood there and thought that if I lived in the house, I would sooner or later have to climb up there and help him. He didn't seem to be really trying." This scene immediately leads the reader to question whether Marlowe is a knight like the one in Chaucer's *Canterbury Tales:*

> Who from the day on which he first began
> To ride abroad had followed chivalry
> Truth, honour, generousness and courtesy.

One soon sees that, to some extent, Marlow is, indeed, such a knight. Much of what he does can be seen as a sort of quest dominated by his compassion for those less fortunate than he. Still, according to Cawelti, he is "a reluctant and ambiguous knight engaged in an obscure quest for a grail whose value he [can] never completely articulate." Throughout the novels readers witness his frustrations over the behavior of the members of the society in which he finds himself. Unlike the classic detective and even some private eyes, he is less concerned with discovering who committed a particular crime than with unveiling hypocrisy, corruption, and moral turpitude while remaining idealistic, albeit poor. And unlike the earlier godlike detective, Marlowe is very much affected by his work, not only physically but also emotionally.

Marlowe's attitude to money (in particular, his own earning power) is key; indeed, several criminals and clients question his motives in light of this attitude. As he tells Taggart Wilde, the district attorney, he earns "twenty-five dollars a day and expenses," to which Taggart responds, surprised, "And for that amount of money you're willing to get yourself in Dutch with half the law enforcement of this county?" Similarly, in *The Long Goodbye,* a hoodlum called Menendez tells Marlowe about all the money he makes, money that allows him to buy the best of everything. He asks Marlowe, "What's the most you ever made on a single job?" and when Marlowe replies "Eight-fifty." He responds, "Jesus, how cheap can a guy get?" By his very attitude toward money, Marlowe distances himself from the unethical gangsters and corrupt "high" society with whom he comes in daily contact. In the same novel, a character repays him for help by sending him a $5,000 note, but Marlowe refuses to spend it because he believes it is tainted, stating, "There was something wrong with the way I got it." It is clear that Marlowe agrees with Lieutenant Bernie Ohls when Ohls says, "There ain't no clean way to make a hundred million bucks."

Marlowe's lack of money is reflected in the way he lives—in particular, his office, with its "five green filing cases, the shabby rust-red rug, the half-dusted furniture, and the not too clean net curtains." This and other descriptions give the reader the strong sense that our detective is an ordinary man. "His way of life may look like failure, but actually it is a form of rebellion, a rejection of the ordinary concepts of success and respectability," says Cawelti.

Chandler describes Marlowe in inordinate detail. He gives so much detail that when D. J. Ibberson wrote to him in 1951, asking for facts about Marlowe's life, Chandler responded on April 19 with several pages of information. He noted, among other facts, his lack of parents and living relatives, the brand of cigarettes he smokes (Camels or any other sort), his height (more than six feet), and his weight ("thirteen stone eight"). Marlowe is, to a certain extent, a knight following a quest, out to save a variety of women in distress. At the same time, he is a fairly ordinary man with whom one can relate simply because he belongs in a tawdry world familiar to his readers. Chandler himself said it best in "The Simple Art of Murder":

> [The detective] must be a complete man and a common man and yet an unusual man. He must be, to use a rather weathered phrase, a man of honor, by instinct, by inevitability, without thought of it, and certainly without saying it. He must be the best man in his world and a good enough man for any world. . . . He is a relatively poor man, or he would not be a detective at all. He is a common man or he could not go among common people. He has a sense of character, or he would not know his job. He will take no man's money dishonestly and no man's insolence without a due and dispassionate revenge.

Even if Chandler may have been exaggerating in this description, it was unusual for an author at that time to flesh out his hero quite so completely, and it allows his readers to see him as a fully rounded individual. Jerry Speir takes exception to the words "complete man"; as Philip Durham points out, however, Marlowe may be an American hero, but he is only a literary one. A true private investigator in California could only investigate, not become involved in murders. "The fictional private eye caught the public fancy because he allowed both sexes to dream, but he was only what his creator intended him to be—pure fantasy." Chandler obviously agreed with Durham's sentiment because he wrote in a letter to Ibberson: "The private detective of fiction is a fantastic creation who acts and speaks like a real man. He can be completely realistic in every sense but one, that one sense being that in life as we know it such a man would not be a private detective."

Marlowe may be "pure fantasy," but his desire to alleviate suffering is evident in *The Big Sleep* when he agrees to help the aged and infirm General Sternwood locate and pay off Arthur Geiger, a purveyor of smut who is blackmailing Carmen, the younger of the general's two daughters. Sternwood already has had to pay another blackmailer, Joe Brody, $5,000 to get out of Carmen's life. Marlowe, having discovered the truth about Sternwood's former son-in-law, Rusty Regan, hesitates to tell Sternwood the truth. The truth about Rusty is that he is dead, shot by Carmen, and lying in an old abandoned oil sump, dumped there by Vivian

Sternwood Regan, helped by Eddie Mars. He feels sorry for Sternwood and does not want him to be "part of the nastiness" of his daughters' lives. The general is depicted as a man who has had a rich and degenerate life but now is a mere shell. He tells Marlowe: "You are looking at a very dull survival of a rather gaudy life, a cripple paralyzed in both legs with only half of his lower belly. There's very little that I can eat and my sleep is so close to waking that it is hardly worth the name." Just in case the reader might begin to feel too much pity for the general, Sternwood later tells Marlowe that neither of his daughters has "any more moral sense than a cat" and nor does he himself. He wants the blackmailer off his back because he is an impatient man and has pride.

Marlowe's compassion for the vulnerable adds to his romanticism. As he tells the district attorney's investigator, Bernie Ohls, in *The Long Goodbye,*

> I'm a romantic, Bernie. I hear voices crying in the night and I go see what's the matter. You don't make a dime that way. You got sense, you shut your windows and turn up more sound on the TV set. Or you shove down on the gas and get far away from there. Stay out of other people's troubles.

Marlowe never stays out of people's troubles, though, even though they cause him pain. In addition, in all the novels Marlowe can be seen as honorable. He refuses to betray a friend in *The Long Goodbye.* In *Farewell, My Lovely* (1940), he is drugged and tied up. When he finally frees himself, he hits his captor, but he does not treat him badly:

> I went back to the man with the white coat. He had too much money for his job. I took what I had started with and heaved him on to the bed and strapped him wrist and ankle and stuffed half a yard of sheet into his mouth. He had a smashed nose. I waited long enough to make sure he could breathe through it.

This sensitivity is remarkable in a private investigator and not characteristic of theprotag onists of many of the other hard-boiled writers.

PHILIP MARLOWE AND WOMEN

The portrayal of women in hard-boiled detective fiction is complicated and prone to disturb the feminist critic. Many women are shown as seductresses, greedy temptresses without morals or ethics. Readers see Marlowe resisting these women, who, in the eyes of the author, are not worthy of his attentions. Just as a worthy knight is not sidetracked by monetary considerations, so, too, Marlowe is not lured into temptation by these women. He is behaving in the tradition of courtly love and thus has to emulate the poetic lover admiring the virginal woman from afar. In *The Big Sleep* the two Sternwood daughters, Vivian and Carmen, both try to seduce Marlowe, but neither succeeds. If the detective is to remain a loner, able to take on quests at a moment's notice, it is important that he not be encumbered by a relationship, especially a committed one. The women he meets most often are blonde and described pejoratively, which supports the traditional representation of woman as Eve, sent to tempt man to fall from grace. Panek posits that the "hard-boiled story . . . may be in part a male response to the change in women's roles that began in the twenties." In this light these female portraits depict a real fear on the part of men of the possible power of women. Certainly, the female hard-boiled novels of the 1980s were written in direct response to the feminist movement of the 1960s and also in contrast to male hard-boiled detective fiction.

In *The Big Sleep* the first description of Vivian Regan sets the scene. "She was worth a stare. She was trouble. She was stretched out on a modernistic chaise-longue with her slippers off, so I stared at her legs in the sheerest silk stockings. They seemed to be arranged to stare at." Later at this first meeting, Vivian tells Marlowe: "My God, you big dark handsome brute! I ought to throw a Buick at you." When he does not respond, she continues, "I loathe masterful men." As the plot unfolds, Marlowe sees Vivian again as she is winning thousands of dollars at the roulette tables of the club owner Eddie Mars. She takes the winnings in a bag and walks outside the casino, only to be held up at gunpoint by a small-time crook, Lanny. Marlowe comes to her rescue by pretending that his pipe is a gun and forcing Lanny to give him the money. Chandler says: "The incident of the masked man with the gun seemed to have made no impression on her at all." Later, after they have had coffee together, Vivian makes a move on Marlowe, and he responds by kissing her "tightly and quickly. Then a long slow clinging kiss." When she asks him where he lives, he counters, "Kissing is nice, but your father didn't hire me to sleep with you." To which she responds calmly, "You son of a bitch." Marlowe rejects Vivian from a sense of nobility and honor toward her father, and her language reinforces her depiction as an unworthy woman.

Vivian's sister, Carmen, also makes several passes at Marlowe, but she is much less attractive to him. She has two main characteristics: lack of intelligence and deformity, not only the physical one of a "curiously shaped thumb" but the psychic one of addiction to drugs and drink. Marlowe's first impression of her is of a small, delicate girl, but she has "predatory" teeth and her slate-gray eyes have "almost no expression." She comments "Tall, aren't you?" When he responds, "I didn't mean to be," she looks puzzled, and Marlowe comments, "I could see, even on that short acquaintance, that thinking was always going to be a bother to her." Carmen is a childlike woman, in need of protection from the world and especially from her own foolishness.

Carmen proves to be trouble throughout *The Big Sleep*. Following the blackmailer Geiger back from his pornographic bookshop to his house, Marlowe waits in his car in the rain. When he hears a shot and a strange, half-pleasurable scream, he breaks the French window and enters the house, only to find Geiger dead on the floor. He had been taking nude photographs of Carmen, who was giggling in a drug-induced state:

> She looked as if, in her mind, she was doing something very important and making a fine job of it. . . . She had a beautiful body, small lithe, compact, firm, rounded. Her skin in the lamplight had the shimmering luster of a pearl. Her legs didn't have quite the raffish grace of Mrs. Regan's legs, but they were very nice. I looked her over without either embarrassment or ruttishness. As a naked girl she was not there in that room at all. She was just a dope. To me she was always just a dope.

When Carmen goes after Joe Brody because he has stolen the nude pictures taken by Geiger and in the fracas is crawling around on the floor, trying to retrieve her gun, Marlowe tells her, "Get up, angel. You look like a Pekinese." The following day, having turned down Vivian's offer of sex, Marlowe returns to his apartment to find Carmen naked in his bed, giggling at him. Her "small sharp teeth glinted," and it is no surprise that he rejects her in a courtly fashion. "It's a question of professional pride. You know—professional pride. I'm working for your father. He's a sick man, very frail, very helpless. He sort of trusts me not to pull any stunts." As he looks at his chessboard on a table close by, he comments to himself: "The move with the knight was wrong. I put it back where I had moved it from. Knights had no meaning in this game. It wasn't a game for knights." Carmen is more than just woman as seductress; she is essentially woman as whore. She will not put on her clothes, and she calls Marlowe by "a filthy name." He feels that by acting in this way she has violated his room, and he tells her that unless she gets dressed immediately, he will throw her out by force, naked. When she finally leaves, the imprint of her "small corrupt body" is still on the bed, which he tears to pieces "savagely."

The last woman of significance in *The Big Sleep* is Mona Mars, the wife of the club owner Eddie Mars, who supposedly ran off with

Vivian's husband, Rusty Regan. She has a "small firm chin" and eyes "the blue of mountain lakes." With her striking blonde, almost silvery hair, she is very attractive. Just as she herself is a fraud, her hair is a wig, and she refuses to accept that Eddie is "a pornographer, a blackmailer, a hot car broker, a killer by remote control and a suborner of crooked cops." Marlowe tries to persuade her to run away with him because he fears for her life with Eddie, but she refuses, and the kiss she gives him is with icy lips. According to William Marling, Mona is considered by some critics an "illusion, the coldness signifying her unreality" or even showing Marlowe's homosexuality. Perhaps this girl with cornflower eyes is "unattainable because she belongs to Chandler's early period of innocence." Maybe she is a real woman with numerous flaws, unacceptable to Marlowe because he prefers fantasy women toward whom he can feel superior.

STYLE IN *THE BIG SLEEP*

Style for Chandler was very important. Many times during his career he discussed style and the effect of language and audience. Like Shakespeare, whom Chandler admired for writing in the language of his time, he also wanted to write in his time and place—that is, in American English as opposed to British English, to appeal to his readers. He was always aware of the power of language and the effects that could be created with it. Because his own personality was tied up in his style, he hated any changes being made to it. Indeed, in a letter to Charles Morton, he points out quite vituperatively that a copy editor changed the word order in one of his articles:

> It is the attitude that gets me, the assumption on the part of some editorial hireling that he can write better than the man who sent the stuff in, that he knows more about phrase and cadence and the placing of words, and that he actually thinks that a clause with a strong (stressed) syllable at the end, which was put there because it was strong, is improved by changing the order so that the clause ends in a weak adverbial termination.

Because Chandler had enjoyed a classical education at an expensive private school in Britain and because he spoke French fluently, much of his writing shows evidence of his own erudition. In addition, his own love of poetry can be seen in the poetic nature of many of his descriptions and in his use of metaphor.

Much has been made of Chandler's use of metaphor, simile, and evocative imagery. There are wisecracks in the dialogue and numerous similes and metaphors to describe each character. At the very beginning of *The Big Sleep,* General Sternwood is said to have "a few locks of dry white hair [which] clung to his scalp, like wild flowers fighting for life on a bare rock." When he begins to speak, the general uses "his strength as carefully as an out-of-work show-girl uses her last good pair of stockings." A few paragraphs later Chandler writes, "The old man nodded, as if his neck was afraid of the weight of his head." Metaphors, too, allow Chandler to give the reader insight into Marlowe's complex character, as he perceives his tawdry world. Dennis Porter describes Chandler's style well when he says that there is an "extravagance" that "gives rise to the creation of grotesques often equal in their vividness to those of the great Victorian novelists." Such "grotesques" are represented, of course, by General Sternwood and, in *Farewell, My Lovely,* Moose Molloy. These characters are, according to Porter, Chandler's "fauna." "In his portraits of 'characters' Chandler sets himself the literary task of finding new combinations of words to express models of ugliness, corruption, squalor, evil, and eroticism."

Throughout *The Big Sleep* women also are described in detail. Carmen is depicted in a mixture of flattering and derogatory terms. When he first meets her, Marlowe says that she walks as if "she were floating," but she has "sharp predatory teeth, as white as fresh orange pith and as shiny as porcelain." Later, she is said to have a smile that would "wash off like water off sand" as she stands in front of Marlowe "like a bad girl in the principal's office." Other women, too, are characterized in equally detailed figurative language. The woman at Geiger's pornographic bookstore approaches Marlowe "with enough sex appeal to stampede a business men's lunch." And Mona Mars has breath as "delicate as the eyes of a fawn."

Chandler's use of metaphor is not limited to his depiction of people. The greenhouse in which Marlowe first meets the general is filled with plants "with nasty meaty leaves and stalks like the newly washed fingers of dead men. They smelled as overpowering as boiling alcohol under a blanket." The furniture in Mona Mars's house "looked as if it had come from one of those places that advertise on bus benches." At the end of the book, when Marlowe finally leaves Vivian Regan, "the bright gardens had a haunted look, as though small wild eyes were watching [him] from behind the bushes, as though the sunshine itself had a mysterious something in its light." Because the use of metaphor is so extensive, it becomes as much a hallmark of Chandler's writing as his characterization and adds greatly to the whole effect of his style.

Chandler's first-person narration is very effective in *The Big Sleep.* First-person narration in a mystery novel has clear disadvantages because the narrator cannot know everything that goes on in the way that an omniscient narrator can. The advantages of the first person for Chandler clearly outweighed these disadvantages. Chandler despised the puzzle formula and the godlike detective of cozy detective fiction, which came out of Britain and was imitated by such American writers as Ellery Queen, Rex Stout, and S. S. Van Dine. Without the traditions, the formality, and the class consciousness that characterized the gentleman detective, the United States could not hope to emulate the golden age writers successfully. If they were to have their own brand of detective fiction, they had to adopt a very different style.

The hard-boiled style was perfect for detective stories about big cities: the vivid descriptions and witty dialogue brought to life the seedy places and sleazy criminals. The first-person style also allowed Chandler to flesh out Marlowe, and his voice acts as the filter, the perspective for all the action. As Frank MacShane explains, Marlowe

> says what the reader might say about the world of Los Angeles were he to encounter it himself. The reader cannot sensibly associate himself with Marlowe as a character in the novel, but he readily accepts his voice. Because it is casual, witty, and forthright, he naturally likes to identify himself with it.

In addition, Marlowe has the voice of the people. When he writes about the houses of the very rich, one hears the implicit resentment toward those who can afford never to work and who can be corrupt and not suffer the consequences. According to Heta Pyrhonen, "Instead of imaginatively identifying with the criminal, the detective-narrator feels himself into the victim, using this relationship as the motivation for his narrative transaction with the reader." This is especially apparent in *Farewell, My Lovely* in Marlowe's sympathy for the protagonist Molloy, who is looking in vain for his former love, Velma.

One criticism that has been voiced of *The Big Sleep* is that the style is uneven. William Marling explains how Chandler used four of his earlier pulp stories to construct *The Big Sleep.* Parts of "Killer in the Rain," "The Curtain," "Mandarin's Jade," and "Finger Man" were combined and enlarged, together with several totally new chapters, to form a fresh story. This "cannibalizing," as Chandler called it, can account for the pulpy nature of some of *The Big Sleep* and for the complexity of the plot. While individual scenes are admirable, the whole does not quite fit. For example, readers never learn who killed the Sternwoods' chauffeur, Owen Taylor, at the start of the story. Other than idle curiosity, there is no real reason for Marlowe to continue searching for the truth about Rusty Regan, but he does so to heighten suspense.

LOS ANGELES AS URBAN WILDERNESS

After living for so many years in California, it was especially fitting that Chandler chose Los Angeles as the setting for his detective stories. The city in the 1930s and 1940s was rife with police lawlessness. According to Frank MacShane, "With so many of its citizens coming from Iowa and Kansas, [the city had] a strong puritanical streak, which [made] it possible for the public to accept summary police proceedings and the harassment of minorities with unpopular opinions." In addition, at this time Los Angeles was transformed from the provincial city it had been at the turn of the century into a vast urban sprawl. Even today the neighborhoods are essentially small cities, with no cohesive whole. Beverly Hills for the rich contrasts with Watts for the poor blacks, and East Los Angeles, where the Mexicans live, is totally different from the San Fernando Valley, the home to middle-class whites. This city of strong contrasts works well as the setting for hard-boiled detective stories; it is easy to imagine it being peopled by such disparate characters as General Sternwood, Eddie Mars, and even Marlowe himself.

In *The Big Sleep* the wealth of minutiae that Chandler depicts in his different settings makes the whole of Los Angeles come alive. Readers know exactly which streets Marlowe is driving on, and when, for instance, he visits Eddie Mars's casino, one can easily imagine the room:

> The light was from heavy crystal chandeliers and the rose-damask panels of the wall were still the same rose damask, a little faded by time and darkened by dust, that had been matched long ago against the parquetry floor, of which only a small glass-smooth space in front of the little Mexican orchestra showed bare. The rest was covered by a heavy old-rose carpeting that must have cost plenty. The parquetry was made of a dozen kinds of hardwood, from Burma teak through half a dozen shades of oak and ruddy wood that looked like mahogany, and fading out to the hard pale wild lilac of the California hills, all laid in elaborate patterns, with the accuracy of a transit.

The hard-boiled stories grew out of frontier fiction, and the violence and lawlessness of Los Angeles, which was so close to the surface of everyday life, was particularly apt as Chandler's setting. Hollywood and the tinsel glamour of the movie industry also highlighted, and even created, the sinful society, gamblers, porn merchants, and blackmailers who preyed on the rich. It is easy to understand why Carmen is being blackmailed, even as Vivian gambles huge sums of money at Eddie Mars's club.

Directly linked to the setting of Los Angeles is Marlowe's attitude to the rich. In all his novels he shines a light on the wealthy, showing how they are corrupt and responsible for numerous societal ills. Just as the female hard-boiled writers showed in the 1980s that even if a particular crime might be solved, the patriarchal institutions that had given rise to the problems generally remained unpunished, so, too, does Marlowe reinforce this fact. In *The Big Sleep*, Geiger, the pornographic bookstore owner, might be shot, but nothing is being done to shut down his shop or limit the trade in pornography. As Captain Gregory of the Missing Persons Bureau tells Marlowe:

> Being a copper I like to see the law win. I'd like to see the flashy well-dressed mugs like Eddie Mars spoiling their manicures in the rock quarry at Folsom, alongside of the poor little slum-bred hard guys that got knocked over on their first caper and never had a break since. That's what I'd like. You and me both lived too long to think I'm likely to see it happen. Not in this town, not in any town half this size, in any part of this wide, green and beautiful U.S.A. We just don't run our country that way.

For Marlowe it is definitely money that corrupts, whether it is the ill-gotten gains of criminals like Eddie Mars or the wealth of the

Sternwoods. Looking at Carmen Sternwood, Marlowe says: "To hell with the rich. They made me sick." She stands, of course, in direct contrast to Marlowe himself, who has little money and a great sense of morality. Panek maintains that some of the social contrasts drawn by hard-boiled writers such as Chandler were directed to readers who were far removed from the wealthy. As he puts it, "The hard-boiled story came to be a paean to the American workman." Whereas the detective hero was a "skilled, honorable, and dedicated workman," society was utterly corrupt.

This corruption usually is caused by money, and it is not only the criminal classes and the rich but also the police who are tainted. *The Big Sleep* shows little police corruption, but in *Farewell, My Lovely* a plainclothes sergeant called Hemingway Galbraith tells Marlowe: "A guy can't stay honest if he wants to. . . . That's what's the matter with this country. He gets chiseled out of his pants if he does. You gotta play the game dirty or you don't eat." Marlowe clearly disagrees with him. In *The Big Sleep,* when Mona Mars says, "As long as people will gamble, there will be places for them to gamble," he responds, "That's just protective thinking. Once outside the law you're all the way outside." It is clear that corruption of any kind, but especially by the police, is against the moral code of a knight. Besides corruption, police brutality adds to the violence of the Los Angeles setting in *Farewell, My Lovely* and *The Long Goodbye.*

FILM ADAPTATIONS

The first cinematic rendition of *The Big Sleep* underwent numerous changes from its original March 1945 filming to its ultimate release in the fall of 1946. With a screenplay by the novelist William Faulkner and the screenwriter Leigh Brackett, with later additions by Jules Furthman and Philip Epstein, the movie picks up much of Chandler's original dialogue. It is in the characters and in key aspects of the plot that most of the changes are apparent. The prerelease version focuses more on Marlowe (played by Humphrey Bogart) than on Vivian Rutledge (played by Lauren Bacall). Bogart plays Marlowe as an insolent guy who is able to pretend without apparent difficulty to be a homosexual when he enters Geiger's bookstore and yet flirts constantly with every female he meets. He admits to being scared when he is tied up in Mona Mars's presence and winces obviously when he is beaten up at different times in the movie. This is clearly a sensitive private investigator, not a macho tough guy. Marlowe retains these characteristics in the final 1946 film release, but the camera angles focused on him are toned down to give more importance to the character of Vivian.

Jack Warner, the movie's producer, determined to give Lauren Bacall (who later married Bogart), in the character of Vivian, several new scenes of an "insolent" nature, to lend the movie a greater love interest between the two protagonists. One scene, in particular, where Marlowe and Vivian sit in a bar and, under the pretext of discussing horseracing, enjoy several minutes of sexual innuendo, was most successful. It was to allow the pair to fall in love that Vivian became the divorced "Mrs. Rutledge" in the movie, and not "Mrs. Rusty Regan," the wife with a missing husband, as she was in the book. This artifice lends her a prominence in the movie that she does not enjoy in the book.

The plot changes in the movie are very much linked to the sexual and social restraints of the 1940s. The homosexuality of Arthur Geiger and his lover, Carol Lundgren, are downplayed but easily identified, if one is aware of the mores of the day. For example, Lundgren always wears a leather jacket and appears very much the he-man. In the novel Carmen is naked when Marlow finds her in Geiger's house and again when she goes to Marlowe's apartment, but, of course, in the movie she is fully clothed. Moreover, her drug habit is merely alluded to, when it is said that she is "high." In the book Carmen is with

Marlowe just before Brody is shot by Carol Lundgren, the homosexual lover of Geiger. Lundgren is under the impression that Brody shot Geiger, but in fact it was Owen Taylor, Vivian Regan's chauffeur, who was in love with Carmen and could not bear to see her demeaning herself by posing naked for Geiger. In the movie both Vivian and Carmen are present, but they have both left Brody's apartment by the time he is killed. The final plot change from the 1945 to the 1946 version concerns the question of who killed Owen Taylor. In the book the killer is never revealed, but in the 1945 movie Bernie Ohls explains that Owen has killed Geiger and Brody followed him, hit him, took the photography, and pushed the car with Taylor in it into the sea.

The second movie version appeared in 1978 and stars Robert Mitchum as Marlowe and Sarah Miles as Vivian (renamed "Charlotte Sternwood Regan"). The director Michael Winner tampers only minimally with Chandler's words, and the fact that Marlowe narrates his thoughts on several occasions, allowing for the full use of Chandler's beguiling metaphors, adds a great deal to the screenplay. Winner's direction also stays closer to Chandler's tone and intent because Marlowe does not have a love interest in Charlotte Regan (Vivian) and the 1970s allowed for nudity and openness about the homosexual Karl (Carol) Lundgren. While Lundgren is portrayed more as a "pretty boy" than a "tough," his relationship with Geiger is made clear when Marlowe tells him, "Joe Brody didn't kill your boyfriend."

Some critics will object that the streets of Westminster, London, and Ramsgate, Kent, are a far cry from Chandler's Los Angeles, but somehow they are just as successful at suggesting greed and dirty dealings as California is. Gene Phillips maintains that "this lurid film wallows too long in the sleazy, voyeuristic world of [the] characters." One could say, however, that the film's openness about showing Camilla (Carmen) naked at Geiger's and allowing Marlowe and the audience to see more naked photos of her is a positive aspect of the film because this was, in fact, Chandler's idea.

Two other aspects of Winner's movie are faithful to the novel. There is a scene with the police and Commissioner Barker that parallels the scene in the 1945 movie where the district attorney explains the death of Owen Taylor. In this 1970s version the death is deemed a suicide, which harks back to Chandler's earlier work "Killer in the Rain." In addition, the ending where Camilla (Carmen) lures Marlowe to where she killed Regan and asks him to teach her to shoot so that she can try to shoot him is included in this movie, whereas it was left out of the earlier version. The inclusion of these two scenes helps to clear up loose ends.

The film also is attractive in that it is in color and seems to move much more swiftly than the earlier black-and-white version. There is a balance in the characterization that is not evident in the earlier version, which at times is a movie so dominated by Bogart and Bacall that Chandler's racy plot and words take second stage. Michael Winner felt that "he didn't adapt the film with sufficient freedom. 'I was so riveted by Chandler, I found it such incredible writing. . . . I didn't want to disturb it with too much trickery in the photography or too much atmosphere.'" Gene Phillips sees this as a major fault on Winner's part, but for many Chandler fans this later version proves the more attractive one, despite or perhaps because of its British setting and director.

RECEPTION AND INFLUENCE

When *The Big Sleep* was first published, it received mixed reviews. Some critics expressed disapproval of the depraved subject matter. This upset Chandler greatly, and he wrote to his American publisher Alfred Knopf on February 19, 1939, saying: "I do not want to write depraved books. I was aware that this yarn had some fairly unpleasant citizens in it, but my fiction was learned in a tough school and I probably didn't notice them much." In the same letter he also admitted the novel was "unequally written." Modern critics, however, continue to hail it as one of the most influential detective novels and a classic. *The Big Sleep* influenced the hard-boiled female writers of the 1980s, and according to the critic William Marling, detective fans ranked it third in a survey of the best mystery stories of all time.

Select Bibliography

EDITIONS

The Big Sleep. New York: Knopf, 1939.

The Big Sleep and Other Novels. London: Penguin, 2000.

OTHER WORKS BY CHANDLER

Later Novels and Other Writings. Edited by Frank MacShane. New York: Library of America, 1995.

SECONDARY WORKS

Cawelti, John G. *Adventure, Mystery, and Romance: Formula Stories as Art and Popular Culture.* Chicago: University of Chicago Press, 1976.

Chaucer, Geoffrey. *The Canterbury Tales.* Translated by Nevill Coghill. London: Penguin Classics, 1973.

Durham, Philip. *Down These Mean Streets a Man Must Go: Raymond Chandler's Knight.* Chapel Hill: University of North Carolina Press, 1963.

Geherin, David. *The American Private Eye: The Image in Fiction.* New York: Frederick Ungar, 1985.

Hornidge, Marilis. "Traditionally Yours." In *The Fine Art of Murder: The Mystery Reader's Indispensable Companion.* Edited by Ed Gorman, Martin H. Greenberg, and Larry Segriff. New York: Galahad Books, 1993.

MacShane, Frank. *The Life of Raymond Chandler.* New York: E. P. Dutton, 1976.

Marling, William. *Raymond Chandler.* Boston: Twayne, 1986.

Panek, LeRoy Lad. *An Introduction to the Detective Story.* Bowling Green, Ohio: Bowling Green State University Popular Press, 1987.

Phillips, Gene D. *Creatures of Darkness: Raymond Chandler, Detective Fiction and Film Noir.* Lexington: University Press of Kentucky, 2000.

Porter, Dennis. *The Pursuit of Crime: Art and Ideology in Detective Fiction.* New Haven, Conn.: Yale University Press, 1981.

Pyrhonen, Heta. *Mayhem and Murder: Narrative and Moral Problems in the Detective Story.* Toronto and Buffalo, N.Y.: University of Toronto Press, 1999.

Slotkin, Richard. "The Hard-Boiled Detective Story: From the Open Range to the Mean Streets." In *The Sleuth and the Scholar: Origins, Evolution, and Current Trends in Detective Fiction.* Edited by Barbara A. Rader and Howard G. Zettler. New York: Greenwood Press, 1988.

Speir, Jerry. *Raymond Chandler.* New York: Frederick Ungar, 1981.

Sarah Orne Jewett's
The Country of the Pointed Firs

KAREN L. KILCUP

FOLLOWING A FARMER with a load of firewood in "A Winter Drive," Sarah Orne Jewett observes:

> It was many years before I ever felt very sorry when woods were cut down. There were some acute griefs at the loss of a few familiar trees, but now I have a heart-ache at the sight of a fresh clearing, and I follow as sadly along the road behind a great pine log as if I were its next of kin and chief mourner at its funeral. There is a great difference between being a live tree that holds its head so high in the air that it can watch the country for miles around,—that has sheltered a thousand birds and families of squirrels and little wild creatures,—that has beaten all the storms it ever fought with; such a difference between all this and being a pile of boards!

Displaying the engaging combination of humor and sensitivity to nature that resonates throughout *The Country of the Pointed Firs* (1896), Jewett here anticipates the ecofeminist perspective that her masterpiece elaborates. This perspective developed during her childhood in rural South Berwick, Maine, where she accompanied her physician father, Dr. Theodore H. Jewett, on his rounds in the countryside and heard the gossip at the family-owned country store.

In "Looking Back on Girlhood" the author reveals,

> My young ears were quick to hear the news of a ship's having come into port, and I delighted in the elderly captains, with their sea-tanned faces, who came to report upon their voyages, dining cheerfully and heartily with my grandfather, who listened eagerly to their exciting tales of great storms on the Atlantic, and winds that blew them north-about, and good bargains in Havana, or Barbadoes, or Havre.

Combined with her excellent education at Berwick Academy, her father's passion for learning, and her access to an outstanding library, hearing the stories of many people in the community enabled Jewett to acquire a concrete experience of human character. All through her life she remembered her father's admonition, "Don't try to write *about* people and things, tell them just as they are!" Jewett's interest in storytelling and affirmative gossip, amply evident in *The Country of the Pointed Firs,* emerges from this personal history.

In addition to biographical factors that converged to empower Jewett's composition of *The Country of the Pointed Firs,* larger cultural forces also informed the text's creation. During her lifetime and before the publication of the book, the New England shipping industry declined significantly, rendering the coastal communities less cosmopolitan and more insular. The Civil War, which occurred while Jewett was in her early teens, radically reduced the number of young men in the community; many of those who remained decided to go west to seek their fortunes, especially after the completion of the transcontinental railroad in 1869. The community that remained at home consisted disproportionately of women, especially older and unmarried women. This imbalance sparked an energetic national discussion about the situation of these "redundant women." At the same time, many of these women formed close long-term relationships—sometimes economic, sometimes emotional and erotic—with other women, as Jewett herself did with her publisher's widow and close friend, Annie Adams Fields. Indeed Lillian Faderman reminds us that "Jewett's most assiduous biographers have been unable to find a trace in her life of even the slightest interest in a heterosexual love affair or marriage," despite the fact that her closest relationship in childhood was not with her mother, Caroline (née Perry), but with her father. Jewett's intimate involvement with women and her experiences in Berwick would lead her to emphasize the lives and psyches of women, especially older women, throughout her work.

Other large social forces were operative as well: the economic crisis of 1873; the upheaval of Reconstruction in the South and its conclusion in 1877; the labor unrest during the century's closing decades; the reemergence of the woman suffrage movement and the emergence of the robber barons; the rapid pace of technological development and concurrent environmental destruction; the rise of environmental consciousness in the United States; accelerating immigration; and the passage of the Chinese Exclusion Act in 1882 and 1892. All of these events affected Berwick as they did the nation as a whole, and all are reflected, either directly or indirectly, in *The Country of the Pointed Firs.* The postwar period also saw the emergence of a substantial middle class that traveled for pleasure and that formed a major audience for what would eventually be called "local color" or "regionalist" writing, enabling many individuals, including white women and writers of color, to earn a living solely by writing. Although Jewett, like the narrator of her great novel, did not need to support herself by her writing, having a family income on which to rely, her efforts were enormously successful

CHRONOLOGY

1849	Jewett is born on September 3 in South Berwick, Maine.
1861–1865	The Civil War. Jewett studies at Berwick Academy, graduating in 1865.
1869	"Mr. Bruce" published in the *Atlantic Monthly.*
1872	Meets Theophilus Parsons, a Harvard law professor and Swedenborgian writer. Jewett's skeptical but long-term interest in spiritualism intensifies.
1877	*Deephaven.*
1878	*Play Days: A Book of Stories for Children.* Jewett's father dies.
1881	James T. Fields dies. Jewett and Annie Fields become closer in a relationship that eventually defined the "Boston marriage."
1884	*A Country Doctor.*
1886	*A White Heron and Other Stories.*
1890	*Tales of New England.*
1896	*The Country of the Pointed Firs.*
1899	*The Queen's Twin and Other Stories.*
1902	Carriage accident after which Jewett writes little.
1908	Meets and mentors Willa Cather.
1909	Jewett dies on June 24 at her home in South Berwick.
1916	*Verses* printed by Jewett's friends.
1925	Willa Cather publishes modified version of *The Country of the Pointed Firs,* naming the book one of three classic American texts, along with *The Scarlet Letter* and *Huckleberry Finn.*

from the beginning—her first major publication occurred when she was only twenty years old—and her work was widely known both in the United States and abroad.

"COME RIGHT IN, DEAR": JEWETT'S INVITATION AND CHALLENGE TO THE READER

In part because of its associative structure, *The Country of the Pointed Firs* is amenable to a wide variety of interpretations. For many early critics the challenge was to construct a reading of the book as a novel, with a traditional conflict leading to a crisis and resolution, but as Elizabeth Ammons has pointed out, the novel's structure is more weblike than linear. Jewett herself acknowledged the unconventional structure of much of her work. In a famous letter to Horace Scudder, the editor of the *Atlantic Monthly,* she writes,

> But I don't believe I could write a long story. . . . In the first place, I have no dramatic talent. The story would have no plot. I should have to fill it out with descriptions of character and meditations. It seems to me I can furnish the theatre, and show you the actors, and the scenery, and the audience, but there is never any play!

Although the narrative in *The Country of the Pointed Firs* represents a variety of tensions, there is no central conflict, no protagonist nor antagonist; instead Jewett elaborates a series of glimpses into rural life at the end of the nineteenth century mediated by the perspective of an affluent writer visiting from the city. The experience of reading her book is more reflective and contemplative and less anxious than for the standard novel, as Jewett interrogates and revises the norms for the genre. At the same time, she explores a number of issues that were of intense concern to her contemporaries and that remain central today, among them gender constructs, race and class relations, and environmental values.

GENDER CONSTRUCTS

When the typical nineteenth-century novel, whether by a male or female writer, discusses relations between men and women, it characteristically focuses on romance. In *The Country of the Pointed Firs,* however, romance appears only as a long-past event evoking loss. In different ways Almira Todd, "Poor Joanna," and Elijah Tilley all mourn the departure of their love partners: Mrs. Todd was rejected by her youthful lover because his mother scorned her lower-class status, and her kind, caring husband, Nathan, died in the waters off Dunnet Landing; Poor Joanna's fiancé "got bewitched with a girl 'way up the bay, and married her, and went off to Massachusetts"; Elijah Tilley so misses his departed wife that he tells the narrator, "I get so some days it feels as if poor dear might step right back into this kitchen. . . . I can't git over losin' of her no way nor no how."

While they form an important substructure and tone for the main narrative, these romances take second place to Jewett's representation of the strength and power of women, especially older women, reflecting the actual demographics of rural northeastern communities and her imagination of a transgendered or androgynous community. Almira Todd, the mysterious herbalist who ministers to the needs of the community, occupies an important role in the imagination of both Jewett and the narrator. Mrs. Todd is first seen dispensing herbal remedies, sometimes with no accompanying instructions and other times with detailed "whispered directions" about the dosage. Mrs. Todd addresses both physical and emotional illnesses: "It may not have been only the common ails of humanity with which she tried to cope; it seemed sometimes as if love and hate and jealousy and adverse winds at sea might also find their proper remedies among the curious wild-looking plants in Mrs. Todd's garden." The conclusion to this set of observations, which completes the important introductory second chapter, elevates Mrs. Todd beyond the realm of ordinary human existence into near-goddess stature:

> She stood in the centre of a braided rug, and its rings of black and gray seemed to circle about her feet in the dim light. Her height and massiveness in the low room gave her the look of a huge sibyl, while the strange fragrance of the mysterious herb blew in from the little garden.

Although Jewett elsewhere humanizes Mrs. Todd—by her criticism of Captain Littlepage and Elijah Tilley, her desire to hide from a cousin whom she unreasonably dislikes, and her disdain for Mari' Harris, an outsider to the village who keeps house for the captain—the author nevertheless presents her as larger than life, a person to be admired.

At the heart of the book, however, is Mrs. Todd's mother, Mrs. Blackett. Together these women offer alternatives to the conventional heroine. The chapters on the visit to Green Island (chapters 8 through 10), Mrs. Blackett's home, represent one of the most idyllic sections of the narrative, with Mrs. Blackett serving as the welcoming deity to her realm of gentle peace and quiet satisfaction. Jewett portrays a psychologically imposing account of the return to the mother, beginning with Mrs. Todd's and the narrator's approach to the island: "A long time before we landed at Green Island we could see the small white house, standing high like a beacon, where Mrs. Todd was born and where her mother lived, on a green slope above the water, with dark spruce woods still higher." Mrs. Todd articulates the mood of the chapter in her remark to the narrator—and readers—that "you never get over bein' a child long's you have a mother to go to." The affectionate interchange between mother and daughter, with the eighty-six-year-old Mrs. Blackett teasing her sixty-seven-year-old daughter about being winded by climbing the hill to the house, reveals their intimacy, as does their chat about the "unlikely" but smart kitten that Mrs. Blackett has chosen from a friend's litter. The tension that saturates the traditional novel transmutes in this instance to friendly banter and comfortable affiliation. Although Jewett risks sentimentality in this episode involving a mother and daughter and a small furry animal, she evades it here and elsewhere with strategies of dialogue, description, and the calmness and plainness of the narrative voice.

Later in the visit Jewett invites readers into Mrs. Blackett's bedroom, where we see "how pleasant it looked, with its pink-and-white patchwork quilt and the brown unpainted paneling of its woodwork." "Come right in, dear," says Mrs. Blackett. "I want you to set down in my old quilted rockin'-chair there by the window; you'll say it's the prettiest view in the house." The narrator sees "a worn red Bible on the light-stand" beside Mrs. Blackett's "heavy silver-bowed glasses" and the "thick striped-cotton shirt that she was making for her son," and she thinks as she sits in the rocker that "it was a place of peace, the little brown bedroom, and the quiet outlook upon field and sea and sky." While she subtly diminishes the importance of the romantic plot in narrative fiction and offers the primacy of contemplative, caring, maternal heroines, Jewett also speaks to her urban contemporaries' desire to escape the bustle and conflict of modern life, as the narrator avers when she concludes, "I never shall forget the day at Green Island. The town of Dunnet Landing seemed large and noisy and oppressive as we came ashore." In the larger social environment of class unrest and racial and ethnic tensions, Dunnet seems to offer an alternative, if vanishing, vision.

Mrs. Blackett's affirmation to the narrator that "I shan't make any stranger of you" epitomizes the goal at the heart of Jewett's narrative, a goal that the narrator highlights in her description of her hostess at the dinner table:

> Her hospitality was something exquisite; she had the gift which so many women lack, of being able to make themselves and their houses belong entirely to a guest's pleasure,—that charming sur-

> render for the moment of themselves and whatever belongs to them, so that they make a part of one's own life that can never be forgotten. Tact is after all a kind of mind-reading, and my hostess held the golden gift.

Mrs. Blackett's "perfect self-forgetfulness" enables the relationship that Jewett elevates above all others in this book: friendship. Heterosexual romantic love, the subject of many American novels, consistently engenders pain in the world of Dunnet Landing, but friendship allows relationships to flourish and to heal worldly wounds.

Jewett's emphasis on friendship forms a dominant thematic strand, from the opening chapter where the narrator privileges it over romantic love, affirming that "the growth of true friendship may be a life-long affair," to her active listening to Captain Littlepage's story and her acknowledgment that "we parted, the best of friends," to the intimate moments with Mrs. Todd during her departure at the story's end. Indeed the matter of durability in relationships, especially among women, forms the core of the book. "The process of falling in love at first sight" suggests an ephemeral and heteroerotic passion, whereas "true friendship" requires the commitment of equals, in this book represented as women, to "life-long" intimacy and shared pleasures.

One episode in which friendship figures crucially occurs during Mrs. Fosdick's visit. The narrator fears being cast aside in Mrs. Todd's affections in favor of this old acquaintance, especially when she meets Susan Fosdick and "the two friends passed on to the kitchen, where I soon heard a hospitable clink of crockery and the brisk stirring of a tea-cup. I sat in my high-backed rocking-chair by the window in the front room with an unreasonable feeling of being left out." Mrs. Todd, however, re-creates the occasion as an opportunity for expanded community, leaving her two guests together to visit and later allowing the narrator to become engaged in the friends' reminiscences about family and friends. When Mrs. Fosdick notes that "conversation's got to have some root in the past, or else you've got to explain every remark you make, an' it wears a person out," Mrs. Todd responds, "Yes 'm, old friends is always best, 'less you can catch a new one that's fit to make an old one out of," as she shares "an affectionate glance" with the narrator.

Although Jewett offers readers appealing, beloved elderly heroines, beautiful in spirit rather than in body, elderly men also represent an important presence in the community. The most disturbed and disturbing of the men in the book is the declined patriarch Captain Littlepage, who cites Milton and imagines a ghostly intermediate world between the living and the dead. Much more attractively portrayed are the feminized characters of Mrs. Todd's brother, William, and of Elijah Tilley. When the narrator visits Green Island, Mrs. Blackett acknowledges to Mrs. Todd that "William has been son an' daughter both since you was married off the island" and notes that "William has very deep affections." William seems as shy as a young girl with strangers; indeed the narrator describes her first encounter with him in terms that suggest his feminine alliances: "I turned . . . and saw an elderly man . . . with a timid air. It was William. He looked just like his mother, and I had been imagining that he was large and stout like his sister." If Almira Todd seems somewhat masculine in her business pursuits and self-assertiveness—we later learn that she takes after her father—William represents her feminized male counterpart.

William's sensibility has the delicacy and attention to detail customarily associated with women, for as he and the narrator return to the house, he

> stopped once or twice to show me a great wasps'-nest close by, or some fishhawks'-nests below in a bit of swamp. He picked a few sprigs of late-blooming linnæa as we came out upon an open bit of pasture at the top of the island, and gave them

> to me without speaking, but he knew as well as I that one could not say half he wished about linnæa.

Ironically Mrs. Todd sees her brother as a failure, at least in the world's terms, but the narrator conveys another perspective. The chapter "The Old Singers" reinforces her appreciation of William's mild, gentle personality, as she describes in highly feminized terms his singing "Home, Sweet Home" with his mother: "His voice was a little faint and frail, like the family daguerreotypes, but it was a tenor voice, and perfectly true and sweet." By portraying William as androgynous, Jewett critiques binarized gender roles and the emergent norm of the manly man, whose prototype would be Theodore Roosevelt.

This blurring of gender boundaries in the portrait of William reemerges in the depiction of Elijah Tilley, who receives the narrator into his home with his knitting, "a blue yarn stocking," in hand. The narrator observes, "There was something delightful in the grasp of his hand, warm and clean, as if it never touched anything but the comfortable woolen yarn, instead of cold sea water and slippery fish." After the death of his wife, Elijah has become domesticated so that his year is divided between feminine and masculine endeavors:

> "No; I take stiddy to my knitting after January sets in," said the old seafarer. . . . "The young fellows braves it out, some on 'em; but, for me, I lay in my winter's yarn an' set here where 'tis warm, an' knit an' take my comfort. Mother learnt me once when I was a lad. . . . They say our Dunnet stockin's is gettin' to be celebrated up to Boston,—good quality o' wool an' even knittin' or somethin'. I've always been called a pretty hand to do nettin', but seines is master cheap to what they used to be when they was all hand worked. I change off to nettin' long towards spring."

The most striking feature of this passage is the convergence of knitting, a traditionally feminine task, with netting, a traditionally masculine one. Even netting possesses feminine overtones in its other meaning of lace-making. Feminine and masculine, domestic and public realms mesh here in the synthesis of these activities by a single individual and even in the similarity of the sounds of the words "knitting" and "netting," virtual homophones.

Initially the narrator misreads Elijah, placing him among the other taciturn old fishermen who are his contemporaries. Returning to the theme of friendship so central to *The Country of the Pointed Firs,* she seems partly envious of these men's ability to communicate by unspoken means, observing that "there was an alliance and understanding between them, so close that it was apparently speechless" and that "arguments and opinions were unknown to the conversation of these ancient friends; you would as soon have expected to hear small talk in a company of elephants." This community of men seems to be one from which the narrator, and women in general, are wholly excluded. The narrator describes Elijah as "such an evasive, discouraged-looking person, heavy-headed, and stooping so that one could never look him in the face, that even after his friendly exclamation . . . I did not venture at once to speak again." But when she remembers Mrs. Todd's assertion that Elijah was "sore stricken and unconsoled at the death of his wife" eight years earlier, she ventures to accept his invitation to visit.

What she—and the reader—discovers is that Elijah's sensibility parallels William's, as he reminisces much as a woman would do and revives his wife for his visitor. Significantly the lost wife's talents parallel those of Mrs. Blackett, including hospitality, sensitivity, and generosity: "'You'd have liked to come and see her; all the folks did,' said poor Elijah. 'She'd been so pleased to hear everything and see somebody new that took such an int'rest. She had a kind o' gift to make it pleasant for folks.'" Sharing intimate details of their life together, such as his wife's pain at breaking a precious tea cup that Elijah had given her and her ability to make beautiful rugs, Elijah affirms, "Her an' me was always havin' our jokes together same 's a boy an' girl. Outsiders never'd know nothin' about it to see us. She had nice manners with all, but to me there was nobody so entertainin." Tangling his yarn because of his tears, Elijah has already admitted what is now clear to the narrator: "I can't git over losin' of her no way nor no how." In her androgynous portrait of Elijah Tilley, as in that of William, Jewett rewrites the hero as she has rewritten the heroine and the domestic romance.

Finally Jewett proposes an intimate relationship—a friendship—between the reader (figured in the character of the narrator, who "reads" the "characters" of Dunnet Landing) and Mrs. Todd herself; she invites readers to envision themselves both inside and outside of this community. In a number of passages in the book she delicately suggests an erotic (but sensual rather than sexual) closeness. The first of these passages arrives early after the narrator has acted as her landlady's amanuensis in the herbalist business and, feeling that she has become too close (and that she has done no writing, which she initially believes requires detachment from others rather than proximity), she says "unkind words of withdrawal to Mrs. Todd." However, Mrs. Todd reaffirms their friendship apart from business, and the narrator confesses that "Mrs. Todd and I were *not separated* or *estranged* by the change in our business relations; on the contrary, a *deeper intimacy* seemed to begin" (emphasis added). At the end of this scene she confides,

> I do not know what herb of the night it was that used sometimes to send out a penetrating odor late in the evening, after the dew had fallen, and the moon was high, and the cool air came up from the sea. Then Mrs. Todd would feel that she must talk to somebody, and I was only too glad to listen. We both fell under the spell.

Nature helps Mrs. Todd to engage her guest in a sensual intercourse whose significance resides less in its explicit content and more in its gesture toward sameness and intimacy, in which Mrs. Todd ultimately tells "all that lay deepest in her heart." In Jewett's fluidly bounded and homoerotic world, differences between author and reader appear to dissolve.

The expedition to Green Island, and especially to Mrs. Todd's favorite pennyroyal patch, seems to mark another moment of equality and same-sex intimacy between women characters in which sensuality replaces passion, as the two women "exhibit what [lesbian feminist critic] Adrienne Rich calls . . . 'a primary intensity' for one another." Mrs. Todd's first gesture, sharing with the narrator the daguerreotypes of her family, signifies the "outsider's" incorporation into that family. As they walk together, the sharing becomes more intense: "Among the grass grew such pennyroyal as the rest of the world could not provide. There was a fine fragrance in the air as we gathered it sprig by sprig . . . and Mrs. Todd pressed her aromatic nosegay between her hands and offered it to me again and again." As if reaching to a lover, Mrs. Todd's gesture resonates with sensuality, and her verbal gesture shortly after indicates the intimacy of their intercourse: "There dear, I never showed nobody else but mother where to find this place; 'tis kind of sainted to me. Nathan, my husband, an' I used to love this place when we was courtin'." The narrator's response confirms their movement together: "I had never heard her speak of her husband before, but I felt that we were *friends* now since she had brought me to this place" (emphasis added). Significantly the narrator underscores not just their sharing of verbal confidence, but also their physical coupling. In this special place she becomes a "reader" who re-creates herself, "waking . . . to new thoughts, and reading a page of remembrance with new *pleasure*" (emphasis added); and Jewett invites her readers—at least her female readers—to respond with similar sensuality, delight, and self-affirmation. This impulse to invite the reader's participation distinguishes Jewett's book from many novels by her predecessors and contemporaries.

RACE, ETHNICITY, AND CLASS RELATIONS

Although early accounts of *The Country of the Pointed Firs* ignore its concern with some of the most charged social issues of the time, more recent critics question Jewett's, and the early critics', relatively idealized portrait of relationships between and among women, pointing out that Jewett's stories demonstrate and perpetuate attitudes of racial, ethnic, and class hierarchy embodied in the larger society. Others, while acknowledging the writer's inevitable participation in attitudes common in her historical moment, defend her relatively progressive views. *The Country of the Pointed Firs* is at the center of these debates, as Jewett's challenge to readers takes on a new angle.

For example, in "Material Culture, Empire, and Jewett's *Country of the Pointed Firs*," Elizabeth Ammons takes Jewett to task for elevating her Norman ancestors over the Saxon strain. During the Bowden family reunion, the narrator offers observations on the assembled family members:

> I had been noticing with great interest the curiously French type of face which prevailed in this rustic company. I had said to myself before that Mrs. Blackett was plainly of French descent, in both her appearance and her charming gifts, but this is not surprising when one has learned how large a proportion of the early settlers on this northern coast of New England were of Huguenot blood, and it is the Norman Englishman, not the Saxon, who goes adventuring to a new world.

This perspective continues as Mrs. Todd observes: "They used to say in old times . . . that our family came of very high folks in France, and one of 'em was a great general in some o' the old wars." Later during the festivities the narrator notes nostalgically, "So . . . their ancestors may have sat in the great hall of some old French house in the Middle Ages, when battles and sieges and processions and feasts were familiar things." By the end of the day, the narrator is consuming the gingerbread prototype of the Bowden house and acknowledging to readers that "I came near to feeling like a true Bowden, and parted from certain new friends as if they were old friends." According to Ammons, "The usual way of reading the Bowden reunion—the way the narrator interprets it for us and thus implicitly instructs us to do likewise—is as a naïve, joyful, old-fashioned rural festival affirming traditional American values of family loyalty, abiding patriotism, and spontaneous benevolent accord with nature." The problem is that "many white feminist critics" have "written fondly of this reunion and of the book as a whole as a celebratory mythologization of a rural matrifocal community in which women . . . have real power and status." By participating in the reunion, says Ammons, and in particular by partaking of the gingerbread with such zest, the narrator signifies her approval of the imperial ambitions of America, which the Bowdens collectively represent: "The reunion celebrates . . . the triumphant colonization of Indian land by white people of British and Norman ancestry."

Certainly during the period in which Jewett was writing—the Colonial Revival—many Americans celebrated traditional (white) values and enjoyed a nostalgia for "simpler" times. However, the period also inaugurated a flurry of self-examination about colonialism and its consequences for Native Americans. Karen Oakes anticipates Ammons' argument in her exploration of the problematic appearance of Native Americans and the "Indian" figure in a variety of Jewett works, including *Deephaven* (1877), the precursor to *The Country of the Pointed Firs.* In Jewett's masterpiece the figure of the Native American haunts the narrative in ways that are difficult to interpret. As an herbalist, Mrs. Todd dispenses "the Indian remedy"—presumably an abortifacient based on her favorite pennyroyal—which, Oakes says, "suggests a subversion of patriarchal control of women's bodies." Moreover, Mrs. Todd cherishes plants "both wild and tame," suggesting at least metaphorically that Indians and whites are of equal value.

A similar ambiguity appears in Jewett's portrait of Poor Joanna, whose home, Shell-heap Island, was, according to Mrs. Fosdick, "counted a great place in old Indian times." But Mrs. Fosdick goes on to express a more sinister perspective:

> I remember when they used to tell queer stories about Shell-heap Island. Some said 'twas an old bangeing-place [a place to idle or loaf] for the Indians, and an old chief resided there once that ruled the winds; and others said they'd always heard that once the Indians come down from up country an' left a captive there without any bo't, an' 'twas too far to swim across to Black Island, so called, an' he lived there till he perished.

Recalling an earlier era of danger among the "savages," this passage precedes a remark by Mrs. Todd that seemingly unsettles such easy and stereotypical associations: "Anyway, there was Indians,—you can see their shell-heap that named the island; and I've heard myself that 'twas one o' their cannibal places, but I never could believe it. There never was no cannibals on the coast o' Maine. All the Indians o' these regions are tame-looking folks." Mrs. Fosdick suggests that the danger lies elsewhere, abroad: "Sakes alive, yes! . . . Ought to see them painted savages I've seen when I was young out in the South Sea Islands!" Again in these remarks lie a troubling domestication and romanticization (along with eradication) of Native Americans. For the affluent white reader such portraits of "exotic" people and places—even at home—may have provided a kind of armchair tourism.

In a similar vein Sandra A. Zagarell points to racist elements of a conversation during the reunion in which Mrs. Caplin, a friend of Mrs. Todd, notes that, to her, Captain Littlepage's housekeeper "Mari' Harris resembled a Chinee." In the context of the recently enacted Chinese Exclusion Act of 1882, this remark is potentially problematic for today's readers. Another way to understand this observation is with an ear simultaneously attuned to nuances of class difference. When the narrator first meets the captain, Mari' is shadowing him and Mrs. Todd:

> Behind this pair was a short, impatient, little person, who kept the captain's house, and gave it what Mrs. Todd and others believed to be no proper sort of care. She was usually called 'that Mari' Harris' in subdued conversation between intimates, but they treated her with anxious civility when they met her face to face.

By this time in the United States, even in old-fashioned parts of rural New England like Dunnet Landing, the distinction between traditionally egalitarian "help" and the more subservient concept of the servant had emerged. The narrator remarks, upon observing the captain's "careful precision of dress," that "I knew Mari' Harris to be a very common-place, inelegant person, who would have no such standards." The narrator seemingly echoes here the opinions of her landlady and offers a model for readers.

The question that arises is where the author stands. In this context Judith Fetterley raises important problems:

> If white women are understood simply as sites of race and class privilege, then one cannot argue that recovering their texts is an act of enfranchising the disenfranchised. Indeed, if one accepts this model, then one can only recover these texts to critique them. And in such a climate, why bother to read them at all?

That is, "inclusion serves as the occasion for orchestrating their redismissal and for effecting their continued exclusion from further literary or historical consideration." Significantly Jewett offers the possibility that her reunion "queen" and heroine, Mrs. Blackett, provides readers with a more appropriate perspective than that articulated by her daughter. When Mrs. Caplin and Mrs. Todd are noting Mari's Asian characteristics, Mrs. Blackett covertly admonishes them: "Mari' Harris was pretty as a child, I remember." When her daughter reverts to criticism, calling the housekeeper "one o' them pretty little lambs that make dreadful homely old sheep" and asserting that Captain Littlepage is "a good sight better company, though dreamy, than such sordid creatur's as Mari' Harris," her mother carefully closes the conversation: "'Live and let live,' said dear old Mrs. Blackett gently"—and then she firmly changes the subject.

Reflecting the mobility of affluent Americans in this period and their proclivity for summer vacations in rural areas, the narrator embodies a class difference from Mrs. Todd that also bears mentioning. A writer, the narrator can afford room and board for spending the summer out of the city, as well as for renting the schoolhouse as an office. While she watches the funeral of Mrs. Begg, the narrator bemoans her separation from the community:

> I began to wonder if I ought not to have walked with the rest, instead of hurrying away at the end of the services. Perhaps the Sunday gown I had put on for the occasion was making this disastrous change of feeling, but I had now made myself and my friends remember that I did not really belong to Dunnet Landing.

Her lack of belonging refers not only to her urban geographical origins but also to her special class status—a status she shares, ironically, with the dreamy Captain Littlepage himself. Citing Darwin she remarks, "There is no such king as a sea-captain; he is greater even than a king or a schoolmaster!" Although there may be an element of kindly humor in this observation, the narrator highlights the captain's elevated manners and perspective, in which he argues nostalgically that the cosmopolitan seafaring men of an earlier generation "lived more dignified, and their houses were better within an' without." This judgment precedes his assertion that "a shipmaster was apt to get the habit of reading. . . . A captain is not expected to be familiar with his crew." Establishing his hierarchical position, Littlepage also underscores his isolation, an isolation similar to the narrator's in this episode.

If the story of her visit represents the process of creating a friendship with both Mrs. Todd and the entire Dunnet community, then the concluding chapter, "The Backward View," paints a portrait of a woman who has engaged the affections of Mrs. Todd but who, as she leaves, detaches herself—and hence readers—from the intimacy she has been at such pains to evoke. As she returns to the city for the winter, her Maine friends become a pleasant yet retreating memory: "When I looked back again, the islands and the headland had run together and Dunnet Landing and all its coasts were lost to sight." Her "work," unlike theirs, is not necessary for survival, and it has far fewer risks, as she acknowledges in this closing chapter:

> Out in the main channel we passed a bent-shouldered old fisherman bound for the evening round among his lobster traps. He was toiling along with short oars, and the dory tossed and sank and tossed again with the steamer's waves. I saw that it was old Elijah Tilley, and though we had so long been strangers we had come to be warm friends, and I wished that he had waited for one of his mates, it was such hard work to row along shore through rough seas and tend the traps alone.

Here Jewett effectively figures the distance—geographical, psychological, and social—that separates the narrator and those like her from this "friend." The marks of Elijah's working life are embodied in his bent shoulders; the hardships he has endured parallel his "hard work" rowing "through rough seas." His friends who could help are absent, and the narrator cannot speak to him across this literal and figurative class divide: "As we passed I waved my hand and tried to call to him, and he looked up and answered my farewells by a solemn nod."

As she does elsewhere in the narrative, Jewett leaves the reader interpretive space: Is Elijah's nod symptomatic of his Yankee reticence? Does it demonstrate his deference to the narrator? Is he indicating his awareness of the transitory nature of their friendship? Although indirectly, Jewett acknowledges her own separation from many people in the Maine community in which she grew up and spent much of her adult life: ultimately Elijah cannot hear the narrator, and their ability to communicate is limited to cryptic body language. In the portraits of Elijah and others, Jewett suggests the frail connections between and among people of different races, ethnicities, genders, and classes, and she invites readers to ponder the possibilities and difficulties of establishing such connections.

NATURE WRITING AND THE ENVIRONMENT

Jewett's writing as a whole, and *The Country of the Pointed Firs* in particular, participates in a tradition of American women's nature writing. In many passages, as well as in the person of Mrs. Todd, Jewett highlights what is for her a restorative affiliation among women, nature, and health (including social health). The opening depiction of Mrs. Todd and her home, with its "bushy bit of a green garden, in which all the blooming things, two or three gay hollyhocks and some London-pride, were pushed back against the gray-shingled wall," articulates this affiliation immediately. This garden is not for show, "the few flowers being put at a disadvantage by so much greenery." Instead it exists for well-being: "The sea-breezes blew into the low end-window of the house laden with not only sweet-brier and sweet-mary, but balm and sage and borage and mint, wormwood and southernwood."

Recalling Henry David Thoreau's *Walden* (1854), the story follows the pattern of the seasons, with the narrator arriving in Dunnet in June, at the beginning of summer, and leaving in late summer. Her stay in the schoolhouse provides the narrator with not only distance from the community but also the distance to view nature. As she tries to write during the funeral procession, nature provokes philosophical meditations: "It was a glorious day early in July, with a clear, high sky; there were no clouds, there was no noise of the sea. The song sparrows sang and sang, as if with joyous knowledge of immortality, and contempt for those who could so pettily concern themselves with death." Envisioning transcendence, the narrator soon discovers that she is unavoidably a part of nature:

> Now and then a bee blundered in and took me for an enemy; but there was a useful stick upon the teacher's desk, and I rapped to call the bees to order as if they were unruly scholars, or waved them away from their riots over the ink, which I had bought at the Landing store, and discovered too late to be scented with bergamot, as if to refresh the labors of anxious scribes.

Familiarly known as bee balm, bergamot represents the necessary connection between nature and art, between the body and meditation. Although the writer purports to have control over her environment (in both senses), this encounter in the schoolhouse suggests that she is not nature's teacher—even if she sits at the desk—but its student, a lesson that Captain Littlepage's story, and Mrs. Todd's later response to it, indicates: "Some thinks he overdid, and affected his head, but for a man o' his years he's amazin' now when he's at his best. Oh he used to be a beautiful man!"

Jewett follows this exclamation with a break in the narrative that suggests readers should contemplate Mrs. Todd's words carefully; then she indicates that we should look elsewhere than to the captain's ethereal stories of another world:

> We were standing where there was a fine view of the harbor and its long stretches of shore all covered by the great army of the pointed firs, darkly cloaked and standing as if they waited to embark. As we looked far seaward among the outer islands, the trees seemed to march seaward still, going steadily over the heights and down to the water's edge.

This view underscores the need to ground oneself by looking at what is present, rather than, as the captain—and the narrator herself, a professional writer—does, imagining other worlds. It also provides a perspective of nature as animate, with the "army" of the "pointed firs" ready to do battle with the sea. In anthropomorphizing the trees Jewett here emphasizes both the beauty and potential conflict in nature.

Nature can also transform itself from moment to moment:

> It had been growing gray and cloudy, like the first evening of autumn, and a shadow had fallen on the darkening shore. Suddenly, as we looked, a gleam of golden sunshine struck the outer islands, and one of them shone out clear in the light, and revealed itself in a compelling way to our eyes. . . . The sunburst upon that outermost island made it seem like a sudden revelation of the world beyond this which some believe to be so near.

Refining her earlier critique of Captain Littlepage's world as too rarified and reminding readers of their interactive interpretive role, Jewett suggests that his vision of transcendence is too remote and too gloomy. That is, if nature—and all it represents—seems to be "growing gray and cloudy," when one looks more steadfastly, a "revelation" of "golden sunshine" suggestive of "the world beyond this" will manifest itself. In some sense Jewett affirms a transcendental view of nature that suggests nature's affinity with the divine; yet her recurrent insistence on *both* bodily existence and imaginative life indicates a profound optimism about the world and a deep faith in nature.

Significantly the transcendental vision in this passage has a human representative: Mrs. Blackett. Ending one paragraph with the vision of the sunburst upon the island that "made it *seem* like a sudden revelation of the world beyond" (emphasis added), Jewett goes on to undercut the vision with subtle humor as Mrs. Todd tells the narrator: "That's where mother lives. . . . Can't we see it plain? I was brought up out there on Green Island. I know every rock an' bush on it." The "world beyond" is actually identical with the natural world, Green Island, whose reigning deity is Mrs. Blackett. Jewett continues this strand of genial humor throughout the visit to Green Island as, for example, when the narrator goes out to dig potatoes: "There is all the pleasure one can have in gold-digging in finding one's hopes satisfied in the riches of a good hill of potatoes." While it mocks the worldly ambitions of many Americans living in what Mark Twain called the Gilded Age, this scene again reminds readers of nature's sensuality as Jewett depicts it in the pennyroyal-gathering episode with Mrs. Todd and the narrator.

In this coastal community nature is also a provider and comforter. Mrs. Todd reminisces to Mrs. Fosdick that, when Poor Joanna moved to Shell-heap Island, "I expect there was always plenty of driftwood thrown up, and a poor failin' patch of spruces covered all the north side of the island, so she always had something to burn." Mrs. Todd notes that Joanna gathers potatoes from her garden and fish, clams, and lobsters from the ocean, concluding: "You can always live well in any wild place by the sea when you'd starve to death up country, except 'twas berry time. Joanna had berries out there, blackberries at least, and there was a few herbs in case she needed them." For company, Mrs. Fosdick notes, "There was her hens." Although city readers who were Jewett's contemporaries may have found this observation amusing, Jewett places it in the context of a "melancholy" discussion about Joanna's love for her friends and her imagined loneliness, again characteristically leaving the reader an interpretive space.

Like Joanna, the narrator, who makes a pilgrimage to Shell-heap Island, envisions nature as a refuge, a "hermitage," to echo the title of chapter 14. The description of her visit continues the overarching narrative's seasonal theme:

> The month was August, and I had seen the color of the islands change from the fresh green of June to a sunburnt brown that made them look like

> stone, except where the dark green of the spruces and fir balsam kept the tint that even winter storms might deepen, but not fade.

Although nature embodies transformation, it also figures permanence. In spite of many dead trees, some elements, such as "low-growing bushes" and "wild morning-glories" survive. Other survivors recall the wild sparrows that Joanna tames, one of which lands on her coffin and sings at her funeral: "The birds were flying all about the field; they fluttered up out of the grass at my feet as I walked along, so tame that I liked to think they kept some happy tradition from summer to summer of the safety of nests and good fellowship of mankind." In these affirmative images Jewett envisions a healing and necessary continuity between human beings and the natural world.

By emphasizing Mrs. Todd's profound respect for the medicinal power of herbs and Poor Joanna's potential for redemption in nature, Jewett underscores the obligation of people to see themselves as part of the natural world. She reinforces this theme during the journey to the Bowden family reunion. As the narrator, Mrs. Blackett, and Mrs. Todd travel inland, Jewett invites readers to consider a tree as one would a person:

> We had just passed a piece of woodland that shaded the road, and come out to some open fields beyond, when Mrs. Todd suddenly reined in the horse as if somebody had stood on the roadside and stopped her. She even gave that quick reassuring nod of her head which was usually made to answer for a bow, but I discovered that she was looking eagerly at a tall ash-tree that grew just inside the field fence.
>
> "I thought 'twas goin' to do well," she said complacently as we went on again. "Last time I was up this way that tree was kind of drooping and discouraged. Grown trees act that way sometimes, same 's folks; then they'll put right to it and strike their roots off into new ground and start all over again with real good courage. Ash-trees is very likely to have poor spells; they ain't got the resolution of other trees."

Mrs. Todd treats the ash tree with respect, and she makes explicit for the narrator and for readers the parallels, even the continuity, between trees and "folks." In effect, as someone who has an intimate acquaintance with plants "both wild and tame," she translates the "body language" of trees into concepts and language accessible to people. Her remarks about "tree nature" and "human nature" often seem bidirectional, with the behavior of one standing in for that of the other. She continues her education of the narrator and reader:

> "There's sometimes a good hearty tree growin' right out of the bare rock, out o' some crack that just holds the roots;" she went on to say, "right on the pitch o' one o' them bare stony hills where you can't seem to see a wheel-barrowful o' good earth in a place, but that tree'll keep a green top in the driest summer. You lay your ear down to the ground an' you'll hear a little stream runnin'. Every such tree has got its own livin' spring; there's folks made to match 'em."

In this worldview, "folks" mirror trees, not the other way around—the natural world is at the center and people are an organic part of the whole. Here Jewett echoes some of the philosophy that she expresses in "River Driftwood," an autobiographical essay (collected in *Country By-ways* in 1881) about the Piscataqua region in which she grew up. The essay underscores human ignorance of the natural world and resistance to hearing its language:

> It is easy to say that other orders of living creatures exist on a much lower plane than ourselves; we know very little about it, after all. They are often gifted in some way that we are not; they may even carry some virtue of ours to a greater height than we do. . . . The day will come for a more truly universal suffrage than we dream of now, when the meaning of every living thing is understood, and it is given its rights and accorded its true value.

The Country of the Pointed Firs concludes in late summer, and by continuing her emphasis on nature Jewett foregrounds the inevitability of human participation in the rhythms of the natural environment. The final chapter opens with an evocation of the narrator's physical connection to place. Indoors is "cool and damp in the morning, and all the light seemed to come through green leaves; but at the first step out of doors the sunshine always laid a warm hand on my shoulder, and the clear, high sky seemed to lift quickly as I looked at it." The friendship that she has established with Mrs. Todd and the other residents of Dunnet Landing seems to extend to nature itself, and the narrator has become more attuned to outdoor rhythms, as she exercises a heightened intensity of the senses:

> There was no autumnal mist on the coast, nor any August fog; instead of these, the sea, the sky, all the long shore line and the inland hills, with every bush of bay and every fir-top, gained a deeper color and a sharper clearness. There was something shining in the air, and a kind of lustre on the water and the pasture grass,—a northern look that, except at this moment of the year, one must go far to seek. The sunshine of a northern summer was coming to its lovely end.

This opening, which is also a closing, reminds readers of human mortality. Time and the seasons propel the narrator toward a greater "clearness" of vision ("no autumnal mist . . . nor any August fog") and a stronger appreciation of detail that contrasts vividly with Captain Littlepage's nebulous and speculative account of human passages into unknown territory. On one level Jewett's vision offers an imaginative respite for Americans, especially urban, privileged ones like the narrator, from the hard edges, pollution, and corruption (in all senses of these words) of modern life. As the critic Josephine Donovan observes, "The world of rural Maine, the land of the pointed firs . . . emerges as a place on the edge of historical time; it is an almost timeless female realm that stands as a counterreality to the encroaching male world of modern technology." *The Country of the Pointed Firs* emerged in the context of increasing national attention to the need for wilderness areas to be set aside and the developing of the national park system, beginning with Yellowstone in 1872. If to some the book's vision seems romantic and escapist, to others it provides a brief for the equal treatment of nature in American society.

IMPORTANCE AND INFLUENCE

Unlike many of her contemporaries, including Rose Terry Cooke, Mary Wilkins Freeman, Alice Brown, Grace King, and Mary Noailles Murfree, Jewett never completely vanished from sight after her death in 1909. During the earlier part of the twentieth century, she received recognition from such major critics as Van Wyck Brooks and a relative of Jewett, the Harvard scholar F. O. Matthiessen, who published a laudatory biography of the author in 1929. Earlier critics and reviewers valued her unique power as a chronicler of vanishing New England culture, as well as her elegant and evocative prose style. In a response typical of her peers, fellow New Englander and writer Alice Brown observed, "No such beautiful and perfect work has been done for many years; perhaps no such beautiful work has ever been done in America." Henry James famously praised Jewett's masterpiece as a "beautiful little quantum of achievement."

Although her work tended to be downplayed by midcentury formalist critics, a handful of scholars, led by Richard Cary, kept Jewett and her work in scholarly conversations through the 1960s, when Jewett figured largely as a writer in the pastoral tradition. *The Country of the Pointed Firs* was a central text for feminist critics of the last quarter of the twentieth century. Beginning in the late 1970s and early 1980s, feminist critics such as Josephine Donovan and Joanna Russ took up the question of "minor" and "major" literature in the context of discussions of literary regionalism as a feminine genre—that is, as a form that achieved its greatest development and fame in the hands of women writers. Others, such as Sarah Way Sherman, extended and complicated earlier discussions of Jewett as a pastoralist by exploring her use of the Demeter-Persephone myth. By the end of the century Jewett's reputation had soared, as new theoretical and critical methodologies emerged enabling renewed appreciation of the writer's complexity and innovation. The durability of Jewett's reputation since her death, especially in contrast to that of other women writers of her period, suggests the hospitality of her work to a variety of readers and interpretations.

Jewett's considerable influence on her contemporaries, including Brown, Freeman, Louise Imogen Guiney, Louise Chandler Moulton, and Celia Thaxter, extends to modern and more recent writers such as H. P. Lovecraft, Willa Cather, Edith Wharton, Mary Ellen Chase, Robert Frost, and Elizabeth Bishop. Although not cited as a direct influence on Toni Morrison, Jewett's work prefigures Morrison's in its use of a folk aesthetic and mythic themes. The most famous connection, between Jewett and Cather, began in 1908, when the younger writer was working for *McClure's* magazine and Jewett became her mentor. The thirty-six-year-old Cather, who at that time had published only a book of poetry and a collection of short stories, worked for the magazine as, in Paula Blanchard's words, "an investigative reporter, researcher, ghostwriter, office manager, and general dogsbody for Samuel McClure, who drove her as mercilessly as he drove himself." Jewett offered the young writer help and encouragement. Together with Annie Fields, Jewett also provided the lesbian Cather an affirmative model of an intimate emotional relationship. Jewett recognized the crushing pressures on Cather and urged her to "find your own quiet centre of life, and write from that," acknowledging that "to work in silence and with all one's heart, that is the writer's lot; he is the only artist who must be a solitary, and yet needs the widest outlook upon the world. . . . You need to have time to yourself and time to read and add to your recognitions."

Cather's tribute to Jewett after the latter's death included dedicating *O Pioneers!* (1913), her first significant work, to her mentor; throughout her career Cather shared Jewett's interest in region and regionalism, gender, and nature, as is evident, for example, in *My Ántonia* (1918). In 1925 Cather published her edition of *The Country of the Pointed Firs* at a time when Jewett was in danger of being forgotten. Ann Romines and others document the problematic changes that Cather made to her mentor's masterpiece by incorporating three later Dunnet Landing stories ("A Dunnet Shepherdess," "The Queen's Twin," and "William's Wedding"; see Cynthia J. Goheen's essay), as well as the younger writer's ambivalence about her mentor's work. Nevertheless Cather's preface expresses her sense of the book's power and importance, an understanding that reemerged several decades later in feminist readings of Jewett: "If I were asked to name three American books which have the possibility of a long, long life, I would say at once, 'The Scarlet Letter,' 'Huckleberry Finn,' and 'The Country of the Pointed Firs.' I can think of no others that confront time and change so serenely."

Like Willa Cather, Edith Wharton both acknowledged and rejected the influence of Jewett and her contemporaries. In her memoir *A Backward Glance* (1934) she observes: "For years I wanted to draw life as it really was in the derelict mountain villages of New England, a life . . . utterly unlike that seen through the rose-coloured spectacles of my predecessors, Mary Wilkins and Sarah Orne Jewett." Priscilla Leder traces the important connections between the writers, pointing out that, "given the popularity of *The Country of the Pointed Firs,* Wharton's acquaintance with Jewett, and the structural similarities of the two works, it seems likely that *Pointed Firs* provided a paradigm of the vision Wharton wished to correct" in *Ethan Frome* (1911). Both stories are told by outsiders to the villages that they visit, but whereas Jewett's narrator becomes at least an honorary community member and friend, inviting readers to assume the same position, Wharton's remains outside and distanced. Nevertheless, in spite of her efforts to separate herself from her famous precursor and to affirm her more realistic and "modern" vision of the world, Wharton's novel shows many traces of a conversation with Jewett's.

Another and perhaps even closer connection between the two writers lies in the similarities between *The Country of the Pointed Firs* and Wharton's *Summer* (1917), which she called her "hot *Ethan*" and which was her favorite novel. Here the narrator is more closely aligned with the central character, Charity Royall, who has been brought down from the Mountain, a mysterious community of outcasts, to become the ward—and eventually the wife—of Lawyer Royall of North Dormer. In *Summer* Wharton again comments negatively on Jewett's conception of rural community, but she does so by critiquing the possibilities for self-development, self-confidence, and independence for poor, uneducated rural women in the face of a community dominated by men's desires and laws.

Love of various kinds is at the center of both *The Country of the Pointed Firs* and *Summer.* In the former, although the women often suffer for romantic love, Jewett depicts them as independent and proud, where someone like Poor Joanna can take her grief over lost love to an island and live a solitary but in many ways comfortable life even in self-exile. Charity Royall, in contrast, betrayed by love—and, significantly, by sexuality—has no choices. Both writers, then, critique the role of romantic love in women's lives, although they do so from different angles. Like many writers, especially women writers determined to make a reputation in a literary world controlled by men, Wharton finds it necessary to distinguish herself from an important predecessor, but she also engages central elements, both substantive and stylistic, in that predecessor's work.

Jewett's influence on Robert Frost was less direct than on Cather and Wharton but no less profound. As a male writer Frost was less subject to diminishment, but as a regional writer he suffered from much of the same prejudice as Jewett did after her death. In "Robert Frost's New England," Perry D. Westbrook observes that it is impossible to ascertain how familiar the poet was with the work of Jewett and other New England regionalists such as Freeman, Cooke, and Brown, but "since they published prolifically in periodicals and in book form, it is hardly likely that he did not have an acquaintance with the work of at least some of them. Indeed only a determined nonreader—which Frost was not—could be entirely ignorant of their work." Westbrook concludes that, "even if he had read nothing by any of them, he is of their company—though admittedly his work as a whole transcends their 'local-colorist' limitations." Many of Frost's earlier critics, including the powerful Amy Lowell, both praised and critiqued Frost for precisely the same qualities that threatened Jewett's reputation in the mid-twentieth century.

As Karen L. Kilcup demonstrates in *Robert Frost and Feminine Literary Tradition,* Frost's affinities with Jewett are often greater than has been recognized in the past. The poet's empathetic style, especially evident in such great early dramatic poems as "A Servant to Servants," "Home Burial," "The Housekeeper," and "The Death of the Hired Man," actualizes feminine voices and subjectivities in ways that recall not only *The Country of the Pointed Firs* but also Jewett's short fiction "The Town Poor," "The Foreigner," and "Martha's Lady" and her dramatic poem "A Farmer's Sorrow." In stories such as "The Gray Mills of Farley" and "Going to Shrewsbury," as well as in her longer masterpiece, Jewett articulates the tension between older, rural ways of life and modern existence, as Frost does in "Out, Out—," "The Vanishing Red," "The Self-Seeker," and other poems. Moreover, Frost shares Jewett's interest in gossip—both positive and negative—as a means of creating community or, alternatively, as a divisive element in rural life.

One of the least explored of Jewett's influences is that on Elizabeth Bishop. In her narratives as well as her poetry, Bishop participates in the tradition of New England regionalism embodied in Jewett's stories, sketches, and poems. Bishop herself describes reading her precursor's work with astonishment and some dismay. In letters to friends Bishop acknowledges the similarity in spite of her reservation that, though the earlier writer's work is "dated," it is "still sometimes marvellous stuff and worth reading. . . . I was appalled when I recently read a whole book—I'm sure anyone who read my story ['In the Village'] would think I was imitating her shamelessly—whole phrases, even—it is very strange; I had really never laid eyes on the ones that are like mine."

The intense imagery and painterly qualities of *The Country of the Pointed Firs* recall Bishop's strengths in these areas, and many of her poems and stories focus on the New England and Nova Scotia of her childhood. Even in those works set outside Jewett's region, however, Bishop displays the careful attention to character and place typical of the earlier regionalist writer's work. Although Bishop's protest to her friend suggests her initial unfamiliarity with Jewett's oeuvre, it also indicates her desire—apparent in relationships with other strong women writers such as her mentor Marianne Moore—to establish her own identity and originality. Such indirect influences as those that Bishop claims Jewett at most had, suggest both the impact of place on character during childhood and the extent to which Jewett's work had become part of New England regional culture during Bishop's formative years. Although Bishop does not say so, it is also possible—indeed likely—that if she read *The Country of the Pointed Firs* or its predecessor, *Deephaven,* the theme of intimate relationships between women that emerges relatively explicitly and affirmatively may have shocked or unnerved Bishop, the closeted lesbian, who, like Cather before her, came of age and lived much of her life in a time of hostility toward homosexuality and who was necessarily more protective of her private affairs.

Jewett's work remains important not only for its influence on her successors but also for its continuing power for readers both inside and outside the academy. Jewett has a loyal group of readers, and her home is a local and regional landmark owned by the Society for the Preservation of New England Antiquities. Like the nearby Hamilton House, which figured in the writer's *The Tory Lover* (1901), a historical romance, it is open to the public, offering visitors a view of her bedroom with her personal belongings such as riding crops, pincushions, and jewelry, as well as her writing area, with the Sheraton secretary she used to compose much of her work. As lesbians have reclaimed Jewett's work as their own, Jewett has entered pop culture. A documentary film titled *Out of the Past* (1998) traces the struggles of a lesbian high school student in Utah to found an extracurricular organization called the Gay-Straight Alliance and compares her to past heroes of the gay liberation movement, including Jewett. Academics from a wide range of perspectives have ensured Jewett's continuing presence on the literary and cultural scene, with numerous editions of *The Country of the Pointed Firs* and other texts widely available from academic and trade presses. Finally, there are numerous websites devoted to Jewett and her work, including Terry Heller's *Sarah Orne Jewett Text Project,* which will eventually make available all of the writer's published work and much of her unpublished work, as well as letters, children's writing, and a portrait gallery.

In addition to her preservation of a particular view of rural New England life, one of Jewett's greatest contributions is to the form and importance of storytelling itself: the stories we tell and how and to whom we tell them are, she suggests, of essential meaning. Critiquing the notion of the novel as a long book with a single plot, tension, and climax, and an attractive young heroine (or hero), Jewett's modern, even postmodern, narrative of friendship offers a network of resonant stories and older characters—with Dunnet Landing and nature itself figuring as important characters—that raise important philosophical and ethical questions about such issues as the shape of authentic relationships, the meaning of community, and the future of America. These questions continue to occupy readers in the twenty-first century no less than they did readers in Jewett's time.

Select Bibliography

EDITIONS

The Country of the Pointed Firs. Boston: Houghton Mifflin, 1896.

Novels and Stories. Edited by Michael Davitt Bell. New York: Library of America, 1994.

The Country of the Pointed Firs and Other Stories. Edited by Alison Easton. London: Penguin, 1995.

The Country of the Pointed Firs and Other Fiction. Edited by Terry Heller. New York: Oxford University Press, 1996.

The Country of the Pointed Firs and Other Stories. Edited by Sarah Way Sherman. Hanover, N.H.: University Press of New England, 1997. (This edition is cited in this essay. The other later editions have useful introductions and a varied selection of stories.)

The Sarah Orne Jewett Text Project. Edited by Terry Heller. Cedar Rapids, Iowa: Coe College, 1997–2002. (http://www.public.coe.edu/~theller/soj/sj-index.htm).

OTHER WORKS BY JEWETT

Deephaven. Boston: J. R. Osgood, 1877.

Country By-ways. Boston: Houghton Mifflin, 1881.

The Tory Lover. Boston: Houghton Mifflin, 1901.

Sarah Orne Jewett Letters. Edited by Richard Cary. Waterville, Maine: Colby College Press, 1967.

SECONDARY WORKS

Ammons, Elizabeth. "Going in Circles: The Female Geography of Jewett's *Country of the Pointed Firs.*" *Studies in the Literary Imagination* 16 (fall 1983): 83–92.

Alaimo, Stacy. *Undomesticated Ground: Recasting Nature as Feminist Space.* Ithaca, N.Y.: Cornell University Press, 2000.

Blanchard, Paula. *Sarah Orne Jewett: Her World and Her Work.* Reading, Mass.: Addison-Wesley, 1994.

Brodhead, Richard H. *Cultures of Letters: Scenes of Reading and Writing in Nineteenth-Century America.* Chicago: University of Chicago Press, 1993.

Brooks, Van Wyck. *New England: Indian Summer, 1865–1915.* New York: Dutton, 1940.

Brown, Alice. Review of *The Country of the Pointed Firs* (1897). In *Critical Essays on Sarah Orne Jewett.* Edited by Gwen L. Nagel. Boston: G. K. Hall, 1984. P. 39.

Cary, Richard, ed. *Sarah Orne Jewett Letters.* Waterville, Maine: Colby College Press, 1967.

———, ed. *Appreciation of Sarah Orne Jewett: 29 Interpretive Essays.* Waterville, Maine: Colby College Press, 1973.

Cather, Willa. Preface to *The Country of the Pointed Firs and Other Stories,* by Sarah Orne Jewett. Garden City, N.Y.: Doubleday-Anchor, 1954.

Donovan, Josephine. *New England Local Color Literature: A Women's Tradition.* New York: Frederick Ungar, 1983.

———. "Women's Masterpieces." In *Challenging Boundaries: Gender and Periodization.* Edited by Joyce W. Warren and Margaret Dickie. Athens: University of Georgia Press, 2000. Pp. 26–38.

Faderman, Lillian. *Surpassing the Love of Men: Romantic Friendship and Love between Women from the Renaissance to the Present.* New York: Morrow, 1981.

Farwell, Marilyn R. "Heterosexual Plots and Lesbian Subtexts: Toward a Theory of Lesbian Narrative Space." In *Lesbian Texts and Contexts: Radical Revisions.* Edited by Karla Jay and Joanne Glasgow. New York: New York University Press, 1990. Pp. 91–103.

Fetterley, Judith. "'Not in the Least American': Nineteenth-Century Literary Regionalism as UnAmerican Literature." In *Nineteenth-Century American Women Writers: A Critical Reader.* Edited by Karen L. Kilcup. Malden, Mass.: Blackwell, 1998. Pp. 15–32.

Folsom, Marcia McClintock. "'Tact Is a Kind of Mind-Reading': Empathic Style in Sarah Orne Jewett's *The Country of the Pointed Firs.*" *Colby Library Quarterly* 18 (March 1982): 66–78.

Foote, Stephanie. "'I Feared to Find Myself a Foreigner': Revisiting Regionalism in Sarah Orne Jewett's *The Country of the Pointed Firs.*" *Arizona Quarterly* 52 (summer 1996): 37–61.

Goheen, Cynthia J. "Editorial Misinterpretation and the Unmaking of a Perfectly Good Story: The Publication History of *The Country of the Pointed Firs.*" *American Literary Realism* 30 (winter 1998): 28–42.

Harrison, Victoria. *Elizabeth Bishop's Poetics of Intimacy.* Cambridge, U.K.: Cambridge University Press, 1993.

Holden, Stephen. "Finding Courage and Anguish along the Road to Gay Pride." *New York Times,* July 31, 1998, late edition, sec. E, p. 22. (Review of the documentary film *Out of the Past.*)

Howard, June. "Unraveling Regions, Unsettling Periods: Sarah Orne Jewett and American Literary History." *American Literature* 68 (June 1996): 365–384.

———, ed. *New Essays on* The Country of the Pointed Firs. Cambridge, U.K.: Cambridge University Press, 1994. (Contains Elizabeth Ammons' essay "Material Culture, Empire, and Jewett's *Country of the Pointed Firs.*")

James, Henry. "Mr. and Mrs. James T. Fields." *Atlantic Monthly,* July 1915, pp. 21–31.

Kilcup, Karen L. *Robert Frost and Feminine Literary Tradition.* Ann Arbor: University of Michigan Press, 1998.

Kilcup, Karen L., and Thomas S. Edwards, eds. *Jewett and Her Contemporaries: Reshaping the Canon.* Gainesville: University Press of Florida, 1999. (Contains Ann Romines' essay "The Professor and the Pointed Firs: Cather, Jewett, and Problems of Editing" and Priscilla Leder's essay "Visions of New England: The Anxiety of Jewett's Influence on *Ethan Frome.*")

McMurry, Andrew. "'In Their Own Language': Sarah Orne Jewett and the Question of Non-Human Speaking Subjects." *Isle: Interdisciplinary Studies in Literature and Environment* 6 (winter 1999): 51–63.

Matthiessen, F. O. *Sarah Orne Jewett.* Boston: Houghton Mifflin, 1929.

Mobley, Marilyn Sanders. *Folk Roots and Mythic Wings in Sarah Orne Jewett and Toni Morrison: The Cultural Function of Narrative.* Baton Rouge: Louisiana State University Press, 1991.

Morgan, Jack, and Louis A. Renza. Introduction to their *The Irish Stories of Sarah Orne Jewett.* Carbondale: Southern Illinois University Press, 1996.

Murphy, Jacqueline Shea. "Getting Jewett: A Response to Sandra A. Zagarell, 'Troubling Regionalism.'" *American Literary History* 10 (winter 1998): 698–701.

———. "Replacing Regionalism: Abenaki Tales and 'Jewett's' Coastal Maine." *American Literary History* 10 (winter 1998): 664–690.

Oakes, Karen. "'Colossal in Sheet-Lead': The Native American and Piscataqua-Region Writers." In *A Noble and Dignified Stream: The Piscataqua Region in the Colonial Revival, 1860–1930.* Edited by Sarah L. Giffen and Kevin D. Murphy. York, Maine: Old York Historical Society, 1992. Pp. 165–176.

Sherman, Sarah Way. *Sarah Orne Jewett, An American Persephone.* Hanover, N.H.: University Press of New England, 1989.

———. Introduction to *The Country of the Pointed Firs and Other Stories,* by Sarah Orne Jewett. Hanover, N.H.: University Press of New England, 1997.

Silverthorne, Elizabeth. *Sarah Orne Jewett: A Writer's Life.* Woodstock, N.Y.: Overlook Press, 1993.

Vicinus, Martha. *Independent Women: Work and Community for Single Women, 1850–1920.* Chicago: University of Chicago Press, 1985.

Westbrook, Perry D. "Robert Frost's New England." In *Frost: Centennial Essays.* Edited by Jac Tharpe. Jackson: University Press of Mississippi, 1974. Pp. 239–255.

Wharton, Edith. *A Backward Glance.* New York: D. Appleton-Century, 1934.

Zagarell, Sandra A. "Narrative of Community: The Identification of a Genre." *Signs: Journal of Women in Culture and Society* 13 (spring 1988): 498–527.

———. "Crosscurrents: Registers of Nordicism, Community, and Culture in Jewett's *Country of the Pointed Firs.*" *Yale Journal of Criticism* 10 (fall 1997): 355–370.

———. "Response to Jacqueline Shea Murphy's 'Replacing Regionalism.'" *American Literary History* 10 (winter 1998): 691–697.

Edith Wharton's Ethan Frome

ANGELA GARCIA

ETHAN FROME (1911) is widely considered to be Edith Wharton's greatest work and her most enduring classic—a technical as well as literary achievement in a form that has been called everything from a novella to a literary fable. Written early-to mid-career during one of her many stays in Paris, and considered shocking and painful by its first readers and critics, *Ethan Frome*'s power has nonetheless been confirmed as the compressed tragedy continues to capture readers' imaginations almost a century after publication.

While this novel, along with *Summer* (1917), marks a departure from Wharton's usual settings of New York society in New York or Europe, its theme—the struggle between love and duty—underlies much of her work. Still, *Ethan Frome*'s abbreviated form and laconic style strive to capture a particularly, even peculiarly, dark intensity. Its portrait of New England life proves a stoic departure from the rose-colored visions of her contemporaries; it leans more heavily toward Nathaniel Hawthorne's tales of puritanical suffering, tinged with the supernatural and etched against the backdrop of a still-wild and desolate New England landscape.

AN ATMOSPHERE OF VOLATILITY

Setting her tale a generation before her own time, Wharton immediately places the snowbound villages of western Massachusetts in a context of brokenness, as (from her *A Backward Glance,* 1934)

> still grim places, morally and physically: insanity, incest, and slow mental and moral starvation were hidden away behind the paintless wooden house-fronts of the long village street, or in the isolated farm-houses on the neighbouring hills; and Emily Brontë would have found as savage tragedies in our remoter valleys as on her Yorkshire moors.

Central to *Ethan Frome* is the idea of spiritual waste, for, according to Wharton, she is conveying a landscape of people who are essentially unfulfilled, people for whom any hope of spiritual, moral, or intellectual sustenance is inexorably eking away. In the phrase "isolated farm-houses" Wharton conveys the lack of social sympathy she finds so debilitating: that aloneness which can harden into what the novel calls "queerness." Indeed, Wharton concerns herself deeply with the metaphor of loneliness as disease, in terms of both character and place. She invests the novel's settings—both Starkfield in general and the Frome farm in particular—with shattered or ruined qualities, but she most effectively suggests ruin through her characters: through the image of a middle-aged Ethan Frome limping in to collect his mail at the post office; through the hypochondria and deep unhappiness of Ethan's wife, Zeena; and, finally, through the epilogue's revelation of the fate of Mattie Silver, formerly like a fairy of springtime, now hunched, immobile, and nagging.

Wharton referred to her characters as her "granite outcroppings," and throughout the novel the characters' pain is exacerbated by their lack of expression, especially in the cases of Ethan and his wife, Zeena; their hurt is completely absorbed and repressed, in effect stunting their spiritual growth and destroying any hope for the salvation of their marriage. As participants in an illicit affair of the heart, Ethan and Mattie also work constantly to veil their mutual hopes and affections in secrecy.

Equally silent are the novel's eternal snowdrifts. A perpetual winter drives *Ethan Frome,* and, indeed, Wharton titled the French translation of her novel *L'Hiver.* Throughout the tale, landscape and hard weather mirror and virtually engulf the emotional and psychological struggles of Ethan and his wife. The snow, omnipresent, indicates the absence of communion and the impotence that is reflected in the town's name, Starkfield. Ethan and Zeena have borne no children, and Ethan finds himself repeatedly frozen in his own storm of emotional confusion: fearful to act on his newfound love for Mattie, fearful to go against Zeena, often fearful to make his outward life, his "real" life, coincide with his inner life, with the fantasies in which he is truly invested.

But, as hope balances brokenness, the wintriness of weather and soul does not go unchallenged in Wharton's novel. In the phrase "savage tragedies" Wharton concedes that a stubborn passion grows hidden in this cold place, and this passion seeps through the grimness to persist in coloring her white and deathlike Starkfield canvas. For example, the many scenes of nature Wharton details serve not only as omens, but

CHRONOLOGY

1862	Wharton is born Edith Newbold Jones on January 24 in New York City.
1885	Marries Edward Wharton of Boston, whose inherited wealth allows the couple to travel to Europe often and spend part of each year in Newport, Rhode Island, then later in Lenox, Massachusetts.
1897	Publishes her first book, *The Decoration of Houses,* then turns to the writing of short stories.
1902	*The Valley of Decision,* her first novel, is published.
1904	Meets Henry James, with whom she maintains a friendship until his death. Edward Wharton's health gradually deteriorates, resulting in protracted trips to Europe.
1905	*The House of Mirth,* based on the New York society of which she was a part, is published to popular and critical success.
1907	The Whartons settle in Paris.
1910	Edward suffers a nervous breakdown.
1911	*Ethan Frome* is serialized in *Scribner's Magazine,* then published in book form.
1913	The Whartons divorce.
1916	Awarded the Legion of Honor for her contributions to France during World War I.
1917	*Summer,* the companion piece to *Ethan Frome,* is published.
1919	Moves to Paris.
1920	*The Age of Innocence.*
1921	Awarded the Pulitzer Prize for *The Age of Innocence:* the first woman to win the Pulitzer.
1923	Awarded an honorary doctorate from Yale University.
1930	Elected to membership in the American Academy of Arts and Letters.
1937	Dies on August 11 in Paris.

also as spiritual consolation for Ethan and Mattie; through landscape, they find a means of expression, and eventually each recognizes in the other a kindred soul who is sensible to this beauty.

Despite Starkfield's long winter seasons of frigid gloom and the deadness of his marriage, Ethan has not absorbed winter as a state of mind. Like a sleeping volcano, his volatile swings of mood—recurrent throes of hope and despair—demonstrate that he has a lively and vulnerable mind and heart just under the surface. In unfolding his tale, the novel's unnamed narrator (an engineer forced to prolong his stay in Starkville because of a labor strike) uncovers the fleeting life and hope—even the emotional whirlwind—beneath Ethan's stony surface.

Ethan Frome's root energy stems from its juxtaposition of health and hope against physical and emotional destruction. Wharton weaves a tight, complex set of motifs into a web of symbols that surround and reinforce the truths that emerge in the novel. On the one hand, within its chief tale the novel promises springtime fertility through the symbolic images that surround and describe Mattie's character; on the other hand, the lovers Mattie and Ethan must constantly vie with real-life frozenness—of Zeena's repressed anger, of Ethan's immobility, of financial limitations, even of moral responsibility—that limits and finally crushes any hope of love's or life's fulfillment.

STRUCTURE AND STYLE

Even among critics who have found fault with the novel, its style and construction are considered a triumph. In her introduction to the Modern Student's Library edition of *Ethan Frome* (published by Scribners in 1922), Wharton discusses the construction of the novel:

> The problem before me, as I saw in the first flash, was this: I had to deal with a subject of which the dramatic climax, or rather the anti-climax, occurs a generation later than the first acts of the tragedy. This enforced lapse of time would seem to anyone persuaded—as I have always been—that every subject (in the novelist's sense of the term) implicitly *contains its own form and dimensions.* . . . The theme of my tale . . . must be treated as starkly and summarily as life had always presented itself to my protagonists; any attempt to elaborate and complicate their sentiments would necessarily have falsified the whole. They were, in truth, these figures, my *granite outcroppings;* but half-emerged from the soil, and scarcely more articulate.

Wharton uses a framing mechanism to sandwich the crucial elements of her tale in a neutral fashion; Ethan's thoughts and his story are conveyed by a man of science, the engineer who has slowly become acquainted with Ethan and his history during his stay in Starkville. The engineer-narrator faces his own physical entrapment in the village—over the long months of winter, and especially in the snowstorm that leads to his invitation from Ethan to stay overnight as a guest at the Frome farmhouse—which parallels Ethan's psychic entrapment.

Although it has been twenty-four years since the events that are the novel's true tale, the events that have made Ethan the man he is today, the narrator recognizes in Ethan an otherworldliness that piques him. Ultimately the engineer cannot resist the mystery that Ethan represents, and he sets aside his other work in an investigative drive for knowledge, determined to uncover the clue to Ethan's strange psyche, the impression he gives of living death. "'Good God!' I exclaimed . . . and I saw his face as it probably looked when he thought himself alone. '*That* man touch a hundred? He looks as if he was dead and in hell now!'" It is not an overstatement to say that the engineer's life and imagination are forever altered by his view of Ethan.

As he obsessively pursues Ethan's mysterious past, the narrator immediately senses the tension between the younger and older Ethan, that hope and possibilities did in fact once exist for him. "I began to see what life there—or rather its negation—must have been in Ethan Frome's young manhood." And so it is the life, or rather the quenched life, in Ethan—his tragic power—that magnetizes this narrator as he follows the decidedly unscientific "vision" that makes the story possible. In order to tell the story of the younger Ethan in the narrator's self-appointed role as bard, he has had to fill in the blanks of some carefully negotiated interviews with townspeople and other reportage with his own inspired or imagined details.

The narrator's tale is the oldest form of story—an oral transmission, even folklore: "I had the story, bit by bit, from various people, and, as generally happens in such cases, each time it was a different story." In his statement the narrator qualifies his tale as a class of fiction, but also of legend, admitting the several versions he has received. In the depth of details that follow, the narrator's avowal that his story is a poetic, inspired gift and not merely a compilation of hearsay, is affirmed. Thus Ethan serves as the narrator's unlikely muse and the key to unlocking his "vision."

The story's dialogue is powerfully imbued with a terseness of idiom; often a few words must carry the weight of the most aggrieved oppression or the most elated hope. Emotionally, the author's reference to the characters as "granite outcroppings" suggests their primal or archetypal needs and desires, which they feel all the more intensely for their inability to express them in language. Ethan, with Mattie, seems forever obstructed by the taciturnity that is his habit: "Her wonder and his laughter ran together like spring rills in a thaw. Ethan had the sense of having done something arch and ingenious. To prolong the effect he groped for a dazzling phrase, and brought out, in a growl of rapture: 'Come along.'" And later: "Again he struggled for the all-expressive word, and again, his arm in hers, found only a deep 'Come along.'"

While Wharton's personification of her characters as "granite outcroppings" might overlook the essential vulnerability and fragility—even complexity—inherent in Ethan's and Mattie's characters, it does reflect their (sometimes regrettable) toughness; the pair at least physically survive their attempt at double suicide—the sledding accident which serves as climax to the novel and propels the characters into the pathetic, enduring triangle of the epilogue. In addition to suggesting the characters' outwards selves as "the tip of the iceberg"—with all their passions buried underground—the phrase "granite outcroppings" also suggests the motif of gravestones—images of silence and death that appear several times in the novel, as the family graveyard lies adjacent to the Fromes' farm.

NATURE'S LANGUAGE AND THE FINER SENSIBILITY

One way that Ethan and Mattie do manage to find a common language is through nature. Landscape provides the articulation that continually evades both Ethan and even a warm soul such as Mattie. Whether through the images of Varnum spruces or a setting winter sun, Wharton demonstrates that snow and sharpness of landscape are not always reflective of despair; on the contrary, stunning tableaux of nature often pierce the characters' psychological anguish and offer relief from isolation. And so, for the lovers, landscape speaks volumes, attesting to the beauty that is possible and validating their unspoken mutual attraction. Their communion is marked by the love of nature. The richest thing Mattie gives Ethan is a feeling of reverberation, as when she shares his sense of wonder and elation at the natural order:

> She had an eye to see and an ear to hear: he could show her things and tell her things, and taste the bliss of feeling that all he imparted left long reverberations and echoes he could wake at will. . . . He had always been more sensitive than the people about him to the appeal of natural beauty. . . . And there were other sensations, less definable but more exquisite, which drew them together with a shock of silent joy.

This is a deep, full, even erotically defined silence, rich with communion. Ethan and Mattie are able to find solace—even, for a time, recompense—for their indoor servitude in the limitless outdoor visions before them: red sunsets, flocks of clouds, and the blue shadows of hemlocks. To Zeena, as perhaps to the general population of the village, these might as well be invisible.

Ethan also finds individual solace in nature's tableaux. Enmeshed in Starkfield's seemingly eternal winter, he nonetheless finds in scene after scene some detail of tree or sky to warm and stimulate his barren existence. For if in Wharton's New England, traditional religion is all but absent, and sympathy rare, the natural world can sustain so that some measure of aesthetic or even spiritual fulfillment is possible, even when one's enthusiasm for its moon, its pines, its snowy fields—along with most everything else—must generally be kept to one's reserved self.

In spite of the alienation that pervades it, the novel, in eliciting sympathy for Ethan, suggests that a finer sensibility (despite its inherent suffering) is preferable to Zeena's hypocrisy and sheer lack of vision. For Ethan, an instinctive curiosity (which ties him to the engineer as his double, or a representation of his potential) and his refined appreciation of nature are life-saving connections to the larger world, a world apart from the very small but nonetheless mind-numbing circumference of Starkfield—in which he feels himself as secluded as the other townspeople he has always known. "His father's death, and the misfortunes following it, had put a premature end to Ethan's studies; but though they had not gone far enough to be of much practical use they had fed his fancy and made him aware of huge cloudy meanings behind the daily face of things." Along with Ethan and Mattie's sharing of their quiet fascination with the natural world, Ethan is able to awe Mattie, for example, by pointing out the Pleiades, or with an impromptu lecture on glaciers and the Ice Age.

Wharton takes pains to portray Ethan as feeling more than most of the villagers. Clearly, the tragic figure at the post office is a man apart, distanced by temperament from the more limited people around him—in a setting, moreover, where the people around him are already essentially alienated from one another. As a dreamer with a heightened sensibility, Ethan merely seeks a sensibility to resonate with his. He has, after all, enjoyed sociability before—he even envisioned moving to the city—and though Mattie has the potential to bring out his dangerous tendency to fantasize, she also elicits his healthier inclination toward human sympathy. When he dreams of his evening by the fire with Mattie, for example, he banishes his fears and aligns himself with his more social college days.

> The sweetness of the picture, and the relief of knowing that his fears of "trouble" with Zeena were unfounded, sent up his spirits with a rush, and he, who was usually so silent, whistled and sang aloud as he drove through the snowy fields. There was in him a slumbering spark of sociability which the long Starkfield winters had not yet extinguished. By nature grave and inarticulate, he admired recklessness and gaiety in others and was warmed to the marrow by friendly human intercourse. At Worcester, though he had the name of keeping to himself and not being much of a hand at a good time, he had secretly gloried in being clapped on the back and hailed as "Old Ethe" or "Old Stiff"; and the cessation of such familiarities had increased the chill of his return to Starkfield.
>
> There the silence had deepened about him year by year.

Wharton works again in this passage to highlight the contrast between Ethan's warm self and his wintry self: his potential for interaction once more threatened by duty and isolation. In this case, the reflex to study or work elsewhere, to escape the family legacy that is the farm, is destroyed by moral obligation. His father's accident and, next, his mother's illness, force him into the role of caretaker. In Ethan's culture,

Wharton suggests, familial duty is unquestionable, and the implicit self-sacrifice is deemed irrelevant, but through Ethan's self-destructive attempt to escape a stifling marriage, the novel works to question the morality of this "moral" duty.

In addition to moral obligation or duty, fear spurs Ethan to act. "Unreasoning dread of being left alone on the farm" in winter, of that creeping isolation, motivates his disastrous marriage to Zeena. He has experience with his mother turning "queer" from loneliness, when traffic ceases on the road past their farm once the local railroad is expanded; and after his mother's death Ethan feels susceptible to a similar insanity. Moreover, the season of her death—in the seemingly endless depths of snowy winter—hastens his ill-chosen marriage. For a warmth-seeking soul that quietly craves social contact, the necessary silence of living alone on the farm would be death.

As he soon learns, marriage in itself is not the antidote for Ethan's feelings of isolation. Locked into his marriage with the unsympathetic Zeena, he remains terribly alone in a spiritual, intellectual, and presumably sexual sense. However, despite his sensitivity of perception, for Ethan to strive for transcendence from his situation of self-sacrifice within a dead marriage is to want more than his lot. When in the coast down the hill Ethan moves to spurn his moral obligation—opting, through the suicide attempt, to leave Zeena alone immediately after he had decided he could not leave her destitute—he is disfigured. Not only this, but he must live with his disfigured lover as well as his despised wife.

Ethan and Mattie's smash-up and its aftermath elicit no sympathy from the villagers but rather only invites silent reproof, an admonition that such passion is fundamentally unattainable—or at least taboo in these parts. Such elation—unless evident within a legitimate relationship such as the engagement of Ruth Varnum and Ned Hale, who are seen happily kissing under the spruces—does not fit into the community's fatalistic and aesthetically insensitive order. Again, as with the stunning visions of landscape, Wharton makes other residents, in their narrow-mindedness, blind or simply indifferent to what Ethan and Mattie see.

REFLECTIONS OF LIGHT

For all the intermittent glories that the natural landscape offers on its canvas, Ethan finds the most soothing earthly vision to be that of the step and voice and hum of Mattie, his hired help. Any hint of her, and Ethan's demeanor thaws further; his range of giddy impulses, with its heights and plunges, proves Ethan very much alive under his hardened exterior. One can almost hear his heartbeat quicken when her character nears his.

In a larger sense, Starkfield's lifetime of winter is offset by the warmth that Mattie brings to the scene, through Ethan's reflections on her. And reflections they are, for she is continually portrayed in terms of metaphors of light almost from the inception of the narrator's story—when Ethan comes around midnight to walk her home from a dance, he searches for Mattie through the lit window of a church basement: a room "seething in a mist of heat." Even her surname, Silver, implies light and enchantment, richness and music.

From the start Ethan draws strength from his (or the narrator's) vision of her, a comfort and meaning that are denied him in his frigid household. Her swiftness and grace as a dancer are also remarked upon, and establish her quickness, her vitality through most of the novel:

> Frome's heart was beating fast. He had been straining for a glimpse of the dark head under the cherry-coloured scarf. . . . As she passed down the line, her light figure swinging from hand to hand in circles of increasing swiftness, the scarf flew off her head and stood out behind her shoulders, and Frome, at each turn, caught sight of her laughing panting lips, the cloud of dark hair about her forehead, and the dark eyes which seemed the only fixed points in a maze of flying lines.

As always, the points of contrast are extreme. The color red is a rare one in the book, and one almost exclusively associated with Mattie, suggesting her liveliness of body and heart—or even the erotic, as when he discovers "a crimson ribbon drawn through her hair" at the start of their one evening at home together. Likewise, the physical rush of Mattie's dancing, symbolized by her flushed cheeks and bound with her character from the reader's first glimpse, distances Mattie from Zeena's slow, ailing movements and sharp, dour character.

Emotionally starved in a loveless marriage, Ethan finds himself, like a moth, increasingly drawn to the cheerful outsider. While Wharton often depicts Mattie in various forms of light, Zeena—whom the narrative, tellingly, always locates in the house—is associated with images of darkness: "Zeena herself, from an oppressive reality, had faded into an insubstantial shade. All his life was lived in the sight and sound of Mattie Silver, and he could no longer conceive of its being otherwise." And all else does fall away in the face of Ethan's obsession.

The light that infuses Mattie is no accident: "But it was not only that the coming to his house of a bit of hopeful young life was like the lighting of a fire on a cold hearth." She provides comfort where there was none. The pitiful irony becomes, of course, that by the end of the work Mattie is inextricably bound with her opposite, Zeena, and any positive light is on the verge of flickering out.

But for the better part of the novel Mattie's sweetness, good nature, youth, and beauty are consistently superimposed against Zeena's harsh angles, sour face, frozen demeanor, and "flat whine." At thirty-five, it is noted, Zeena "was already an old woman." A hypochondriac given to spending money that Ethan, a farmer, cannot afford, her selfish spinster temperament and ultimately opaque solitude give way not only to indifference but also to thinly disguised smugness at her ability to inflict punishment on Ethan. Furthermore, no ailment is ever specified or confirmed firsthand in the novel by an authority; the reader must take Zeena's word for the "complications" purported by the doctor in Bettsbridge, and given her self-indulgent character and steadily growing neurosis, the prospect seems dubious.

Zeena's real work appears to be that of projecting her meanness of spirit or temperament upon others, although Ethan and Mattie are impervious to these spells for a time. The sharp contrast that candlelight and firelight often throw on the female pair serves as another important motif in the novel and accompanies one of the most revelatory moments for Ethan. When he returns from the (for him) intimate journey home escorting Mattie from the church dance, the pair panic to find the door locked against them; their guilty fear at being found out for their undefined passion, their terror at the prospect of a godlike Zeena, pervades the scene.

> Then the door opened and he saw his wife.
>
> Against the dark background of the kitchen she stood up tall and angular, one hand drawing a quilted counterpane to her flat breast, while the other held a lamp. The light, on a level with her chin, drew out of the darkness her puckered throat and the projecting wrist of the hand that clutched the quilt, and deepened fantastically the hollows and prominences of her high-boned face under its ring of crimping-pins. To Ethan, still in the rosy haze of his hour with Mattie, the sight came with the intense precision of the last dream before waking. He felt as if he had never before known what his wife looked like.

Another motif prevalent in *Ethan Frome* is the literal and symbolic waking moment, which usually intrudes harshly in the novel. In this threshold scene the novel's dramatic intensity deepens, and, with it, Ethan moves one step closer to his ruin. Ethan, in his romantic fervor, convinces himself of his wife's physical (and, by implication, moral) ugliness; he demonstrates his repulsion toward her by attempting to remain downstairs rather than follow her to bed. But Ethan's impulse to act truthfully is checked, as the household teaches him that such illicit expression is impermissible. Zeena sees all—most likely catching Mattie's furtive warning glance in this scene: the lovers' first, typically silent conspiracy. And Ethan, cowed again, ends up following his bony wife upstairs to their sterile marital bed.

In the case of *Ethan Frome,* love's repression causes a stasis, a failure to grow much like the bourgeois, tense, erotic, yet unconsummated love between Newland Archer and Countess Ellen Olenska in Wharton's later work, *The Age of Innocence* (1920). In this later exploration of character, even though it is ensconced in turn-of-the-century New York society, Archer too represents a buried sensibility, and Olenska represents Archer's light. In both cases the seemingly pure love is thwarted by marital obligation, leaving the lovers tantalized but duty-bound and essentially virginal. Yet Archer—forced by social mores into an equally impossible dilemma—realizes his situation, forgoes his chance at passion, and ultimately fulfills his marital duty. Ethan, who cannot reconcile himself to such untruthfulness, refuses to withdraw from his beloved. But such stubborn rebelliousness of character, Wharton shows, merely evokes greater tragedy; Ethan's and Mattie's degeneration of body and spirit graphically illustrate a deeper barrenness than Archer's and Olenska's passive destinies. None of the four are fulfilled. Tellingly, when the narrator enters the Fromes' farm in the epilogue, it is nighttime, and indoors the hearth is cold.

THE STRUGGLE AGAINST IMPOTENCE

In his lone battle against mental and moral starvation—and he is a truly embattled character—Ethan tries desperately to break from the bankruptcy that is his loveless marriage. Although always bound by social convention and the fear of isolation, he seeks, largely unconsciously, to establish his own code that thrives on the affirmation of life rather than its negation—from his first searching glance in Mattie's direction. When, after Zeena dismisses Mattie (ostensibly to hire a girl to help with Zeena's medical "complications"), he comes upon her note to him—"Don't trouble, Ethan"—and tries to rebel.

> For the life of her smile, the warmth of her voice, only cold paper and dead words!
>
> Confused motions of rebellion stormed in him. He was too young, too strong, too full of the sap of living, to submit so easily to the destruction of his hopes. Must he wear out all his years at the side of a bitter querulous old woman? Other possibilities had been in him, possibilities sacrificed, one by one, to Zeena's narrow-mindedness and ignorance. And what good had come of it? She was a hundred times bitterer and more discontented than when he had married her: the one pleasure left her was to inflict pain on him. All the healthy instincts of self-defence rose up in him against such waste.

This passage especially testifies to Wharton's sympathetic portrayal of Ethan. According to the narration, this granite is being slowly eroded by his spouse. Wharton clearly wishes to embody in Ethan the healthier and more generous impulse of the marriage. By reemphasizing the "storm" of rebellion in Ethan at his loss of potential, Wharton wishes to place Ethan firmly on the side of life and health—and opposed to Zeena's self-absorption and premature decrepitude. She further conveys his kindness in the scenes that occur a generation later, when Ethan goes out of his way to be helpful as the engineer-narrator's carriage driver, exhibiting a gradual break in his reserve. In speaking of his mother to the narrator, Ethan essentially lets him into his confidence. The narrator, as a stranger to the town, is permitted this rare rapport with the icy Ethan, who shows himself both helpful and helpless.

Thus defined by contradiction, in turn rooted and rootless, the energy of *Ethan Frome* is brought to bear on the reader's sympathy for Ethan: a sick man who seeks to heal himself, though not at a cost to others. He tries not to incur damage, and ultimately he abandons his final escape route by refusing to request that the builder Andrew Hale loan him money under false pretenses. His awareness of Hale's own dire economic straits is coupled with, and complicated by, the sympathy that Mrs. Hale expresses for Ethan and his plight: a rare gift for Ethan and one that strikes deep. He also claims he cannot leave Zeena destitute, to care for herself. In fact, while fear and chronic immobility flaw Ethan deeply, moral responsibility might play the crucial role in preventing Ethan from running away with Mattie.

In the face of life-denying repression domestically and socially, Ethan's drive for a receptive soul is, for most if not all the novel, irrepressible. And this is no mean feat, considering the ghostly community in which he resides. In the microcosm that is Starkfield, the novel suggests that the only real moral bankruptcy, or active sin, would be to remain *without a struggle* in the loveless marriage that has buried him before his time. Aside from the natural world, Ethan's love for Mattie remains the only pure or redemptive force in the novel. For Ethan, then, its call—although representing the slimmest of chances—is irresistible, signifying his greatest chance for emotional survival in an otherwise unbearable daily existence.

In observing so accurately the wistfulness of the human soul, Wharton also designs the unsanctioned love of the novel's main characters to draw the reader's sympathy. Essentially unfulfilled, Ethan and Mattie try to draw strength, purpose, and vitality from even the most timid attempts to love each other. And, in pursuing that seemingly unstoppable passion, they run a conscious risk. In the moral universe Wharton has created, love, at least for a time, swells beyond even the most extreme or unnatural distress of the material world.

Meanwhile, however, Ethan's nemesis (and easily the most unsympathetic character in the novel) derives much of her potency from silence. She who has Starkfield and convention on her side regularly instills fear in her husband while she plots her own survival. If Ethan disguises his love awkwardly—doing Mattie's chores, suddenly shaving every morning—Zeena is a master at long-practiced secrecy. In fact, branded into the unhappy household is an elaborate pattern of hiding.

Bereft as she is of love, Zeena focuses much of her energy on undoing what Ethan and Mattie have to hide: a mutual passion. As she quickly and resolutely affirms her husband's poorly hidden attraction for the girl—for his too-honest nature betrays itself in subtleties Zeena would alert to, in voice and step, gesture and action—Zeena effectively nullifies the threat. First she taunts him with an idea of Mattie's impending marriage, then she orchestrates a motive to remove the girl from the household.

Indeed, Zeena, as the true obstacle to their union, provides another important tension in Ethan and Mattie's relationship. That they persist in their affection and passion is their private triumph. However, Zeena keeps the pair laced in doubt, and possibly the doubt and fear that inhabits them within the long shadow cast by Zeena is part of what keeps them entranced with each other, united as they are against a common enemy. She might be love's catalyst, as well as its foil.

Zeena's omnipotence, even in her absence, is most telling during the one evening Ethan and Mattie have alone together while Zeena is gone. At one point Mattie sits on Zeena's rocking chair, only to nervously jump right up again. Even the cat seems to embody a witchlike Zeena, and fear overwhelms them to a needless whisper when Mattie breaks a fancy, never-used pickle dish (its newness reemphasizes the barren marriage). The next day, like a disobedient and penitent child, Ethan goes to extremes in snowy conditions and narrow time constraints to find the glue needed to fool his wife; but, as in their moral lives, the damage has been done, and they are found out. The simile Wharton uses for

Zeena's handling of the dish, "as if she carried a dead body," and Zeena's spasm of sobs implying the misplaced sorrow over the bits of broken glass, reflect the waste of her marriage and prefigure the deeper waste of the useless bodies that is to follow.

Truly, Zeena's power knows no equal in the novel. Cushioned within his daydream, within the cozy domestic intimacy that presents itself to his fancy, Ethan's torment and emasculation are complete. Though he is painted throughout the evening as a sympathetic though powerless character, tasting the teasing, fleeting blissfulness of a fulfilling domestic life—and his erotic handling and kissing of Mattie's "strip of stuff" is charged enough—the cat, the rocking chair have won the day.

Through his reassurances regarding the broken pickle dish, which Mattie accepts reverentially and which soothe her, Ethan tastes potency. He takes explicit pleasure in momentarily mastering Mattie—in noting her awe of him and his abilities. In contrast, he never can feel any power over Zeena; he can only distance himself from her and ignore her.

But when Zeena says too much, when she openly exposes her hatred and resentment of Ethan (in saying it was his duty to marry her because she had lost her health caring for his mother), he silently, psychically, unleashes long-nesting hatred. What comes next is, paradoxically, their most intimate moment in the novel; in the poisonous darkness each wishes to destroy the other.

> Through the obscurity which hid their faces their thoughts seemed to dart at each other like serpents shooting venom. Ethan was seized with horror of the scene and shame at his own share in it. It was as senseless and savage as a physical fight between two enemies in the darkness. . . . It was the first scene of open anger between the couple in their sad seven years together, and Ethan felt as if he had lost an irretrievable advantage in descending to the level of recrimination.

His shame at their squalid arguing is significant. Ethan is still striving to rise above his wife's level of meanness. But each one's continuous blame of the other has eroded any foundation that is left for their marriage. In spite of his regained composure and his clear moral superiority (in the universe of the novel), when Zeena announces her dismissal of Mattie, she takes away her husband's one reason for living, and Ethan is denied—or denies himself—any shred of the manhood he has left.

> Ethan looked at her with loathing. She was no longer the listless creature who had lived at his side in a state of sullen self-absorption, but a mysterious alien presence, an evil energy secreted from the long years of silent brooding. It was the sense of his helplessness that sharpened his antipathy. There had never been anything in her that one could appeal to; but as long as he could ignore and command he had remained indifferent. Now she had mastered him and he abhorred her. Mattie was her relation, not his; there were no means by which he could compel her to keep the girl under her roof. All the long misery of his baffled past, of his youth of failure, hardship and vain effort, rose up in his soul in bitterness and seemed to take shape before him in the woman who at every turn had barred his way. She had taken everything else from him; and now she meant to take the one thing that made up for all the others. For a moment such a flame of hate rose in him that it ran down his arm and clenched his fist against her. He took a wild step forward and then stopped.

This passage and others like it suggest Ethan's Job-like character as well as the trials inflicted by Zeena's cruel and underhanded omnipotence. Since the power is hers to retain or dismiss her second cousin from their household, Zeena's substance gradually grows to more than that of a shade Ethan can ignore; her transformation from pathetic woman to superhuman—whether god, devil, or witch—is, in Ethan's mind, complete. As their relationship develops this imbalance of power, any response becomes useless against her. For Zeena, having made a decision, never changes her mind.

Ethan also displays a latent violence in his desire for mastery, which he immediately chokes. Forever repressing passion's wild urges, accustomed to hushing his mind and heart, he is left prone to a habitual pent-up violence. Sometimes this slips out in shards of dialogue that come across as verbal forms of a clenched fist, especially when he is overwhelmed by the stormy jealousy he feels toward Mattie's suitor, Denis Eady (a jealousy that lends the novel part of its intensity). "I don't know how it is you make me feel, Matt. I'd a'most rather have you dead than that!" At this point Ethan has already, understandably perhaps, imagined Zeena's death (indoors) at the hands of tramps, but when his wishfulness spreads to Mattie, the violence of his expression seems a bit startling.

The dread of isolation that brings about his aggressive frame of mind is as constant as winter to Ethan's psyche and nearly as palpable. It is the same dread that brings Ethan to mindless agreement with Mattie when she proposes that they die together. In their winding, intimate route to the train station, Ethan discovers their love is mutual. At the point of their coast down the hill—an erotic climax of sorts—their love has been expressed most openly to date, but a violence too must be shared, must consecrate their love: "Her sombre violence constrained him: she seemed the embodied instrument of fate." With Mattie's urging Ethan toward the suicide pact, she effectively masters Ethan much the way Zeena has. No longer servant, she moves into the role of siren. That the blame spreads to Mattie as a personification of fate further points to Ethan's ultimate submission. At this juncture, he is unable to act or take responsibility for his acts.

In the rising action of the suicide attempt, which might be classified as action ending in obliteration, it is as though all the passivity that has built up in his nature must erupt at once, in a blast. Wharton's dialogue in the coasting scene is almost blinding in its desperation and intensity, in repeated lines like operatic refrains: Ethan's "I can't let you go!" to Mattie's "Where'll I go?" then finally Ethan's "Get up! Get up!" His final command to Mattie is to convince her to sit behind him in the sled, so that when the sled slams into the elm tree toward which they are suicidally aiming, he will hit the elm first. But of course the failure of his supposedly sharp eyes at this most important moment of his life exposes all his former bragging as full of air, his supposed mastery as a farce. The brief, dream-like intercession of Zeena's face seems to thwart even Ethan's ability to master his target; she either supernaturally prevents his and Mattie's death, or, in an alternate reading, Ethan's overactive imagination has once more passed responsibility for his most terrible failure onto his dominant wife, whom he mortally fears. It also echoes the earlier apparition that virtually looms over the pair's heads and interposes itself eerily by name or motion or vision on the evening Ethan and Mattie think themselves alone:

> Zeena's empty rocking-chair stood facing him. Mattie rose obediently, and seated herself in it. As her young brown head detached itself against the patch-work cushion that habitually framed his wife's gaunt countenance, Ethan had a momentary shock. It was almost as if the other face, the face of the superseded woman, had obliterated that of the intruder.

Whether it causes the accident or not, this second supernatural visage fulfills Ethan's deepest fears and mocks his one attempt at decisive action. And the wholesale destruction—of love, passion, anything that matters to Ethan—is complete with the failure of the sled to hit the big elm square on. The novel's motif of brokenness here manifests itself supremely.

It must be conceded, however, that, while Mattie might be desirous of a master, and Ethan toys with that role, what he truly seems to seek and enjoy is a cooperative, collaborative love. The reverberation of souls that he feels when viewing a wondrous natural scene with Mattie satisfies not only his aesthetic, but also his social and emotional sensibilities.

At the same time, Ethan can neither master nor collaborate with death. His powerlessness is mocked even in his death wish. In the couple's twisted, wizened, or deadened bodies, their death-in-life, the novel presents the failure of the will to die as the most horrible failure. And, to Ethan's further shame, Mattie in her resultant spinal disease carries the brunt of his failure and defeat. The dancing bird is reduced to a half-conscious twittering.

> Then he understood that it must be in pain: pain so excruciating that he seemed, mysteriously, to feel it shooting through his own body. He tried in vain to roll over in the direction of the sound, and stretched his left arm across the snow. And now it was as though he felt rather than heard the twittering; it seemed to be under his palm, which rested on something soft and springy. The thought of the animal's suffering was intolerable to him and he struggled to raise himself, and could not. . . . and all at once he knew that the soft thing he had touched was Mattie's hair and that his hand was on her face.

This blindingly painful and moving scene, when Ethan reaches to find Mattie after the sled has crashed, vies with that of the epilogue for raw poignancy, more so because Mattie's pain *is* Ethan's pain—in effect, they for a moment become the other—and their first words in their re-creation as invalids are each other's names. Wharton's passage is remarkable, in its nightmare twist on the ecstasy of sexual fulfillment, for its symbolic merging and separation of the lovers as well as its realization of Mattie's transformation to a new state. Her birth to an animal-like existence relies on sound and touch rather than visual sensation. She is "it" now, the slightest of creatures. Amid Ethan's blind confusion, there could be no ruder awakening.

Whether it is a penalty for illicit love, a supernatural blow from Zeena, or a random occurrence, whether it is a result of Ethan's fear or a result of convention, the consequence of Ethan's and Mattie's love is undeniable. In their coast down the hill the lovers ultimately cannot extinguish themselves. They are refused even that power—although the possibility that they might continue living was something neither, in their cautious and finally open passion, in their climax of inseparability, could rationally consider.

In having thus foreshortened their already brief passion, the tale rebukes not only its transgression of convention but its irrationality. Critics generally consider the lovers' relationship a foolhardy romance, as characteristically adolescent or immature as the individuals involved rather than as an adult manifestation of genuine, steadfast devotion. The lovers' humility, which was already considerable, is complete, and their lives plummet more deeply into tragedy. If to fail is human, they are Adam and Eve—quintessentially human. The lovers become personifications of indefinite spiritual suffering, and the village takes two more hopeful souls, two living victims, into its frozen grip.

THE EMASCULATION OF POVERTY

While Wharton condemns individual repression as a damnable state in *Ethan Frome,* she extends this critique to the community of Starkfield (that is, the novel's social structure). As the narrator states, "During the early part of my stay I had been struck by the contrast between the vitality of the climate and the deadness of the community." Through his vision—and he, like Ethan, is endowed with a higher sensibility—Wharton's narrator reveals how virtually all the characters in the novel's universe suffer from economic, physical, or emotional hardship, from Andrew Hale's money difficulties and Zeena's chronic hypochondria to the deformity and paralysis that finally wreak havoc with Ethan Frome's and Mattie Silver's bodies.

In particular, the novel offers a commentary on the economic system that is inextricable from any individual moral fear or failure. While the antiheroes in the vast majority of Wharton's oeuvre typically belong to a middle- or upper-middle-class society, Wharton's antihero Ethan Frome marks a departure from this trend. A working-class farmer always on the verge of bankruptcy, as a young man Ethan ekes the barest of means from the soil, and indeed he emerges even more destitute twenty-four years later, in the epilogue.

In his blatantly dependent financial position, he never strays far from suggesting a parallel with Wharton's middle-class heroine, Lily Bart, in her earlier novel and first popular and critical success, *The House of Mirth* (1905). Similarly trapped by a restricted income (relative to her social class), and even more extremely dependent on others for allowance or inheritance, Lily is finally forced to work in a hat factory in order to pay off a debt. Even in that role she finds failure, as she cannot do the work as well as the others. Her challenge is to find an honorable relationship to money, but even in her noble choice to work—although she is as unsuited for this as Mattie—love continues to evade her. Like Ethan, she remains honorable yet unfulfilled, finding only tragically unhappy dignity.

Ethan's relationship to one of the few other male characters in the story, the builder Andrew Hale (to whom he sells lumber), is almost completely defined by money. From the beginning he approaches Hale for a loan; the first time he is turned away, and the second time he turns away himself: the open pity and compassion of Mrs. Hale shames him from deceiving his friend into giving him the fifty dollars to go out west with Mattie.

Some critics argue that lack of vision spurs the lovers on to the attempted suicide as much as lack of money or moral responsibility—that they might, with patience and rational thought, have discovered an alternate solution. On the contrary, Wharton works hard to make sure that the characters appear utterly trapped, that every alternative *that they can see* is exhausted; in doing so, she strives to make their (lack of) choice consistent with their limitations, in this setting and under these circumstances.

Creativity certainly fails them at this dark juncture. But a solution might not be possible, especially in the frame of mind that poverty creates. Not only does poverty limit options, but *Ethan Frome* shows how it forces options, especially in a desperate state of mind. Every time the protagonist has attempted to educate himself, to move away from Starkfield, duty—in the guise of his father's accident and then his mother's illness—has called him back to the gravelike farm.

Ethan's idea of going out west disintegrates as he begins to feel his shackles (one of many prison images in the novel) and sense his incarceration, uncolored by the rosy hue of infatuation. After weighing the possibilities of getting the money he needs, and exhausting them, Ethan submits.

> Borrowing was out of the question: six months before he had given his only security to raise funds for necessary repairs to the mill, and he knew that without security no one at Starkfield would lend him ten dollars. The inexorable facts closed in on him like prison-warders handcuffing a convict. There was no way out—none. He was a prisoner for life, and now his one ray of light was to be extinguished.
>
> He crept back heavily to the sofa, stretching himself out with limbs so leaden he felt as if they would never move again. Tears rose in his throat and slowly burned their way to his lids.

Along with the immobility that the prison metaphor presents, the motif of light returns as impending darkness. Repression is also symbolized in the last image; Ethan is terribly alone, but, significantly, is only half able to cry. This raw expression of feeling goes only as far as his lids, not running down his cheeks. Nevertheless, the picture maintains Ethan's sensitive and sincere qualities. In his lucid confrontation of practical circumstances, he appears no longer torn between hope and despair but deeply distraught. When Ethan allows himself temporarily to encounter the bitter truth, he sees the dimness of his future—that regardless of any action, he will be forced to remain in isolation. The alternative presents itself again as inaction. Only the beauty of nature intervening—a pure moon outside the window—answers him, not in consolation this time but as if "to mock his wretchedness."

An impoverished man in emotional turmoil—facing imminent loss—is not likely to make clearheaded, rational choices. After this psychological state of emergency, he wakes to familiar denial: "I guess things'll straighten out," he assures Mattie. When they do not, Ethan breaks out in another fit of rebellion, grasping at yet another spindly plan. This is the point at which he walks purposefully to the village to lie to Andrew Hale for money. But Mrs. Hale's unexpected appearance and compassionate words make him suddenly aware and ashamed of himself. He feels himself momentarily less alone, so it is not that familiar dread which thwarts him, but his decency. The event switches him suddenly back to reality, the only reality that can matter, the community of Starkfield.

> With the sudden perception of the point to which his madness had carried him, the madness fell and he saw his life before him as it was. He was a poor man, the husband of a sickly woman, whom his desertion would leave alone and destitute; and even if he had had the heart to desert her he could have done so only by deceiving two kindly people who had pitied him.
>
> He turned and walked slowly back to the farm.

Ethan's is the madness of passion but also the madness of impoverishment. When the fantasies drop away, the crudeness and squalor come into sharp relief. But what is most remarkable in this lucid, decidedly unromantic passage is the protagonist's "heart." Ethan's basic kindness and civility—even to a wife who has wished him nothing but ill—seems almost his downfall as it has rooted him to the most hopeless of circumstances and conceded him to the loss of his life's light. Just as romantic transport is crumpled in the novel, the notion of virtue leading to a character's happy ending is also subverted.

WOMEN IN *ETHAN FROME*

In spite of Ethan's more fully developed plight, the female characters in the story stand most helpless when it comes to economic power. Without any legal right to the purse strings, they can only manipulate to achieve their ends. As the critic Elizabeth Ammons attests in her fairytale reading of the story as a woodcutter and two witches, neither Zeena nor Mattie has any viable future to lose. But without economic power, neither had any future to begin with. Zeena is, as the other women of her day, completely economically dependent on her husband. She had entered the Frome household as a nurse to Ethan's dying mother, and after her marriage to Ethan, her only real power comes in manipulating her husband. Zeena relegates her unmet needs and desires to the realm of ill health, according to Ammons:

> Zeena's hypochondria, her frigidity, her taciturnity broken only by querulous nagging, her drab appearance—these make her an unsympathetic character. They also make her a typically "queer" woman of the region, a twisted human being produced by poverty and isolation and deadening routine. . . . Mattie Silver is merely spared the gradual disintegration into queerness that Ethan had witnessed in Zeena and his mother. The accident, like magic, swiftly transforms the girl into a whining burdensome hag.

Hungry for even a small measure of self-affirmation, Zeena's vague complaints and insistence on new treatments well illustrate the plight of women. Illness was one of the few avenues open to a poor or middle-class woman to gain power and attention—even social connections—as she seeks advice from other women and from doctors, not to mention that illness enhanced the otherwise unlikely possibility of attaining household help. Although an ill woman may be seemingly passive, her assertion of a string of ailments can work as a method for increasing her status. And, of course, the medical and quasi-medical establishments were only too glad to sell these women remedies.

It is convenient and foolproof for Zeena to use illness as an excuse to hire a girl, rather than keep Mattie, despite the fact that Mattie receives only room and board. Zeena's self-victimization and special status in this respect lend her a martyred and pitiful air, and Ethan cannot win any argument in the arena of his wife's health, even when it involves spending an inordinate amount of money. It is Zeena's only territory, and she is adept at taking advantage of the benefits it offers her.

Throughout the course of *Ethan Frome,* for example, she does little or nothing to help around the house, although she freely criticizes Mattie's awkwardness. And even after the smash-up, when Zeena has turned to doctoring the invalids, and the household is barely in a subsistence position financially, the narrator sees Ethan at the post office duly picking up envelopes addressed to Zeena from patent medicine companies. In the ironic depiction of a crippled man picking up useless prescriptions for a hypochondriac, the prologue demonstrates that after twenty-four years, Zeena's insensitivity remains unchanged.

Although she is painted as supremely insensitive and neurotic, Zeena's feigned illnesses seem deeply connected to an emotional hunger. The only response she can elicit from her husband is that of duty, the only nurturing that of paying for her medicines and doctors. By claiming to be sick, she has improved her standing in her household and in her community the only way she can. Her marriage is unsalvageable, but she can still use the pretext of her health to save face among the villagers who, she insinuates, know of the affair and feel it mandatory that she dismiss Mattie. The importance of the community and its gossip in the statement "I know well enough what they say of my having kep' her here as long as I have" cannot be denied.

Mattie's relationship to money is also crucial to the events of *Ethan Frome.* Her mother's death and father's bankruptcy put her in the position of needing to work for room and board at Ethan's farm in the first place, and Zeena makes her own generosity and mercy in the role of benefactor clear, as Mattie takes the role of grateful servant. But in her affection for Zeena's husband, it is clear that, to Zeena, Mattie is not grateful enough—on the contrary, she is an ingrate and usurper to her wifely (though lonely) place.

Mattie is the innocent outsider with nowhere to go, truly at the mercy of relations. She has been left desolate and has proven herself unfit for work behind a counter. Even at the farm, Ethan must help her out, as her only skills are of no practical use: "He did his best to supplement her unskilled efforts, getting up earlier than usual to light the kitchen fire, carrying in the wood overnight, and neglecting the mill for the farm." Ironically, it is Zeena's discovery of his surrogate scrubbing of the kitchen floor that initiates her "queer looks" and kindles her early suspicion of and increasing hostility toward her husband.

Brute economic reality intrudes finally and desperately on the hill, as Ethan and Mattie acknowledge the financial impossibility of her situation—"Where'll I go if I leave you?"—and the moral impossibility of his. His power to intercede as her benefactor has vanished: "I'm tied hand and foot, Matt. There isn't a thing I can do." When Mattie bursts out, "There's never anybody been good to me but you," Ethan reemphasizes his paralysis: "Don't say that either, when I can't lift a hand for you!"

Not all the female characters share the broken destinies that afflict Ethan's mother, Zeena, and Mattie, however. In the same way that the engineer serves as Ethan's alter ego—as the man he might have been had he escaped the shackles of life in Starkfield—the middle-class Ruth Varnum, who becomes Mrs. Ned Hale, embodies the least "queer," most sympathetic future for a female character—a future that might have been Mattie's had she married the prosperous businessman Denis Eady. Ruth Hale's trait of compassion, rare for Starkfield, gives her the clear and merciful vision she shares with the narrator.

THE TRIUMPH OF SILENCE

Many critics have found Wharton's sliver of an epilogue, with its characteristic terseness, so blunt that it is merciless. After the hopeful buildup and the tentativeness of Ethan's and Mattie's love, the reader is once again shut out from Ethan's myriad thoughts and feelings. He resumes, on the outside, his place as a common man of Starkfield except for his pronounced limp, his shrunken right side, and the power that great suffering gives. But for the reader, who has been allowed to experience his life from the inside, the horror that unfolds is much greater than it would be for any other man in the village. As Ethan knows too well what he has lost in beholding Mattie's invalid figure and whine, the reader too mourns her spirit, his spirit, and all those "healthy instincts of self-defence" Ethan had worked to keep alive.

In view of the torturous epilogue, silence triumphs, Mrs. Ned Hale at last seems willing to share with the narrator her recollections of the events that crippled the bodies and lives of Ethan and Zeena and Mattie. Nonetheless, in alluding to the unspeakable misery of Mattie having lived, Mrs. Ned Hale's empathy, significantly, keeps her from repeating Mattie's hopeless words when she awoke after the accident she wished never to awake from. In this recollected scene the power is in the gap: the unspeakability and ultimate inaccessibility of those words become Mattie's real assessment of her state. (In contrast, her survival in a paralyzed condition reflects an understatement of her true, deathlike condition.) This void becomes her context, her norm.

Almost a quarter-century later, even the most sympathetic female in the story only sees the friend who was to be her maid of honor once or twice a year. And in Mrs. Ned Hale's final remark a chill of truth darts out: "And the way they are now, I don't see's there's much difference between the Fromes up at the farm and the Fromes down in the graveyard; 'cept that down there they're all quiet, and the women have got to hold their tongues."

As the family graveyard lies en route to the farm's main entrance, gravestones form another motif beckoning throughout *Ethan Frome.* Most strikingly, the inscription noting "Endurance" (which also implies a silent endurance) both names Ethan's mother (who dwindled into a silent, mad existence) and prophesies her son's burdened fate. Wharton's striking placement of this word equates a life of endurance or continuous self-sacrifice with living death.

Mrs. Ned Hale's comment seems to imply that Ethan is equally dead, whether buried in the graveyard or at the farm, but that Zeena and Mattie are distinguished from their dead relatives only by their senseless prattling—a further reference to the "querulous drone" that both Zeena and Mattie emit and that has dissolved them into virtually one and the same person.

The repetition of the word "querulous" contains a pointed reference to what is being said, or more precisely (to borrow the narrator's phrase), its negation. By characterizing the women's words in these terms, the novel suggests the nagging's substancelessness and essential pettiness; by implication, when language or even life is devoid of passion or power, it is devoid of meaning.

Ethan craves nurturing but concludes literally motherless and virtually wifeless. As the removal of the "L" of the house attests, his home has lost its feminine center. It is clear that although Ethan married Zeena to escape a lonely silence, silence or death is preferable to the type of complaining that occurs again and again, ad infinitum, in Ethan's house—the complaining that he had learned to shut himself off from when Zeena engaged in it and that now accosts him in the person of his former beloved. Having finally removed any possibility of a warm voice, in its struggle against silence, *Ethan Frome* stresses the all-too-human need for the life-giving qualities of a sympathetic soul.

IRONY AND MOTIF

Opposing characters in *Ethan Frome* blur in the startling epilogue as the narrator records the picture he views as he steps into the kitchen of the Frome house. In providing the jigsaw's last piece, and allowing the narrator to solve the mystery of Ethan Frome, Wharton—paradoxically—ushers the reader into a universe of brokenness. The ending of *Ethan Frome* shockingly defies a reader's expectation, as it becomes evident that it was Mattie's—and not Zeena's—voice heard "droning querulously" in the prologue.

After (to follow the sound imagery) the animal-like twittering and the witchlike drone, the sight of those beady eyes and immobile frame brings to the reader—along with the narrator—his own waking moment, as it were. That the cackling belongs to Mattie is a crumbling realization. It terrifies. All the springtime metaphors disintegrate, the promise of fertility is abandoned, and the reader is ushered into Zeena's universe: cold and sharp. Through the frame of the querulous droning, then, Wharton completes the transference of beloved into abhorred.

As their voices merge, the premature decrepitude of Zeena and the humming youthfulness of Mattie meet in a sameness of no longer premature but actual old age—and a sameness of days that resembles death. Wharton implicitly criticizes the women's plight and draws attention to their powerlessness, as symbolized by Mattie's paralysis.

Furthermore, the two women's diametrically opposed characters have turned into symbols not of a typically fulfilling whole but of a terrible oneness—their "marriage" is a nightmare image of what the union of Ethan and Mattie might have been. With the perverseness of the ending, Ethan's earlier exclamations of "Oh, Matt, I can't let you go!" and his recurrent wish for inseparability from Mattie all come true. They are still together, but unexpectedly, sharing a cold, barren home with Zeena, in their fifties and sixties, with Ethan expected to live for decades more.

In a further irony among countless ironies, Ethan, the frozen one, has survived better than the gay, active Mattie. Even the silent dignity of death is not to be hers, for she emerges "twittering," then "querulous." Her character, which never attains the depth of Ethan's multidimensionality, has literally been flattened out. Despite Ethan's resolve to sit in front, it is Mattie who takes the brunt of the accident, who comes closest to death in her resulting paralysis. And in her dwindled form, she mocks Ethan's intellectual and emotional paralysis, his inability to act. Mattie's forlorn figure demonstrates the ridiculousness of his pretensions toward being a master of anything, much less his own future, and serves as a final reprimand against Ethan's fairytale, romantic tendencies.

Wharton develops the elements of the lovers' mirroring or doubling from the beginning of the novel. As Ethan patiently takes on her chores, he wishes Mattie to defy Zeena when he dares not, to intercede for him: "Ethan alternately burned with the desire to see Matty defy her and trembled with fear of the result." Now she has interceded for him in the worst way, and he, who can still walk, must take the blame for his failure of vision in both the literal and symbolic sense. His bent shoulders and shrunken right side symbolize the burden of this responsibility.

Light and warmth are notably absent in this anti-home. Even hope and despair blur into a kind of numbness. Although Mattie enters the tale as "the lighting of a fire on a cold hearth," in the final tableau, when Ethan invites the engineer into his impoverished farmhouse, the room where they find Mattie and Zeena is bitterly cold, and the fire is almost out because

Zeena had fallen asleep. The substance of Mattie's drone is to ask Zeena to restart the fire: to petulantly ask for the warmth she can no longer provide in her graceful dancing, her innocent words, the way her eyelids sank or fluttered.

Ethan has of course been asking for warmth silently throughout his life. His stoic nature, though a part of his dignity, is after all only a symptom of his disease: repression. Through his household's diminishment, Ethan internalizes the value of community over self. Starkfield has taught him that warmth is not, in fact, possible—and that the result of defiance is not death but increased torture.

Typified by the center Ethan has had to remove from the house, its heart—the "L"—the power of the novel lies on its unremitting symbolic evocation of what is missing. Everything lost—the lovers' passion, the thrum of their operatic coming together on the hill and the subsequent desperation—still echoes in the epilogue's frozen scene. Because of the catastrophic nature of the change, Mattie the girl still feels palpably more real than this ghost. And so, while the characters appear wholly defeated, twenty-four years has been a moment; the twitter still contains the birdsong, and the hunched figure still hints of the dance. In this way, Wharton's chronology of the novel is more emotional than literal.

IMPORTANCE AND INFLUENCE

Although the technique Wharton employs is largely considered that of realism, her heavy use of symbol—those ironic motifs so tightly interwoven in the story—brand the novel with an otherworldly immediacy. Primal emotions are brilliantly and uncomfortably conveyed in an American setting. Contemporary readers remote from old New England villages easily access Ethan's psychology—the intermittent numbness, passion, and alienation—and at the same time absorb the love story's truth through its powerful archetypes.

Historically, however, waves of skeptical, or at best, qualified criticism have limited *Ethan Frome*'s influence. Often condescending in tone, reviews of the slim novel have compared it unfavorably to works ranging from Emily Brontë's *Wuthering Heights* and novels by Leo Tolstoy and Gustave Flaubert, for example, to novels by Wharton's friend and contemporary Henry James. Wharton herself, although she never discussed the work in depth, felt obliged to come to its defense regarding structure or realism in a few of her writings.

Nonetheless, since the (psychological and biographical) feminist criticism that emerged in the 1970s, and the many film versions of Wharton's novels produced in the 1990s, her work has enjoyed a popular and critical revival. Most critics now use the resources of Wharton's letters, for example, to establish and enrich connections between her life and her writing. At the same time, more scholars are likely to explore sexual symbolism, repression, and silence—among other ideas—as themes running throughout *Ethan Frome.*

This novel in particular has bucked critical trends and naysayers to enjoy its status as a great American classic. While a seeming lack of redemption characterizes and even contemporizes the novel, mere amorality or moral inertia as a central theme would not account for the work's longevity. Consequently, the reader might need to resist fixating overmuch on the epilogue and look to the source of the novel's energy.

Finally, it is a question of the resilient element. What lies deepest in the novel's heart—and what pulls the reader along? The critic Blake Nevius, as early as 1968, responded to the wave of often pointedly reductive criticism of *Ethan Frome* that would last from at least the mid-1950s through 1975 in words that speak to the lasting and hypnotic effect of this fascinating work:

> Written over half a century ago, *Ethan Frome* has survived not only the changes in literary fashion

but the occasional efforts, by critics of such imposing reputation as John Crowe Ransom and Lionel Trilling, to make us view it more severely and ask whether after all it is not merely a tour de force. "It is sometimes spoken of," says Mr. Trilling ruefully, "as an American classic." Despite the reservations of some critics, the view that *Ethan Frome* is a classic has persisted, and attempts to chip away at the monument have left it strangely intact.

Select Bibliography

EDITIONS

Ethan Frome. New York: Scribners, 1911. (The Scribner paperback edition, reissued 1997, is cited in this essay.)

Ethan Frome: The Modern Student's Library Edition. New York: Scribners, 1922. (Significant for Edith Wharton's brief introduction, discussing the origin and the construction of the novel.)

Edith Wharton's Ethan Frome: *The Story with Sources and Commentary.* Edited by Blake Nevius. New York: Scribners, 1968. (Among many fascinating analyses, contains the skeptical essays of John Crowe Ransom and Lionel Trilling, which effectively silenced critics until the late 1970s.)

Ethan Frome: Authoritative Text, Backgrounds and Contexts, Criticism. Edited by Kristin Lauer and Cynthia Griffin Wolff. New York: Norton, 1995.

OTHER WORKS BY WHARTON

The House of Mirth. New York: Scribners, 1905.

Summer. New York: Scribners, 1917.

The Age of Innocence. New York: Appleton, 1920.

A Backward Glance. New York: Appleton, 1934.

SECONDARY WORKS

Ammons, Elizabeth. *Edith Wharton's Argument with America.* Athens: University of Georgia Press, 1980. (A groundbreaking work of feminist criticism on the novel, most notably in its analysis of *Ethan Frome* as a subverted fairytale.)

Bell, Millicent, ed. *The Cambridge Companion to Edith Wharton.* Cambridge, U.K.: Cambridge University Press, 1995.

Bendixen, Alfred, and Annette Zilversmit, eds. *Edith Wharton: New Critical Essays.* New York: Garland, 1992.

Bloom, Harold, ed. *Edith Wharton.* New York: Chelsea House, 1986.

Fedorko, Kathy. *Gender and Gothic in the Fiction of Edith Wharton.* Tuscaloosa: University of Alabama Press, 1995. (Focuses on an examination of the dream states of both Ethan and the storyteller.)

Fryer, Judith. *Felicitous Space: The Imaginative Structures of Edith Wharton and Willa Cather.* Chapel Hill: University of North Carolina Press, 1986. (Interesting for its discussion of the narrator as counterpart to Ethan as well as the psychological implications of the Frome farm's architecture.)

Gimbel, Wendy. *Edith Wharton: Orphancy and Survival.* New York: Praeger, 1984.

Howe, Irving, ed. *Edith Wharton: A Collection of Critical Essays.* Englewood Cliffs, N.J.: Prentice-Hall, 1962. (Contains the influential Lionel Trilling essay.)

Joslin, Katherine. *Edith Wharton.* New York: St. Martin's, 1991. (Includes commentary on the critical reception of Wharton's novels.)

Killoran, Helen. *The Critical Reception of Edith Wharton.* Rochester, N.Y.: Camden House, 2001. (Provides an up-to-date synopsis of the relatively sparse *Ethan Frome* criticism in a chapter titled "The Murder of a Masterpiece.")

Lewis, R. W. B. *Edith Wharton: A Biography.* New York: Harper and Row, 1975. (One of the two 1970s biographies that resparked interest in Wharton's work.)

Lyde, Marilyn. *Edith Wharton: Convention and Morality in the Work of a Novelist.* Norman: University of Oklahoma Press, 1959.

McDowell, Margaret. *Edith Wharton.* Rev. ed. Boston: Twayne, 1990. (Helpful analysis of the endurance of Wharton's art.)

Nevius, Blake. *Edith Wharton: A Study of Her Fiction.* Berkeley: University of California Press, 1953. (An illuminating discussion of elements such as the "trapped sensibility" in the novel.)

Raphael, Lev. *Edith Wharton's Prisoners of Shame: A New Perspective on Her Neglected Fiction.* New York: St. Martin's, 1991. (Valuable close reading of shame and pride as central themes in *Ethan Frome.*)

Singley, Carol. *Edith Wharton: Matters of Mind and Spirit.* Cambridge, U.K.: Cambridge University Press, 1995.

Springer, Marlene. *Ethan Frome: A Nightmare of Need.* New York: Twayne, 1993. (Rare for the sustained discussion on this particular novel, this is an entire work devoted to analyses of *Ethan Frome.*)

Tuttleton, James, Kristin Lauer, and Margaret Murray, eds. *Edith Wharton: The Contemporary Reviews.* Cambridge, U.K.: Cambridge University Press, 1992.

Wershoven, Carol. *The Female Intruder in the Novels of Edith Wharton.* Rutherford, N.J.: Fairleigh Dickinson University Press; London: Associated University Presses, 1982.

Wolff, Cynthia Griffin. *A Feast of Words: The Triumph of Edith Wharton.* 2d ed. Reading, Mass.: Addison-Wesley, 1995. (This definitive biography of Wharton helped to resurrect her status and establish biographical connections to the themes in her work—for instance, the marital difficulties and illicit affair said to have inspired *Ethan Frome.*)

Wright, Sarah Bird. *Edith Wharton A to Z: The Essential Guide to the Life and Work.* New York: Facts on File, 1998.

F. Scott Fitzgerald's

The Great Gatsby

CHARLES R. BAKER

IN 1922 F. Scott Fitzgerald was twenty-six years old and rapidly nearing the peak of his fame and fortune. His first two novels, *This Side of Paradise* (1920) and *The Beautiful and the Damned* (1922), were critical and commercial successes, and he was enjoying the earliest, happiest days of his marriage to the second girl of his dreams, Zelda Sayre. He felt confident and secure enough in his abilities as a writer to tell his editor, the legendary Maxwell Perkins of Charles Scribner & Sons, "I want to write something *new*—something extraordinary and beautiful and simple + intricately patterned." He expanded on that desire in a letter to fellow novelist Thomas Boyd in March of 1923: "I shall never write another document-novel. I have decided to be a pure artist + experiment in form and emotion." After extricating himself from the debts incurred by his failed stage play, *The Vegetable; or, From President to Postman* (1923), Fitzgerald took his wife and daughter to Europe in 1924. In the French Rivera town of St. Raphael, Fitzgerald wrote the first draft of what is recognized as his masterpiece, *The Great Gatsby* (1925).

THE PRINCIPALS GATHER

Key to any first-person narrative is the reliability of the narrator. Nick Carraway, the narrator of *The Great Gatsby,* presents his credentials immediately. He is from a prominent midwestern family, a graduate of Yale University, and a veteran of World War I. His father impressed on him at an early age that he should not be quick to judge others: "'Whenever you feel like criticizing anyone,' he told me, 'just remember that all the people in this world haven't had the advantages that you've had.'" Nick has tried hard to remember his father's words, reserving judgment when he has found himself the tolerant recipient of unsought secrets, griefs, and intimate revelations. But such conduct has its limits, and he admits, "When I came back home from the East last autumn I felt that I wanted the world to be in uniform and at a sort of moral attention forever; I wanted no more riotous excursions with privileged glimpses into the human heart." Here Fitzgerald alerts the reader that this story is composed of Nick's recollection of events that have already occurred. One of the intriguing narrative effects Fitzgerald incorporates in this novel is an absence of strict chronological order, a technique used most effectively by an author Fitzgerald greatly admired, Joseph Conrad. Like Conrad's narrator Marlow in *Lord Jim* and "Heart of Darkness," Nick was only partially involved in the events he relates, but he is the sole source and readers therefore have no choice but to accept his version of the story. The bits and pieces of information Nick gathers from other characters and those he collects from Gatsby himself are artfully arranged to present a picture of a man and his times that is rather like a Cubist painting: a masterpiece of angles and perspectives, darkness and light.

Nick is clearly disgusted with the people and events that populate his picture of the summer he spent on Long Island in 1922; only one person "was exempt from my reaction," Jay Gatsby. He says there "was something gorgeous about him," that he possessed "some heightened sensitivity to the promises of life," an "extraordinary gift for hope," a "romantic readiness" that Nick is unlikely to find in any other person. "No—Gatsby turned out all right at the end; it is what preyed on Gatsby, what foul dust floated in the wake of his dreams that temporarily closed out my interest in the abortive sorrows and short-winded elations of men."

When Nick returned home from the war, he was restless and unsure about what direction his life should take. Because everyone he knew had gone into the bond business, he decided to give it a try. His father agreed to finance his desire for one year, and Nick went east in the spring of 1922 to New York to learn the trade. Instead of doing the practical thing and taking rooms in the city, Nick, who had grown up around lawns and trees, chose instead to rent a bungalow in the community of West Egg on the eastern side of Long Island, about twenty miles outside of the busy metropolis. "It was a matter of chance that I should have rented a house in one of the strangest communities in North America. I was on that slender riotous island which extends itself due east of New York and where there are, among other natural curiosities, two unusual

CHRONOLOGY

1896	Francis Scott Key Fitzgerald born on September 24 to Edward Fitzgerald and Mary (Mollie) McQuillan Fitzgerald in St. Paul, Minnesota.
1911	Attends Newman School, a boarding school in Hackensack, New Jersey.
1913	Enters Princeton University.
1915	Meets Ginevra King, his first serious romance and the inspiration for many of his fictional heroines.
1917	Ginevra ends the romance. Leaves Princeton for Fort Leavenworth. Commissioned as 2nd Lieutenant in the infantry.
1918	Meets Zelda Sayre while stationed in Alabama. Peace declared, so he is not sent overseas. Early version of *This Side of Paradise* rejected by Scribners.
1920	*This Side of Paradise* published by Scribners. Marries Zelda Sayre in New York. First collection of short stories, *Flappers and Philosophers,* published.
1921	Birth of only child, Frances Scott "Scottie" Fitzgerald, on October 26.
1922	*The Beautiful and the Damned* and *Tales of the Jazz Age.*
1923	Production of his play, *From President to Postman,* closes after one week in Atlantic City, New Jersey.
1924	First draft of *The Great Gatsby* written on the French Riviera and revised in Rome.
1925	*The Great Gatsby* published on April 10.
1926	Third collection of short stories, *All the Sad Young Men,* published.
1927	Works for two months as a screenwriter for United Artists in Hollywood.
1930	Zelda suffers first in a series of mental breakdowns.
1931	Fitzgerald returns from fifth trip to Europe and works for Metro-Goldwyn-Mayer in Hollywood.
1934	*Tender Is the Night.*

1935	Fourth collection of short stories, *Taps at Reveille,* published. Begins writing essays that will be published posthumously as *The Crack-Up.*
1936	Zelda institutionalized in Highland Hospital, Asheville, North Carolina.
1940	Freelancing for motion picture studios in Hollywood. Begins work on *The Last Tycoon.* Dies of a heart attack on December 21. Buried in Rockville Union Cemetery, Rockville, Maryland.
1941	*The Last Tycoon.*
1945	*The Crack-Up.*
1948	Zelda dies in fire at Highland Hospital. Buried with her husband.

formations of land." West Egg is a peninsular formation that juts out into Long Island Sound and is separated from its twin formation, East Egg, by a narrow bay. Although both communities boast glittering mansions of the wealthy, East Egg is the home of old money while its neighbor to the west is the playground of the nouveau riche and is therefore considered less fashionable. This does not matter to Nick who is happy to have, for eighty dollars a month, a little house tucked unobtrusively between two palaces, a view of the Sound, a patch of lawn, a Finnish woman to cook and clean, and the close proximity of millionaires.

After settling comfortably into his new surroundings, Nick drives to East Egg to have dinner with Tom and Daisy Buchanan and thereby becomes innocently yet inextricably involved in events that culminate in tragedy. Daisy is Nick's second cousin once removed, and Tom was his classmate at Yale. Tom is a huge, hulking man prone to cruelty and sarcasm; a star football player in his college days, he now seems to Nick to be "one of those men who reach such an acute limited excellence at twenty-one that everything afterwards savours of anticlimax." He has inherited an enormous amount of money but seems unhappy and angry. All that his money can buy—mansions, polo ponies, women—cannot replace the lost glory days of his youth. Despite his brutishness, Tom is a frightened man. He tells Nick at dinner that a book he is reading has greatly disturbed him. Tom's book is *The Rise of the Coloured Empires* by Goddard. (Fitzgerald chose not to use the actual title and author: *The Rising Tide of Color* by Lothrop Stoddard, which was published in 1920.) The book's author warns that white supremacy is in danger of being overrun by what he considers inferior races. Tom declares that something must be done to stem the tide or civilization (meaning his own wealth and position in society) is doomed. Tom is a powerful man who will defend the privileges afforded him in a society that rewards his class and race. "The idea is if we don't look out the white race will be—will be utterly submerged. It's all scientific stuff; it's been proved." He continues, "This fellow has worked out the whole thing. It's up to us who are the dominant race to watch out or these other races will have control of things." The racism Tom espouses is certainly hateful, but it is not fanatical for the time and indeed may be only a feeble attempt to present himself to his guest as an intelligent man who keeps up with the latest scientific theories. Evidence of this possibility is found later in the novel when Tom is again seeking to impress: "I read somewhere that the sun's getting hotter every year. . . . It seems that pretty soon the earth's going to fall into the sun—or wait a minute—it's just the opposite—the sun's getting colder every year." The combination of intellectual pretension, anger, frustration, and muddle-headed thinking makes Tom a dangerous man.

Tom's wife, Daisy, is initially presented as his opposite in every way: beautiful, delicate, silly, and romantic. As the story progresses, however, she is revealed to be just as ruthless and amoral as her spouse. She seems to be held in her marriage by sheer laziness, not love, as if remaining in a comfortable and familiar position, regardless of Tom's brutish behavior and infidelities, is preferable to exerting the energy it would take to leave it. Whereas Tom is "a great big hulking physical specimen," Daisy is rather insubstantial, not possessing the physical presence Fitzgerald gives to other, even minor, characters. Her mutability is emphasized by Fitzgerald's inconsistencies the few times he gives a description of her. For instance, in chapter 7 Tom and Daisy's daughter, Pammy, is described as having "yellowy hair," and her mother says "She's got my hair and shape of face." In chapter 8, however, Gatsby kisses Daisy's "dark shining hair." This may be nothing more than an oversight on Fitzgerald's part (if read closely enough, he does make a mistake concerning Daisy's chronology, a mistake that is examined in Richard Lehan's *The Great Gatsby: The Limits of Wonder),* but the change in hair color underscores the difficulties the reader has in developing a clear picture of Gatsby's beloved. Or it may be Fitzgerald's intention to keep her physicality vague, thereby impressing on the reader that it is the "idea" of Daisy that is important. She is more an embodiment of a romantic dream—a dream Tom may have had once and has forgotten, a dream that controls Gatsby's life.

Daisy is one of many desirable young women who populate Fitzgerald's work who were inspired by his ill-fated romance with Ginevra King. Fitzgerald met Ginevra in 1915 when he was a nineteen-year-old student at Princeton and she was a sixteen-year-old debutante from a wealthy family. The ledger Fitzgerald kept chronicles their joyous times together: attending dances, parties, football games, and the latest entertainment form, the movies. As the ranks of Ginevra's wealthy suitors grew, Fitzgerald's hopes diminished. In August 1916, while he was visiting Ginevra in Lake Forest, Illinois, her hometown, he records overhearing someone say, "Poor boys shouldn't think of marrying rich girls." The wound caused by Ginevra's rejection of him in 1917 never healed. His psyche was shaken but his art was born. In Andrew Turnbull's biography, *Scott Fitzgerald,* Fitzgerald is quoted as saying, "The whole idea of Gatsby is the unfairness of a poor young man not being able to marry a girl with money. This theme comes up again and again because I lived it."

The fourth member of the dinner party is Jordan Baker, a professional golf champion who is rumored to have cheated during her first tournament win. Jordan is based on Ginevra King's friend, Edith Cummings, who won the women's golf championship in 1923. Nick is attracted to her cool self-sufficiency.

> She was extended full length at her end of the divan, completely motionless and with her chin raised a little as if she were balancing something on it which was quite likely to fall. If she saw me out of the corner of her eyes she gave no hint of it—indeed I was almost surprised into murmuring an apology for having disturbed her by coming in.

Just before dinner is served, Jordan tells Nick that she knows he lives in West Egg and remarks that he must know Gatsby. "'Gatsby?' demanded Daisy, 'What Gatsby?'" Her question goes unanswered. "Before I could reply that he was my neighbor dinner was announced; wedging his tense arm imperatively under mine Tom Buchanan compelled me from the room as though he were moving a checker to another square." Tom receives a phone call during dinner and Jordan confides to Nick, "Tom's got some woman in New York." Daisy is visibly upset and leaves the dinner table to regain her composure. Soon after Tom and Daisy return to their guests the phone rings again but "Daisy shook her head decisively at Tom," and he stays put. The tension is broken when dinner ends and Tom and Jordan stroll the grounds of the Buchanan estate. Nick and Daisy move to a wicker settee on the veranda. After struggling with her turbulent emotions, Daisy confesses, "Well, I've had a very bad time, Nick, and I'm pretty cynical about everything." To impress on Nick just how cynical she has become, she tells Nick about the birth of her daughter.

> It'll show you how I've gotten to feel about—things. Well, she was less than an hour old and

> Tom was God knows where. I woke up out of the ether with an utterly abandoned feeling and asked the nurse right away if it was a boy or a girl. She told me it was a girl, and so I turned my head away and wept. "All right," I said, "I'm glad it's a girl. And I hope she'll be a fool—that's the best thing a girl can be in this world, a beautiful little fool."

She feels that she is in vogue with "the most advanced people" by thinking that "everything's terrible." "'And I *know.* I've been everywhere and seen everything and done everything.' Her eyes flashed around her in a defiant way, rather like Tom's, and she laughed with thrilling scorn. 'Sophisticated—God, I'm sophisticated.'"

Nick drives back home confused and disgusted. "It seemed to me that the thing for Daisy to do was to rush out of the house, child in arms—but apparently there were no such intentions in her head." At this early stage of the story Fitzgerald hints that nothing that follows will change her mind. As he sits outside his house Nick notices a man facing the bay that divides West Egg from East Egg, his arms stretched toward a distant green light. Nick thinks it must be Gatsby.

> I decided to call to him. Miss Baker had mentioned him at dinner, and that would do for an introduction. But I didn't call to him for he gave a sudden intimation that he was content to be alone—he stretched out his arms toward the dark water in a curious way, and far as I was from him I could have sworn he was trembling. Involuntarily I glanced seaward—and distinguished nothing except a single green light, minute and far away, that might have been the end of a dock. When I looked once more for Gatsby he had vanished, and I was alone again in the unquiet darkness.

THE VALLEY OF ASHES

One Sunday afternoon, Tom decides to take the train into New York and insists that Nick accompany him. The train makes a stop about halfway between West Egg and Manhattan in a place called the valley of ashes, an area of swampland that is being filled with refuse. It is, indeed, an American version of T. S. Eliot's *The Waste Land* (1922) a poem that Fitzgerald knew by heart. A side-by-side reading of these two masterpieces is an enlightening experience. Apart from the thematic and symbolic similarities, both works share a pattern of dramatic language; a good example is this passage from Fitzgerald's novel: "'What'll we do with ourselves this afternoon,' cried Daisy, 'and the day after that, and the next thirty years?'" compared with lines 131 through 134 of the poem,

> What shall I do now? What shall I do?
> I shall rush out as I am, and walk the street
> With my hair down, so. What shall we do to-
> morrow?
> What shall we ever do.

The desolate landscape is watched over by a huge pair of blue eyes (Fitzgerald writes that the retinas are one yard high but he must have meant either the irises or pupils) that peer out of yellow eyeglass frames on an old fading billboard advertising the services of a specialist in the treatment of eye disorders, Dr. T. J. Eckleburg. Tom and Nick get off the train and make their way to a nearby gas station and car repair garage owned by George B. Wilson, husband of Tom's mistress, Myrtle. Wilson seems to be as insubstantial as the ashy dust that covers everything, "He was a blonde, spiritless man, anæmic and faintly handsome." But Myrtle is colorful, vibrant, and fleshy. "She was in the middle thirties, and faintly stout, but she carried her surplus flesh sensuously as some women can. Her face, above a spotted dress of dark blue crêpe-de-chine, contained no facet or gleam of beauty but there was an immediately perceptible vitality about her as if the nerves of her body were continually smouldering." Wilson is a defeated man; he has seen his version of the American Dream (his own business with living quarters above and a once-faithful wife) become like the ash heaps that encroach on the once thriving crossroads.

> The only building in sight was a small block of yellow brick sitting on the edge of the waste land, a sort of compact Main Street ministering to it and contiguous to absolutely nothing. One of the three shops it contained was for rent and another was an all-night restaurant approached by a trail of ashes.

The third shop is Wilson's garage. "The interior was unprosperous and bare; the only car visible was the dust-covered wreck of a Ford which crouched in a dim corner." Tom has long held out to Wilson the possibility that he might sell one of his cars to the garage owner, a possibility that Wilson relishes, knowing he can resell the car for a profit. "When he saw us a damp gleam of hope sprang into his light blue eyes." But it is not to be; Tom merely uses the possibility to divert Wilson's attention away from the fact that Tom comes there to make contact with Myrtle.

Tom manages to convey to Myrtle that he wants her to slip away and join him and Nick on the train. Soon all three, together with an assortment of guests, are drinking the night away in an apartment on 158th Street that Tom keeps for his assignations with Myrtle. Nick is disgusted by the vulgarity of the party but is too fascinated by its grotesqueness to leave. Things turn even uglier when a thoroughly drunken Myrtle taunts Tom by repeating Daisy's name over and over, a name, Tom tells her, she has no right to mention. She persists, and he deftly breaks her nose. Clearly Tom is the sort of man who believes that the use of violence is a suitable way to deal with his problems.

GATSBY AND HIS PARTIES

Over the four weeks he has lived near Gatsby, Nick has noticed the elaborate preparations for his neighbor's weekend parties but has not been invited to attend.

> On week-ends his Rolls-Royce became an omnibus, bearing parties to and from the city, between nine in the morning and long past midnight, while his station wagon scampered like a brisk yellow bug to meet all trains. And on Mondays eight servants including an extra gardener toiled all day with mops and scrubbing-brushes and hammers and garden shears, repairing the ravages of the night before.

One Saturday morning, however, one of Gatsby's many servants appears at Nick's door with an invitation to that weekend's festivities. Nick wanders over in the evening and mingles with the huge crowd of guests, hearing snatches of rumors about his host. Some speak of his generosity, but others claim that he is a sinister character who has perhaps committed murder. Nick joins Jordan in a search for the mysteriously absent Gatsby but gives up around midnight and devotes himself to drinking enormous glasses of champagne. A man greets him with the unlikely declaration that he recognizes Nick from the war. He tells Nick that he has just bought a hydroplane and invites him to come along on its test flight the next morning. He asks, "Want to go with me, old sport?" Nick is surprised to learn that his new acquaintance is Gatsby, who apologizes for being a poor host. "Old sport" has been used as a clue in discovering the identity of the man Fitzgerald used as the model for Gatsby. The most likely is Max Gerlach, an alleged bootlegger who had lived near Fitzgerald in Great Neck (West Egg) and who sent him a newspaper clipping in 1923 on which he had written, among other things, "How are you and the family, old sport?" One of the many rumors regarding Gatsby's wealth is that it was gained through the illegal sale and transportation of alcohol—"bootlegging." Nick notices that the smile Gatsby turns on him is almost hypnotic—reassuring without being ingratiating. He also notices that Gatsby is very formal in his speech, searching for the precise word to convey the desired impression. But Nick glimpses a small crack in the facade, "Precisely at that point it vanished—and I was looking at an elegant young rough-neck, a year or two over thirty, whose elaborate formality of speech just missed being absurd."

Gatsby is informed by a butler that there is a telephone call for him from Chicago, and he leaves Nick with a promise to join him later. But when the butler returns, he says that Gatsby would like to speak to Jordan alone. When Jordan comes back to Nick an hour later, she teases him by saying she has just heard the most extraordinary thing but has promised not to tell anyone.

THE GANGSTER CONNECTION

At the end of chapter 3, Nick tells the reader that his summer has not been all fun and games among the rich on Long Island. He has a job at Probity Trust in lower Manhattan that keeps him very busy during the week. He has also had a brief affair with a girl in his office who lives in Jersey City. He is curious about Jordan but feels no real love for her. Indeed, he sees her as careless and dishonest but fascinating.

Although he has been to two of Gatsby's parties and has ridden in his hydroplane and used his private beach, Nick's initial curiosity about the man has waned because of Gatsby's tight-lipped reserve. He is surprised when Gatsby arrives in one of his extravagant cars at Nick's house one morning and, because they are meeting for lunch that afternoon in New York, offers to drive him to work. As they make their way toward Manhattan, Gatsby suddenly asks Nick, "Look here, old sport. . . . What's your opinion of me anyhow?" Nick manages to politely evade the question, and Gatsby proceeds to tell him the story of his life in the hopes of dispelling any wrong impressions Nick may have formed based on the rumors Gatsby knows he has heard. He claims that he is from the Midwest, born into a wealthy family whose men have always been educated at Oxford University in England. He further claims that his heroic actions in World War I earned him decorations from all the Allied governments. He offers in proof two items he just happens to have in his pockets: a medal engraved "Major Jay Gatsby for Valour Extraordinary" and a photograph of himself and five other young men taken at Trinity College, Oxford. He is the only member of his family still living, and he has inherited a vast fortune. Nick is willing to believe Gatsby despite the fact that when asked where in the Midwest he was born, Gatsby answers, "San Francisco."

Gatsby explains that it is important for Nick to know that he is a well-bred gentleman in light of the favor he wants from Nick: "I didn't want you to think I was just some nobody." But instead of asking him outright, Gatsby tells Nick that Jordan will fill him in later on the details of "the sad thing that happened to me" and what Nick can do for him. Nick is somewhat bothered that Gatsby knows that he is joining Jordan for tea at the Plaza Hotel that afternoon but says nothing. That Nick's life is about to change is symbolized by two examples of change that America was experiencing: the arrival of immigrants from eastern Europe and African Americans from the southern states. As he rides in Gatsby's Rolls-Royce, Nick sees a funeral procession drive by and look at the magnificent car "with the tragic eyes and short upper lips of south-eastern Europe." Later he sees a limousine with three well-dressed blacks "driven by a white chauffeur, in which sat three modish Negroes, two bucks and a girl. I laughed aloud as the yolks of their eyeballs rolled toward us in haughty rivalry." (Almost every character in the book displays a degree of racism. Nick's observations here regarding the eastern Europeans and the African Americans, though certainly racist, are mild compared to Tom's hateful denunciations and are suggestive of Nick's gradual moral decline.)

At noon, Nick leaves his office and meets Gatsby for lunch at a little restaurant on 42nd Street that is, appropriately enough, underground. He finds Gatsby in conversation with an older man who is introduced as Meyer Wolfshiem. From his stories of the old days and the human molars he wears mounted as cufflinks, it is clear that Wolfshiem is an aging gangster. It is also clear that he has known and admired Gatsby for some time. After Wolfshiem leaves their table, Gatsby tells Nick that the old man is responsible for fixing the 1919 World Series. This bit of information makes a strong case for Arnold Rothstein being the gangster whom Wolfshiem is based upon. Rothstein was suspected of bribing the Chicago White Sox to purposefully lose to the Cincinnati Reds. Investigators never found enough evidence to convict him, but Rothstein had bet heavily on the underdog Reds. As Gatsby says of Wolfshiem, "They can't get him, old sport. He's a smart man."

A MEETING AFTER MANY YEARS

Later that same afternoon, Nick joins Jordan for tea at the Plaza Hotel, and she tells him of a chain of events that began one October day in 1917 in Louisville, Kentucky. She was sixteen and her friend, Daisy Fay, the most popular girl in their hometown, was eighteen. Jordan remembers walking along Daisy's street and being called to by her friend who is sitting in her white roadster with a young, infatuated lieutenant. Daisy introduced her beau as Jay Gatsby. Jordan tells Nick that she lost touch with Daisy the following year but had heard rumors about her and a young officer whom her parents forbade her to visit in New York before he was to leave for the war overseas. Daisy was devastated, but by June of 1919 she had recovered enough to marry a wealthy Chicagoan, Tom Buchanan. The night before the wedding, Jordan came into Daisy's room and found her drunk and inconsolable, a bottle of wine in one hand and a letter in the other. Fitzgerald does not reveal the contents of the letter or the name of its author, but it is safe to assume it was from Gatsby, swearing his eternal love. The next afternoon, Daisy went through with the planned wedding. Jordan ends her recollections with a description of the traveling circus that is the marriage of Tom and Daisy and a nasty indiscretion involving Tom and a chambermaid in Santa Barbara. The picture of Daisy she presents is that of a terribly unhappy woman who must patiently endure her husband's infidelities.

Jordan explains that Gatsby wants Nick to make his home available for a surprise meeting with Daisy. Nick agrees, and when he returns home that evening, he sets a time and date with Gatsby, who had been anxiously awaiting Nick's decision. Gatsby is very grateful and clumsily offers Nick a confidential business deal that could be worth a lot of money. Although Gatsby assures him that he "wouldn't have to do any business with Wolfshiem," Nick tactfully declines. "I realize now that under different circumstances that conversation might have been one of the crises of my life."

A heavy rain is falling the morning of the meeting, yet Gatsby has sent someone over to mow Nick's unkempt yard and has others deliver a houseful of fresh-cut flowers. Gatsby, dressed to impress in a white suit, silver shirt, and gold tie (subliminal suggestions of wealth), arrives an hour before the agreed-upon time of four, petulant and restless. When he hears Daisy arrive, he leaves through the back door only to walk around the house in the pouring rain and knock on the front door. After meeting her, he goes to the kitchen and admits to Nick that this whole idea of seeing Daisy is a terrible mistake. Nick tells Gatsby that he is acting like a little boy and sends him back into the room where Daisy sits alone. The meeting is awkward; Daisy is formal. "I certainly am awfully glad to see you again." And soon after, she says, "We haven't met for many years." Gatsby is quick to interject, "Five years next November." The time element is emphasized by Gatsby's accident with a mantel clock in Nick's house and, later, when a guest of Gatsby's, Mr. Klipspringer, plays a 1920s favorite, "Ain't We Got Fun," on the piano as the trio wanders through Gatsby's mansion. Lines from that song perfectly describe Gatsby's dilemma, "In the meantime, / In between time—" Gatsby is indeed in between time, the five years he has spent preparing for this moment have come to an end, and an uncertain, possibly disappointing, future looms.

Nick dashes through the rain to a sheltering tree and after an hour returns to his house. Readers do not know what the reunited lovers discussed during Nick's absence, but Gatsby is glowing as brightly as the sun that has finally broken through the storm clouds. Even so, after Gatsby has led Daisy and Nick on a giddy tour of his mansion, Nick sees a trace of doubt in Gatsby's features; as though having finally grasped his long desired grail, he has found that it is just that, only a grail whose substance is formed by his imagination and yearning and nothing more.

> The expression of bewilderment had come back into Gatsby's face, as though a faint doubt had occurred to him as to the quality of his present happiness. Almost five years! There must have been moments even that afternoon when Daisy tumbled short of his dreams—not through her own fault but because of the colossal vitality of his illusion.

DRIVING ON TOWARD DEATH

Now Fitzgerald accelerates his story. Events occur more quickly, and the summer heat becomes stifling. Nick chooses this time to tell the reader the true story of Gatsby's early years, facts, he explains, that he learned from Gatsby much later in the chain of events. Jay Gatsby came into the world as James Gatz, the son of poor North Dakota farmers. At the age of seventeen, unable to accept who he was, he left home in search of who he could become. Although his image of who that might be was blurry, it did have a name: Jay Gatsby. For more than a year he drifted along the southern shore of Lake Superior, doing whatever work he could for food and shelter. Dissatisfied with that life, he enrolled in a small college in southern Minnesota, but he was dismayed that the school did not see his potential greatness and embarrassed by the janitorial work he had to do to pay his way. After two weeks he left the school and returned to Lake Superior, where he was instrumental in helping a yacht owner avoid certain disaster. The yachtsman is fifty-year-old Dan Cody, who represents a Horace Greeley type of success that is no longer feasible for Gatz's generation. Cody, whose millions were pulled from the copper mines of Montana, takes the boy, who now calls himself Jay Gatsby, under his wing and sails to exotic ports of call with him for five years, showing the wonders that can be had with wealth. Cody dies, and Gatsby, cheated out of an inheritance of $25,000 by Cody's mistress, drifts away with nothing more than a fervent desire to achieve greatness. When Dan Cody died, Jay Gatsby was born.

> I suppose he'd had the name ready for a long time, even then. His parents were shiftless and unsuccessful farm people—his imagination had never really accepted them as his parents at all. The truth was that Jay Gatsby, of West Egg, Long Island, sprang from his Platonic conception of himself. He was a son of God—a phrase which, if it means anything, means just that—and he must be about His Father's Business, the service of a vast, vulgar and meretricious beauty. So he invented just the sort of Jay Gatsby that a seventeen year old boy would be likely to invent, and to this conception he was faithful to the end.

Tom, who has grown suspicious of his wife's absences, accompanies Daisy to one of Gatsby's parties to see if he can discover the reason for them. Also, he is curious about Gatsby and how he is able to create such lavish entertainments. While he wanders through the crush of famous and infamous guests, his wife and Gatsby slip away to Nick's house for some time alone. After the party Gatsby lays out his and Daisy's plans to Nick. She will confess to Tom that she has never loved him. Once free of him, she will return to Louisville and be married to Gatsby at her family home—just as she should have done five years ago. Nick cautions Gatsby not to expect too much and warns that the past cannot be repeated. Incredulous, Gatsby insists that it can.

Several days later Gatsby and Nick are lunch guests at the Buchanan mansion on the hottest day of the summer. Daisy is nervous, knowing that Gatsby wants to confront Tom with their plans. Tom, through his observations of the two lovers over lunch, sees that his suspicions about his wife are well founded. The party decides to drive into Manhattan to escape the heat—Gatsby and Daisy in Tom's blue coupe and Tom, Nick, and Jordan in Gatsby's yellow "circus wagon," as Tom derisively calls it.

Tom stops at Wilson's garage to get the gas tank filled and finds Wilson almost too sick to do the job. He tells Tom that he has learned something about Myrtle and plans to take her far away. As Tom drives away in Gatsby's car, Nick sees Myrtle staring down at them from an upstairs window, her face a picture of desperate and rapidly changing emotions.

The group agrees to take a room at the Plaza Hotel, and Tom orders glasses, ice, and crushed mint to go with the whiskey he has brought along. His temper is as hot as the room. He knows Gatsby is trying to steal his wife, and he learned moments ago that his mistress is moving west. Tom goads Gatsby about his mannerisms and his claim of having gone to Oxford. Gatsby manages to answer politely, but when Tom pushes him too far on the matter of his involvement with Daisy, he tells the enraged husband that Daisy has never loved him and that she is going to leave him. Tom tells Gatsby that he is crazy, that Daisy would never leave him for a man of such low character. He goes on to expose Gatsby as a man who gained his wealth through illegal activities: bootlegging, gambling, and something so awful that Tom's private investigator was afraid to report it. An expression passes over Gatsby's face briefly, but Nick sees in it the possibility that Gatsby could be capable of murder.

> It passed, and he began to talk excitedly to Daisy, denying everything, defending his name against accusations that had not been made. But with every word she was drawing further and further into herself, so he gave that up and only the dead dream fought on as the afternoon slipped away, trying to touch what was no longer tangible, struggling unhappily, undespairingly, toward that lost voice across the room.

Tom may have scored his winning point by revealing the source of Gatsby's wealth. Gatsby was correct in his assumption that he could buy Daisy away from her husband, but he was tragically mistaken in thinking Daisy would not distinguish between his money and Tom's. The Buchanan fortune may have had origins equally as sordid as Gatsby's, but the Buchanans had the advantage of time, of being "old money" that lost its history after being handed down for generations.

Gatsby's insistence that she tell Tom that she never loved him is too much for her; the best she can give Gatsby is the pathetic declaration that she did love Tom once but she loved Gatsby too. This wounds Gatsby. He has never loved anyone but Daisy and he expects the same exclusivity from her. Tom is quick to act on his advantage, shouting that even that is a lie; that Daisy did not even know Gatsby was alive until recently. Gatsby's anger and panic are evident as he desperately tries to defend himself to Daisy against Tom's accusations. It is clear, however, that Daisy has neither the strength nor the desire to do anything but plead with her husband to put an end to this horror and allow her to go home. In an act that expresses his supreme confidence in his marriage and his utter contempt for Gatsby, Tom tells Daisy to go back home with Gatsby; he and the others will follow in Tom's blue coupe. Daisy is alarmed but Tom says to her, "Go on. He won't annoy you. I think he realizes that his presumptuous little flirtation is over." Gatsby and Daisy leave without speaking another word. "They were gone, without a word, snapped out, made accidental, isolated like ghosts even from our pity."

Tom breaks the silence they leave behind by asking Jordan and Nick if they want a drink.

Nick is too stunned by the scene he has just witnessed to answer. Tom asks again and Nick declines the offer, remarking that he just remembered that today is his thirtieth birthday; another indicator from Fitzgerald that time passes, youth fades, dreams die. As Tom drives toward home with Nick and Jordan they see what they assume to be a car wreck. A small crowd and a few cars are gathered in front of Wilson's. Tom had intended to drive on but something in the faces of the crowd makes him stop to have a look. He pushes his way through the door of the garage and finds Myrtle's body wrapped in a blanket. A policeman is questioning a witness, and Tom overhears that Myrtle had run out into the road and into the path of a speeding yellow car. She was killed instantly. The yellow car never even slowed down; indeed it is reported to have increased its speed after hitting Myrtle. Tom finds Wilson and impresses upon the distraught and nearly senseless man that although Tom was driving the yellow car that morning, he was not driving it that night. Tom and Jordan and Nick leave the tragic scene, Tom cursing Gatsby's cowardice.

Tom drives straight home, forgetting in his anger to drop Nick off in West Egg. He has his butler call for a taxi and Nick wanders down Tom's driveway to wait for it on the road. He is surprised to find Gatsby lurking in the dark shrubbery. Gatsby asks if Nick had seen any trouble along the road home. When Nick relates what he knows of the accident, Gatsby tries to explain what happened. He says that a woman who appeared to know them and want to talk to them suddenly ran into the road. There had been a car coming in the other direction and they were going to hit either the car or the woman. When he tells Nick that he tried to grab the wheel, Nick guesses the truth: Daisy was driving. It is interesting to speculate on whether Daisy knew she was killing her husband's mistress or was simply choosing the direction that would avoid a collision with an oncoming car, saving herself and Gatsby from harm. Fitzgerald is silent about this.

Although he is sorry about Myrtle's death, Gatsby is more concerned about Daisy and how Tom may mistreat her as a result of the events in the room at the Plaza. He tells Nick that he will stay where he is, watching Daisy's window for a signal that she needs rescuing or until it is obvious that she has safely gone to bed. Nick offers to take a look through the windows to see if there is indeed any commotion; all he sees is Daisy and Tom sitting at the kitchen table, an untouched meal between them. Nick sees Tom talking earnestly and intently and Daisy occasionally nodding her head; to Nick they look like a pair of conspirators. "They weren't happy, and neither of them had touched the chicken or the ale—and yet they weren't unhappy either. There was an unmistakable air of natural intimacy about the picture and anybody would have said that they were conspiring together." So much of the sheer tragedy of this novel hangs on that one word, "conspiring." Fitzgerald tells nothing of their conversation, leaving the possibilities to the reader's imagination: Does Daisy tell Tom that she was behind the wheel and is bullied into a murderous scheme that will eliminate the only other person who knows that? Or does she maintain her innocence knowing that Tom will find a way to avenge the death of his lover? Either way, Daisy, in order to avoid any personal unpleasantness and inconvenience, is shown to be willing to sacrifice the man who has dedicated his life to the idea of her perfection. Gatsby's fate is sealed at that kitchen table. Tom feels "entirely justified" in destroying the man who threatens his marriage. "They were careless people, Tom and Daisy—they smashed up things and creatures and then retreated back into their money or their vast carelessness or whatever it was that kept them together, and let other people clean up the mess they had made." Nick returns to Gatsby and tells him that all is quiet in the Buchanan mansion and advises him to go home and get some sleep. Gatsby chooses to stay. "So I walked away and left him standing there in the moonlight—watching over nothing."

Sometime just before dawn, Nick hears a taxi in Gatsby's driveway. He walks over and finds a dejected Gatsby leaning against a table in the hall. Nick is concerned that the police will eventually trace the car that killed Myrtle and advises Gatsby to get away for a while. Gatsby will not even consider it, not until he knows what Daisy intends to do. The two men sit and watch the gray dawn turn to gold, and, now that his carefully created persona has been shattered and exposed by Tom, Gatsby tells Nick the truth about his early years, Dan Cody, and his romancing of Daisy under false pretenses. He admits that he led her to believe that he was of the same social and economic status as she. When Gatsby returned from the war, he was, like so many other soldiers, ignored by an uncaring America that had no further use for him. He had received a letter from Daisy while he was at Oxford telling of her marriage to Tom, but he traveled to Louisville on the last of his army pay anyway in the vain hope that he would find the lost thread of their romance that would lead him back to her. A week later he gave up and boarded a train to New York.

After breakfast Nick and Gatsby stand on the porch and notice that there is an autumnal feel in the air. One of Gatsby's servants says that he plans to drain the swimming pool before the falling leaves clog the pipes. Gatsby tells him to wait; he has not used the pool all summer. For some reason, Nick is reluctant to leave Gatsby's side. He misses two trains into Manhattan before he finally decides to go. When he reaches the hedges at the beginning of Gatsby's property, he turns, "They're a rotten crowd," Nick calls out. "You're worth the whole damn bunch put together." Gatsby nods and gives Nick a radiant and understanding smile.

While the two men are thus engaged, a neighbor of Wilson's, Michaelis, is trying to comfort the bereaved garage owner. Michaelis knew that Wilson had suspicions regarding his wife and another man and had locked her in their room over the garage, where he had planned to keep her for a couple of days, until a car deal with Tom earned him the money to take her far away. He had taken Myrtle to the window and shown her the unblinking eyes of Dr. Eckleburg's billboard and told her that she might have been able to fool him but God saw everything and knew what she had been doing. She managed to get away from him and run out into the road; perhaps she recognized the yellow car and thought Tom was behind the wheel as he had been earlier in the day or perhaps she was hoping to flag down anyone who would get her away from her deranged husband. Wilson is certain the driver of the yellow car was both his wife's lover and her murderer, and he tells Michaelis that he knows how to find out who that person is. While his friend is distracted, Wilson pockets a revolver and walks down the road to East Egg.

After several attempts to reach Gatsby by telephone, Nick leaves a fruitless day at his office and hurries to Gatsby's home. The servants tell him that Gatsby had taken an air mattress to the swimming pool earlier in the afternoon. His chauffeur admits that he had heard gunshots but, being one of Wolfshiem's associates, he had not given the matter much thought. Nick, the chauffeur, the butler, and the gardener hurry to the pool, where they find Gatsby floating aimlessly. The bullet that killed him did not puncture the air mattress. As they carry his body to the house, they discover Wilson dead by his own hand. Fitzgerald maintains Gatsby's grace, elegance, and privacy even in his death. The unpleasant events occur "offstage," as it were, and there are no ear-shattering gunshots, no agonized cry, no gaping wounds.

> There was a faint, barely perceptible movement of the water as the fresh flow from one end urged its way toward the drain at the other. With little ripples that were hardly the shadows of waves, the laden mattress moved irregularly down the pool. A small gust of wind that scarcely corrugated the surface was enough to disturb its accidental course with its accidental burden. The touch of a cluster of leaves revolved it slowly, tracing, like the leg of a compass, a thin red circle in the water.

Nick finds himself Gatsby's spokesman and sole friend in the rush of publicity that follows. Haunted by the events of the summer, he decides to return home to the comforts of the Midwest. But first he arranges one final favor for his friend, a proper burial. He is dismayed that, even though the murder of Gatsby is headline news, no one visits the house or makes inquiries. Those friends and associates of Gatsby's that he can contact offer self-conscious excuses for not being able to attend. He attempts to reach the Buchanans but is told that Tom and Daisy hastily packed some bags the afternoon of the murder and left for an undisclosed destination for an undisclosed period of time. (Nick runs into Tom on a New York street some weeks after the murder and is told, as Nick already suspected, that Wilson had arrived at the Buchanan mansion armed and demanding to know who owned the yellow car that had struck and killed his wife. Tom, in fear for his life, told the man that it belonged to Gatsby and silently allowed him to act on his incorrect assumptions that Gatsby had been Myrtle's lover and that Gatsby had been driving the car that killed her.)

In the midst of Nick's disappointment and disgust, a bewildered, embarrassed, and grief-stricken old man arrives at the mansion three days after the murder; he is Henry C. Gatz, who had read of his son's death in the Chicago newspaper. He carries, with obvious pride, a picture of the mansion and a book his son had read as a youth, *Hopalong Cassidy.* Opening it to a flyleaf in the back of the tattered book, he shows Nick a handwritten schedule and list of resolves aimed toward self-improvement that his son had written at the age of sixteen, just one year before he left home.

On the morning of the funeral, Nick goes to New York to see Meyer Wolfshiem. Wolfshiem reminisces about meeting the young Gatsby, who had wandered into Winebrenner's poolroom on 43rd Street hungry, penniless, and looking for work. Wolfshiem, who was having lunch in the poolroom, invited him to join him at his table. Gatsby ate four dollars worth of food in half an hour, an incredible amount by the standards of 1919. Wolfshiem saw possibilities in the handsome, gentlemanly young soldier and groomed him to become his right-hand man. He tells Nick that he would like to come and pay his respects but cannot get mixed up in what has happened.

At five o'clock in the afternoon, a funeral procession consisting of three cars makes it way through the thick mist to the cemetery. In the end only a Lutheran minister, Mr. Gatz, a perpetual party guest Nick calls "Owl Eyes," the postman, and some of Gatsby's servants join Nick to bid farewell to a man who "paid a high price for living too long with a single dream." Dan Cody had shown the seventeen-year-old Gatsby the style of life that could be bought with vast amounts of money; Meyer Wolfshiem had taught the twenty-nine-year-old the quickest way to make it. What his mentors had failed to do was tell him that no amount of money can buy the past. But even if they had, the Great Gatsby would not have believed them.

FROM OBSCURITY TO GREAT AMERICAN NOVEL

When *The Great Gatsby* was published on April 10, 1925, critics were quick to announce that it was a failure. The *New York World* printed a headline on April 12, 1925, that read, "F. Scott Fitzgerald's Latest a Dud." A reviewer for that newspaper, Laurence Stallings, wrote ten days later that he found the novel to be unlike anything Fitzgerald had attempted in terms of character development and "in the design and integrity of the novel"; nonetheless, he stated that he did "not think for one moment in reading the book that 'here is a great novel' or even, that 'here is a fine book.'" On May 2, 1925, H. L. Mencken, writing for the *Baltimore Evening Sun,* considered the novel to be "in form no more than a glorified anecdote," although he did praise "the charm and beauty of the writing." In 1926 Conrad Aiken offered this judgment in the

October 1926 issue of the *New Criterion:* "If only he can refrain altogether in future from the sham romanticism and sham sophistication which the magazines demand of him, he may well become a first-rate novelist."

A few voices held a minority opinion. William Rose Benét wrote in the May 9, 1925, issue of the *Saturday Review of Literature,* "For the first time Fitzgerald surveys the Babylonian captivity of this era unblinded by the bright lights. He gives you the bright lights in full measure, the affluence, the waste, but also the nakedness of the scaffolding." And in the August 1925 issue of *The Dial,* the magazine's managing editor, Gilbert Seldes, wrote, "Fitzgerald has more than matured; he has mastered his talents and gone soaring in a beautiful flight, leaving behind him everything dubious and tricky in his earlier work, and leaving even farther behind all the men of his own generation and most of his elders." Despite such high praise, the reading public was not greatly attracted to the novel. After an initial printing of 20,870 copies, Scribners released a second printing four months later of only 3,000. At the time of Fitzgerald's death, fifteen years later, copies of the second printing still remained in the Scribner warehouse.

It was Fitzgerald's editor at Scribners, Max Perkins, who first attempted to breathe some life back into the author's reputation. He did this through a brilliant piece of literary marketing; he published Fitzgerald's unfinished novel, *The Last Tycoon,* together with a selection of short stories and *The Great Gatsby.* The influential critic Edmund Wilson edited the omnibus edition. Four years later, Perkins published Fitzgerald's collection of autobiographical essays, *The Crack-Up.* That same year, 1945, saw the publication of Viking Press's *The Portable F. Scott Fitzgerald,* which included *The Great Gatsby, Tender Is the Night* and nine short stories, edited by Dorothy Parker and introduced by John O'Hara. In 1949 the moviegoing public saw Hollywood's version of Fitzgerald's novel starring the film favorite Alan Ladd as Gatsby. Bantam, hoping to draw the moviegoers to the novel, published a paperback edition of *The Great Gatsby* with Ladd on the cover.

As public interest in the man who had shown such early promise, who had soared like a brilliant skyrocket only to disappear in the darkness, was growing, serious evaluations of Fitzgerald and his work began to appear, thanks in large part to Scottie Fitzgerald's donation of her father's papers to the Princeton University library in 1950. The first biography of Fitzgerald, *The Far Side of Paradise,* was written by Arthur Mizener and published by Houghton Mifflin in 1951. Since then Fitzgerald has been the subject of an enormous publishing industry with library and bookstore shelves boasting dozens of books about the man, his work, and his times.

The Great Gatsby reached perhaps the highest point of its popularity with the release in 1974 of the sumptuous motion picture version starring Robert Redford and Mia Farrow. Suddenly Gatsby became a cultural phenomenon and Gatsby theme parties were the rage. Commercial enterprises were quick to cash in by producing such things as Gatsby-styled clothing, music, and furniture—anything that captured the essence of the Roaring Twenties. But in all the glitz and glamour, something was ignored: Fitzgerald's indictment of the American Dream.

Fitzgerald made it clear that he intended *The Great Gatsby* to be the Great American Novel. He wrote to Perkins in August 1924, "I think my novel is about the best American novel ever written." And he struggled unsuccessfully with his editor to title the work *Under the Red, White and Blue.* In Gatsby we recognize the touch of larceny that to some degree is in all of us, a willingness to bend the laws of the land or God for our own convenience or gain or pleasure. But we also recognize in Gatsby the loss of our personal and national dreams. Everyone has a green light at the end of a dock, a longing for something that is just beyond reach in his or her life; some have several. Wanting more than we have or really need has long been a part of the American way of life. In a culture of runaway commercialism, dissatisfaction is encouraged and personal contentment is almost un-American. We have a unique and tenacious ability to forget history, to ignore what has failed, to make the same mistakes over and over. We dream big, but, entangled in illusions, we do not dream wisely. It is Gatsby's illusion about Daisy that brings about his downfall, but it is the same illusion that gives meaning to his life. As Fitzgerald wrote to his friend Ludlow Fowler in 1924, "Thats the whole burden of this novel—the loss of those illusions that give such color to the world so that you don't care whether things are true or false as long as they partake of the magical glory."

The Great Gatsby is in many ways the Great American Novel, and Gatsby is our American Everyman. Indeed, the novel is the archetype of the American idea of self-invention. Gatsby is a model for success because he appeals to our remarkable ability to reinvent ourselves and adjust our personal code of ethics in order to get what we think we somehow deserve. And if we fail to reach that blissful new world, we will simply imagine a bigger and better one, believing like Gatsby "in the green light, the orgastic future that year by year recedes before us. It eluded us then, but that's no matter—tomorrow we will run faster, stretch out our arms farther. . . . And one fine morning—."

It is tragic that Fitzgerald's "one fine morning" never dawned during his lifetime. Despite brief moments of fame, his life was a disappointment, burdened by alcohol, debt, and an unstable wife. His reputation as one of America's finest writers is firmly established today not only by popular sales but also by continuing academic interest. *The Great Gatsby* is found on numerous required reading lists for secondary schools, and Penguin publishers announced in 2003 that annual sales of the novel number close to half a million copies. It has become such a part of the American consciousness that it is hard to imagine that Fitzgerald could have penned these heart-breaking lines just a few months before his death: "I wish I was in print. It will be odd a year or so from now when Scottie assures her friends I was an author and finds that no book is procurable."

Select Bibliography

EDITION

The Great Gatsby. New York: Charles Scribner's Sons, 1925. (The novel is widely available is several editions. The 1995 Scribner paperback edition is cited in this essay.)

SECONDARY WORKS

Bloom, Harold. *F. Scott Fitzgerald's* The Great Gatsby. New York: Chelsea Publishing House, 1986. (Includes eight essays and Bloom's introduction in which he contends that *The Great Gatsby* is a part of the Romantic tradition of Keats and Shelley.)

———, ed. *Gatsby.* New York: Chelsea House Publishers, 1991. (Thirteen fascinating essays plus several critical extracts. Bloom's introduction explores Fitzgerald's use of Joseph Conrad's *Lord Jim* as a model for the narrative style in *The Great Gatsby.*)

Bruccoli, Matthew J. Introduction to *F. Scott Fitzgerald's Ledger: A Facsimile.* Washington, D.C.: NCR Microcard Books, 1973.

———. *Some Sort of Epic Grandeur: The Life of F. Scott Fitzgerald.* New York: Carroll and Graf, 1993.

———. *Fitzgerald and Hemingway: A Dangerous Friendship.* New York: Carroll and Graf, 1994.

———, ed. *The Great Gatsby.* The Cambridge Edition of the Works of F. Scott Fitzgerald. New York: Cambridge University Press, 1991. (In addition to the text of the novel, this volume includes exhaustive notes, two maps, a photograph of "The Valley of Ashes," and seven appendixes covering such topics as the evolution of the title and the selection of the cover art.)

Bryer, Jackson R., ed. *F. Scott Fitzgerald: The Critical Reception.* New York: Burt Franklin, 1978. (Contemporary reviews of Fitzgerald's works.)

Donaldson, Scott, ed. *Critical Essays on F. Scott Fitzgerald's* The Great Gatsby. Boston: Hall, 1984.

Kazin, Alfred, ed. *F. Scott Fitzgerald: The Man and His Work.* Cleveland: World, 1951.

Kuehl, John, and Jackson R. Bryer, eds. *Dear Scott / Dear Max: The Fitzgerald-Perkins Correspondence.* New York: Scribners, 1971.

Lehan, Richard. The Great Gatsby: *The Limits of Wonder.* New York: Twayne, 1990. (A thorough examination of the novel with chapters devoted to each of the principal characters.)

Lockridge, Ernest, ed. *Twentieth Century Interpretations of* The Great Gatsby. Englewood Cliffs, N.J.: Prentice-Hall, 1968.

Long, Richard Emmet. *The Achieving of* The Great Gatsby: *F. Scott Fitzgerald, 1920–1925.* Lewisburg, Pa.: Bucknell University Press, 1979. (A good overview of Fitzgerald's writing technique and the influence of Joseph Conrad on his early work.)

Mellow, James R. *Invented Lives: F. Scott and Zelda Fitzgerald.* Boston: Houghton Mifflin, 1984.

Milford, Nancy. *Zelda: A Biography.* New York: Harper and Row, 1970.

Mizener, Arthur. *The Far Side of Paradise.* Boston: Houghton Mifflin, 1951. Revised edition, 1965.

———, ed. *F. Scott Fitzgerald: A Collection of Critical Essays.* Englewood Hills, N.J.: Prentice-Hall, 1963.

Parker, Dorothy, ed. *The Portable F. Scott Fitzgerald.* Introduction by John O'Hara. New York: Viking, 1945, 1949.

Piper, Henry Dan, ed. *Fitzgerald's* The Great Gatsby: *The Novel, The Critics, The Background.* New York: Scribners, 1970.

Tate, Mary Jo. *F. Scott Fitzgerald A to Z: The Essential Reference to His Life and Work.* Foreword by Matthew J. Bruccoli. New York: Facts on File, 1998.

Turnbull, Andrew. *Scott Fitzgerald.* New York: Scribners, 1962.

———, ed. *The Letters of F. Scott Fitzgerald.* New York: Scribners, 1964.

Saul Bellow's Herzog

SANFORD PINSKER

IN MUCH THE same way that William Faulkner created the necessary conditions for serious literature about the modern South—and in the process, inspired generations of literary followers—Saul Bellow made serious literature about modern urban Jewish Americans possible. His fiction brought the immigrant Jewish sensibility, in all its restless striving and ethnic vividness, to national attention. With novel after impressive novel he slowly emerged as the only contemporary fictionist who could be mentioned in the same breath with Henry James and William Faulkner. *Herzog* (1964) is arguably Bellow's most poignant novel because it chronicles the struggle—and the triumph—of a man who confronts both the outer world and his inner self with humor, dignity, and wisdom. As the child of Russian Jewish immigrants, the protagonist Moses Herzog is formed by a culture that never entirely leaves him, even as he moves into the mainstream of secular American life. Thus, *Herzog* is a detailed, richly textured account of what it means to be a Jewish intellectual in the late twentieth century.

Solomon Bellows, later known as Saul Bellow, was born in Lachine, Quebec (a suburb of Montreal), on June 10, 1915. His parents, Liza Gordon and Abraham Bellows, had emigrated from St. Petersburg, Russia, just two years before. His father was a daring but largely unsuccessful businessman (Bellow remembers him as a "sharpie circa 1905"), but he cast a large, often oppressive shadow over Saul, the youngest of his four children, because he did not believe that anyone could make a living as a writer.

The Bellows family moved to Chicago when Saul was nine years old, and there the future writer spent much of his youth trying to prove his father wrong and to earn his blessing. The task was a daunting one, not only because he received little encouragement at home (his mother hoped he would become a Talmudic scholar) but also because white Anglo-Saxon Protestants controlled the avenues of high culture. Nonetheless, Bellow made his way through the public library stacks, not, as he puts it, "to read the Talmud, but the novels and poems of Sherwood Anderson, Theodore Dreiser, Edgar Lee Masters, and Vachel Lindsay" (cited in James Atlas's *Bellow: A Biography*). To this muscular, thoroughly realistic, and American prose, Bellow added the Yiddish, Hebrew, and French of his childhood.

As an undergraduate at Northwestern University, he majored in anthropology because he was told that anti-Semitism would thwart his literary ambitions. From the beginning, however, everything in his life that militated against Bellow's success as a writer was met by his stiff resistance. Later, when intellectuals made much of alienation, Bellow said kind words about accommodation; when Marxism was fashionable, Bellow quickly outgrew the fashion; and when New York intellectuals of the 1950s sought sexual freedom through Reichian psychology, Bellow's fascination with orgone boxes and other pieces of Reichian apparatus quickly faded. Decades later, Bellow would find himself embroiled in controversy because he was less than enthusiastic about the large claims made on behalf of multiculturalism. Bellow has always been his own man, even if this meant earning the disapproval of critics who mounted a number of angry charges against him: elitism, misogynism, racism. As a serious artist, he regarded elitism as a badge of honor rather than one of shame; as for the other accusations, his best defense has always been a careful reading of his fiction.

"As the external social fact grows larger, more powerful and tyrannical," Bellow wrote in a 1951 application to the Rockefeller Foundation, "man appears in the novel reduced in will, strength, freedom and scope." Bellow proposed to write a novel brave enough to talk directly about the human spirit, and to do this he developed a style that merged the vocabulary of high culture with urban slang. The foundation turned down his request for badly needed funding, but he continued to explore ways in which fiction might speak for man at a time when most writers were too embarrassed to talk about the soul, much less about God.

Bellow has been showered with every important literary prize —three National Book Awards, the Pulitzer Prize, and, in 1976, a Nobel Prize in Literature—but he has not generated the wide public adulation associated with the careers of American modernists such as

CHRONOLOGY

1915	Bellow born on June 10 in Lachine, Quebec, Canada.
1924	Moves with his family to Chicago.
1931–1933	Attends Tully High School.
1933	Enters the University of Chicago.
1934	Transfers to Northwestern University.
1937	Receives bachelor's degree from Northwestern with honors in sociology and anthropology.
1938–1942	Teaches at the Pestalozzi-Froebel Teachers College in Chicago. Employed by Works Progress Administraton Writers' Project.
1941	Publishes first story, "Two Morning Monologues," in *Partisan Review.*
1942	Moves to New York. Publishes "The Mexican General," also in *Partisan Review.*
1943	Works in the editorial department of the *Encyclopaedia Britannica* on the Great Books of the Western World project.
1944	Publishes first novel, *Dangling Man.* Serves briefly in the merchant marine at the end of World War II.
1947	*The Victim.*
1948	Awarded a Guggenheim Fellowship. Travels in Europe for the next two years.
1953	Publishes *The Adventures of Augie March,* which wins the National Book Award for fiction (1954).
1953–1954	Teaches at Bard College. Lives at Tivoli in Duchess County.
1956	*Seize the Day.*
1959	*Henderson, the Rain King.*
1960–1962	Coedits the literary magazine *The Noble Savage* with Keith Botsford. In 1962 becomes a member (and later chairman) of the Committee on Social Thought at the University of Chicago.
1964	Publishes *Herzog,* which wins his second National Book Award (1965).
1968	*Mosby's Memoirs and Other Stories.* Awarded the Croix de Chevalier des

	Arts et Lettres by the French government.
1970	Publishes *Mr. Sammler's Planet,* which wins his third National Book award (1971).
1975	Publishes *Humboldt's Gift,* which wins the Pulitzer Prize (1976).
1976	Wins Nobel Prize for literature. Publishes *To Jerusalem and Back.*
1982	*The Dean's December.*
1984	*Him with His Foot in His Mouth and Other Stories.* Wins Malaparte Award.
1987	*More Die of Heartbreak.*
1989	*A Theft* and *The Bellarosa Connection.*
1992	*Something to Remember Me By.*
1994	*All Adds Up: From the Dim Past to the Uncertain Future.*
1997	*The Actual.*
2000	*Ravelstein.*

William Faulkner, F. Scott Fitzgerald, and, most especially, Ernest Hemingway. Of his books only *Herzog* spent a stretch of time on the best-seller list (*Ravelstein,* published in 2000, made a brief appearance), but Bellow's works have generated considerable attention from reviewers, critics, and scholars. Literally hundreds of articles, dozens of book-length studies, and a healthy number of Ph.D. dissertations explore his novels and dissect his themes. The Bellows industry gives no sign of slowing down, even if Saul Bellow himself is not the household word that Ernest Hemingway once was (and in many ways, still is).

FICTION BEFORE HERZOG

Bellow began his career in the mid-1940s, at a time when Ernest Hemingway dominated the literary landscape and his sparse style was being imitated by many aspiring young authors. A man was defined, Hemingway argued, by the manner in which he faced his death—for instance, on a battlefield or in the bullring. At such existential moments in a Hemingwayesque world, action spoke louder than words, and a character's inner life was often sacrificed to more pressing external facts. In complete contrast to the Hemingway model, *Dangling Man* (1944) was Bellow's strenuously inward-looking account of a man waiting to be drafted who finds himself uneasily "dangling" between a civilian life that no longer matters and a military call-up that keeps being postponed. The novel announced a new direction in American literature, not only because it was a study in alienation, isolation, and claustrophobia or because it was a "proof" book—one that showed Bellow's intimate acquaintance with the masterpieces of world literature—but also because *Dangling Man* criticized the Hemingway aesthetic of manly stoicism: "Most serious matters are closed to the hard-boiled. They are unpracticed in introspection, and therefore badly equipped to deal with opponents whom they cannot shoot like big game or outdo in daring." By contrast, Bellow's testy protagonist, who writes up his thoughts in the form of a journal, is—like many of Bellow's protagonists to follow—a character study in introspection. The poet and critic Delmore Schwartz in the *Partisan Review* (May/June 1944) praised the novel for its catalog of "the typical objects of a generation's sensibility," whereas Bellow's biographer, James Atlas, felt that *Dangling Man* was about "the struggle to sustain a sense of identity and worth amid the patriotic clamor of wartime."

Saul Bellow began his career as a writer at virtually the same time that the cultural critic Philip Rahv was complaining in the *Kenyon Review* (in 1939) about the state of literary life in America—which, Rahv said, "has seldom been so deficient in intellectual power." Rahv got the intellectual he had wished for when Saul Bellow began publishing in the pages of *Partisan Review,* the "little magazine" Rahv had cofounded with William Phillips in the late 1930s. Fiercely independent of mind since its first issue, *Partisan Review* joined an anti-Stalinist leftism with a commitment to literary modernism. Early on, Bellow's unapologetic intellectualism seemed to satisfy both parts of the *Partisan Review* formula, but in subsequent years Bellow's ideological quarrels with the magazine made it clear that he was not really part of the *Partisan Review* crowd—or for that matter, of any crowd.

In *Dangling Man* Joseph, the novel's moody protagonist, casts his eye over the buildings outside his window and wonders about what, in all this dreary urban landscape, "speaks for man." For Bellow, this remains an abiding question—along with those questions generated by the ongoing project of constructing a sturdy soul. In some novels, such as *The Victim* (1947) or *Seize the Day* (1956), Bellow broods about an interior life in great disarray; with other novels (e.g., *The Adventures of Augie March,* 1953, or *Henderson, the Rain King*, 1959), comic energy tends to dominate the landscape. Bellow's justly admired "style" is a function of his content. When dreamy protagonists ruminate about why they are out of step with life's messier complications (as is often the case in *Herzog*), form and function merge into a seamless whole. Herzog's richly textured rationalizations make a kind of sense but so do the counter-arguments of his former wives and assorted enemies. No-nonsense realists and assorted sharpies, immigrants on the make, and women who, as Herzog puts it, "eat green salad and drink human blood" provide the tension that makes the eventual victories of his protagonists (however small or ambivalent they might be) at once credible and impressive. No contemporary American writer managed to pack as many "ideas" or as much urban "stuff" into a single paragraph. The measure of such a novelist, of course, is how good were his ideas (as it turned out, very good indeed) and how vivid were his details (again, very vivid indeed).

A NOVEL OF IDEAS, WITH A COMIC TWIST

Herzog is the novel toward which Bellow had been pointing from the beginning—and in his protagonist's effort to free himself from the grip of mental collapse, one sees the larger crisis of contemporary culture: a pervasive sense of spiritual emptiness. By the early 1960s the "wasteland" that the poet T. S. Eliot had explored in his 1922 epic poem had become a widespread sociological condition. Herzog rails against everything that diminishes the human spirit, but contemporary life often seems much larger—and certainly more brutal—than the individual person.

Herzog is the story of a man who is plunged into despair when his wife suddenly leaves him and he discovers that she has been sleeping with his best friend for years. Herzog suffers the cruel fate of the cuckold: the derision of those who knew that he was being sexually deceived and, moreover, who concluded that Herzog is to blame for the sexual misfortune. As if this were not trouble enough, Herzog is also a historian of ideas who has been suffering through a protracted writing block. Indeed, as he takes stock of his tattered life during five frantic days of introspection, what he sees, often in extended flashbacks, is a life badly lived.

At the same time, however, Herzog is able to balance a hard, uncompromising look at himself with an equally tough sense of how others have betrayed him. Through the sustaining effort to lay his life bare, Herzog's flashes of wit and unflagging good humor make him one of the most attractive "losers" in contemporary literature. Herzog may be a dreamy egghead, a man who fiddles with ideas while his version of Rome burns, but he is also resilient enough to survive every obstacle, including himself. The madness that threatens to destroy him lifts off in the novel's final pages, partly from Herzog's physical exhaustion and partly because he (finally) comes to the point where there was nothing left for him to say. To accept what he can do, and also what he cannot, and even more important, to know that there are some things one can only pray toward, makes it clear that Herzog has not suffered in vain: he has managed to turn suffering into insight and to know—at long last—who he is.

Contemporary novels are replete with antiheroes, and although Herzog is hardly meant to be a flawless character, the positive aspects of his soul far outweigh the negative ones. He is, in short, a "mentsch," the Yiddish term for a human being. "If I am out of my mind," Herzog muses in the novel's opening sentence, "it's all right with me." But having thought this, it must occur to Herzog, as well as to readers, that his madness is decidedly *not* all right. For an intellectual, a mind is what most matters, and even though pain has taught Herzog that books cannot teach him about how to *live,* he is not willing to completely abandon the high-flown ideas that define him as an intellectual. Moses Herzog is also a master of irony, which is sometimes directed at others, but just as often is painfully directed at himself.

In *Herzog,* as in other Bellow novels, humor is a key ingredient because wit is how oppressed peoples have traditionally countered the fists and guns of a majority culture. Moreover, humor is, in Bellow's words, "more manly" than complaint because it relies on resources inside the person rather than on efforts to extract sympathy from outsiders. At a time when Jews were not especially welcome in mainstream American society and when Bellow was told that no college teaching jobs would be open to him, humor was simultaneously a shield and a weapon against a world that regarded his "kind" as inferior. Thus, Bellow explores the human comedy, as did Shakespeare, Dante, and James Joyce before him, but he does so with a distinctively Yiddish flavoring. An intellectual cut in the Herzog mold moves easily—sometimes *too* easily—from flinty seriousness to flat-out playfulness.

Herzog is, among other things, the story of what happens when a man suddenly realizes that the roles of scholar and citizen, husband and father, no longer define him as they once did. The Naragansett Foundation, a think tank, has been paying Herzog's bills as it waits for the great scholarly book he can neither organize nor finish. His scholarship, once so brilliant, is now a heap of incoherent pages. His current marriage to Madeleine is also in shambles and moving inexorably toward divorce. Indeed, Herzog's life increasingly resembles the eyesore of a house in the Berkshires that was bought with Papa Herzog's money and that now stands as a symbol of his ruin. Some wonder, then, that "Late in spring Herzog had been overcome by the need to explain, to have it out, to justify, to put in perspective, to clarify, to make amends." Bellow's exhausted protagonist ends the novel five days after he began it—seeking renewal in the natural environs of the Berkshires even though the decaying house situated there is a constant reminder of his grief. Lying on a hammock, Herzog shuffles through moments from his past as if they were playing cards, and in these flashbacks he eventually comes to terms with what it means to be an intellectual, a husband, a father, and a citizen.

When some reviewers wondered if *Herzog* was so densely packed with ideas that only readers with a Ph.D.—or perhaps several of them—need apply, Bellow quickly reminded them that he meant his novel to be "funny," that it was designed to show how little a conventional education, however rigorous, has to say about the spiritual and moral complications of adulthood. On one level, *Herzog* is surely meant to satirize pedantry and to take a few satiric jabs at parlor intellectuals, but it is also clear that Bellow often uses Herzog, a more genuine, more committed intellectual, as a mouthpiece for his own disgust with what he regards as trendy intellectualism.

Throughout the novel, Herzog insists that the "Herzog heart" is a better test of what is true. Herz, the German word for heart, is embedded in his name, and Herzog uses the phrase as a way of remembering the vivid, deeply passionate days of his Canadian childhood. What the various people he met on Napolean Street showed him—in their laughter and tears, their grit and unswerving love—later found a prominent place in the adult "Herzog heart." If Herzog often sees himself in a less than heroic mold, this does not mean that he has abandoned the effort to bring about a world more attractive and more just. At one point he puts it this way: "*Lord, I ran to fight in Thy holy cause, but kept tripping, never reached the scene of the struggle.*" He is a comic failure, but some of the novel's most important moments occur when he acknowledges just how pathetic, how laughable, he can sometimes be. If it is true that Herzog often wears his heart on his sleeve, it is even truer that he *has* a heart while most of those who surround (and torment) him decidedly do not. A conventional education, though valuable, cannot teach one how to understand the heart, much less minister to it. Herzog would have no trouble engaging in a discussion about the Socratic question "How should a good person live?" but many of his intellectual colleagues might think of the activity as dreamy foolishness. The world, they would insist, operates on the principles of brutal reality, and that, in a nutshell, is why they regard poor Herzog as lovable but very naive.

HERZOG, LEOPOLD BLOOM'S AMERICAN COUSIN

The sheer range of material high and low, serious and playful, that makes its way through Herzog's stream of consciousness reminded many Bellow critics of Leopold Bloom in James Joyce's *Ulysses.* Here is a representative sample of Bloom's hyperactive interior life as he sets out for yet another day in dear dirty Dublin:

> The sun was nearing the steeple of George's church. Be a warm day I fancy, Specifically in these black clothes feel it more. Black conducts, reflects, (refracts is it?) the heat. But I couldn't do in that light suit. Make a picnic of it. His eyelids sank quietly often as he walked in happy warmth, Boland's breadvan delivering with trays our daily but she [his wife, Molly] prefers yesterday's loaves turnovers crisp crowns hot.

Bloom's inner thoughts are filled with misinformation, along with bits and pieces of advertising jingles (Bloom himself is a seller of ads) and popular songs. He remembers learning about how fast a falling body travels from a high school physics course (Bloom, unlike Herzog, did not attend college, much less graduate school). Indeed, so much popular culture swirls through Bloom's overly active brain that it is often difficult to keep his half-understandings straight. The result makes Bloom one of the funniest characters in modern literature.

In certain respects, Herzog is Bloom's literary cousin, at least in the sense that Herzog's mental letters are often meant to be humorous comment rather than dead serious argument. Herzog invites readers to share in what passes through a trained mind, greatly troubled. Traveling on a high-speed train the novel's protagonist remembers a train ride forty years earlier, and he muses about the existential differences.

> Now the train was ribbed for speed, a segmented tube of brilliant steel. There were no pears, no Willie, no Shura, no Helen, no Mother. Leaving the cab, he thought how his mother would moisten her handkerchief at her mouth and rub his face clean. He had no business to recall this, he knew, and turned toward Grand Central in his straw hat. He was of the mature generation now, and life was his to do something with, if he could. But he had not forgotten the odor of his mother's saliva on the handkerchief that summer evening in the squat hollow Canadian station, the black iron and the sublime brass. All children have cheeks and all mothers spittle to wipe them tenderly. These things either matter or they do not matter. It depends upon the universe, what it is.

What the two novels share is a richness of texture as each sets out to capture the conditions that, taken together, add up to "culture." Bloom is at once the most ordinary of men (he is thoroughly lower middle class) and modern literature's most multidimensional character. We know more about him than almost anybody else fixed on the printed page—his peccadilloes and passions, his antiheroic folly and the ways in which he is a legitimate avatar of Odysseus. Bloom is, in short, the history of modernity rolled up into a single person.

With some important caveats, the same might be said of Herzog. He, too, contains "multitudes" (as Walt Whitman cheerfully declared about his own persona), and he (Herzog), too, partakes in nearly equal measures of the noble and the base. The two characters differ, however, when it comes to education. In *Ulysses* Joyce uses the young-and-heady Stephen Dedalus when he wants to introduce knotty discussions of literature in general and aesthetic theory in particular. At his more rarified moments Stephen is a talking head, a brain disconnected from its body. By contrast, Bloom is earthy. He never lets readers forgets that he is a body, and that the body eats and later defecates. He is also a heart, one that spends Bloomsday worrying about his wife's afternoon meeting with a man out to seduce her and to cuckold him.

During the years that Bellow taught seminars as part of the University of Chicago's prestigious Committee on Social Thought, he often chose *Ulysses* as one of the central texts. Among the literally hundreds of minor characters in Joyce's novel is one Moses Herzog. He and Bloom are, presumably, the only Jews in turn-of-the-century Dublin. Bellows denies that he plucked his character's name from Joyce's pages, but the novel named after Moses Herzog certainly carries over, as well as alters, the central spirit of the century's most epic novel.

Bloom's head most resembles a sponge, and through it runs all manner of material: snatches of song, snippets of slogans, speculations large and small. Bloom wonders about the precise meaning of "parallax" and whether the word he is fishing for is "reflects" or "refracts." He thinks, incorrectly, that nuns invented barbed wire and that the initials INRI on a crucifix (Latin for "Jesus Christ, King of the Jews") means "Iron Nails Ran In." His misinformation makes him lovably human and increases our sense that pain often wears a tragicomic face.

Moses Herzog is in many ways Bloom's opposite: he is a man who cannot *not* know the facts of history, and more important, what those "facts" imply about culture, then and now. Bloom looks at Catholic Ireland as an outsider, one consigned to the margins. What he observes may indeed be riddled with errors, but his sociological comments about everything from burial customs to engrained anti-Semitism ring true. Herzog, the child of immigrants, is similarly consigned to playing the role of outsider—this despite the fact that Herzog represents a generation that had elbowed itself into academia's higher orbits. Herzog is no Bloom, however; when it comes to reviewing weighty books, even if his comments come as mental letters, he knows precisely where arguments miss the mark, just as he knows (painfully) how his own work has shriveled away to nothing.

THE MULTI-FACETED MOSES HERZOG

Herzog's project as a scholar is to connect the life lessons he learned as a child growing up in a cramped, poverty-ridden immigrant neighborhood with the intellectual scaffolding he acquired at America's best universities. "*Ours is a bourgeois civilization,*" Herzog writes in a "mental letter" to a fellow professor,

> *I am not using this term in its Marxian sense.* Chicken! *In the vocabularies of modern art and religion it is bourgeois to consider that the universe was made for our safe use and to give us comfort, ease, and support. Light travels at a quarter of a million miles per second so that we can see to comb our hair or to read in the paper that ham hocks are cheaper than yesterday.*

Herzog's ability to link the rarified idea (e.g., the speed of light) with its mundane application (e.g., combing our hair; perusing the newspaper) perfectly captures his extraordinary eggheadedness. His heritage (no other word will quite do) as the child of Russian Jewish immigrants gives a peculiarly Yiddish twist to his assessments of the world. He is skeptical (as a language Yiddish seemed wonderfully equipped to pull down vanity) at the same time that he is fully committed to helping to repair the world. Most of all, he has comic qualities that can be slapstick (his students cannot fail to notice that he has absentmindedly tucked the bottom of his sports coat into his trousers when returning from the bathroom) and a sense of humor that can be subtle: "Lead me not into Penn Station," he ruefully prays to the Lord as the world threatens to overwhelm him.

Herzog's troubles, though uniquely his own, seem to represent the uncertainties of the modern world—and in his struggle to exorcize his inner demons, to make a full accounting of the inner self, Herzog spares himself nothing. His self-examination leads him to conclude that

> he had been a bad husband—twice. Daisy, his first wife, he had treated miserably. Madeleine, his second, had tried to do *him* in. To his son and his daughter he was a loving but bad father. To his parents he had been an ungrateful child. To his country, an indifferent citizen. To his brothers and his sister, affectionate but remote. With his friends, an egotist. With love, lazy. With brightness, dull. With power, passive, With his own soul, evasive.

As a novel, *Herzog,* goes on to unpack each of these self-accusations, giving them a local habitation and specific set of references. For example, the scenes involving Daisy and the residue of a first marriage that could not survive his selfishness are simultaneously poignant and painful. People grow apart, as did Daisy and Herzog, but few husbands remember how a marriage went sour with such an unsparing honesty:

> I had that room in Philadephia—that one-year job—and I was commuting to New York three or four times a week on the Pennsylvania train, to visit Marco [his son]. Daisy swore there would be no divorce. . . . Papa got wind of my dissolute life, and was angry. Daisy wrote him all about it, but it was none of Papa's business. What actually happened? I gave up the shelter of an orderly, purposeful, lawful existence because it bored me.

Herzog is attracted to women who, unlike Daisy, are dangerous and ultimately destructive. Romantic literature is filled with examples of *la belle dame sans merci,* the woman without pity, and, indeed, that is one of the roles that Madeleine, Daisy's replacement, will play. In his personal life, Herzog equates the orderly with the boring and the chaotic with the exciting. This too can be seen as a small "r" romantic notion, quite different from the capital "R" Romanticism that Herzog investigated so thoroughly in his first book, *Romanticism and Christianity.* There, the account of the ways in which religion and Romanticism were historically entangled cleared the way for revisionist thinking about how ideas worked their way through history.

Herzog is considerably less impressive when one turns the spotlight on his personal life. He is drawn to sexual destruction in much the same ways that moths seek out hot, killing lights. Herzog is a womanizer whose many mistresses were more than willing to minister to his emotional and sexual needs. Herzog writes to them in ways that differ from the usual missives he sends to fellow intellectuals. Here, there is no insider gossip about this or that intellectual celebrity, no Big Questions for big minds, or carping, review-like comments, but, rather, memories of tender moments. One would think that Herzog would acknowledge his own dalliances as he rages at Madeleine for her affair, but he does not. A double standard, not uncommon in the early 1960s, is firmly in place.

Thus, each woman in his life represents a part of Herzog's multifaceted personality. His mistress Ramona, who owns a flower shop where she is surrounded by the delicious odors and textures of hothouse plants, represents the considerable pull of sensuality. As Ramona serves Herzog a meal that is riddled with seduction, Herzog's senses reel because intellectual though he may be, "a woman's breasts mattered greatly," and Ramona is amply endowed in this department. Still, she is no Madeleine, and that is a sticky point because, for Herzog, a woman must not only be beautiful but also smart and, perhaps most of all, a challenge.

Madeleine, his second wife, has dimensions that his first wife, the placid *hausfrau* Daisy, does not, but Madeleine has turned out to be more of an adventure than Herzog had bargained for. At times she is competitive, filling their marital bed with all manner of dusty, erudite tomes meant to swell her graduate school research; at other moments she sets out to replace the bohemianism of her parents with the ritual and rigid certainties of the Catholic church. She surrounds herself with obscure scholarly works and is perfectly at ease shooting the breeze with Herzog's academic pals, but there is something both forced and ultimately fake about her enthusiasms. In short, she dabbles with ideas and intellectual passions without making a firm commitment to any of them. A wounded Herzog sees these passions—and a good many others—as evidence of Madeleine's duplicity. She puts on (and takes off) roles with apparent ease, including those of wife, mother, and soul mate. And ultimately she has left him for their mutual friend, the culture maven and intellectual wannabe Valentine Gersbach. "We can't live together any more," Madeleine's well-rehearsed speech begins, and a thoroughly shocked, absolutely unbelieving Herzog has no choice but to hear his beautiful wife through:

> Her speech continued for several minutes. Her sentences were well formed. This speech had been rehearsed and it seemed also that he had been waiting for the performance to begin. . . . "It's painful to have to say I never loved you. I never will love you either," she said. "So there's no point in going on."

Herzog is also a novel about a protagonist's relentless effort to drive to the very bottom of sexual grief as it manifests itself in divorce. Most outsiders to such sad business know enough to know that blame is probably equally divided, but assessing blame is quite a different matter when one is surfing through a participant's stream of consciousness. Herzog can, for example, call up the eighteenth-century maxim that equates grief with idleness, but this bit of lore, like countless others in his throbbing head, brings him little comfort:

> He went on taking stock, lying face down on the sofa. Was he a clever man or an idiot? Well, he could not at this time claim to be clever. He might once have had the makings of a clever character, but he had chosen to be dreamy instead, and the sharpies cleaned him out.

Any number of subsequent Bellow protagonists could, of course, make the same confession: idleness is often a component of grief. Herzog knows this just as surely as he knows his eighteenth-century poetry. But this does not help him to decide if that makes him clever or simply an even bigger idiot. Herzog may "know" that he is being taken in by con men but something inside him cannot quite resist. In some ways he, like other Bellow characters before and after him, is oddly attracted to the hard-edged world in which success is determined by whoever walks away with the most hard cash. The central burden of a Bellow novel is to show how a man broken by the world—and, yes, his own flaws—can move painfully, but inexorably toward something akin to health.

At the top of his game, Herzog is both funny and wise, and one feels that he will somehow "make it." At the bottom of his game, however, Herzog is an unshaven, gaunt, and slightly shaking mess. His agitation sometimes manifests in manic acts of atonement, as when, for example—against all that common sense would dictate—he wants to paint an old piano green (hardly an accidental choice given the pastoral themes in the novel) and ship it to his daughter. Herzog's brother looks on in horror and tries, as best he can, to convince this broken man that he badly needs professional help—all the while trying hard to preserve Herzog's fragile dignity.

For many New York intellectuals, Herzog seemed to be a study of the there-but-for-the-grace-of-God sort. They followed his heartbreak with mixtures of pity and fear—sorry that this large, generous heart has not got a prayer amid the world's hustle and sharp elbowing, and afraid that his story is but a slight exaggeration of their own. Such readers knew that everything Herzog was trained to believe in no longer exists quite as it did, and they feared that "things" would only get worse, far worse, in the decades that followed—and indeed, one might say, things did. Among those inclined to keep tabs on an author's cultural politics, many felt that Bellow first flew his neoconservative colors with *Herzog.* The assessment may or may not be true, but it is clear enough that Bellow's protagonist means to lead those around him (and thereby readers) out of the shoddy cultural wasteland he sees swirling all around him.

In the world Herzog describes shoddiness is often a matter of the way that certain intellectuals, usually tenured academics, appropriate language that used to shiver with authenticity—"the void" is one example he cites—and then allow it to fall too easily off their tongues. Mermelstein, one of Herzog's contemporaries, is an example of this phenomenon. Not surprisingly, Herzog is jealous (that is the only word that will do) about the success that Mermelstein has garnered for his book while he (Herzog) continues to be mired in hundreds of unrevised manuscript pages. Even more upsetting, Mermelstein has written a book very similar to the history of modern ideas that Herzog has in mind. Herzog, being Herzog, insists that his book, when it finally gets finished, will be much better than Mermelstein's, but not even Herzog is entirely convinced by the rationalization. Mermelstein represents the loss of authentic culture in the early 1960s. (Only a few years later, *Mr. Sammler's Planet* will explore how the countercultural late 1960s made matters even worse, and by the turn of the century, Bellow had made no secret of the fact that he stands four-square against political correctness, hence, the suspicion, fair or not, that Bellow moved full circle from his early days as a radical and sometime Marxist to a neoconservative traveler.) What Herzog cannot understand is how Mermelstein, a man who should know better, can settle for such glib, reductive formulations:

> *You see how gruesomely human beings are destroyed by pain, when they have the added torment of losing their humanity first, so that their death is a total defeat, and then you write about "modern forms of Orphism" and about "people who not afraid of suffering" and throw in other such cocktail-party expressions. Why not say rather that people of powerful imagination, given to dreaming deeply and to raising up marvelous and self-sufficient fictions, turn to suffering sometimes to cut into their bliss, as people pinch themselves to feel awake. I know that my suffering, if I may speak of it, has often been like that, a more extended form of life, a striving for true wakefulness and an antidote to illusion. . . .*

It is hardly an accident that Bellow's protagonist is named Moses, and that his vision of a life purposefully lived echoes the biblical Exodus. He means to lead not only the brilliantly mistaken Mermelstein out of his errors about the possibilities of modern life but also all the other New York intellectuals who babble half-knowingly about American culture while ordinary citizens are literally dying (this is no metaphor, Herzog insists) for the lack of something *real* to believe in at the end of the day. At bottom, Herzog's vision is religious, although not traditionally so. He remembers the various religious figures who pop up in memory (not only assorted rabbis but also priests, ministers, and nuns), but what marks him more distinctly is the compassion he feels for those, human and animal, who make his sufferings—real and painful as they are—seem relatively meaningless by comparison. In a New York courtroom, the brutal details in a child murder case drives Herzog to tears; the scene in which he tries to "rescue" his daughter Junie from his nemesis and wife's lover, Valentine Gersbach, is simultaneously comic and heartbreaking. With a gun in his hand (Papa's revolver, brought from Russia and unloaded), Herzog is only a source of our pity and fear as he watches Gersbach gently give Junie her evening bath.

Herzog's suffering has served to burn away the fat from his soul. He sees with a clarity that is not easily transported to paper, but his extended mental letters provide the essentials of his argument-in-progress. Paradoxically, the "argument" comes, as it must, to the conclusion that silence is more trustworthy, and truer, than more high-flown rhetoric. Herzog has moved to the stage of acceptance, and that is where he decides not to tell Mrs. Tuttle, housekeeper of his decaying Ludeyville estate, that she should dampen her broom lest she kick up clouds of dust. If the result of silence is particles swarming through the air, so be it. There are times when it is best to let go, to divest the world of Herzog's advice.

Earlier in the novel, and at his best moments, there are enough solid ideas to feel that Herzog still "has it" and that his mind is not completely bent on justification and revenge—although these goals have their parts to play as Herzog spins out a conspiracy theory in which psychoanalysts, lawyers, and priests join Madeleine in deceiving him or as he imagines the violent turns that justice might take. But these machinations, vividly memorable though they are, do not reflect Herzog at his deepest or his best. The novel is filled with flashes of Herzog that make it clear he is not simply a portrait in madness, and in the novel's final pages, he begins the process of acceptance—of himself as well as others—that suggests a healthier Herzog in the near future.

For the bulk of the novel, however, Herzog strikes readers as a man easily duped because he is absentminded about everything except the knotty intellectual material he is trying to tame—and this absentmindedness, alas, includes his beautiful wife. And he is a tender man, even with a pistol inside his shaking palm. Herzog cannot pull the trigger because this would deny everything he fundamentally is. Herzog may no longer be a contender for the intellectual throne, but he will become something infinitely richer: a person content to leave metaphors (including those explaining himself) to others, and a final understanding to God. Whatever it is that Herzog most wants—for the "mental letters" to stop, for peace to form a protective pocket in his heart, for grace to descend—he can only "*pray toward it.*"

MOSES HERZOG'S EPISTOLARY EXERCISES

Herzog's imaginary epistles—the "mental letters" he resorts to writing as his mental state becomes ever more aggravated—comprise an increasingly large share of the novel. In this sense, *Herzog* harkens back to the beginnings of the novel in the eighteenth century and the exchanges of letters that was its staple ingredient. Herzog's letters are not nearly so polished nor do they exhibit the elevated diction and decorum of that earlier era. Rather, Herzog often shoots from the hip, responding to current events as they swirl around him in much the same way that irate newspaper readers do when they fire off an angry letter to the editor. "*Dear Mr. President,*" he writes to Dwight Eisenhower, "*Internal Revenue regulations will turn us into a nation of bookkeepers. The life of every citizen is becoming a business. This, it seems to me, is one of the worst interpretations of the meaning of human life history has ever seen.*" Sometimes Herzog's letters are clearly meant to be playful, as is the case when he writes to Herr Docktor Heidegger and wonders where he was standing when he talks about our collective "fall into the quotidian," but there are also times when Herzog rages in all seriousness against those who are glib popularizers of the idea that there is no hope for humankind: "*We must get it out of our heads,*" Herzog imagines writing to Mermelstein, whose book he both admires and hates, "*that this is a doomed time, that we are waiting for the end, and the rest of it, mere junk from fashionable magazines. Things are grim enough without these shivery games.*" The book's mental letters give snippets of Herzog's mind at its most salient, its most impressive, as well as at its most self-serving and mean-spirited.

In short, the mental letters give a glimpse into Herzog's complicated heart. To his dead mother he writes, "*Dear Mama, As to why I haven't visited our grave in so long . . . ,*" with a matter-of-fact tone that does not disguise how deeply sorrowful he in fact is. Because "mental letters" do not require postage stamps or a trip to the mailbox, they can easily flit in and out of Herzog's unconscious. Moreover, Herzog's mental letters span the globe. Some are written to fellow scholars Herzog knows from international conferences, and some are written to the women he slept with as he traveled. Either way, Herzog's inner thoughts turn to them as mechanisms to cope with the fact that his friend Valentine Gersbach has cuckolded him and his wife has left him.

In an age that pays not merely lip service but produces hard cash to reward the special importance of intellect, Bellow's brilliant protagonists grow to expect the gingerly treatment due an endangered species. Herzog's first book, *Romanticism and Christianity,* appeared on many required reading lists, and his growing reputation as a scholar with first-rate potential allowed him to pick and choose among a wide variety of enviable academic posts. As a scholar, Herzog is nicely positioned. But he has hit something of a brick wall in his private life and one of the consequences of his breakup with Madeleine is that he is forced to confront certain truths about himself and the people he once regarded as friends. He has become a crank, not only about the scholarly work he cannot bring into focus but also about the wife he did not regard seriously until she walked out the door. Only Herzog—or so Herzog imagines—can have grand thoughts, but Madeleine also has a mind and yearns to use it. So when things fall apart in the Herzog household, both a marriage and Herzog's scholarly career are destroyed. There are times when Herzog realizes what he has become, but he struggles with it. As each new thought grips his heart, he races to write it down. The resulting "mental letters," such as the one he writes to President Eisenhower objecting to Internal Revenue Service regulations, amply demonstrate that Herzog has a quixotic side; he is willing, sometimes even anxious, to tilt at any windmill that strikes his fancy as undermining the human condition: "Man's life is not a business," he chides in his letter to the president. Herzog's letters speak out for individual man at a time when everything seems to militate against the individual, and his abiding faith, his unshakable innocence, are what make him such an attractive character.

During the first day of the novel, and Herzog's bout with madness, many of his wild musings are literally written down; he transcribes whatever flashes across the screen of his inner life, usually on scraps of paper that come to hand and often in the middle of teaching a class. In these flashbacks, Herzog realizes that his students must have regarded this behavior as strange, but he was, and still is, a deeply preoccupied man, and this is the best instruction on the costs of "romanticism" he is able to give them. Many of Herzog's random thoughts fall into the category of *trepverter,* a Yiddish term he defines as "retorts that came too late, when you were already on your way down the stairs." Having so badly missed the chance to say something as the affair between his friend Gersbach and his wife Madeleine began and then progressed, Herzog says it now, and in full agitated throat. This, unfortunately, only makes his social situation worse as many in Herzog's former circle, who knew about the affair but betrayed him by keeping silent, now regard him as so benighted, so foolish, that he did not see the writing on the domestic walls of the large ramshackle house in rustic Ludeyville, where he had isolated Madeleine from the cultural pleasures of New York. No doubt Herzog hoped that arranging for the Gersbachs to join them in Ludeyville would help, but, ironically enough, the move sealed Herzog's fate.

THE PLACE OF PLACE

Homes matter dearly to Herzog, from the squalor of his childhood on Montreal's Napoleon Street to the large, albeit crumbling, house in Ludeyville. Herzog's most vivid memories are those of his childhood on Napoleon Street, where despite the widespread poverty and cramped conditions of that immigrant world, he was left with the nostalgic feeling that nowhere else had he experienced emotions as wide or as deep. His father and mother loom especially large in Herzog's memories. Papa Herzog is a man who failed in virtually every enterprise he put his hand and mind to:

> First Father Herzog failed in Petersburg, where he went through two dowries in one year. He had been importing onions from Egypt. Under Pobedonostsev the police caught up with him for illegal residence. He was convicted and sentenced. . . .
>
> In 1913 he bought a piece of land near Valleyfield, Quebec, and failed as a farmer. Then he came into town and failed as a banker; failed in the drygoods business; failed as a jobber; . . . failed as a junk dealer. Then he became a marriage broker and failed—too short-tempered and blunt. And now he was failing as a bootlegger, on the run from the provincial Liquor Commission. Making a bit of a living.

Thus, on the face of it, Herzog comes from a long line of comic failures. He is often the architect of his misfortune, so he fits the classic definition of the *schlemiel:* the man who ensures his own defeat by buttering his bread on both sides and then watching as it falls to the floor. Herzog recalls his father in larger-than-life proportions as a man who simply could not make it because he was not willing to be as ruthless as the times required: "He looked for business opportunities—bankruptcies, job lots, mergers, fire sales, produce—to rescue him from illegality. He could calculate percentages mentally at high speed, but he lacked the cheating imagination of a successful businessman." By all tough-minded measures, Papa Herzog was a flop; nonetheless, what remains in Herzog's consciousness is an unfailingly warm memory of the evenings when he and his brothers licked the labels for the bottles of moonshine his father hoped to sell to American rumrunners. But even here, where so many made large fortunes, Papa Herzog was betrayed and eventually beaten up.

Mother Herzog is the smothering immigrant mother drawn large. She spoiled Moses shamelessly, even if she lacked the funds to lavish him with expensive gifts. Instead, Herzog remembers, she provided homier services: "she was cook, washerwoman, seamstress on Napoleon Street in the slum. Her hair turned gray, and she lost her teeth, her very fingernails wrinkled. Her hands smelled of the sink." Others in the family had money—Aunt Zipporah, for example—but not mother and father. Still, Herzog was made to feel that he was the "prince" that the family's name suggests:

> Once, at nightfall, she was pulling me on the sled, over crusty ice, the tiny glitter of snow, perhaps four o'clock of a short day in January. Near the grocery we met an old baba in a shawl who said, "Why are you pulling him, daughter!" Mama, dark under the eyes. Her slender cold face. She was breathing hard. She wore the torn seal coat. . . . "Daughter, don't sacrifice your strength to children," said the shawled crone in the freezing dusk of the street. I wouldn't get off the sled. I pretended not to understand.

Add boyhood friends such as Nachman, a perennially down-on-his-luck poet who aged badly as he fell ever deeper into madness, and Herzog's memories of Napoleon Street take on a substance and a weight that makes it culturally—and humanly—significant: "Napoleon Street, rotten, toylike, crazy and filthy, riddled, flogged with harsh weather—the bootlegger's boys reciting ancient prayers. To this Moses' heart was attached with great power. Here was a wider range of human feelings than he had ever again been able to find." When he compares his parents and other people from his childhood on Napoleon Street with the heartless, petty beings who have brought him such grief in his adult life, the differences are clear: the former is a vivid instance of Paradise Lost while the latter suggests the rings of a Dantean hell. The immigrant Jewish world had both soul and a sense of oversized passion while, by contrast, the contemporary world seems smaller and unsavory.

REALITY INSTRUCTION

Bellow once told an interviewer that Reality Instructors are people who know the score, and who know that a sad sack such as Herzog does not. So they better him with reasons of the Real and make it clear that he had better wise up. Many of those who hector Herzog happen to be lawyers who will continue to get a bad rap in Bellow's subsequent fiction. Often they are representing a character's wife in a nasty divorce case; tough postures come with the territory, especially when it is important to bluff in ways that will make an agitated husband throw in the towel and hand over everything.

Sandor Himmelstein emerges as the toughest, most vividly etched lawyer in *Herzog*. Unlike the dreamy Herzog, Himmelstein knows how brutal reality can be, and he accepts the covenant. Nothing surprises or particularly upsets him; he cynically expects the worst, and he is fully prepared to hit back—quickly and hard. Still, he "likes" Herzog, largely because, as Himmelstein puts it:

> You're not like those other university phonies. You're a *mensch*. What good are those effing eggheads! It takes an ignorant bastard like me to fight liberal causes. Those silk-stocking Yale squares may have a picture of Learned Hand in the office, but when it comes to getting mixed up in Trumbull Park, or fighting those yellowbellies in Deerfield.

Himmelstein prides himself on being a scrapper, and he is particularly proud of his willingness to get his hands dirty fighting liberal causes. But the time he spends ingratiating himself with Herzog is time postponed from confronting the *real* issue: custody of Herzog's children. Himmelstein urges him to abandon the fight for custody, arguing that a man does not have a chance in this kind of court battle. (Later, Herzog wonders if his old friend is, in fact, betraying him, but this may be yet another instance of Herzog's paranoia.) "Speaking as a lawyer," Himmelstein says, he imagines the courtroom scene:

> I can see you with a jury. They'll look at Madeleine, blooming and lovely, then you, haggard and gray-haired, and bam! there goes your custody suit. That's the jury system. Dumber than cave men, those bastards—I know this isn't easy for you to hear, but I better say it. Guys at our time of life must face facts.

Himmelstein does not mince words, but he also does not lose sight of his goal—namely, to manipulate Herzog into abandoning a custody fight for Junie. As Herzog keeps insisting that all is not lost—he could dye his hair, for example—it becomes clear that he has pitted himself against "mass man," the entity he defines as "a man of the crowd. The soul of the mob." This is precisely what the boorish, no-nonsense Himmelstein is, and when he gets wind of what Herzog is suggesting, a blowup quickly follows. Himmelstein has no patience for academic speculation or abstract language (especially when it is directed his way), and as the discussion drags on, Himmelstein pulls out the heavy artillery, laying down the brutal truths of domestic litigation: "[They'll] tie your guts in knots," he tells Herzog; "They'll put a meter on your nose, and charge you for breathing. You'll be locked up back and front. Then you'll think about death. You'll pray for it. A coffin will look better to you than a sports car."

No doubt a part of Bellow is attracted to the likes of a Reality Instructor such as Sandor Himmelstein, especially in those moments when he wonders what good a first-class education is. That it is not likely to prepare one for life as a citizen, husband, or father seems true enough (here, Herzog is Exhibit A), yet Herzog (and Bellow) is not quite ready to concede entirely to the life defined by the Reality Instructors. Nonetheless, with Himmelstein he gives in, agreeing to take out an expensive life-insurance policy for his wife and child. Here, vengeance (temporarily) gives way to sacrifice.

Not all of Herzog's instruction in reality takes a form as coarsely grained as the tirades from Himmelstein. Sometimes "reality" makes its way into Herzog's extended flashbacks embodied as priests who know canon law and who can aid Madeleine in her effort to marry the Jewish Herzog; sometimes it is embodied as relatives from both sides of the Herzog marriage who listen to Herzog, shaking their heads (literally or figuratively) as his frenetic story tumbles out. All of them know the plain-as-the-nose-on-your-face truth: that Herzog was cuckolded and that he should have known better. They savor the fact that Herzog, the world-beating intellectual, does not know this, but they do—and their "instruction" on this point, so confident its understanding of what matters most in the world, is galling to Herzog, who depends upon his heart as a barometer for behavior and as a measuing rod for the soul. The Good, the True and the Beautiful—benchmarks for the Romanticism that Herzog writes about—have no place in the quotidian world where "reality" means what is tangible, what can be bought or sold. "Hard-boiled" is the term usually given to the people Herzog labels as Reality Instructors, with the additional proviso, in Herzog's definition, that their superiority is both brutal and relentless. Reality Instructors do not concern themselves with such niceties as tolerance. Much less with fair play they live in the Hobbesian jungle without knowing (or caring) about who Thomas Hobbes was. A part of Herzog is eminently capable of giving an impromptu session in the history of ideas, but no one is eager to take him up on it.

A VALENTINE FOR GERSBACH

If Herzog has collected a large number of people who find him heartbreakingly ridiculous, Valentine Gersbach, the one-legged man who "limps off" with Herzog's dish of a wife, never ceases thinking of him as an intellectual role model. Gersbach is sensual, witty, and, most of all, there for Madeleine when Herzog becomes preoccupied with his heady thought. But essentially, Gersbach is a fraud—as an intellectual (he merely follows, as best he can, whatever the current fashion might be), as a poet (when he gives a reading he has the back doors locked so that people cannot leave), and most of all, as somebody who passed himself off as Herzog's best friend. That Gersbach's first name is "Valentine"—associated with a commercialized holiday of candy, flowers, and sentimental greeting cards—is only one indication among many that Bellow will spare this character nothing.

To Herzog, Gersbach can be represented with a single word: betrayer—that, and enemy to Junie. Here, for example, Herzog reads from a real, rather than "mental," letter written by a babysitter worried about the possible damage that Valentine and Madeleine are doing to Junie's frail psyche:

> *Mr. Gersbach, who has an ambiguous position in this household, is very amusing to the child, on the whole. She calls him Uncle Val, and I often see him giving her a piggyback, or tossing her in the air.* Here Herzog had set his teeth, angry, scenting danger. *But I have to report one disagreeable thing, and I talked this over with Lucas. This is that, coming to Harper Avenue the other night, I heard the child crying. She was inside Gersbach's car, and couldn't get out, and the poor little thing was shaking and weeping. . . . Then I found out that her Mama and Uncle Val were having a quarrel inside, and Uncle Val had taken her by the hand and led*

> *her out to the car and told her to play a while. He shut her up and went back in the house.*

The letter infuriates Herzog, who is certain that he alone has the qualities of goodness and patience to effectively nourish his child. Moreover, his paranoia about Junie's situation is reinforced and inflamed after he stumbles into a city courtroom searching for the lawyer handling his divorce. What Herzog hears is heart-rending testimony about an abused child who has died of neglect:

> The medical examiner was on the stand. Had he seen the dead child? Yes. Did he have a report to make? He did. He gave the date and circumstances of the examination. . . . The child, he said, was normally formed but seemed to have suffered from malnutrition. There were sings of incipient rickets, the teeth were already quite carious, but this was sometimes a symptom that the mother had had toxemia in pregnancy. Were any unusal marks visible on the boy's body? Yes, the little boy had apprently been beaten. Once, or repeatedly? In his opinion, often beaten. . . . The boy's liver had been ruptured. The hemorrhage caused by this may have been the immediate cause of death. There was also a brain injury. "In your opinion, then, the child died violently?" "That is my opinion. The liver injury would have been enough."

The mood of the courtroom testimony is emotionless and matter-of-fact, whereas Herzog, as he listens to the testimony—obviously thinking about his own daughter's fate—can barely control the range of throbbing emotions that roll over him. Like an epic hero whose journey takes him on a descent into the underworld—and there he learn truths not available to normal mortals—Herzog has descended into the bowels of Chicago's criminal justice system, where he encounters some of the cruelest instruction in reality that he has faced yet.

Herzog's experience in the courtoom gives a new, frightening dimension to Valentine Gersbach. True, nothing that Valentine Gersbach ever did escapes Herzog's sour notice. For example, when Gersbach mispronounced a Yiddish word, Herzog takes him to task, and then worries that this insistence on "proper" Yiddish is probably foolish. Still, if Gersbach cannot get the details straight, is there any reason to believe that he could synthesize Big Ideas (as Herzog does) or put together a presciption for humanist living in the postmodern world? But now, after hearing how children are brutalized, Herzog imagines that Gersbach is capable of violence, and moreover, that he must be stopped. Hence, Herzog's frenetic flight to Chicago, where he will cease being the egghead and become Junie's savior.

MINOR CHARACTERS AS COUNTERWEIGHTS

Overcome by "a need to explain, to have it out, to justify, to put in perspective, to clarify, to make amends," Herzog spends much the novel in the grip, often a comic one, of his own hyperconsciousness. He firmly believes himself to be, like Shakespeare's King Lear, a man "more sinned against than sinning." Others, justifiably or not, are less sure. They respond to Herzog's high-mindedness with nearly equal doses of admiration and thinly veiled condescension: "Though Simkin was a clever lawyer, very rich, he respected Herzog. He had a weakness for confused, high-minded people with moral impulses like Moses. Hopeless! Very likely he looked at Moses and saw a grieving childless man trying to keep his dignity." In Herzog's case, the populist wisdom that figures "If you're so smart, why ain't you rich?" becomes the unspoken "And if you were *really* so smart, how come you got cuckolded?" Such back-biting is bad enough, but those who would instruct poor Herzog in the nature of the Real are even worse. They elbow their way into his life with teeth bared and a stomach for the brutalities of quotidian life. Why, Herzog wonders, must the word "reality" always be modified by the adjective "brutal"? Even Herzog, who has been as schooled by the streets as he had been by books, knows the answer: because "brutal realities" are what we see around us and are therefore what we believe in.

Meanwhile, Herzog continues to ponder the questions that matter deeply to him. What our country badly needs, he half-jokingly insists, is a "good five-cent synthesis" (a play on the once-popular quip that what the American economy needs is a good five-cent cigar), one that would provide "a new angle on the modern condition, showing how life could be lived by renewing universal connections; overturning the last of the Romantic errors about the uniqueness of the Self; revising the old Western, Faustian ideology; investigating the social meaning of Nothingness." Herzog's "synthesis" is merely a grand, wonderfully nutty dream; everything militates against him creating such a synthesis and thus making good on his early promise as a scholar: the sleazy cultural moment, assorted "operators" (Mermelstein, Shapiro, and other competing academics), Reality Instructors, Potato Lovers, lawyers representing a former wife, virtually *any* woman, and of course, himself.

The minor characters who swim their way through Herzog's stream of consciousness serve to demonstrate the way much of our popular culture coarsens the atmosophere by substituting junk for what were once regarded as great books and by lowering formerly high standards. In Herzog's day, adults flocked to evening classes in the hope that they would find some measure of truth there; now undergraduate students can major in television shows or video games at many colleges. Herzog, meanwhile, sees himself as a warrior in the struggle against this decay. But he is equally at war with the corruptions within himself. His largely interior battle reminds one that the human spirit continues to matter in the life of an individual citizen, no matter how much the size and power of his society outweighs him. And if this extended spiritual exercise ultimately exhausts Herzog, the very fact that he no longer feels the compunction to write "mental letters" is an optimistic sign, one that speaks to Herzog's resilience and his health, or at least of its possibility in the near future. Readers feel the change in his mental status because he can, at long last, let go—accepting that he is "*pretty well satisfied to be, to be just as it is willed,*" and that he has no "messages for anyone. Nothing. Not a single word."

HERZOG'S AUTOBIOGRAPHICAL ASPECT

One of the things that gives Bellow's novel both a richness of texture and a feeling of importance is that Herzog's soul has many sides. Those who wrote *Herzog* off as a novel in which Bellow tells his side of a nasty divorce were not careful readers. Although Bellow's protagonist has more than a few similarities to the tumultuous life of its author, especially in the way that both found themselves going through messy divorces, the novel's most remarkable accomplishment is in Bellow's uncanny ability to put his finger squarely on the pulse of his cultural times. Nonetheless, biographers who have tried to pluck the mystery of Bellow's life and art have found an abundance of details about the connections between *Herzog* the novel and the biographical facts upon which it draws. "Bellow made no effort to disguise the models of his characters—and they weren't pleased," James Atlas writes.

> "I'm not just a flower girl," complained Rosette Lamont, the model for Herzog's hot-blooded mistress, Ramona. Jonas Schwartz, the Minneapolis lawyer who had represented Sondra [Bellow's second wife] in the divorce, was furious to find himself represented as the hectoring, dwarfish Sandor Himmelstein. "Have you read *Herzog*?" he ranted to Bellow's lawyer, John Goetz, grabbing him by the lapels in an elevator: "He makes me into a son of a bitch." Sondra was to spend years trying to explain to Adam [her son, who became a literary figure in his own right] that it hadn't been like that at all. Only [Professor Jack] Ludwig was reported to be happy with his likeness. "I'm Valentine Gersbach," he boasted to his students, predicting that someday he would show up "in a lot of books."

Bellow made no secret that that *Herzog* had its autobiographical side: "When a writer runs out of other people to write about," Atlas quotes him as saying, "there's no reason why he can't use himself." But Bellow's characters are most often composites, and as the decades have passed since the novel's publication, Herzog's biographical models are of diminishing interest to general readers outside the Bellow circle, and even this "interest," much of it indistinguishable from gossip, will only grow fainter as years go on. Bellow's accomplishment in *Herzog* is to have shaped his raw, autobiographical material into a piece of fiction that holds up over time as a lively commentary on the times and places that gave rise to its impassioned pages.

Select Bibliography

EDITION

Herzog. New York: Viking Press, 1964. (The novel is widely available in paperback through Penguin Books. The 1976 Penguin paperback is cited in this essay.)

OTHER WORKS BY BELLOW

The Adventures of Augie March. New York: Viking Press, 1953.

Dangling Man. New York: Vanguard Press, 1944.

Henderson the Rain King. New York: Viking Press, 1959.

Humboldt's Gift. New York: Viking Press, 1975.

Mr. Sammler's Planet. New York: Viking Press, 1970.

Seize the Day. New York: Viking Press, 1956.

The Victim. New York: Vanguard Press, 1947.

SECONDARY WORKS

Atlas, James. *Bellow: A Biography.* New York: Random House, 2000.

Bloom, Harold, ed. *Saul Bellow.* New York: Chelsea House, 1986.

Bradbury, Malcolm. *Saul Bellow.* London and New York: Methuen, 1982.

Braham, Jeanne. *A Sort of Columbus: The American Voyages of Saul Bellow's Fiction.* Athens: University of Georgia Press, 1984.

Clayton, John J. *Saul Bellow: In Defense of Man.* 2d ed. Bloomington: Indiana University Press, 1979.

Cohen, Sarah B. *Saul Bellow's Enigmatic Laughter.* Urbana: University of Illinois Press, 1974.

Cronin, Gloria L., and Ben Siegel, eds. *Conversations with Saul Bellow.* Jackson: University Press of Mississippi, 1994.

Dutton, Robert R. *Saul Bellow.* Boston: Twayne, 1982.

Furman, Andrew. "Ethnicity in Saul Bellow's *Herzog:* The Importance of the Napolean Street, Montreal, Memories." *Saul Bellow Journal* 13 (1995): 41–51.

Galloway, David. "Moses Bloom-Herzog: Bellow's Everyman." *Southern Review* 2 (1966): 61–76.

Goldman, L. H. *Saul Bellow's Moral Vision: A Critical Study of the Jewish Experience.* New York: Irvington, 1983.

Poirier, Richard. "Bellows to *Herzog.*" *Partisan Review* 32 (1985): 264–271.

Schulman, Robert. "The Style of Bellow's Comedy." *PMLA* 83 (1968): 109–117.

Tanner, Tony. *Saul Bellow.* Edinburgh and London: Oliver and Boyd, 1965.

Trachtenberg, Stanley, ed. *Critical Essays on Saul Bellow.* Boston: G. K. Hall, 1979.

Wilson Jonathan. Herzog: *The Limits of Ideas.* Boston: Twayne Publishers, 1990.

Ralph Ellison's Invisible Man

D. QUENTIN MILLER

INVISIBLE MAN (1952) is one of the most enduring, ambitious, and important American novels. Published at the dawn of the civil rights movement, it reflects on a period of African American protest (the 1930s and 1940s) and anticipates a period of African American revolution (the late 1950s and 1960s). It is also a novel that examines the American Dream in general; challenges accepted wisdom; tests the assumptions of modernism, Marxism, and psychoanalysis; and addresses complex moral issues without attempting to resolve them. It is densely allusive, at times humorous, deeply philosophical, and never dull. Its scope is enormous. Like other complex, intricately crafted, and ambitious narratives such as Herman Melville's *Moby-Dick,* Thomas Pynchon's *Gravity's Rainbow,* and Toni Morrison's *Beloved, Invisible Man* is a likely choice for the great American novel.

Like all great novels, *Invisible Man* is about a quest, specifically the quest for the understanding of one's individual identity in modern America. The fact that the narrator of *Invisible Man* (called "Invisible Man" or "the narrator" hereafter) is never named throughout the novel might indicate that his quest for identity fails. Yet a name is only a superficial identity, something given at birth rather than earned; as Kimberly Benston writes in "I Yam What I Am," "the refusal to be named invokes the power of the Sublime, a transcendent impulse to undo all categories." Invisible Man ends up with something more important than a name: a coherent voice. The narration of the novel is his greatest accomplishment, for it allows him to understand himself and to connect with others—the readers of the novel. Walter Slatoff points out that, like Whitman's poem "Song of Myself," *Invisible Man* "begins with the word *I* and ends with the word *you.*" Yet Invisible Man would not be able to tell his story without first reflecting on his experiences, many of which are based on humiliation, abuse, and the loss of self-control. In short, he has to pay a price before he learns to narrate, and he must sacrifice his dignity and his ambition for conventional success in order to earn a more mature identity.

PROLOGUE: "THE END IS IN THE BEGINNING"

Invisible Man is framed by a prologue and an epilogue, both of which originate from the mature (if jaded) identity of the narrator in the present. He begins the book by describing his life in a hole, a subterranean cavern underneath New York City lit by 1,369 light bulbs powered by stolen electricity. Also, in the novel's opening pages he describes how he once viciously beat up a white man who uttered a racial slur. He thus projects an image of himself as a thief and a thug while he sets up the theme of invisibility. Although the narrator's introduction might make the reader suspicious and distrustful, it is peppered with moments of clarity and understanding that encourage the reader's interest; the narrator realizes, as he is about to slit the throat of the white racist, "that the man had not *seen* me, actually; that he, as far as he knew, was in the midst of a walking nightmare!" His hole in the ground is brightly lit, yet his invisibility (and the fact that he lives underground) would seem to make light unnecessary. He addresses this apparent contradiction: "I love light. Perhaps you'll think it strange that an invisible man should need light, desire light, love light. But maybe it is exactly because I *am* invisible. Light confirms my reality, gives birth to my form." First-time readers of the introduction will most likely be confused, but they are encouraged to accept the absurdity of his situation, for "contradiction . . . is how the world moves." The difficulty of holding two opposing concepts in the mind is part of what the narrator has learned to do over the course of the novel. This skill is an outgrowth of the condition of invisibility, which is linked to, but not synonymous with, being black in modern America.

The prologue of the book explains so much of what is to follow that it seems a more fitting conclusion than an introduction. Invisible Man alludes to the major episodes and characters of the novel in his prologue, long before the reader can understand his meaning. He occasionally catches himself and says, "But that's getting too far ahead of the story" or, "Bear with me"; yet his method is deliberate, for the reader is forced to do what Invisible Man has done all his life: to move forward without a clear understanding of what is coming next. The important parts of this

CHRONOLOGY

1914	Ralph Waldo Ellison born on March 1 in Oklahoma City, Oklahoma, to Lewis Alfred and Ida Millsap Ellison.
1933	Begins his study of classical music at Tuskegee Institute in Alabama.
1936	Leaves Tuskegee for New York City due to financial difficulties. Expects to return for his senior year but fails to earn enough money to return.
1937	Begins his literary career by writing a review published in *New Challenge,* edited by Richard Wright.
1938	Joins the Federal Writers' Project, a New Deal program that encourages writing about folklore and urban life.
1942	Becomes editor of short-lived *Negro Quarterly.*
1939–1944	Publishes eight short stories.
1946	Marries Fanny McConnell in July. It is his second marriage; the details of his first are unavailable.
1952	*Invisible Man.*
1953	Receives the National Book Award.
1955–1957	Receives a fellowship from the American Academy of Arts and Letters to live in Rome, where he begins work on a second novel.
1964	Publishes *Shadow and Act,* a collection of essays.
1967	A fire destroys Ellison's summer home in Plainfield, Massachusetts, including about 350 pages of his long-awaited second novel.
1969	Receives the Medal of Freedom.
1986	Publishes his second collection of nonfiction, *Going to the Territory.*
1994	Dies of pancreatic cancer in Harlem on April 16 without having completed his second novel.
1999	*Juneteenth* published posthumously. Edited by John F. Callahan, Ellison's literary executor, the novel receives poor reviews.

life lesson are all addressed in the prologue: to learn how to see (even "to *see* around corners"), to accept contradiction, and to understand "a slightly different sense of time." All of these hard-earned skills give the narrator power.

In order to earn this power, the narrator must suffer and alter his notion of reality. He admits that he is prone to violence, a destructive and irrational response to "being bumped against by those of poor vision":

> You wonder whether you aren't simply a phantom in other people's minds. . . . You ache with the need to convince yourself that you do exist in the real world, that you're a part of all the sound and anguish, and you strike out with your fists, you curse and you swear to make them recognize you. And, alas, it's seldom successful.

By admitting this, he suggests that violence is not the best solution to invisibility, yet it does have some merit, for it may *occasionally* be successful. The narrator's acceptance of contradiction—which explains his fondness for puns and for other language play—is a more productive response to invisibility.

The notion that one can manipulate time is perhaps his most powerful revelation, though it is difficult to explain. In the prologue he describes how he once listened to Louis Armstrong after smoking marijuana. He says, "Perhaps I like Louis Armstrong because he's made poetry out of being invisible. I think it must be because he's unaware that he *is* invisible." The narrator, by contrast, is all too aware of his invisibility, which might be why he feels the need to alter his mind-set with marijuana or sloe gin when he listens to Armstrong. He attempts to describe what the experience is like:

> It was a strange evening. Invisibility, let me explain, gives one a slightly different sense of time, you're never quite on the beat. Sometimes you're ahead and sometimes behind. Instead of the swift and imperceptible flowing of time, you are aware of its nodes, those points where time stands still or from which it leaps ahead. And you slip into the breaks and look around. That's what you hear vaguely in Louis' music.

The marijuana gives him "a new analytical way of listening to music . . . I found myself hearing not only in time, but in space as well. I not only entered the music but descended, like Dante, into its depths." After he descends into the music he hears a slower tempo, then enters a cave and hears an old woman singing a spiritual. He falls to lower levels where he sees a naked white woman "pleading in a voice like my mother's" as "slaveowners . . . bid for her naked body," then to an even lower level where he hears the call and response of a church congregation meditating on the contradictory meaning of blackness: "*Black will git you . . . an' black won't . . . It do . . . an' it don't.*" He arrives at the very core of the music and has a conversation with the old woman who had been singing spirituals about the meaning of freedom, whose meaning is "in loving," she insists, but when pressed she admits that her notion of freedom is "all mixed up. First I think it's one thing, then I think it's another."

The section on Armstrong's music and the out-of-time hallucination that follows it dominate the prologue and advance many of the important themes that recur throughout the novel. Even the reader who does not understand the meaning of these passages is encouraged to be patient and to foster a new method of reading that requires closer attention to music, to dream-like sequences, to irrational forces, and to the deeper meaning of words like freedom, blackness, and invisibility. The reader may feel assaulted by this barrage of unfamiliar words, images, and concepts, but that is precisely the narrator's objective. He is inviting readers down into his underworld, after all, and if they are going to understand him, they must be willing to descend to his level, out of their comfort zone, just as he descended "beneath the surface" of Armstrong's music. In retrospect he found the experience "exhausting . . . And yet, it was a strangely satisfying experience." It is likely that the reader of *Invisible Man* will feel the same way.

PORTRAIT OF THE ARTIST AS A YOUNG INVISIBLE MAN

As baffling as the prologue is to the first-time reader of *Invisible Man,* it is unlikely that it would cause many readers to put the book down, for it is filled with the action, ideas, and imagery that make the novel so pleasurable. Nevertheless, the narrator is aware of the limits of abstraction and so begins the body of the book in a much more conventional manner by describing the origins of his story. He gives the final lesson of his story right away: "It took me a long time . . . to achieve a realization everyone else appears to have been born with: That I am nobody but myself." The narrator is a slow learner, a fairly common characteristic among narrators. Yet his circumstances are unusual: he is an invisible man, after all, and his grandparents had been slaves in a land that proclaims that its residents are free and equal to one another. He immediately links his identity to his grandparents' status as slaves and initiates the question of fate: "I was in the cards, other things having been equal (or unequal) eighty-five years ago." Although the narrator grows into a strong proponent of Emersonian self-reliance, he is acutely aware of the role of fate and the limitations of free will to a black/invisible man in America. One of Ellison's early published stories, "King of the Bingo Game" (1944), also employs the metaphor of gambling to describe the relationship between choice and fate. The main character of that story believes that he controls his fate by pushing a button that stops a bingo game's spinning wheel. Yet a security guard knocks him down at the end of the story even though he has won the bingo prize. He has failed to understand the way individual will and culture interact. The narrator of *Invisible Man* is more aware of the meaning of this idea; he says he was "in the cards" two generations before his birth. The control he gains over the course of the narrative is in realizing that he does not have the power to shuffle or deal the cards but rather that, as an invisible man, he can hide within the deck or drop out of the game altogether.

The narrator's grandfather is much more prominent throughout the novel than the narrator's immediately family. The narrator barely mentions his parents in the first chapter of the book and never indicates whether he has siblings, but he dwells on his grandfather's mysterious deathbed pronouncement to the narrator's father:

> Son, after I'm gone I want you to keep up the good fight. I never told you, but our life is a war and I have been a traitor all my born days, a spy in the enemy's country ever since I give up my gun back in the Reconstruction. Live with your head in the lion's mouth. I want you to overcome 'em with yeses, undermine 'em with grins, agree 'em to death and destruction, let 'em swoller you till they vomit or bust wide open. . . . Learn it to the younguns."

These dying words stay with the narrator throughout his life, yet they are contradictory and difficult to grasp. The narrator as a young man does not take them seriously, either because he does not understand them, because his parents told him to forget them, or because he is blinded by ambition. He begins his story of his own experiences by describing his role in a "Battle Royal" that coincides with his graduation from high school.

The Battle Royal is an important formative scene because it illustrates so vividly the novel's themes. In fact, the novel can be compared to a theme-and-variation pattern in music, with the Battle Royal as the initial statement of the theme. The narrator and a number of his black, male classmates are brought before the town's wealthy, white power brokers in order to provide them with a perverse kind of entertainment in the form of a chaotic fight. Prior to fighting, the young men, dressed only in shorts and boxing gloves, are shown a naked white woman, and the narrator notes that he feels "a wave of irrational guilt and fear," which is a precursor to the violence that will follow. The narrator's feelings give way to a contradictory set of responses:

> I wanted at one and the same time to run from the room, to sink through the floor, or go to her and cover her from my eyes and the eyes of the others with my body; to feel the soft thighs, to caress her and destroy her, to love her and murder her, to hide from her, and yet to stroke where below the small American flag tattooed upon her belly her thighs formed a capital V.

She is a human being as well as a symbol, both of the forbidden sexual appeal of white women and of the forbidden dream of America. The narrator responds to her humanity with tenderness but cannot reconcile those feelings with his desire to destroy or murder her. It is noteworthy that white men carefully orchestrate this response in order to control black boys. The men blindfold the aroused boys, place them in the boxing ring, and encourage them to beat one another as the only outlet for their confusion.

Because he is in the ring, the narrator's choices are limited: he must take his irrational feelings and direct them toward his peers or submit to the flying fists around him. The black community is thus pitted against itself, and the narrator is a participant in the ritualized violence that ensues. Moreover, his blindfold partially slips, and he discovers that he can see the other fighters:

> I moved carefully, avoiding blows, although not too many to attract attention, fighting from group to group. . . . I played one group against the other, slipping in and throwing a punch then stepping out of range while pushing the others into the melee to take the blows blindly aimed at me.

This is the first triumph of his discovery of invisibility and its attendant attribute of sight: he is able to minimize his physical harm. Yet he does not have full control over his situation: he must suffer a few blows so as not to attract attention, and any individual gain is offset by someone else's loss.

The narrator is obsessed with delivering a speech that he had delivered at his school, and he is so fixed on doing so that he loses his sense of timing and invisibility that had earlier given him an advantage. Yet the humiliation and abuse continue: the boys are encouraged to scramble for prize money on a carpet that has been rigged to send electric shocks through them. After suffering a severe shock, Invisible Man learns again how to work within his surroundings: "Ignoring the shock by laughing, as I brushed the coins off quickly, I discovered that I could contain the electricity—a contradiction, but it works." As before, he has seized some control of his fate, but the problem again is that he has lost his dignity, even as he prepares to deliver his speech to the men who sponsored the event.

The battle can be interpreted in terms of conscious and subconscious forces at war with one another, and after the narrator discovers the trick of laughing and containing electricity, he violates the code of the spectacle by grabbing the leg of one of the drunken white patrons: "It became a real struggle. I feared the rug more than I did the drunk, so I held on, surprising myself for a moment by trying to topple *him* upon the rug. It was such an enormous idea that I found myself actually carrying it out." This idea begins with some unconscious desire to redirect his anger in order to make a white man suffer along with himself and with the other black boys on the electrified rug. Although this impulse is not truly an idea, it does reveal something powerful about the importance of impulses in this novel. The narrator does not realize the meaning of what he is doing, and this same pattern is repeated when he actually delivers his speech, which derives directly from Booker T. Washington's 1895 Atlanta Exposition address. The drunken men laugh and taunt the narrator as he tries to deliver his speech, humiliated, bloodied, and exhausted by the Battle Royal. His unconscious desires again surface as he substitutes the words "social equality" for "social responsibility" in the speech. The instantly sobered audience scrutinizes him and asks him to repeat the phrase; he says "social responsibility," the less threatening of the phrases, and claims that "equality" was a mistake attributable to the fact that he "was swallowing blood." The men reward him with a briefcase containing a "scholarship to the state college for Negroes." He is overjoyed and completely forgets about the humiliation he had to endure at the Battle Royal. Yet his unconscious mind is troubled, and he dreams that night of his grandfather, who asks him to read a letter inside a briefcase. The message written on it is "Keep This Nigger-Boy Running." The dream ends with the grandfather's mocking laughter, and the narrator is again left with this old man's ambiguous wisdom, which is masked by the narrator's own blind ambition.

"HEARING AIN'T 'SPERIENCING": EVALUATING COLLEGIATE WISDOM

Presumably the narrator sees college as a compulsory step on the path to success. In order to gain insight into the meaning of the post–Battle Royal dream, he says, "I had to attend college," as though there is no choice in the matter. Yet the lessons he learns during college do not derive from conventional instruction and study. If Ellison's namesake, Ralph Waldo Emerson, was right when he said that "Books are for the scholar's idle times," then the narrator is a model of "The American Scholar," at least as he describes his experience. He describes his "beautiful" college with an almost rapturous attention to the details of nature as opposed to the particular subjects of his reading: "The buildings were old and covered with vines and the roads gracefully winding, lined with hedges and wild roses that dazzled the eyes in the summer sun. Honeysuckle and purple wisteria hung heavy from the trees and white magnolia mixed with their scents in the bee-humming air." In Emerson's "American Scholar" formula, "The ancient precepts 'Know thyself' and 'study nature'" merge. Invisible Man apparently learns only the nature part of this formula at college, yet his experience there is a significant step toward knowing himself, a quest that culminates in his narrative.

The narrator's description of the college is nostalgic, but it quickly changes from this rapturous praise of nature and white buildings to an awareness of "the forbidden road . . . sloping and turning, paralleling the black powerhouse with its engines droning earth-shaking rhythms in the dark, its windows red from the glow of the furnace." The road, described with sexual imagery, leads to an insane asylum, reminiscent of T. S. Eliot's *The Waste Land,* "barren of buildings, birds, or grass." The description reveals the lush beauty of the college campus to be a facade, masking the poverty and madness of the land that surrounds it. But it is also significant that the narrator associates the college buildings with whiteness, in contrast to the black powerhouse that the college trustees never see. This invisible building is where the work is done and where the energy comes from. This description forecasts the Liberty Paints section of the book and recalls the Battle Royal scene.

Even as he praises his college, the narrator trains readers to look for the contradictions in this "flower-studded wasteland." Recalling the mechanical horror of the recent world war, the narrator recalls how he and his classmates "drilled four-abreast down the smooth asphalt and pivoted and entered the chapel on Sundays, our uniforms pressed, shoes shined, minds laced up, eyes blind like those of robots to visitors and officials on the low, whitewashed reviewing stand." They gather around a statue that is identical to the one of Booker T. Washington at Tuskegee Institute, the obvious model for the college in the novel and the college where Ellison studied music from 1933 to 1936. Recalling his college years from the isolated safety of his hole, the narrator says:

who fears the Brotherhood and who claims to be the true source of power and knowledge within Liberty Paints. Brockway instructs the narrator how to read gauges and reminds him that *"we the machines inside the machines."*

Brockway works underground, as the narrator eventually will, but he is so much like Bledsoe in his threatening, arrogant conception of his own importance that he causes a new reaction in the narrator: "Something uncoiled in my stomach and I was moving toward him, shouting, more at a black blur that irritated my eyes than at a clearly defined human face." Moreover, he fights Brockway—his first physical battle since the Battle Royal—and is surprised to find that "my anger was flowing fast from action to words." His anger is finally finding its appropriate outlet: fighting, though it empowers him temporarily, yields to the more lasting effect of language. It is not coincidental that the hospital scene that follows is characterized by verbal defiance, even when the narrator does not fully understand the importance of what he is saying or thinking.

The hospital scene following the explosion at Liberty Paints is redolent with birth imagery. Invisible Man cannot recall his name or his mother's name when asked, and he fantasizes that his mother is one of the machines he is connected to. He cannot remember his own name either, but he does remember the identity of certain stock characters from childhood stories like Brer Rabbit. He has been damaged by the explosion, and he is once again subject to the humiliation of powerful whites (doctors and nurses) who joke about his dancing as they send electric shocks through his body. He appears somewhat mad in the hospital and in the scenes following, but with this madness comes a certain insight and self-possession. He articulates his crisis for the first time: "I could no more escape than I could think of my identity. Perhaps, I thought, the two things are involved with each other. When I discover who I am, I'll be free."

His recollection and partial identification with Brer Rabbit also connects him to the characters he meets in the North whose importance he has denied. The character Peter Wheatstraw, based on a folk singer of the same name, had asked him the cryptic question, "Is you got the *dog*?" prior to his arrival at Liberty Paints. Wheatstraw is a kind of blues-singer folk hero who attempts to connect the narrator with his past, but the narrator has repressed all memories of his youth: "I liked his words though I didn't know the answer. I'd known the stuff from childhood, but had forgotten it; had learned it back of school." After the Liberty Paints explosion the narrator is in a better position to recall the importance of his origins and of the lessons learned in the schoolyard as opposed to the classroom. He meets another version of a blues hero in the form of a yam-seller on the streets: "I stopped as though struck by a shot, deeply inhaling, remembering, my mind surging back, back." Ecstatically eating the yams, the narrator experiences "an intense feeling of freedom" which leads him to laugh off his deep-seated hatred of Bledsoe and unleashes in him a repressed humorous strain that causes him to admit, "I yam what I am."

MAKING SPEECHES: FINDING A LASTING VOICE

In a 1968 interview Ellison said, "fiction, at its best, moves ever toward a blending of the tragic with the comic—or towards that mode which we know as the Blues." It is no accident that Invisible Man's latent sense of humor coincides with his newfound appreciation for the impromptu blues singers he meets on the streets of New York—Wheatstraw and the yam-seller—or that his post–Liberty Paints rebirth into a new identity accompanies his own version of the blues: a tendency toward spontaneous speechmaking. In contrast to the speech he made after the Battle Royal that earned him a scholarship, the speeches he makes in New York are improvised and succeed most where rhetoricians would say they fail. When he allows feeling to overtake thinking and to lull himself out of a conventional sense of timing, as Armstrong does, he reveals the blues singer within himself and prepares for his final, most lasting accomplishment: the narration itself.

It is evident from the narrator's language alone that he is not a blues singer like Trueblood, Peter Wheatstraw, or the yam-seller. Yet he has deeply buried the part of himself that connects with these bluesmen, which is why he either hates them or cannot quite understand them. It is the blues that gives both *Invisible Man* and Invisible Man their unique strength. The prologue teaches that the key to the blues is in reaching deep, which is exactly what the narrator is in the process of learning as he begins his lengthy speechmaking career after being reborn in the Liberty Paints hospital. The tension between wanting to accomplish something meaningful and wanting to suffer in solitude snaps when the narrator notices an old black couple being evicted. Seeing their sorrow and their discarded possessions, which together describe a history of black America, the narrator hears himself "talking rapidly without thought but out of my clashing emotions." He is unsure about the action that will result from his speech, which is characterized by the kinds of repetitions and improvisations one hears in the blues; but he is aware that his speech comes from within him. He finds that he is "no longer struggling against or thinking about the nature of my action" when he leads the crowd back inside the house with the couple's possessions. The narrator barely escapes the ensuing melee, but he is in touch with his humanity for the first time in the novel.

The remainder of the novel, nearly half its length, is dominated by his involvement with the Brotherhood, a communist organization dedicated to the plight of the underclass. The organization's leader, Brother Jack, admires the narrator's rhetorical gifts at the eviction even as the narrator claims, "I made no speech." Arguing that "individuals" such as the old evicted couple "don't count," Brother Jack enlists the narrator in his cause by praising him, yet he cautions him not to be sentimental about such people:

> You're not like them. Perhaps you were, but you're not any longer. Otherwise you'd never have made that speech. Perhaps you were, but that's all past, dead. You might not recognize it just now, but that part of you is dead! You have not completely shed that self, that old agrarian self, but it's dead and you will throw it off completely and emerge something new. *History* has been born in your brain.

The irony is that the part of the narrator that Jack sees as dead is exactly the part that has just been reborn. The narrator should recognize the insincerity of Brother Jack's analysis; the reason he fails to is his persistent desire for fame and wealth. The Brotherhood immediately seduces him with both and gives him a new name. The budding identity he feels after his eviction speech has been immediately co-opted, and the voice he has found is quickly altered to accommodate the Brotherhood's rhetoric. As evidence of how thoroughly immersed in the system he has become, the narrator gives his landlady Mary "a *hundred*-dollar bill," the very denomination that Norton gave Trueblood after hearing his story.

Whether the Brotherhood is ultimately beneficial or detrimental to the narrator is a matter of debate. In a sense the Brotherhood is no different from college: the narrator is supposed to do as he is told even as he enjoys a sense of belonging. In both cases he has only limited control over his environment. Yet the Brotherhood recognizes the narrator's achievements and value even as it tries to convince him that individuals do not matter. Before *Invisible Man,* Bigger Thomas, the protagonist of Richard Wright's *Native Son* (1940), was the most recognized fictional character in African American literary history. Wright's depiction of the Communists' connection to the black community was much more favorable than Ellison's. Yet although the Brotherhood does not allow

Invisible Man to speak freely, it does allow him to speak, something Bigger is not permitted by his Communist lawyer Boris Max in the final section of *Native Son.*

The most controversial piece written about *Invisible Man* is undoubtedly Irving Howe's 1963 essay "Black Boys and Native Sons." The essay denounced Ellison and James Baldwin for failing to "accept the clenched militancy of Wright's posture as both novelist and man." Howe specifically attacks Ellison's depiction of the Communists, which he says "does not ring quite true." Beyond that, Howe says that Ellison "makes his Stalinist figures so vicious and stupid that one cannot understand how they could ever have attracted him or any other Negro." Ellison responded virulently to the attack in his essay "The World and the Jug" (1964): "I can only ask that my fiction be judged as art; if it fails, it fails aesthetically, not because I did or did not fight some ideological battle." Ellison does not call the Brotherhood the Communist Party; yet the similarities between them are so evident that readers and critics are tempted to take either Howe's perspective or Ellison's here: *Invisible Man* may be a work of art, but it clearly has the potential to become a political battlefield. The debate mirrors the narrator's response to his eviction speech and to his involvement in the Brotherhood, both of which contain the dual impulses to join and to flee.

Throughout his involvement with the Brotherhood the narrator embodies the controversy that *Invisible Man* raised. Three major events—the narrator's stadium speech, his interview with a prominent magazine, and his funeral speech following Brother Tod Clifton's death—are all subjected to public debate and dissent among the Brotherhood's leadership. During the stadium speech, which occurs after a minimum of training in the Brotherhood's rhetoric, he is plagued by an almost mystical loss of vision, and he admits with some surprise, "I realized that the flow of words had stopped." Feeling at once powerful and vulnerable, he throws away any script he might have rehearsed and gives in to his deeper impulses: "'Look at me!' The words ripped from my solar plexus. . . . '*Something strange and miraculous and transforming is taking place in me right now. . . .* I feel suddenly that I have become *more human.*'" This admission causes one of the Brotherhood leaders to denounce the speech as "wild, hysterical, politically irresponsible and dangerous . . . and worse than that, it was *incorrect!*" The debate over his speech causes the Brotherhood to send Invisible Man away for a period of training, and although this period might enable him to become a more effective speaker for the Brotherhood, the real effect is to prevent him from exposing his individual humanity in public.

The narrator accepts his redefined role in the Brotherhood because he continues to believe that his work for them is important. This conviction is tested when he is introduced to Brother Tod Clifton, a vigorous man his age whose appearance elicits the narrator's effusive admiration: "I saw that he was very black and very handsome, and as he advanced mid-distance into the room, that he possessed the chiseled, black-marble features sometimes found on statues." Although he initially feels competitive, he quickly realizes that Tod Clifton is his friend, the only true one he has in the novel.

Clifton's fall from Brotherhood prominence to a peddler of racist puppets is unexpected and unexplained. It is somehow connected to his battle with Ras the Exhorter, a black nationalist loosely modeled on Marcus Garvey who opposes the Brotherhood because it does not specifically advance the cause of black people or their separation from white people. Opposite to the Brotherhood's ultra-rationality, Ras operates from his emotions, and he confronts the narrator and Clifton about their involvement with the Brotherhood: "I ask both of you, are you awake or sleeping? What is your pahst and where are you going?" The narrator dismisses Ras as a bitter, poisoned soul who does more damage than good, but Clifton is troubled by Ras's rhetoric; he tells the narrator, "I suppose sometimes a man *has* to plunge outside history. . . . Plunge outside, turn his back . . . Otherwise he might kill somebody, go nuts." This statement precedes Clifton's disappearance, but it also foreshadows the narrator's ultimate plunge into the hole from which he narrates.

The narrator has a difficult time analyzing Clifton's choice to plunge, specifically his decision to sell dolls that demean his own race: "'To plunge,' he had said. But he knew that only in the Brotherhood could we make ourselves known, could we avoid being empty Sambo dolls. . . . I'd forget it and hold on desperately to Brotherhood with all my strength." He continues to turn a blind eye to the nature of the Brotherhood partially because Clifton's fate seems so wretched, especially once he is shot down in the street and immediately forgotten. This event is troubling to him because of history's indifference to people like Clifton, who is also like him:

> The cop would be Clifton's historian, his judge, his witness, and his executioner, and I was the only brother in the watching crowd. And I, the only witness for the defense, knew neither the extent of his guilt nor the nature of his crime. Where were the historians today? And how would they put it down?

The narrator experiences a significant realization at this moment: he is underground at the time, watching the subway trains move like time, quickly forgetting the past:

> What did [historians] ever think of us transitory ones? Ones such as I had been before I found Brotherhood—birds of passage who were too obscure for learned classification, too silent for the most sensitive recorders of sound, of natures too ambiguous for the most ambiguous words, and too distant from the centers of historical decision to sign or even to applaud the signers of historical documents? We who write no novels, histories or other books.

Although he still clings to the Brotherhood for his life's meaning, the narrator realizes that he is more connected to the anonymous souls overlooked by history, and he commits himself to becoming their historian. His decision to write this book has been made.

His speech at Clifton's funeral is the obituary that sets up his own autobiography. Prior to the speech he meditates more on history and resolves, "although I knew no one man could do much about it, I felt responsible." His speech, almost completely improvised, is characterized by a compulsive repetition of Clifton's name followed by the bare facts of his life: "He was standing and he fell. He fell and he kneeled. He kneeled and he bled. He bled and he died." He describes Clifton as a version of "the same old story," yet he succeeds in restoring his individualism, and his perspective shifts decidedly away from the Brotherhood that claims that individuals do not matter: "I saw not a crowd but the faces of individual men and women."

THE FINAL PLUNGE

The narrator is able to see the Brotherhood for the dehumanizing organization it is, and his awareness of its nature sends him scrambling for a new identity. He refuses to follow Ras, who has renamed himself "Ras the Destroyer" as he leads the people of Harlem into a full-scale riot over the injustice of Clifton's death. The narrator is mistaken for a man named Rinehart, a protean, streetwise numbers runner. The narrator dresses the part when he realizes that being Rinehart can work to his advantage, yet he is bothered by the easy loss of himself: "If dark glasses and a white hat could blot out my identity so quickly, who actually was who?" He suffers an existential crisis: "Well, I *was* and yet I was invisible, that was the fundamental contradiction." Invisibility is "frightening" because it puts him on a level with Clifton: forgotten, unimportant, essentially dead from history's viewpoint.

Although many people mistake him for Rinehart, the narrator returns to his own fragile identity. A drunken woman from the Brotherhood tries to elicit forceful sex from him, and when she passes out he writes, "Sybil, you were raped by Santa Claus surprise" on her belly, but he erases it when he realizes "such games were for Rinehart, not me." He knows who he is not—Rinehart, or a member of the Brotherhood, or Bledsoe's heir apparent, or Ras—but he is still in the process of discovering who he is. That discovery can only take place outside of society's contradictory forces, especially when those forces turn violent as they do in the Harlem riot that concludes the body of the book. The streets of Harlem become a massive re-creation of the Battle Royal, where the only choices are "either run or get knocked down." The instinctive fight or flight response sends the narrator running and eventually dropping into the safety of a hole. He is different from Clifton, who died fighting, yet he has also plunged outside of history. He stops running, and thus ends the prophecy from his grandfather's dream that connects him to the control of others:

> Knowing now who I was and where I was and knowing too that I had no longer to run for or from the Jacks and the Emersons and the Bledsoes and Nortons, but only from their confusion, impatience, and refusal to recognize the beautiful absurdity of their American identity and mine.

He is finally prepared for the self-knowledge that he has sought throughout the book, a knowledge he can only discover when he is profoundly alone, reflecting on his culture like a modern Thoreau.

Few have questioned the brilliance and importance of *Invisible Man,* but the narrator's exile at the end of the book caused some controversy when it was interpreted as cowardice by radical black activists in the 1960s. Larry Neal summarized these responses when he called *Invisible Man* "a profound piece of writing but the kind of novel which, nonetheless, has little bearing on the world as the 'New Breed' sees it. . . . We know who we are, and we are not invisible." These readers were apparently more sympathetic with Ras than with the narrator, who suffers paralysis: "Fully awake now, I simply lay there as though paralyzed. I could think of nothing else to do." This admission might not have suited the political ambitions of black revolutionaries, but the word "awake" is important here and throughout the novel. What has been awakened in the narrator is his consciousness of his humanity, which he sees as more fundamental than commitment to political activism. Though invisible, he is a man, not a robot, a zombie, "a spook like those who haunted Edgar Allan Poe; nor . . . one of your Hollywood movie ectoplasms."

Moreover, he is a man with a voice, something that his critics overlook when they interpret his time in the hole as inactivity. Through his narrative he has gained the power to name or refuse to name himself; as he says in the epilogue, "I have also been called one thing and then another while no one really wished to hear what I called myself." He asks, "Being invisible and without substance, a disembodied voice, as it were, what else could I do?" To suggest that he should fight, or organize, or burn down a city is to overlook the whole novel in which he actually witnesses how those solutions hinder his humanity. Although it is difficult to imagine what he might do when he makes good on his promise to emerge from his hole, it is clear that speaking and writing are his blues, and through them he becomes visible.

The grand irony in terms of Ellison's life is that *Invisible Man* dug a hole for its author, who did not manage to publish another novel during his lifetime. Ellison's efforts were dispersed among a number of public roles as he served on a number of foundations, taught and lectured at prestigious academic institutions, and published essays. The public waited eagerly for over four decades as Ellison churned out material that would become the follow-up novel, published posthumously as *Juneteenth* (1999), which received tepid reviews. Although Ellison was set back by a 1967 fire that destroyed much of the work in progress, his writer's block was probably due to the extraordinary power of his first novel. F. Scott Fitzgerald's observation that there are "no second acts in American lives" was never truer than in Ellison's case. Yet *Invisible Man* reads more like a complete oeuvre than a first act. All of the energy and power poured into it might have exhausted the author, but the result is a book that transformed American literature more dramatically than a lifetime of lesser works could have.

Few twentieth-century American novels are read and studied more frequently than *Invisible Man,* which Robert Bone, in his survey *The Negro Novel in America* (1958), proclaimed "by far the best novel yet written by an American Negro." The novel continues to fascinate and reward readers for a number of reasons. First, it was a breakthrough work of African American literature in that it merged the artistic experimentation of the Harlem Renaissance with the protest literature of the 1930s and 1940s. Second, it called attention to the motif of invisibility that has been a cornerstone of African American literature and thought throughout the twentieth century. Third, it took stock of the great American literature of the nineteenth and early twentieth centuries while placing it in a modern context. The narrator's maturity parallels the nation's maturity, in a sense, and the unsettling application of Emersonian thought to the terrifying reality of twentieth-century life is what fuels the beauty and richness of the novel. The appeal of *Invisible Man* is ultimately both historical and literary, though, and the novel's greatest achievement is that it renewed the power of printed fiction in an era when most Americans had given up on believing in literature or anything else. Upon accepting the National Book Award for *Invisible Man,* Ellison said, "there must be possible a fiction which, leaving sociology to the scientists, can arrive at the truth about the human condition, here and now, with all the bright magic of a fairy tale." In terms of truth and magic, Ellison's novel has few rivals.

Select Bibliography

EDITION

Invisible Man. New York: Random House, 1952. (This essay cites the Vintage Books edition, 1989.)

OTHER WORKS BY ELLISON

Shadow and Act. New York: Random House, 1964.

"Flying Home" and Other Stories. Edited by John F. Callahan. New York: Random House, 1996.

Juneteenth: A Novel. Edited by John F. Callahan. New York: Random House, 1999.

SECONDARY WORKS

Benston, Kimberly W. "I Yam What I Am: The Topos of (Un)naming in Afro-American Literature." In *The Signifying Monkey: A Theory of Afro-American Literary Criticism.* Edited by Henry Louis Gates Jr. New York: Oxford University Press, 1988. Pp. 151–172.

———, ed. *Speaking for You: The Vision of Ralph Ellison.* Washington, D.C.: Howard University Press, 1987.

Blake, Susan. "Ritual and Rationalization: Black Folklore in the Works of Ralph Ellison." *PMLA* 94, no. 1 (1979): 121–125.

Bloom, Harold, ed. *Ralph Ellison.* New York: Chelsea House, 1986.

Bone, Robert. *The Negro Novel in America.* New Haven, Conn.: Yale University Press, 1958.

Busby, Mark. *Ralph Ellison.* Boston: Twayne, 1991.

Butler, Robert J., ed. *The Critical Response to Ralph Ellison.* Westport, Conn.: Greenwood, 2000.

Callahan, John F. "Chaos, Complexity, and Possibility: The Historical Frequencies of Ralph Waldo Ellison." *Black American Literature Forum* 11, no. 4 (winter 1977): 130–138.

———. "'Riffing' and Paradigm-Building: The Anomaly of Tradition and Innovation in *Invisible Man* and *The Structure of Scientific Revolutions.*" *Callaloo* 10, no. 1 (1987): 91–102.

———. *In the African-American Grain: Call-and-Response in Twentieth-Century Black Fiction.* 2d ed. Middletown, Conn.: Wesleyan University Press, 1988.

———. "Frequencies of Memory: A Eulogy for Ralph Waldo Ellison." *Callaloo* 18, no. 2 (1995): 298–320.

Curtin, Maureen F. "Materializing Invisibility as X-Ray Technology: Skin Matters in Ralph Ellison's *Invisible Man.*" *LIT: Literature Interpretation Theory* 9, no. 4 (1999): 281–311.

Dickstein, Morris. "Ralph Ellison, Race, and American Culture." *Raritan* 18, no. 3 (1999): 30–50.

Fabre, Michel. "The Narrator/Narratee Relationship in *Invisible Man.*" *Callaloo* 8, no. 3 (1985): 535–543.

Gates, Henry Louis, Jr. *The Signifying Monkey: A Theory of Afro-American Literary Criticism.* New York: Oxford University Press, 1988.

———, ed. *Black Literature and Literary Theory.* New York and London: Methuen, 1984.

Gottesman, Ronald, comp. *The Merrill Studies in* Invisible Man. Columbus, Ohio: Charles E. Merrill, 1971.

Graham, Maryemma, and Amritjit Singh. *Conversations with Ralph Ellison.* Jackson: University Press of Mississippi, 1995.

Hersey, John, ed. *Ralph Ellison: A Collection of Critical Essays.* Englewood Cliffs, N.J.: Prentice Hall, 1974.

Jackson, Lawrence. *Ralph Ellison: Emergence of Genius.* New York: Wiley, 2002.

Lee, Kun Jong. "Ellison's *Invisible Man:* Emersonianisms Revised." *PMLA* 107, no. 2 (1992): 331–344.

McSweeney, Kerry. Invisible Man: *Race and Identity.* Boston: Twayne, 1988.

Marvin, Thomas F. "Children of Legba: Musicians at the Crossroads in Ralph Ellison's *Invisible Man.*" *American Literature* 68, no. 3 (1996): 587–608.

Nadel, Alan. *Invisible Criticism: Ralph Ellison and the American Canon.* Iowa City: University of Iowa Press, 1988.

Napier, Winston. *African American Literary Theory.* New York: New York University Press, 2000.

Neal, Larry. "And Shine Swan On." In *African American Literary Theory.* Edited by Winston Napier. New York: New York University Press, 2000. Pp. 69–80.

O'Meally, Robert G. *The Craft of Ralph Ellison.* Cambridge, Mass.: Harvard University Press, 1980.

———, ed. *New Essays on* Invisible Man. Cambridge, U.K.: Cambridge University Press, 1988.

Parr, Susan Resneck, and Pancho Savery, eds. *Approaches to Teaching Ellison's* Invisible Man. New York: Modern Language Association, 1989.

Porter, Horace A. *Jazz Country: Ralph Ellison in America.* Iowa City: University of Iowa Press, 2001.

Reilly, John M., ed. *Twentieth-Century Interpretations of* Invisible Man. Englewood Cliffs, N.J.: Prentice Hall, 1970.

Schor, Edith. *Visible Ellison: A Study of Ralph Ellison's Fiction.* Westport, Conn.: Greenwood, 1993.

Slatoff, Walter. "Making *Invisible Man* Matter." In *Approaches to Teaching Ellison's* Invisible Man. Edited by Susan Resneck Parr and Pancho Savery. New York: Modern Language Association, 1989. Pp. 31–36.

Stepto, Robert B. *From behind the Veil: A Study of Afro-American Narrative.* 2d ed. Urbana: University of Illinois Press, 1991.

Sundquist, Eric J., ed. *Cultural Contexts for Ralph Ellison's* Invisible Man. Boston: Bedford, 1995.

Trimmer, Joseph F. *A Casebook on Ralph Ellison's* Invisible Man. New York: Crowell, 1972.

Watts, Jerry Gafio. *Heroism and the Black Intellectual: Ralph Ellison, Politics, and Afro-American Intellectual Life.* Chapel Hill: University of North Carolina Press, 1994.

Wolfe, Jesse. "'Ambivalent Man': Ellison's Rejection of Communism." *African American Review* 34, no. 4 (2000): 621–637.

Robert Lowell's Life Studies

PETER FILKINS

THE PUBLICATION OF Robert Lowell's *Life Studies* in 1959 marks the beginning of contemporary American poetry. Few books can claim to be a watershed event in the development of how poetry is written, but along with T. S. Eliot's *The Waste Land,* published in 1922, *Life Studies* is just such a volume. Within it, Lowell's forging of what would come to be known as the confessional mode granted poets the authority to mine their personal lives to an extent never seen before. *Life Studies* represents a breakthrough not only in how poems were written but also in what poets and readers came to think of as the stuff of poetry. Before it, poets influenced by Eliot wrote dense, complex works riddled with symbolic meaning. Afterward, poetry sprang from quotidian biography, tone having replaced symbol as poetry's central means of expression.

Revolutions never occur in a complete vacuum, and many writers and works prepared the way for Lowell's achievement. As early modernists, Eliot and Ezra Pound reshaped poetry to include serious social and political commentary, as well as to revivify and make new the language available to them. From there William Carlos Williams went on to tap the rhythms of colloquial American speech in order to formulate a free verse structured by cadence and breath rather than the artifice of meter and rhyme. Robert Frost, however, shaped a formal poetry that sprang from the naturalness of conversation, demonstrating as well that art could be found in the commonalities of rural life. In addition, Beat poets such as Allen Ginsberg, Gregory Corso, and Charles Olson pushed the formal parameters of verse while also arguing for a greater engagement with history and politics. W. D. Snodgrass, a student of Lowell's at the University of Iowa, also discovered a way to write directly about deep personal pain at the very same time as his more famous teacher. *Heart's Needle,* Snodgrass' searing account of his divorce and the sadness of being separated from his daughter, was published the same year as *Life Studies* and was even thought by some to be the stronger book at the time.

Lowell, however, was the lightning rod through which the energies of all these separate writers came to pass, and it was *Life Studies* that split the contemporary poetic idiom wide open with a single strike. Part of the reason why lies in his prominence as a poet who had gained early fame with his 1946 volume, *Lord Weary's*

Castle, which garnered Lowell the Pulitzer Prize at age thirty and was itself an example of the clotted, symbol-ridden verse he would come to reject. Lowell's pedigree as a member of a famed Boston family that traced its ancestry back to the Mayflower also had an effect. In *Life Studies* he set out to dissect his family's Brahmin noblesse, revealing a downward spiral matched only by what Lowell saw as the corruption and despair of America in the 1950s. Lowell was also simply the right poet working at the right time. Schooled in the hermeneutics of New Criticism (his mentors included Allen Tate, John Crowe Ransom, and Cleanth Brooks); morally courageous (in 1943 he accepted a jail sentence for violating the Selective Service Act in protest of the American bombing of civilian targets in World War II); possessed of a gift for both formal intricacy and authoritative, nuanced speech; and a victim of a manic-depressive condition that both altered his perception of reality and led to deep suffering—Lowell's background, education, experience, talent, and personality were equally matched by his readiness to forge a style in which, as Williams said in a letter to him, "There is no lying permitted to a man who writes that way" (quoted in Steven Gould Axelrod's *Robert Lowell: Life and Art,* 1978).

Life Studies is as much a record of the poet's journey to a new open style as it is the earliest example of it. Within the volume, a reader can follow a mini-progression from the more formal metrics of Lowell's earlier work, seen in the four poems that open the book, to the eventual free verse metrics used to explore family history and his own haunted self at the book's end. In this way the book's arrangement lays out a set of formal challenges, resolving each of them as it proceeds. The content of the poems also makes clear that *Life Studies* is a very great book that survived a very troubled author. The tension between Lowell's formal experimentation and his own relentless self-examination is key to the book's artistry, as well as a source of the debate long forwarded about the merits of Lowell's

CHRONOLOGY

1917	Robert Traill Spence Lowell Jr. is born March 1 in Boston, the son of Robert Traill Spence Lowell and Charlotte Winslow Lowell.
1930–1935	Attends St. Mark's School, where he studies with the poet Richard Eberhart and meets Frank Parker. Is nicknamed "Cal," for Caligula, which stays with him throughout his life.
1935–1937	Attends Harvard University.
1937	Spends spring and summer in Tennessee with Allen Tate and Caroline Gordon. Against his parents' wishes, transfers to Kenyon College.
1937–1940	Studies at Kenyon with John Crowe Ransom. Graduates summa cum laude in Classics.
1940	Converts to Roman Catholicism. Marries Jean Stafford on April 2.
1940–1941	Teaches at Kenyon. Studies with Robert Penn Warren and Cleanth Brooks at Louisiana State University.
1942–1943	Lives with Allen Tate and Caroline Gordon while working on *Land of Unlikeness.*
1943	Writes Franklin Roosevelt and refuses induction into armed service as protest against bombing of civilians in Dresden. Is sentenced to a year and a day in jail. Serves five months in federal prison in Danbury, Connecticut, and West Street Jail in New York City, before being paroled.
1944	*Land of Unlikeness.*
1946	Publishes *Lord Weary's Castle,* which wins wide critical acclaim and the Pulitzer Prize.
1947	Wins American Academy–National Institute of Arts and Letters grant and a Guggenheim Fellowship.
1947–1948	Serves as poetry consultant to the Library of Congress.
1948	Divorces Stafford.
1949	In March, Lowell is institutionalized for a nervous breakdown. Returns to

	New York. Marries Elizabeth Hardwick on July 28.
1950	*Poems 1938–1949.* His father dies.
1950–1953	Lives and travels in Europe.
1951	Publishes *The Mills of the Kavanaughs.* Wins Harriet Monroe Poetry Award.
1953	Teaches with John Berryman at University of Iowa, where W. D. Snodgrass is one of his students.
1954	Mother dies. Moves to Boston. Begins correspondence with William Carlos Williams.
1955–1960	Teaches at Boston University, where his students include Sylvia Plath, Anne Sexton, and George Starbuck.
1957	A daughter, Harriet Winslow Lowell, is born.
1959	*Life Studies.* Wins the National Book Award and shares the Guiness Poetry Award with W. H. Auden and Edith Sitwell.
1960	Moves to New York, where he and Hardwick will live for the next ten years.
1961	Publishes *Imitations,* a book of translations, and a translation of Racine's *Phaedra.* Wins Bollingen Prize for Translation and the Harriet Monroe Poetry Award.
1963	Given a lifelong teaching appointment at Harvard.
1964	Publishes *For the Union Dead* and *The Old Glory,* a trilogy of plays. Wins Obie Award for best play and Ford Foundation grant for drama.
1965	Publically declines President Lyndon Johnson's invitation to the White House Festival of the Arts in protest against the Vietnam War.
1967	Publishes *Near the Ocean.* Participates in antiwar march on the Pentagon.
1969	Publishes *Notebook 1967–68* and *Prometheus Bound.*
1970	Publishes *Notebook.* Appointed Visiting Fellow at All Souls College, Oxford.
1970–1976	Residence in England, where he teaches at Essex University in 1970–1972.
1971	A son, Robert Sheridan Lowell, is born to Lowell and the novelist Caroline Blackwood.
1972	Divorces Hardwick and marries Blackwood in October.
1973	Publishes *The Dolphin, For Lizzie and Harriet,* and *History* all on the same day. *The Dolphin* wins the Pulitzer Prize.
1976	*Selected Poems.*
1977	Publishes *Day by Day,* which wins the National Book Critics Circle Award. Awarded the American Academy and Institute of Arts and Letters National Medal for Literature. Returns to residence in United States without Blackwood and spends summer with Hardwick in Maine. Dies of heart failure in a New York taxi cab upon return from England on September 12.

career. Though it gained instant recognition and a National Book Award, *Life Studies* was also greeted with a high degree of skepticism by critics who found the poet's turn to free verse a falling off from his earlier metrical work, and his inclusion of such personal material a self-indulgence. Allen Tate, Lowell's early mentor, went so far as to advise against publication. And John Bayley in "Robert Lowell: The Poetry of Cancellation" would later say, "If there *is* a moving quality in these poems—and in a muffled way there can be—it is that of a drama without an audience, even that of the poet himself. We have the intimation of a human life in a state of shock, remembering, like Wordsworth's Old Man, 'the importance of his theme'—or at least its human potentiality—'but feeling it no longer.'"

Lowell's appeal was and is not universal, but there can be little question of the need to come to terms with his achievement. One of the problems in doing this has always been the tendency of readers to treat the poems either as an unvarnished biography or to see the book's style as a revolutionary break with the past aimed at destroying all links with the tradition that preceded him. This latter tendency leads to a dismissal of Lowell's earlier work as too rhetorical, or it generates consternation about the poet's later return to more formal structures in books such as *Near the Ocean* (1967) and *History* (1973). Meanwhile, emphasis on biographical content equates all confessional poetry as being the same without any attempt to discern stylistic differences between poets such as Sylvia Plath, Anne Sexton, Randall Jarrell, and John Berryman. In this guise, one is either a fan of this "type" poetry or one is not, despite the intricacies of each poet's individual expression.

The sturdiness and longevity of *Life Studies* and the ability of individual poems to still speak to us would argue against a simplistic appreciation of the book as biography in verse or a confessional *ur*-text. The "shock" of the material Lowell chose to write on has long since worn off, and with time Lowell's style has come to seem more engaged with the tradition than opposed to it. Poems such as "A Mad Negro Soldier Confined at Munich," "To Delmore Schwartz," "My Last Afternoon with Uncle Devereux Winslow," "Waking in the Blue," "Memories of West Street and Lepke," and the masterful "Skunk Hour" remain as fresh and vital as they did on first appearance. Add to this the oddity of Lowell's inclusion of the autobiographical prose section titled "91 Revere Street" and how over the years it has come to seem the wellspring of the book's genius, and it becomes clear that *Life Studies* is not just a seismic event along the continuum of American poetry but rather a complex work of art whose meaning has evolved and changed with time.

LIFE AS LANDSCAPE

The writing of the poems that eventually would form *Life Studies* must have provided Lowell with a great deal of solace, if not even therapeutic relief. However, it is not the pain with which the poet grapples that sustains the book's greatness but rather its pattern. To say this does not mean that Lowell sat down with a conscious pattern to work out as he proceeded, or even to what extent he himself was aware of the many echos and repetitions that help weave together what at first seems a rather loose and uneven collection. In fact, the prose section that Lowell eventually chose to include in the book (though it was left out of the first British edition) was clearly written as an act of therapy during Lowell's recovery from a severe breakdown in 1954, and was not something the poet immediately planned to publish. This in itself blurs the line between poetry as a means of survival versus the work of a conscious artist rendering the experience that he has survived.

Nonetheless, Lowell clearly had the idea of making certain assertions through the arrangement of the poems. It is no accident that the volume begins with "Beyond the Alps," a poem that leaves behind the Rome of Lowell's early Catholicism, as well as the overheated religious imagery of his earlier work. It is also clear that Lowell intended his progression to end with the bruising awareness gained through the more confessional poems of Part Four, titled "Life Studies." However, one must be careful not to reduce such a progression to a step-by-step process either of recovery or dissolution. "Skunk Hour," the book's culminating poem in both thematic and stylistic terms, was in fact the first of the confessional poems that Lowell completed. Similarly, "91 Revere Street" is not the only piece of autobiographical prose Lowell worked on during his therapy, but it is the most polished of the several that he wrote. Though at the time the writing of it may have served a therapeutic function, Lowell's later inclusion and positioning of it in the book's overall sequence remains an artistic choice rather than a psychological or biographical necessity.

As many critics have observed, the organization of *Life Studies* is the tightest and most intricate of all of Lowell's books. Three of the book's four sections of poetry (if Part Four is counted as two sections, as Lowell divided it) contain only four poems each. By far the book's longest section, "91 Revere Street," takes up more than one-third of the finished collection, its prose appearing in smaller type than that with which the poems are printed. Without it, the book would run to roughly forty-five pages, just over half the length of the slimmest of volumes normally published. Critics, however, have paid little attention to the prose section (Jerome Mazzoro, for instance, devotes only one paragraph to it in his seminal study), choosing for the most part to see it simply as background material that prepares the way for the confessional breakthrough of Part Four. In addition, with sections of four poems each bracketing it, clearly a great deal of pressure is brought to bear on both the prose memoir and the first eight poems offered. By the end of Part Three one is beyond halfway through the entire book. With Part Four carrying the title "Life Studies," it would almost seem that, indeed, the first three sections can be read together as one kind of book in its own right, whereas the final section is another.

Such a unique, if not odd, arrangement argues that Lowell is making more specific artistic choices than would be required by an account of the departure from his early style or the preparation for the psychological and stylistic breakthrough in the later confessional mode. Instead, what the first three sections of *Life Studies* illustrate is the arduous process of working through one kind of expression toward another, and that such a turn demands not just a change in poetic style but also a reshaping of the poet's entire approach to life and the experience of it as manifested through an artistic crisis. In this manner, each of the first three sections works as a failed attempt to solve Lowell's crisis, as well as a demonstration of a different facet of it. However, like so many of the cowed, helpless, or incarcerated figures of his poems, the poet seemingly can do nothing but put one foot in front of the other, his own "subnormal boot-/black heart . . . pulsing to its ant-egg dole" of solid new ground as he claws his way through the mire of his own remaking.

The conventional wisdom is that Part One depicts Lowell turning his back on his desire for religious and moral justice, only to accept and record the spiritual detritus of a flawed world. As Irvin Ehrenpreis wrote in "The Age of Lowell," this made it possible for Lowell "not only to treat himself as part of history but to treat history as part of himself." Lowell's journey in "Beyond the Alps" is from the religious seat of Rome to the modern secular world of Paris, "our black classic, breaking up / like killer kings on an Etruscan cup." The move from a God-bound idealism to the flux and disappointment of history also means that "Life changed to landscape" for Lowell, a new and troubled dawn breaking within "the blear-eyed ego kicking in my berth" as the train of his poetic and historical journey heads west toward Boston and home. The transition, however, is not a simple one. As Lowell acknowledges:

> . . . Much against my will
> I left the City of God where it belongs.
> There the skirt-mad Mussolini unfurled
> the eagle of Caesar. He was one of us
> only, pure prose. . . .

Admitting that he envies "the conspicuous / waste of our grandparents . . . / while breezing on their trust funds through the world," Lowell longs for an escape that he knows will not be offered him. Submitting himself to the kind of "agonizing reappraisal" that will never trouble the gangster Czar Lepke, depicted in "Memories of West Street and Lepke," Lowell will soon identify himself with the historical tyrant Mussolini, through his own immersion into "pure prose" in "91 Revere Street." His journey "Beyond the Alps" corresponds not only to the religious and political demise he suffers and records, but also the descent into prose, an event that will, for the time being, obliterate Lowell as a poet and complete "the miscarriage of the brain" inspired here by Minerva in order for him to reemerge a new and different poet.

"Beyond the Alps" pitches Lowell onto the plain of his dilemma, but it does not solve it for him. Rather, in the next two poems of Part One, the poet reverts back to both his penchant for dramatic verse and for sweeping political commentary. The first manifests itself in "The Banker's Daughter," a poem that harks back to the wooden monologues of *The Mills of the Kavanaughs* (1951), Lowell's least successful book. "Inauguration Day: January 1953" is a more effective rendition of the moral condemnation found in *Lord Weary's Castle* and the political engagement that Lowell would later turn to in *Near the Ocean* (1967) and *History* (1973). The poem, however, does little to resolve the sense of a self at loose ends with the world around him. While "the Republic summons Ike, / the mausoleum in her heart," the "brutal girlish mood-swings" that plague Marie de Medici in "The Banker's Daughter" evoke Lowell's own volatile attacks, and no amount of political invective could cure that. Instead, Lowell has yet to find a way to "treat history as part of himself." The poem on Dwight Eisenhower's inauguration serves as a reminder that the train set in motion in "Beyond the Alps" has already succumbed to stasis as "Our wheels no longer move."

The last poem of the first section, "A Mad Negro Soldier Confined at Munich," is quite another matter. Possibly based on a fellow patient in a Munich military hospital where Lowell stayed during a breakdown in 1952, as Philip Hobsbaum points out, here there is a much closer identification between the poet and his subject. "We're all Americans," announces the speaker, the confinement and repression of his spirit at the hands of brutal attendants linking to both Lowell and all of America in "the tranquillized *Fifties*" ("Memories of West Street and Lepke"). Though the poem is written in rhyming quatrains, both its conversational tone and varied rhyme patterns suggest an urge to break its own bonds. But Lowell, as if trying to chain down such experience, will not entirely let go. Because of his close identification with the mad Negro, he in essence ends up chaining himself down as well, the animal submission outlined at the poem's end becoming a collective one that includes himself as

> . . . "We file before the clock,
>
> and fancy minnows, slaves of habit, shoot
> like starlight through their air-conditioned bowl.
> It's time for feeding. Each subnormal boot-
> black heart is pulsing to its ant-egg dole"

In expressing the fragility of a mental state he knew all too well, Lowell is left with an impossible choice. On the one hand, if he reverts to his old manner of writing, he chains the very spirit with which he empathizes. On the other hand, any naturalistic expression of such a state dissolves the poem into the lonely, nonsense babbling of the insane that Lowell hints at, but can only imitate when the soldier says cryptically,

> "In Munich the zoo's rubble fumes with cats;
> hoydens with air-guns prowl the Koenigsplatz,
> and pink the pigeons on the mustard spire.
> Who but my girl-friend set the town on fire?"

As a sort of frustrated compromise, the entire poem is set in quotes, unlike the earlier "The Banker's Daughter," which is also spoken as a monologue. This lands the poet in a kind of netherworld between styles, the vibrancy of the mad Negro's voice seeming closer to Lowell's very own, the quotation marks even allowing the poet to step to the front of the stage to talk aloud within his own book. However, those same demarcations, like the residue of meter and rhyme that controls the speaking voice, also mark the mask behind which the poet still hides.

THE RIVERBOTTOM OF PROSE

In *Robert Lowell: Life and Art,* Steven Gould Axelrod observes a link between Lowell's 1953 review of Robert Penn Warren's verse-novel *Brother to Dragons* and the journey traced in "Beyond the Alps":

> Reviewing the book at the same time as he was composing "Beyond the Alps," and apparently thinking in images of the poem, [Lowell] wrote: "Warren . . . has crossed the Alps and, like Napoleon's shoeless army, entered the fat, populated riverbottom of the novel." In *Life Studies,* Lowell likewise intended to stress experience over form, and enter "the fat, populated riverbottom" of life.

Lowell's prose memoir, "91 Revere Street," turned out to be the express train to this destination, though likely not even the poet himself could have predicted the turns it would take or the paradoxical manner in which it would see him through.

Lowell's "91 Revere Street" is more a pool of powerful memories than a polished memoir. As Vereen Bell points out in *Robert Lowell: Nihilist as Hero,* throughout the piece "Lowell frequently forces transitions across the flimsiest of associations, and manages by this device to subvert or call into question thematic unity at the same time that he sustains it." Within this autobiographical fragment, Lowell ranges from the memory of a painting of his great-great-grandfather Major Mordecai Myers, "a Grand Old Man, who impressed strangers with the poise of his old-time manners," to debilitating views of his failed father and domineering mother, to memories of childhood battles and embarrassments at school, and finally to a lengthy account of Commander Billy "Battleship Bilge" Harkness, his father's naval academy roommate and lifelong friend who boozes and bellows his way through Sunday dinners at 91 Revere Street as the nine-year-old Lowell looks on with a mixture of puzzlement and chagrin. Direct linkages between these narrative threads, however, are never made, and Lowell often moves from one to the other without the slightest reference to historical time or sequence.

In one passage, for instance, Lowell recalls his expulsion by "Officer Lever" from the Boston Common after he bloodies the noses of two of his playmates. He then follows the anecdote with an entirely new and seemingly unrelated memory:

> New England winters are long. Sunday mornings are long. Ours were often made tedious by preparations for dinner guests. Mother would start airing at nine. Whenever the air grew so cold that it hurt, she closed the den windows; then we were attacked by sour kitchen odors winding up a clumsily rebuilt dumb-waiter shaft. The windows were again thrown open. We sat in an atmosphere of glacial purity and sacrifice. Our breath puffed whitely. Father and I wore sleeveless cashmere jerseys Mother had bought at Filene's Basement. A do-it-yourself book containing diagrams for the correct carving of roasts lay on the arm of Father's chair. At hand were Big Bill Tilden on tennis, Capablanca on chess, newspaper clippings from Sidney Lenz's bridge column, and a magnificent tome with photographs and some American's nationalist sketch of Sir Thomas Lipton's errors in the Cup Defender races. Father made little progress in these diversions, and yet one of the authors assured him that mastery demanded only willing readers who understood the meaning of English words. Throughout the winter a gray-whiteness glared through the single den window. In the apoplectic brick alley, a fire escape stood out against our sooty plank fence. Father believed that churchgoing was undignified for a naval man; his Sunday mornings were given to useful acts such as lettering his three new galvanized garbage cans: R.T.S. LOWELL–U.S.N.

From here Lowell goes on to the extended account of the ribald and embarrassing Commander Billy Harkness, but no further mention is made of his previous expulsion from the Common, or before that the memory of the embarrassment he feels for Elie Norton, a classmate who loses control of her bladder and runs weeping from the third grade. Instead, the reader is left to extract and connect the thematic threads. Lowell's point is then revealed when the boy identifies more strongly with the embarrassed

Elie in all her natural helplessness, himself committing an open act of rebellion in the public sphere of the Common almost in anticipation of his father's pathetic study of how to carve a roast or those Sunday mornings spent lettering his garbage cans. In addition, those garbage cans will reverberate later in "Memories of West Street and Lepke,"

> where even the man
> scavenging filth in the back alley trash cans,
> has two children, a beach wagon, a helpmate,
> and is a "young Republican"

or in "Skunk Hour" where the untamed mother skunk "swills the garbage pail / . . . / and will not scare."

Such a passage establishes the themes of failure and rebellion that haunt the biography of Lowell and also provides images and metaphors that resonate in later poems. In *Robert Lowell: The First Twenty Years,* Hugh Staples observes Lowell's emphasis on places such as Revere Street or Dunbarton or Beverly Farms, and his "skillful use of physical detail as a means of illuminating character." As Vereen Bell goes on to note in his insightful discussion of "91 Revere Street" quoted earlier, "Such details float at random in the memoir, this way and that, but then unpredictably make contact with one another and radiate implication, creating a progressively enriched but complex thematic context." A large part of why such details become so numinous is their own detachment from narrated experience, for much of "91 Revere Street" depicts an experience of memory rather than the memory of an experience. By acknowledging that "New England winters were long," Lowell establishes an air of perpetuation, as if all winters were alike, or that he and his father wore "sleeveless cashmere jerseys" *every* Sunday, or that the Commander's garbage cans required re-lettering each and every week. This then makes such details iconic and menacing while their return in the later poems both allows them further resonance and provides Lowell with the opportunity to gain control and transform them.

Lowell's submission of his life and art to the subtle rigor of "pure prose" is the regenerative catalyst for both Lowell as a writer and *Life Studies* as a sequential progression. For the most part critics have seen the memoir as a "backdrop" to the later poems. However, the demands of prose as an art form were of great concern to Lowell. During a 1957 West Coast reading tour he began adding syllables to lines as he read them aloud in order to make them easier to speak, despite the metrical violations that would ensue. In his 1961 *Paris Review* interview with Frederick Seidel, republished in Lowell's *Collected Prose,* Lowell would go on to worry the relation between poetry and prose to a great extent, at one point admitting:

> Prose is in many ways better off than poetry. It's quite hard to think of a young poet who has the vitality, say, of Salinger or Saul Bellow. Yet prose tends to be very diffuse. The novel is really a much more difficult form than it seems; few people have the wind to write anything that long. Even a short story demands almost poetic perfection. Yet on the whole prose is less cut off from life than poetry is.

Concerned about "this business of direct experience" and wanting to accomplish "the virtue of a photograph but all the finish of art," Lowell envies prose writers, as well as the ability of Frost and his

> sense of rhythm and words and composition, and getting into his lines language that is very much like the language he speaks—which is also a work of art, much better than other people's ordinary speech and yet natural to him; *he has that continuity with his ordinary self and his poetic self* [emphasis added]—he's made what with anyone else would be just flat. A very good prose writer can do this and make something of it. . . . When it comes to verse the form is so hard that all of that gets drained out.

"91 Revere Street" was Lowell's means of inventing a continuity between his "ordinary

argue for the opposite, for especially in the first section, Lowell offers a study of a family's decline matched only by William Faulkner for the corruption and despair depicted. Beginning with three poems on his grandparents, Lowell laments the loss of their Edwardian stability and charm at the same time that he sees such decline as both natural and inevitable. "My Last Afternoon with Uncle Devereux," perhaps the strongest of the family poems, is a snapshot of Lowell at five as he becomes aware of the impending death of his uncle Devereux from Hodgkin's disease at age twenty-nine. The pressure and tragedy of becoming an adult are heightened for the young child when, despite the certain loss of his son, Grandfather Winslow admonishes Devereux for extravagantly forsaking his responsibilities:

> My Uncle was dying at twenty-nine.
> "You are behaving like children,"
> said my Grandfather,
> when my Uncle and Aunt left their three baby
> daughters,
> and sailed for Europe on a last honeymoon . . .
> I cowered in terror.
> I wasn't a child at all—
> unseen and all-seeing, I was Agrippina
> in the Golden House of Nero. . . .

Throughout the poem Lowell grants the reader a view into the submerged consciousness of himself as a child. In an eery dreamlike manner he observes that "I picked with a clean finger nail at the blue anchor / on my sailor blouse washed white as a spinnaker" without ever making clear the significance or precise meaning of the image, just as elsewhere he seems to sit both inside and outside his grandfather's porch, noting that

> One of my hands was cool on a pile
> of black earth, the other warm
> on a pile of lime. . . .

But lest one be deceived into thinking that Lowell is detailing precise and accurate memories of Lowell as a child, Steven Gould Axelrod notes that "the authorial awareness includes both the consciousness of the remembered child and that of the remembering adult poet." Hence Lowell refers to himself as Agrippina, and even makes the bald admission that "I wasn't a child at all." Even the reference to Devereux sailing to Europe echoes back to the voyage that marks the death of Lowell's former poetic self recorded in "Beyond the Alps." As both vehicle and voice of the poem, Lowell is indeed "Unseen and all-seeing" as any artist must be.

A symmetry in the sequence of the family poems again suggests a certain symbolism. The three poems on his grandparents are followed by three poems on his father, then three on his mother, and finally two on himself as an adult. Richard Fein observes the wonderful progression from grandparents to parents to Lowell as adult son, husband, and father in the section, which is marked by a countertension of the adult poet still trapped in the wounded consciousness of the child. In addition, the movement from three sets of three to the final grouping of two would also suggest a gradual reduction in the family through death, whereas the solitary speaker of "Skunk Hour" in the second section posits Lowell's existence as a man at last freed from his family, but also cut adrift and alone.

One effect of such careful handling is that, despite the steely eyed view the poems take of Lowell's family, there is also a great amount of tenderness within them. One needs only to compare the earlier catalog from "91 Revere Street" of Commander Lowell's books on tennis and carving, and the pathetic image of his lettered garbage cans, to the catalog of objects Lowell lists in "Father's Bedroom":

> blue threads as thin
> as pen-writing on the bedspread,
> blue dots on the curtains,
> a blue kimono,
> Chinese sandals with blue plush straps.
> The broad-planked floor
> had a sandpapered neatness.

The clear glass bed-lamp
with a white doily shade
was still raised a few
inches by resting on volume two
of Lafcadio Hearn's
Glimpses of unfamiliar Japan.
Its warped olive cover
was punished like a rhinoceros hide.
In the flyleaf:
"Robbie from Mother."
Years later in the same hand:
"This book has had hard usage
on the Yangtze River, China.
It was left under an open
porthole in a storm."

Gone is the pained embarrassment of the earlier memoir. Instead the poem evokes a feeling of a life battered down and yet ennobled somewhat by the storm of experience. The repeated mention of "blue" restores the father to his naval career and potential heroism, just as the "sandpapered neatness" of the floor hints at military discipline and its corresponding dignity. Lowell's description of the "blue threads as thin / as pen-writing" also acknowledges a paternal presence engendering his own work, just as the final identification of his father with a book mirrors the establishment of Lowell's identity through his own volume. Both father and son, and *Life Studies* as well, have seen "hard usage" while "left under an open / porthole in a storm." It is as if, in accomplishing an art that would allow him to be himself, Lowell can at last accept and acknowledge the presences from which both he and his work have sprung. His may be a series of relentless, uncompromising "studies" of their pitiful shortcomings, but first and last they represent "life," without which there would be no art at all.

Steven Gould Axelrod also points out a crucial lapse in the chronology suggested by the order of the poems in Part Four, a lapse that underscores the manipulation of reality that is part of the so-called confessional mode. Though the last two poems of the first section of Part Four "portray Lowell's mental decline, institutionalization, and partial recovery, [they] are clearly intended to take place *after* the harrowing psychotic episode in section two." In other words, when Lowell arrives "Home After Three Months Away" at the end of the first section, he may declare, "I keep no rank nor station. / Cured, I am frizzled, stale and small," but such a state is a recovery from the "dark night" of "Skunk Hour," where Lowell admits, "I myself am hell; / nobody's here—." Conversely, the fact that Lowell arrives at a state of recovery, however tentative, at the end of the first section would also imply that he should be in greater balance in the last section. On the surface, this would seem paradoxical, given the implied breakdown not only in "Skunk Hour" but also in "Man and Wife" and "'To Speak of the Woe That Is in Marriage.'" Even Lepke concentrating

on the electric chair—
hanging like an oasis in his air
of lost connections. . . .

would seem to suggest that Lowell ends the book on the brink of extinction. However, the mad Lowell depicted in the second section is rendered by a Lowell who is rested and restored to sanity at the end of the first. Even the return of a four-poem sequence in this last section would argue the same, for once again the same concerns of social history are combined with personal anguish orchestrated in the quartet of poems in both Parts One and Three.

Lowell's "Life Studies," then, are just that: studies of life rendered as artful depictions, their seemingly sketchy nature revealing more permanent and careful organization only later. In some ways the reader is no closer to Lowell than to any other poet, but rather is in the hands of a poet more skillful at manipulating personal material to powerful effect. In fact, the breakthrough Lowell made was to show how much of the quotidian self could be used for art, and how it could be done with intricacy, complexity, irony, and wit. As Marjorie Perloff perceptively concludes in *The Poetic Art of Robert Lowell:*

> In *Life Studies,* . . . Lowell is trying to fuse the romantic mode, which projects the poet's "I" in the act of self-discovery, and the Tolstoyan or Chekhovian mode, usually called realism. I would posit that it is his superb manipulation of the realistic convention, rather than the titillating confessional content, that is responsible for the so-called breakthrough of *Life Studies* and that distinguishes Lowell's confessional poetry from the work of his less accomplished disciples.

Perloff's evaluation points to why "Skunk Hour" is able so powerfully to depict the nadir of Lowell's mental anguish and at the same time represent the apex of his new style. Although the sufferings of the man were no doubt very great, it is the poet who discovered the means to make them cohere, echoing both St. John of the Cross and John Milton as he arrives at the most private of monologues:

> One dark night,
> my Tudor Ford climbed the hill's skull;
> I watched for love-cars. Lights turned down,
> they lay together, hull to hull,
> where the graveyard shelves on the town. . . .
> My mind's not right.
>
> A car radio bleats,
> "Love, O careless Love. . . ." I hear
> my ill-spirit sob in each blood cell,
> as if my hand were at its throat. . . .
> I myself am hell;
> nobody's here—

Anchoring the book as a whole, the voice of this poem is a conglomerate of all those that have come before it. The mind that is "not right" is a collective one; the inept father, domineering mother, poignant grandfather and uncle, suffering artist, mad soldier, corrupt state, and fallen Church are all rolled into a single representative psyche one is inclined to name "Robert Lowell." Thus, "nobody's here" might also be taken more literally, whereas "I myself am hell," lifted from Milton's Lucifer, assures readers that behind the scenes a finely tuned literary mind is working the ropes. Meanwhile, the mother skunk and her kittens at the end of the poem attest to something natural and more permanently real, a condition that the poem aspires to as a work of art. The rude matriarch's stubborn survival counters the exhausted suicidal figure when

> She jabs her wedge-head in a cup
> of sour cream, drops her ostrich tail,
> and will not scare.

Lowell, however, has also survived to note: "I stand on top / of our back steps and breathe the rich air." The subtle mention of that collective "our" acknowledges that the poet has been restored to a viable social relation through, and because of, the uncompromising nature of his art.

IMPORTANCE AND INFLUENCE

Perhaps the greatest influence any work can have is the permission it grants to those coming after it to work in a new way. *Life Studies* did this more than any other book of poetry from the second half of the twentieth century. Though Sylvia Plath's *Ariel* certainly opened poetry to a wider array of women, it too owes a tremendous debt to Lowell. After him, it became possible, even expected, for poets to explore and exploit the hidden mysteries of their own personalities, and readers came to understand that a poem could consist simply of the tonal nuance with which an object or setting was described. In addition, as Mark Rudman points out, the family entered American poetry to a degree never seen before, something that has distinguished it in nature from other poetries of the world since. The techniques Lowell forged in *Life Studies* have also been used by poets who hold little in common with Lowell's life or voice. Plain-style poets such as Stephen Dunn or Carl Dennis, who would shy away from heightened rhetoric or such extreme states of mind, are beholden to Lowell for the authority granted them to write about their direct personal experience and have it matter. James Merrill also turned from obtuse convolution to an elegant yet direct handling of his own family history and personal life in a way that is traceable to the influence of Lowell.

But Lowell himself did not rest on his laurels or remain stuck in the confessional mode. In many ways he returned to the more public voice of *Lord Weary's Castle,* but only by filtering his work through the prose cadence he discovered in *Life Studies.* His next book, *For the Union Dead,* which appeared in 1964, continued his personal exploration, but on a more public stage. Though he says in "Eye and Tooth" that "Everyone's tired of my turmoil," the volume looks outward toward the world and its ruin in poems such as "The Mouth of the Hudson," "Fall 1961," "The Public Garden," "July in Washington," and the title piece, perhaps the best poem Lowell ever wrote. In the early 1960s, "For the Union Dead" was even placed as the last poem in a revised edition of *Life Studies,* a symbol of the more public turn Lowell's work would later take in *Near the Ocean* and *History.* From the more formal venturings in the blank verse sonnet undertaken by Lowell in those books, the poet eventually returned to the free-verse confessional mode in his last book, *Day by Day,* published in 1977 just weeks before he died. Much of his later work is considered uneven by many, but what Lowell never lost after *Life Studies* was the ability and willingness to try anything in poetry. His was not a "career" molded by the careful repetition of an achieved and recognized mode but rather the evolution of an artist constantly in search of protean change. Some of that change was not always successful, and much of the poetry that it produced will be forgotten, but little of Lowell's writing was done with anything less than complete daring.

If nothing else, *Life Studies* showed that both life and art are serious business, and that the recording and transformation of life's flux is no mean task. As Mark Rudman writes in *Robert Lowell: An Introduction to the Poetry:*

> The transformation of raw experience into art, as Lowell practiced it, is a more radical act than it would seem and exists at a very high level of abstraction. It immediately sacrifices the universal; archetypes have to be unearthed, found amidst the myriad details of the recreated, remembered world. Lowell has been dubbed a "confessional" poet, but his is not a poetry of confession, it's a poetry of revelation.

Life Studies laid down the challenge of such transformation to the poets who followed it, but more as a general approach than a restricted mode of writing. Nonetheless, the confessional mode did for a while become a dominate style, even though Lowell worked to break free and write a more public poetry of protest and moral conviction. These strands in his work would also become influential, spurring poets such as Denise Levertov and Adrienne Rich to contribute ongoing and complex critiques of American politics and culture while poets such as James Wright and Galway Kinnell felt emboldened to write more imagistic and lyrical poems that in their own way criticized the waste and horrors of the Vietnam era. More important, though, *Life Studies* demonstrated the connection between the personal and the political. Simply by mediating on the distress within his own heart, Lowell was able to strike at the disturbance within that of the republic. As Richard Fein writes in *Robert Lowell,* in this way "Lowell finds himself undertaking a historical role, not by reaching for one, but by showing us most intimately the forces and frustrations that went into the making of him." After *Life Studies,* any poet writing had permission to do the same.

But few would go on to do it as well as Lowell, or to have such a personal search play out on such a public stage. Berryman, Plath, and Sexton followed most closely in his footsteps, but none of them enjoyed the same kind of celebrity and pedigree, nor has there been a poet since whose public presence was as commanding. Given the wounded, fragile air that always seemed to surround Lowell's genial smile, this last aspect is surprising, but the tumult of the 1960s cast him into a limelight that few poets have experienced. The Pentagon marches, the McCarthy campaign, President Johnson's anger at Lowell's refusal of an invitation to a White House luncheon—these were heady times full of protest and rage, and because of Lowell, poetry suddenly became something that mattered in America. Lowell, however, also understood that there was a price to pay. The carnage of the Vietnam War was a poor excuse for fame and notoriety, and his own struggles were only the raw material of his art and not its end. As he would confess in "The Dolphin," the title poem to his 1973 volume,

> I have sat and listened to too many
> words of the collaborating muse,
> and plotted perhaps too freely with my life,
> not avoiding injury to others, not avoiding injury
> to myself—

However, the ability to freely plot his life with the artistry first laid down in *Life Studies* is also what allowed Lowell to arrive at a weathered equilibrium at the end of "The Dolphin" as he acknowledges that "my eyes have seen what my hand did."

That Lowell was and is an important poet can hardly be disputed. That he was the greatest of his time is probably not as useful of a description simply because he was an even more interesting and influential figure than perhaps even the best of his poems live up to. Yet it is hard to separate the two, for the combination of life as poetry and poetry as life, each lived and written at its highest intensity, remains the foundation of his achievement, the cornerstone for which was laid in *Life Studies.* Thankfully, our idea of what a poet is or does has transcended the suicidal costs of living that the confessional poets seemed helpless to avoid. But though the grim and troubled lives that bore the fruit of so many wonderful poems are not to be envied, the craft and courage that set them down remains no less admirable. As with any artist, Lowell's legacy is the inventiveness and complexity of his craft and imagination. *Life Studies* remains the epitome and apex of his creative gift.

Select Bibliography

EDITIONS

Life Studies. New York: Farrar, Straus and Cudahy, 1959.

Life Studies and For the Union Dead. New York: Noonday Press, 1964. (This is the edition cited in this essay.)

OTHER WORKS BY LOWELL

Lord Weary's Castle. New York: Harcourt, Brace, 1946.

For the Union Dead. New York: Farrar, Straus and Giroux, 1964.

Near the Ocean. New York: Farrar, Straus and Giroux, 1967.

The Dolphin. New York: Farrar, Straus and Giroux, 1973.

History. New York: Farrar, Straus and Giroux, 1973.

Day by Day. New York: Farrar, Straus and Giroux, 1977.

Collected Prose. Edited by Robert Giroux. New York: Farrar, Straus and Giroux, 1987.

SECONDARY WORKS

Axelrod, Steven Gould. *Robert Lowell: Life and Art.* Princeton, N.J.: Princeton University Press, 1978. (An excellent overview of Lowell's life and work that also collects early versions of "My Last Afternoon with Uncle Devereux Winslow" and "Skunk Hour.")

———, ed. *The Critical Response to Robert Lowell.* Westport, Conn.: Greenwood Press, 1999. (Collects both contemporary and later reviews and assessments, including M. L. Rosenthal's review from *The Nation.*)

Bell, Vereen M. *Robert Lowell: Nihilist as Hero.* Cambridge, Mass.: Harvard University Press, 1983. (An intelligent study that reads Lowell as a poet of despair whose protean art is his only means of survival.)

Bloom, Harold, ed. *Robert Lowell.* New York: Chelsea House,1986.

Cooper, Phillip. *The Autobiographical Myth of Robert Lowell.* Chapel Hill: University of North Carolina Press, 1970.

Cosgrave, Patrick. *The Public Poetry of Robert Lowell.* London: Gollancz, 1970; New York: Taplinger, 1972.

Crick, John. *Robert Lowell.* New York: Barnes and Noble, 1974.

Doreski, William. *Robert Lowell's Shifting Colors: The Poetics of the Public and the Personal.* Athens: Ohio State University Press, 1999. (Insightful assessment of the relationship between the public and personal aspects of Lowell's poems.)

Fein, Richard. *Robert Lowell.* 2d ed. Boston: Twayne, 1979. (The chapter on *Life Studies* provides a useful discussion of the book's formal arrangement.)

Hamilton, Ian. *Robert Lowell: A Biography.* New York: Random House, 1982. (Still the best biography of Lowell, though somewhat dour in its handling of his life.)

Hart, Henry. *Robert Lowell and the Sublime.* Syracuse, N.Y.: Syracuse University Press, 1995.

Hobsbaum, Philip. *A Reader's Guide to Robert Lowell.* London: Thames and Hudson, 1988. (Brief overview of the major themes and developments.)

Kalstone, David. *Becoming a Poet: Elizabeth Bishop with Marianne Moore and Robert Lowell.* New York: Farrar, Straus and Giroux, 1989. (Though focused primarily on Bishop, this well-written study sheds light on the importance of Bishop to Lowell's development.)

London, Michael, and Robert Boyers, eds. *Robert Lowell: A Portrait of the Artist in His Time.* New York: David Lewis, 1970. (Provides stimulating and wide-ranging views of Lowell's strengths and weaknesses as a poet written by his contemporaries. Includes disparaging views of Lowell's art by John Bayley and Robert Bly.)

Mariani, Paul. *Lost Puritan: A Life of Robert Lowell.* New York: Norton, 1994. (Adds new information gathered from Elizabeth Bishop's correspondence, but rather sketchy on the poems.)

Martin, Jay. *Robert Lowell.* Minneapolis: University of Minnesota Press, 1970.

Mazzaro, Jerome. *The Poetic Themes of Robert Lowell.* Ann Arbor: University of Michigan Press, 1965. (An important early study that traces the change from Lowell's early religious poetry to a poetry of experience.)

Meiners, R. K. *Everything To Be Endured: An Essay on Robert Lowell and Modern Poetry.* Columbia: University of Missouri Press, 1970.

Frank Norris' McTeague

DEANNA K. KREISEL

McTEAGUE IS A strange novel. In the literary history of the United States, its place is more that of intriguing oddity than flawless masterwork. Judged by contemporary literary standards, its characters seem flat and stereotypical, its symbolism strained and obvious, its situations contrived and unrealistic. And yet it is a compelling, gripping work—a page-turner—whose influence has been vast and whose fascination is undeniable. In fact, the very flaws of the novel are part of a deliberate design on the part of Frank Norris, its young author, who saw *McTeague* (1899) as an American version of the literary philosophy and techniques practiced by his hero, the French naturalist author Émile Zola. Norris was a staunch advocate of realism in literature, as opposed to what he saw as the sentimentality of much nineteenth-century fiction. For Norris, the grittiness of everyday life was the appropriate subject matter of a new, realistic, "muscular" kind of writing, a point he makes in "The True Reward of the Novelist," published in *Novels and Essays* (1986):

> The difficult thing is to get at the life immediately around you, the very life in which you move. No romance it in? No romance in you, poor fool. As much romance on Michigan avenue as there is realism in King Arthur's court. It is as you choose to see it. The important thing to decide is which formula is the best to help you grip the Real Life of this or any other age. . . . The difficulty then is to get at the immediate life, immensely difficult, for you are not only close to the canvas, but are yourself part of the picture.

Norris might seem to be contradicting his own advice in *McTeague,* a novel that, after all, features murder, domestic violence, pathological miserliness, and a not-very-realistic showdown between two men handcuffed to each other in California's Death Valley. Yet the characters and situations of the novel are very much drawn from "Real Life," the unglamorous work-a-day surroundings of San Francisco's urban working class. There is nothing unusual about the slightly dim-witted dentist, the sweet young girl he courts, and the working people who are their friends, neighbors, and family. And this is precisely Norris' point: remarkable things happen to unremarkable people every day; the characters of *McTeague* are ordinary in their very extraordinariness.

For Norris, real life is the proper subject of the novelist's art. However, this seemingly simple statement belies the complexity (and occasionally contradictory nature) of his literary philosophy. In fact, Norris saw "life" and "literature" as diametrically opposed. As Donald Pizer, one of Norris' most famous interpreters, claims in his introduction to *The Literary Criticism of Frank Norris* (1976):

> To Norris, "life" included the emotions and the instincts. It incorporated both the world of nature (the outdoors and the country) and the kind of life which Norris believed "natural" (the life of passion and violence, and the life of the low and fallen) because such life was closest to the primitive in man and furthest from the cultivated. "Literature," on the other hand, included thought, culture, overeducation, refinement, and excessive spirituality.

As bizarre and out-of-the-ordinary as some of the situations in *McTeague* may seem, then, they are real for Norris precisely because they demonstrate the true nature of human beings—violent, passionate, primitive—when the refining influences of education and polite society are stripped away. Most of the characters in Norris' novels struggle to maintain the outer trappings of socially accepted behavior. McTeague's powerful impulse to molest Trina while she is under ether in his dental parlors, Trina's gradual descent into pathological miserliness, and the ultimate murderousness of McTeague and Marcus are all examples of thinly civilized characters whose true natures eventually emerge throughout the course of the novel. Indeed, one could argue that the revelation of these natures is one of the central goals of Norris' narrative project.

The unusual events of Norris' plots and the sordidness of the situations he narrates have not always found favor with readers and critics: Norris' literary significance has fluctuated greatly in the past century. He worked quite consciously to build a national reputation for himself, and by the last years of his life was widely considered to be a major American novelist; in fact, the last novel published while he was alive, *The Pit,* was hailed by the *New*

CHRONOLOGY

1870	Norris is born on March 5 in Chicago.
1878	The Norris family travels to Europe and spends the winter in Brighton.
1885	Family moves to San Francisco. Frank begins attending Belmont Academy, a preparatory school. After breaking his arm playing football, he is withdrawn from school.
1886	Attends Boys' High School in San Francisco, then later transfers to the San Francisco Art Association School to study painting.
1887	The Norris family travels to England and France, and Frank studies painting in London and Paris.
1889–1890	Returns to the United States. Publishes his first article, "Clothes of Steel," a history of armor, in the *San Francisco Chronicle.* Begins studying at the University of California at Berkeley and starts work on *Yvernelle,* a book-length narrative poem.
1891	Publishes *Yvernelle,* which is subsidized by his mother. Joins Phi Gamma Delta fraternity.
1894	Completes final year at Berkeley but does not receive degree, having failed the mathematics matriculation exam. Frank's parents divorce, and he moves with his mother and brother Charles to Cambridge, Massachusetts, where he begins studying creative writing with Lewis Gates at Harvard and begins drafts of *McTeague* and *Vandover and the Brute.*
1895	Returns to San Francisco, then travels to Cape Town and Johannesburg, South Africa, as a correspondent for the *San Francisco Chronicle.*
1896	Develops tropical fever and is expelled from the Transvaal by the Boers. Returns to the United States, where he recuperates at the Big Dipper Mine in California. Becomes staff member of The Wave, where he contributes fiction, essays, and reviews for nearly two

> flowed in his veins. Why should it be? He did not desire it. Was he to blame?

Other characters in the novel also show signs of hereditary predilections toward degeneracy. After Trina and McTeague are engaged and she wins the lottery, she begins to scheme about how to maximize their income through investment and even decides to start making wooden toys on the side for extra money. This is the first sign in the novel of what will become her pathological hoarding:

> It soon became apparent that Trina would be an extraordinarily good housekeeper. Economy was her strong point. A good deal of peasant blood still ran undiluted in her veins, and she had all the instinct of a hardy and penurious mountain race—the instinct which saves without any thought, without idea of consequence—saving for the sake of saving, hoarding without knowing why.

Trina's fatal flaw is traced back to the quality of the "blood in her veins," just as McTeague's predilection toward violence is attributed to the "evil of an entire race" that flows through his. This is the hallmark of Lombroso, whose theory of human degeneracy greatly influenced Norris: both Trina and McTeague are able to function normally in society for a time, under a thin veneer of civilizing influence, until some triggering event unleashes their true criminal and animalistic natures and they begin to act like "brutes."

Yet this focus on heredity and blood should not overshadow the other deterministic factors at work in Norris' novel. While readers are told that McTeague's father's brutality is one of the reasons the dentist himself is inherently violent, according to the language of the passage (the "vices and sins of his father . . . tainted him"), this inheritance could be as much due to childhood social conditioning as to genes. While Norris emphasizes McTeague's "blood" later, he is careful to point out that a combination of factors triggers the dentist's violence: not only genetic predilection but also luck and circumstances play their role. (None of the subsequent tragedy would have happened had Trina not won the lottery ticket in the first place.) Norris is careful to point to other environmental factors that influence his characters' natures and behavior. For example, McTeague has had only a spotty education at best and learns his dentistry from a traveling charlatan—he "had read many of the necessary books, but he was too hopelessly stupid to get much benefit from them. Marcus is trained in his profession of veterinary assistant in a similar way: his "knowledge of the diseases of domestic animals had been picked up in a haphazard way, much after the manner of McTeague's education." They have hardly had the opportunity to raise themselves very far from their backgrounds of poverty and struggle; while they may be doing slightly better than their parents and grandparents, it is only by the slimmest possible margin, and as soon as a piece of bad luck strikes, they are plunged right back into a life of hardship and penury.

The socioeconomic status of the characters is thus of crucial importance. It is no accident that naturalist writers tend to populate their novels with the poor and uneducated: a predilection toward violence or a genetic inheritance of criminality would not necessarily be sufficient for tragedy in the privileged environs of the upper classes. However, as Donald Pizer argues in *Twentieth-Century American Literary Naturalism,* "the ideological core of American naturalism—a sense of man more circumscribed than conventionally acknowledged—does not precede this exploration of the 'low' and 'irrational' but rather derives from it." In other words, writers like Norris do not deliberately concoct novelistic experiments wherein helpless character-subjects are tortured and killed in order to prove some abstract point about the tragic nature of all human life. Rather, these writers are attempting to depict a truth of contemporary society as they see it: that, as Pizer puts it, "the poor—in education, intellect, and worldly goods—are indeed pushed and forced, that the powerful do control the weak." If one focuses only on the inherent or genetic side of the determinist equation, one will lose sight of this more political point, and of the radical and subversive potential of the naturalist movement.

GENDER IN *McTEAGUE*

One of the crucial environmental factors for the characters in *McTeague* is their gender. Whether or not Norris consciously intended to explore the question of gender as a determining force in his novel, it is impossible to think critically about what happens to the characters in *McTeague* without considering their sex. One of Norris' central themes is the effect of the gold Trina wins in the lottery—and the characters' obsession with it—on traditional roles of man and woman, husband and wife.

The novel traces Trina's decline from a frail and feminine creature—"innocent, confiding, almost infantile"—to a "slatternly, dirty, coarse" old miser, whose figure has grown "coarse, stunted, and dumpy" from self-deprivation. Conversely, Trina's hoarding causes the gradual emasculation of McTeague, who begins the novel as a "young giant" with "immense limbs, heavy with ropes of muscle" and hands "hard as wooden mallets." After his slow starvation due to Trina's refusal to give him money for food, he is still huge, but now his face is "lean and pinched," and there are "deep black shadows in the shrunken cheeks." On a purely physical level, Trina's obsession with the gold causes a reversal of masculine and feminine characteristics, yet it is the crossing of more intangible gender barriers with which Norris is primarily concerned. Norris pathologizes Trina's obsession with money and acquiring money because it represents a dangerous encroachment on the part of a woman into traditionally masculine terrain.

The story of Trina hoarding more and more money is the story of a woman gathering more and more power to herself—and thus necessarily draining power from her traditional superior, her husband. As the struggle between Trina and McTeague draws to its tragic conclusion, it becomes apparent that Norris sees Trina's hoarding almost as more dangerous than McTeague's brutality. As already seen, McTeague is predisposed to violence, yet it is Trina's unreasonableness, her unhealthy avarice, which ultimately causes McTeague's murderousness. Her desire for power, in the form of gold, is pathologized partly because she is a woman; she is a dangerous and unnatural creature. Norris' novel can be read as a woman's potentially subversive search for cultural power and legitimacy.

The question is, how does money become a representation of, a symbol for, power? The most obvious answer is that the desire for money is the desire for purchasing power, the ability to choose freely what one will consume. This form of power is one that is routinely denied women in the Victorian age. A popular song of the period, "A Bird in a Gilded Cage" (words by Arthur A. Lamb and music by Harry von Tilzer) in Margaret Bradford Boni's *Songs of the Gilded Age* (1960), dramatizes the plight of a young woman who has married for economic security:

> She's only a bird in a gilded cage,
> A beautiful sight to see.
> You may think she's happy and free from care,
> She's not, though she seems to be.
> 'Tis sad when you think of her wasted life,
> For youth cannot mate with age;
> And her beauty was sold
> For an old man's gold,
> She's a bird in a gilded cage.

The young wife may seem to be "happy and free from care," but her economic security is an illusion; as long as the money belongs essentially to her husband ("old man's gold"), she is effectively imprisoned by her dependence on him. The image of a bird in a gilded cage is, of course, one of the most memorable parts of *McTeague.* In the context of the popular image depicted in the song, it takes on added resonance as a representation of Trina. She is imprisoned not only by her avarice but also by the knowledge that McTeague has at least potential control over her money; she will attempt to escape from this figurative prison through hoarding.

Trina does see her marriage to McTeague as a potential loss of the economic power and independence she has gained through her lottery money. When McTeague appeals to their solidarity as an economic unit ("Well, it's all in the family. What's yours is mine, and what's mine is yours, ain't it?"), Trina recoils and asserts her independence: "No, it's not; no, it's not; no, it's not. . . . It's all mine, mine. There's not a penny of it belongs to anybody else." Clearly, Trina sees marriage, with its traditional character of property sharing, as a threat to her economic power and independence.

This is not the only arena in which the power struggle between Trina and McTeague takes place. It also takes place in their home, the womanly domain in which Trina can rule supreme: "Her household duties began more and more to absorb her attention, for she was an admirable housekeeper, keeping the little suite in marvellous good order." The home in the nineteenth century was seen as a utopian space, a retreat for the husband from the harsh world in which he must make a living. Alfred Habegger, in his book *Gender, Fantasy, and Realism in American Literature* (1982), describes how

> the home was supposed to be a perfect retreat and marriage a perfect union. . . . Men were more and more absorbed in the egotistic struggle for wealth, place, and power. While the home turned into a shrine, the rest of the world became a fierce, competitive arena for the rough and tumble of primitive capitalism.

Yet if the home is popularly imagined as a utopian "retreat" for the man, what is it for the woman? Her "arena" for the "struggle" for "power" surely must be there, and her main competitor is her husband. According to Habegger, this struggle manifests itself in the wife's adherence to rules of etiquette and womanly niceties and in her desire to "tame" her husband into her image of gentility. This paradigm operates in *McTeague* when Trina cleans up her husband's act:

> Gradually the dentist improved under the influence of his little wife. He no longer went abroad with frayed cuffs about his huge red wrists—or worse, without any cuffs at all. . . . She broke him of the habit of eating with his knife, she caused him to substitute bottled beer in the place of steam beer, and she induced him to take off his hat to Miss Baker, to Heise's wife, and to the other women of his acquaintance.

This last "improvement" is particularly telling, for it crystallizes the relations that Habegger sees at work between men and women: wives effectively browbeat their husbands into submission to particularly female rules of behavior. (Likewise, Trina forces her husband to stop being "gruff and indifferent to his female patients" and to accompany them to the door and "h[o]ld it open for them.") Thus, according to Habegger's argument, the home ultimately ceases to be a place of retreat for the beleaguered husband, who begins to keep company with his buddies instead of with his increasingly shrewish wife.

While Habegger does acknowledge that the scene of the "enormous conflict" between men and women in the late nineteenth century is frequently the home, in his focus on the retreat of men from this supposed haven to the real haven of the tavern and saloon, he barely hints at the fact that this is a manifestation of a grave power struggle between husband and wife. The home may lose its utopian character for the husband, but while so doing it remains the sole source of power for the wife. Trina's home is her domain, as she tacitly admits when she bewails the fact that she and McTeague must move because of their financial circumstances: "We've got to leave here—leave this flat where I've been—where *we've* been so happy."

In Trina's case, this territoriality is complicated by her growing miserliness. Her pride in housekeeping described above is also a passion for "regulating the schedule of expenditure with an economy that often bordered on positive niggardliness. It was a passion with her to save money." And in the very next sentence, amid the description of Trina's housekeeping skills, readers learn that she hides her money "in the bottom of her trunk, in the bedroom." Her home is not only an arena for power struggles with her husband but also a space for her consolidation of money, the medium through which she recuperates power over her husband. The two compulsions are often represented by Norris as occurring on the same psychological plane in Trina's mind. Thus, when she and McTeague end one of their many fights over finances (which, significantly, she has won), she orders him from the room: "I'd like to have my kitchen to myself, please."

The concentration of female power in the home, as opposed to the male "struggle for wealth, place, and power" in the marketplace, is revealed quite clearly when this division of space breaks down. When McTeague loses his practice and thus stops bringing in the main income (his correct place in the home/marketplace opposition), Trina's miserliness becomes even more irrational: "Trina had become more niggardly than ever since the loss of McTeague's practice. It was not mere economy with her now. It was a panic terror." This heightened avarice cannot be completely explained by their new poverty, for Trina has more than enough money saved to make their living conditions comfortable, even without touching the principal of her lottery money. Instead, it seems more like a reaction to the shrinking of the space over which she had previously ruled, particularly the woman's own space, the kitchen:

> What a pleasure it had been to invade that little brick-paved kitchen every morning, . . . proud in the sense of her proprietorship and her independence! How happy she had been the day after her marriage when she had first entered that kitchen and knew that it was all her own! . . . And now it was all to go.

The word "invade" here is particularly appropriate, for Trina's "proprietorship" does take the form of a sort of militaristic occupation and defense against the forces of McTeague, whom she is so fond of ordering from her domain. When Trina's power base shrinks as she is forced to lose her kitchen and her "pretty things," she compensates by becoming even more tightfisted and jealous of her other power resource, money. (The erosion of the separateness of the gendered spheres, home and marketplace, takes its toll on McTeague, as well. He cannot abide the fact that his wife is supporting them single-handedly: "Her industry was a constant reproach to him. She seemed to flaunt her work defiantly in his face. It was the red flag in the eyes of the bull.")

Of course, the marriage of the two forms of power at Trina's command, money and domestic space, only goes so far. When forced to make a decision between the two, Trina chooses the money. A long description of Trina's pathological love for her money toward the middle of the book—"I'm going to get more; I'm going to get more, more, more; a little every day"—is directly followed by the revelation that "she was still looking for cheaper quarters." Although the move from the suite to the small whitewashed room is "a long agony," she is willing to tolerate the further diminution of her living space in order to save more money. While the domestic sphere is for women—and had been for Trina—a resource of power, the true power is concentrated in money. This is not the perception of Trina alone, for clearly true freedom and independence for women can accrue only with economic independence; the power of domestic space is but a consolation prize. This perception is not diminished by the fact that money in *McTeague* routinely is the source of tragic downfall. While it is true that in the novel, as Lewis Fried has noted, "money is not so much a medium of exchange, not so important as a means of allowing man to realize his desires, as it is a symbol of the transformation of life's dreams and hopes into junk," the fact remains that as Norris depicts them, the characters in *McTeague* still see it as a means of satisfying their needs. They therefore still try to acquire money, along with the power it represents, because its ultimate desirability still lies in its power to transform. As Karl Marx wrote about this phenomenon in "The Power of Money in Bourgeois Society": "The extent of the power of money is the extent of my power. Money's properties are my properties and essential powers—the properties and powers of its possessor." This possible source of power must be doubly tantalizing to someone from whom power systematically has been denied; Trina, as a woman, sees it as an effective weapon in her battles with McTeague.

But this interpretation can only go so far. The power that money confers in the form of economic decision making and independence cannot account for many of the baffling characteristics of Trina's obsession with it. There is the sexual nature of her love for money, for one thing, and the fact that she refuses to spend any of it—effectively denying the very economic power which she may be seen as trying to accumulate. In order to understand the puzzling nature of Trina's obsession, one will have to try to comprehend another aspect of the power of money for Trina.

NORRIS' ECONOMICS

McTeague is a novel shot through with gold. Critics of the novel often cite the heavy-handedness of the gold imagery as an example of Norris' clumsiness and lack of subtlety. Not just one, or even two, but four characters are obsessed with gold: Trina, of course; McTeague, as he starts to feel stinted by Trina's miserliness; the maid Maria Macapa, who is obsessed with her imagined dinner service of pure gold; and Zerkow, who marries her solely to get his hands on it. Then there is the giant gold-tooth sign McTeague longs to hang outside his dental parlors, the gold he uses in his dentistry practice, the gold mining that occupies the last part of the novel, even the gilt cage in which the canary is kept. The word "gold" appears in *McTeague* nearly two hundred times. The novel is not merely a product of the "Gilded Age" but also one reason why the decades before and after the turn of the twentieth century were given that nickname.

As many critics of the novel have noted, the obsession with money and gold in *McTeague* can best be described as fetishism. While the words "fetish" and "fetishism" are commonly used to refer to an excessive or unhealthy attachment to a (usually physical) object, in order to understand the love of money in *McTeague* one must look more closely at how fetishism actually works. There are three intellectual traditions that concern themselves with the concept of fetishism: the anthropological, the Marxist, and the psychoanalytic. According to Roy Ellen in his essay "Fetishism," the term traditionally has been used in the anthropology of religion to refer to an attribution of agency or other human characteristics to a nonhuman entity. The important factor is that "there tends to be an inner ambivalence as to whether it is the objects themselves which effect material changes in some mysterious way, or whether it is some spiritual force which is either represented by or located in (but separate from) those objects."

This explanation of the mechanism of fetishism, in which the fetish object is somehow confused with an imagined source of agency or power, is a particularly compelling description of prevalent attitudes toward gold in the late nineteenth century. In his book *The Gold Standard and the Logic of Naturalism,* Walter Benn Michaels has outlined nineteenth-century attitudes toward gold in an effort to explain the paradoxical nature of hoarding as depicted in *McTeague.* As he puts it, "Trina . . . is never glad to get rid of her gold. . . . Why, then, does Trina save?" In the debates over the gold standard in the late nineteenth century, those who advocated the free coinage of silver feared that because the amount of gold in the world was fixed (and small), money would soon run out, whereas those who advocated remaining on the gold standard felt that gold was "natural" money, with superior intrinsic value. Given this historical conception of precious metal as having a natural, intrinsic value somehow outside of human agency, Trina's fetishization of gold can be more readily understood. In positing a value that inheres in the coins themselves, she assigns to them a power akin to that which religious fetish objects assume. The concept of value takes on an almost godlike quality. Trina certainly has "an inner ambivalence" as to whether the gold itself "effects material changes in some mysterious way, or whether it is some spiritual force" located in the gold itself (that is, its intrinsic value). Thus her overwhelming desire to "have her money in hand." She wants to have the money "itself," not just the paper that represents it, so that she can "plunge her hands into it, her face into it, feeling the cool, smooth metal upon her cheeks." In religious fetishism, it is often the case that physical contact or proximity to the fetish object is crucial. Norris' depiction of Trina's obsession adheres to this classical conception of fetishism: the need for a physical representation as an aid to worshipping some abstraction, in this case the mysterious value of money.

But why is this value mysterious? Why is Trina, and why were the gold advocates, so convinced of the powerful, independent value of money that they posited that value as somehow existing already in nature, waiting to be "discovered" by man? Karl Marx proposed the existence of a process that he called the "fetishism of commodities," in which workers perceive the exchange value of the products of their labor under capitalism as being inherent in the objects themselves. If in a free-market society all commodities can be exchanged for other commodities, and everyone's position in that society is determined by his or her ability to acquire commodities, then people start to think of relations between human beings (workers and capitalists) as relations between commodities. Buyers and sellers attribute human qualities to exchanged objects when they imagine that those objects have a fixed and inherent value and forget that they are the products of human society. Thus the commodity is mysterious, as stated in Marx's *Selected Writings,* "simply because in it the social character of men's labour appears to them as an objective character stamped upon the product of that labour." Money can be seen as a special case of commodity fetishism. And in the case of money, which is a universal in the process of exchange, this mysterious character becomes a very real sense of power. For Marx, money in a market society *is* all-powerful:

> By possessing the *property* of buying everything, by possessing the property of appropriating all objects, *money* is thus the *object* of eminent possession. The universality of its *property* is the omnipotence of its being. It therefore functions as the almighty being.

This tendency of the Marxist notion of commodity fetishism to blend into a classical anthropological (or religious) model is similar to the process of confusion operating in Norris' description of Trina's obsession with gold. Her perception of the mysterious power of gold (which commodity fetishism attempts to explain) is inseparable from her need for contact with the physical object itself (which is documented in the anthropological literature).

In the third model of fetishism, the Freudian, the fetish object is a means specifically for sexual gratification. Not only is the fixation on the object a source of gratification for the subject, he (for fetishism in women, according to Sigmund Freud, is rare) is not likely to feel that it interferes with his normal life. In his essay "Fetishism," Freud notes that "though no doubt a fetish is recognized by its adherents as an abnormality, it is seldom felt by them as the symptom of an ailment accompanied by suffering. Usually they are quite satisfied with it." The fetishist, according to Freud, is compensating for his perception of woman's lack of a penis. This perception has led to an anxiety that he may himself be castrated (as she has been); thus, he denies that she does not have a penis:

Carson McCullers' The Member of the Wedding

LOUIS H. PALMER III

CARSON McCULLERS IS often seen as a kind of poster child for the gothic or grotesque school of southern fiction, specifically representative of the post–Southern Renascence generation. Her group—which includes Flannery O'Connor, Eudora Welty, Truman Capote, Harper Lee, and Tennessee Williams—is seen, in such a perspective, to continue in the tradition of the fiction of William Faulkner and Erskine Caldwell, whose works responded to the pressures of modernism by emphasizing the peculiar, violent, bizarre, and exotic qualities of the American South, often focusing on lower-class characters. The early Faulkner and Caldwell were labeled "Southern Gothic" by Ellen Glasgow in the mid-1930s, a term she used disparagingly. By implication, their rich style and violent subject matter contrasted unfavorably with Glasgow's own version of social realism. The term stuck and came to be seen in contrast with the land-based and traditionalist values espoused by the Agrarian movement, values which are sometimes also assumed to be those of the late Faulkner.

Flannery O'Connor defined the major challenge for McCullers' generation of fiction writers: "The presence alone of Faulkner in our midst makes a great difference in what the writer can and cannot permit himself to do. Nobody wants his mule and wagon stalled on the same track the Dixie Limited is roaring down." The McCullers group, if they may be so called, had the misfortune—in O'Connor's opinion—to be southern writers in the shadow of Faulkner. But writing in Faulkner's wake also provided opportunities. Faulkner's heirs responded to this situation by exploring fields in which the master was uncomfortable: particularly gender and sexuality. This enhancement of perspective added to the southern focal dynamic of family, class, and race and resulted in a unique body of southern fiction during the 1940s and 1950s.

But McCullers was not just a southern writer. She was writing in the age of World War II, of Rosie the Riveter, of a generation of women who were encouraged to participate as workers and supervisors in American manufacturing industries, with all the gender-bending and gender-role violation that such a reversal implies in a culture where gender boundaries were normally strictly policed. Critics and reviewers often cite McCullers' interest in gender ambiguity—for example, Leslie A. Fiedler refers to Frankie Addams from *Member of the Wedding*

(1946) and Mick Kelly from *The Heart Is a Lonely Hunter* (1940) as "boy-girl" characters, a term Ihab Hassan intensifies to "men-women freaks"—but few acknowledge the pressure on gender roles created by the war effort as having anything to do with it. Critics more often portray McCullers as having androgynous or homosexual tendencies—a reputation that she actively encouraged, although, as Lori J. Kenschaft argues, she does not fit easily into gender-opposed categories, such as "lesbian," either. Emerging as an *enfant prodige* with the publication of her first novel, *The Heart Is a Lonely Hunter,* the twenty-three-year-old author became a legend in Greenwich Village literary circles. She was tall, thin, and moonfaced, with huge eyes and a wide mouth, and she tended to dress either in men's clothing or in wispy, ultrafeminine gowns—that is to say as "masculine" or as "feminine," portraying self-conscious gender roles. A photo of her taken at the Yaddo arts colony in 1941 shows her in a striped sailor's jersey, loose shorts, and loafers, holding a cigarette in one hand and a thermos (reputed to be full of sherry "tea") in the other. Here she looks very much like an adolescent female—an age type she would return to again and again in her fiction.

McCULLERS' MAJOR FICTION

The Heart Is a Lonely Hunter is an ambitious first novel. It follows five unusual characters through a few episodes in their lives in a small southern city. Mick Kelly is an adolescent girl with artistic ambitions. Doctor Benedict Copeland is an African American who works hard toward ending the Jim Crow system. Jake Blount is a self-styled labor activist and a drunk. Biff Brannon owns the New York Café and is an unreflective observer of human eccentricities. Each of the five trusts and confides in John Singer, a deaf-mute who has a limited ability to read lips. When Singer commits suicide as a result of the death of his love interest, a Greek deaf-mute with a mental disability who had been

CHRONOLOGY

1917	Born as Lula Carson Smith on February 19 in Columbus, Georgia.
1933	Graduates from high school. Writes first short story, "Sucker."
1934	Moves to New York to study at Julliard but loses money. Works at various jobs and takes creative writing classes at Columbia and New York University.
1935	Meets Reeves McCullers while at home in Georgia.
1936	Publishes first story, "Wunderkind."
1937	Marries Reeves. They live in Charlotte, North Carolina.
1940	*The Heart Is a Lonely Hunter.* Serial publication of *Reflections in a Golden Eye* in *Harper's Bazaar.* Separates from Reeves. Joins group of artists and writers living in Brooklyn Heights. Attends Breadloaf Writers' Conference in Vermont.
1941	Suffers a stroke in February. Attends Yaddo, an arts colony in Saratoga Springs, New York, where she will return periodically for several years. *Reflections in a Golden Eye* published in book form. Experiences health problems.
1942	Divorces Reeves.
1945	*Ballad of the Sad Café* in *Harper's Bazaar.*
1945	Remarries Reeves.
1946	*The Member of the Wedding.*
1947	Travels to France. Suffers two strokes and is partly paralyzed.
1949	The play version of *The Member of the Wedding* opens in Philadelphia.
1950	*The Member of the Wedding* opens on Broadway on January 5 and eventually runs for 501 performances.
1952	Moves with Reeves to a farmhouse in Bachivillers, France.
1953	Leaves Reeves in France; he commits suicide.
1957	*The Square Root of Wonderful,* a play, opens on Broadway and closes after 45 performances.

1961	*Clock without Hands,* her final novel.
1962	Operation for breast cancer.
1963	The play version of *Ballad of the Sad Café* opens on Broadway.
1964	*Ballad of the Sad Café* closes after 123 performances.
1967	Dies of massive brain hemorrhage on September 29.

institutionalized, the act reverberates though the lives of the other four, precipitating crises which leave them isolated and disillusioned.

After *The Heart Is a Lonely Hunter,* McCullers published two short novels in *Harper's Bazaar: Reflections in a Golden Eye* (1940) and *The Ballad of the Sad Café* (1943). *Reflections in a Golden Eye,* which was serialized in two installments in 1940, was reviewed and is generally regarded as a disappointing second novel. In it, life in a southern "army post in peacetime" is presented as both oppressive and intense. A complex tangle of unique and eccentric characters interact in a plot that involves homosexual attraction, infidelity, voyeurism, self-mutilation, nervous disorders, and, finally, murder. It presents people, even sensitive and intelligent ones, as victims of overwhelming internal drives and instincts, before which they appear to be helpless. The bizarre characters and events seem both gratuitous and overly earnest, and the novel's grotesqueries never quite become humorous.

The Ballad of the Sad Café, which was not serialized but published in one issue of *Harper's Bazaar* (August 1943) in order "to maintain the cadence of the lyric form," stands in contrast to *Reflections.* It develops a similarly twisted plot and similarly strange characters into a series of episodes that *work* because of the humorous detachment of the narrative voice and the almost mythic quality of the setting—a dusty, forgotten southern mill town without the historical immediacy of a contemporaneous army base and the popular-magazine Freudianism of the characters' complexes. The main characters consist of a mannish superwoman, a trickster hunchback, and a brutish convict, who form a love triangle in which there is no reciprocation. Cousin Lymon, the hunchback, develops a crush on convict Henry Macy, who teams up with him in order to get back at Miss Amelia, his ex-wife, who did not exert her influence to keep him out of jail and who, ironically completing the triangle, loves Lymon. The hunchback's betrayal destroys her, and she boards up her store (the site of the "sad café") and withers away, watching helplessly out of an upstairs window. The events are described with gusto and sympathy by an ironic narrator, who seems to be both a part of and separate from the townspeople. In psychological terms, these characters seem to function more as paradigms or allegories for interior states, avoiding the clinical case-study feel of the character treatment in *Reflections in a Golden Eye.*

McCullers wrote *Reflections in a Golden Eye* in 1939, just before the publication of *The Heart Is a Lonely Hunter* in 1940, and she wrote *The Ballad of the Sad Café* the year after that. In an interview which the cinema writer Rex Reed conducted with McCullers shortly before her death in 1967, she reflected on this time: "I became an established literary figure overnight, and I was much too young to understand what happened to me or the responsibility it entailed. I was a bit of a holy terror." According to her biographer Virginia Spencer Carr, McCullers separated from her husband Reeves in late 1940 and moved into a house in Brooklyn Heights with George Davis (literary editor at *Harper's Bazaar*) and a series of boarders, including the poet W. H. Auden, the dancer Gypsy Rose Lee, and the novelist Richard Wright, along with many other literary and artistic figures from the wartime bohemian scene in New York.

Throughout this period and for the next four years McCullers worked on a story she called first "The Bride" and then "The Bride of Her Brother." In this novel, published in 1946 as *The Member of the Wedding,* she returned to the setting and some of the themes of her first novel.

The central character is again an adolescent girl with a male name in a middle-class family in a small southern city. Again, the plot is transitional, tracing the character's shift from a tomboyish freedom into a more restrictive, gendered young adulthood. In both cases the young woman's dream or fantasy is frustrated, but with important differences. In *The Heart Is a Lonely Hunter,* Mick's ambition is artistic—she wants to study music and become a concert pianist and composer, and this is frustrated by the financial realities of depression-era poverty. Ultimately she must set her dream aside to earn money for her family. Her frustration is mirrored by that of the people she associates with, who are all outsiders, and by the frustration of Singer, to whom they all talk without any idea of his inner state, which they wonder about after he commits suicide. This diffuse structure places Mick in a larger context and presents her crisis as part of that larger picture, more appropriate, perhaps, to the social drama fiction of the 1930s.

In *The Member of the Wedding,* McCullers follows the same kind of narrative economy that she displayed in *The Ballad of the Sad Café*—her focus is on Frankie's interaction with two other characters: Frankie's six-year-old cousin John Henry and the African American cook and housekeeper Berenice. One can survey McCullers' first four novels in simple numerical terms—a long novel with six major characters, then a short novel with six, followed by a short novel and then a longer one, both with three central characters. In this progression McCullers is developing her narrative focus from a broad social spectrum to a more narrow and personal one. As Klaus Lubbers describes it, "The multi-level structure of *The Heart Is a Lonely Hunter* and the emotional intimacy of *Reflections in a Golden Eye* have yielded to simpler organization, the constantly shifting focus now resting on one character." This allows for a novel that is "simpler to read and requires less explanation" than the earlier books, but it also allows for a much more intricate and profound exploration of Frankie's crisis and transition. Because of its adolescent protagonist, and because of the easily accessible "surface brilliance," as Oliver Evans calls it, *The Member of the Wedding* has become a staple of adolescent reading lists and curricula, a categorization leading to interpretive misunderstandings. The novel's themes and issues are profoundly adult. Frankie's issues devolve as much from what she does not acknowledge—adult sexuality, with all of its complex interactions, and the compromises and limitations of adult life, clearly delineated by Berenice—as from what she understands—the adult language and behavior she imitates.

CRITICAL RECEPTION

In her study *Wunderkind: The Reputation of Carson McCullers, 1940–1990* (1995), Judith Giblin James provides an outline of the development of McCullers criticism. The general phases she outlines for *The Member of the Wedding* begin with an initial emphasis on universality in the 1950s, when Frankie is taken quite literally as a type of Everyman and her situation of loneliness and alienation generalized as representative of the human condition. Readings focusing on her fascination with freaks and her gender instability combine, starting with Leslie A. Fiedler, to present the novel as a celebration of aberration and the grotesque as normal (or abnormal) outgrowths of adolescence or the southern setting. The women's movement of the 1960s and 1970s brought readings of the novel as a specifically female bildungsroman that concludes with Frankie's capitulation to a gendered and secondary social role (see Barbara A. White) or that celebrates her brief flirtation with an androgynous ideal. The publication of Virginia Spencer Carr's biography in 1975 gave readers intimate knowledge of McCullers' own life and personal issues, including bisexual or lesbian tendencies and a firm opposition to the politics of segregation in the South. Much criticism since Carr's biography has focused on issues of politics, race, and sexuality.

position than Berenice, she must learn to police her behavior and her appearance. F. Jasmine has attempted to modify her appearance, to "fix [her]self up nice in [her] dress," but she has not learned the proper gender and class behaviors: "speaking sweetly and acting sly."

Although Berenice is the agent in F. Jasmine's instruction in such things, she seems somewhat ambivalent about what she is teaching. When F. Jasmine suggests Berenice marry her boyfriend, T. T. Williams, Berenice refuses for a purely emotional reason: he does not make her shiver. After the conversation about the dress, the narrative flashes back to earlier evenings in the summer when each of the three would discuss his or her ideal world. John Henry's world is quickly summarized as "a mixture of delicious and freak" and focused around bodily awareness and power: "chocolate dirt" and abilities such as superhuman vision and "the sudden long arm that could stretch from here to California." Berenice would envision a just world with no racial distinctions, no war, no violence, and food for all. "The old Frankie" would agree with Berenice but look for belonging—"a world club with certificates and badges." Also she would wish "that people could instantly change back and forth from boys to girls, whichever way they felt like and wanted." Berenice would disagree, stating that "the law of human sex was exactly right just as it was." These ideal worlds again demonstrate the characters' allegorical placements, with Frankie's position a liminal border zone between social awareness and bodily fantasy. Her decision to join the wedding is equivalent to a decision to change from a girl to a boy at will, as she soon discovers. But her description of momentarily seeing the wedding couple out of the corner of her eye and then turning to realize that there were "two colored boys in an alley" gains Berenice's attention, and their roles shift. They are now no longer teacher and pupil: "It was the first time ever they had talked about love, with F. Jasmine included in the conversation as a person who understood and had worth-while opinions."

Berenice has recognized something in F. Jasmine's experience, and this allows her to treat her as an adult, even letting her smoke one of her cigarettes. The corner-of-the-eye experience has reminded Berenice about how she recognized pieces of her dead husband in the subsequent men she married. "I had to go and copy myself forever afterward. What I did was to marry off little pieces of Ludie whenever I come across them. It was just my misfortune they all turned out to be the wrong pieces." She finds a correspondence between her misreadings of her former husbands and F. Jasmine's misreading of the wedding. As she begins to tell about the final husband, presumably a story with some sexual content, she realizes her danger again and calls F. Jasmine and John Henry "two little pitchers and four big ears," thus relegating F. Jasmine back into the role of a child who is not allowed to hear such things. She warns F. Jasmine about changing her name: "Things accumulate around your name. . . . One thing after another happens to you, and you behave in various ways and do things, so that soon the name begins to have a meaning." Berenice speaks in two voices here. Obviously she is speaking about reputation, important in retaining middle-class status, but she is also telling the reader how to read Frankie/F. Jasmine/Frances as each name acquires its own accumulation.

PART 2 CONTINUED: F. JASMINE'S JOURNEY

The culminating episode in part 2 is F. Jasmine's more perilous nighttime journey. First she visits Big Mama, Berenice's mother, a fortune-teller who basically repeats Berenice's warnings about her plans. She predicts that F. Jasmine will return after her journey, and she remarks on F. Jasmine's growth: "You look like a regular grown girl." After trying to seem shorter by hunching her shoulders, "F. Jasmine felt the power of the wedding; it was as though, on this last evening, she ought to order and advise." Or it is as if in this liminal phase she could move fluently between being a child whose physical growth everyone talks about and being an adult. She addresses Honey, Berenice's nephew, who, according to Big Mama, is "a boy God had not finished," and who is, significantly, "leaning against the door jamb." Taking the tone Berenice uses to address her, F. Jasmine suggests to Honey that he go to Cuba or Mexico, where he could learn the language and pass for white. Honey laughs at her suggestion. The scene is a missed opportunity—if F. Jasmine wanted a "we of me," a companion in the unfinished zone, Honey would be an obvious choice. Like her he is a misfit—sensitive, musical, and misunderstood according to conventional standards. But she cannot imagine him as an equal, and so she patronizes him from her race- and class-advantaged position, telling him that trying to be white elsewhere is "the best thing you can do" as "a colored boy." F. Jasmine's failure of sympathy for Honey or for John Henry, who, dressed like a girl, has followed her into the night, sets the scene for the failure of judgment that nearly leads to her rape. She sends John Henry home and then meets the soldier, who seems only marginally less sober than before. Their conversation, in which he tries to be flirtatious and she tries to be adult, does not work:

> Nor would he talk about the war, nor foreign countries and the world. To his joking remarks she could never find replies that fitted, although she tried. Like a nightmare pupil in a recital who has to play a duet to a piece she does not know, F. Jasmine did her best to catch the tune and follow. But soon she broke down and grinned until her mouth felt wooden. The blue lights in the crowded room, the smoke and the noisy commotion, confused her also.
>
> "You're a funny kind of a girl," the soldier said finally.

She goes to his room, and as he pulls her onto the bed she realizes through a set of "separate glimpses" into memory that the threat is sexual, "but she did not let those separate glimpses fall together, and the word she repeated was 'crazy.'" She has enough presence of mind to bite the soldier's tongue, then hit him on the head with a water pitcher. He collapses and she escapes out the window and down the fire escape.

This trauma prepares her for the trauma of the wedding, and the breakdown in language demonstrates her inability to integrate the various aspects of the real adult world, where sexuality is both a serious stake and a consequence in the game. Allegorically, the near-rape scene is an inversion of the wedding as a socially sanctioned and ceremonial sexual liaison, and both are equally nightmarish experiences for F. Jasmine. They are equally out of her control, and both fail to speak her language, to fit into her conception of the world.

PART 3: DISASTER AND DISSOLUTION—FRANCES COPES

After all this, readers miss the actual wedding and are introduced, in part 3, to its immediate consequences. Frances is sulking and crying, having been dragged from the car when she tried to accompany her brother and his wife on their honeymoon. "Flinging herself down in the sizzling dust, she cried out for the last time: 'Take me! Take me!'—from the beginning to the end the wedding was unmanaged as a nightmare." Frances has repeatedly been asked what grade she is in at school—a question for a child. On the bus ride home, Berenice tries to comfort her, imagining a party split for her two halves, a bridge party inside with a costume party in the yard: "One party dainty and the other one rough."

When she gets home Frances tries to run away, planning to become a dainty Hollywood starlet or a rough New York marine, but is picked up by a policeman in the Blue Moon Café. The novel's final episode is months later and represents the end of the novel's world. Frances and her father are moving to the suburbs, Berenice has quit her job with them and decided to marry T. T., and John Henry has died a sudden and painful death from meningitis. Frances and Berenice sit in the empty kitchen, where all of John Henry's weird drawings have been painted over. In like manner, Frances has painted over her rough side and is playing the dainty girl, and Berenice has relented to social and economic pressure by marrying the man who does not make her shiver, after tending to John Henry in his horrible suffering and death. Honey is in jail on a drug charge. Frances has shed the accumulations associated with her previous names, the rough and boyish Frankie and the loose and liminal F. Jasmine. She has become a "nice little white girl" in the worst senses of the phrase, full of class pretensions and white supremacist snobbery. Of her new friend Mary Littlejohn she says to Berenice, "There's no use our discussing a certain party. You could not possibly ever understand her. It's just not in you." She does this as a consequence of an imagined tone in Berenice's voice, and she repeats the insult because she "knew that the words had hurt." Her projected plans now include a world tour with Mary, an unlikely outcome since she and her father are moving in with relatives, not a sign of financial prosperity. She is, she tells Berenice, "just mad about Michelangelo."

Frances is venturing out again, but her name and her language prove that she is taking a conventional role that barricades her against accumulating any elements to her latest name that might be criticized. She is playing her class status, her whiteness, and her femininity defensively, shutting out anything that might be rough or unconventional. Her creativity is no longer expressed in costumes and shows that might suggest or allow the performance of a more fluid gender, class, or racial identity, but in reproductions of classic works of art "pasted in an art book." Frankie had fantasized about "the Law" as a Black Maria swarming with policemen, who storm into her house in search of her shoplifted penknife; F. Jasmine had imagined a similar arrest for her attack on, even murder of, the soldier. For Frances, the law that finds her in the Blue Moon is a tired policeman who will not meet her eyes; ultimately the law has become her own ability to police herself, to keep "safe" in socially sanctioned, acceptably narrow role categories. Perhaps the only thing unusual about the final Frances is her interest in radar, which was an exciting new technology first used during World War II. Young women during this war were encouraged to imagine ways to help with the war effort. But the war effort will not last, and by the time Frances is ready to become a member of her own wedding it will be the era of "containment." Indications are that she will have left her more unusual ambitions, such as radar, behind in favor of more gender-appropriate pursuits, like art.

John Henry, doomed avatar of the bodily consciousness of childhood, sums up the wedding disaster which has so devastated Frances: "'The show is over and the monkey's dead,' John Henry quoted, as he settled himself in the next to the last bus seat beside her father. 'Now we go home and go to bed.'" This infuriates Frances because it allows her to see that for him "the wedding had only been a great big show, and he had enjoyed her misery at the end as he had enjoyed the angel cake." Indeed the wedding, from angel cake to Frances' breakdown, had fit into John Henry's world as a "mixture of delicious and freak." (This trip, Frances' emotional nadir, is one of the few times in the novel when she seems to be aware of other people's perspectives, a necessary relational quality that she generally lacks.) John Henry's use of a "known saying" involving a monkey brings into juxtaposition two threads that give one access to the novel's function as allegory.

Other references to monkeys appear in the narrative at odd times. F. Jasmine goes looking for the organ-grinder and his monkey in the second section, and when she finds them she also finds the soldier, who is drunkenly trying to buy the monkey. The childish Frankie, with her rough and greedy ways and dirty elbows, is a simian creature to be sure, but she becomes less understandable to those around her when, as F.

Jasmine, she actually begins to "ape" adults—to imitate their behaviors without understanding the reasons for those behaviors. In a way the soldier does buy the monkey when he walks off with F. Jasmine—he is getting an imitation of a young woman. In a like fashion John Henry's final summation of the wedding demonstrates that the imitation has failed, the dead monkey is Frances rolling in the dust after the departing honeymoon car fails to take her. In her final armored insensitivity, Frances is again aping adulthood, but in a much more carefully guarded and conventional fashion. In such a manner does allegory intrude into the story's realistic narration.

Allegory intrudes also through "sayings." Clichés constantly reappear in the novel, mostly in the mouths of Berenice and Frankie's father, two representatives of the adult social realm. Berenice sums up her critique of F. Jasmine's wedding plans by pointing out repetitiously:

> "Two is company and three is a crowd. And that is the main thing about a wedding. Two is company and three is a crowd."
>
> F. Jasmine always found it hard to argue with a known saying. She loved to use them in her shows and in her conversation, but they were very hard to argue with. . . . Berenice refused to follow F. Jasmine's frame of mind. From the first it was as though she tried to catch F. Jasmine by the collar, like the Law catches a no-good in the wrong, and jerk her back where she had started—back to the sad and crazy summer.

Known sayings are the voice of the law, of those who are in the adult social world, "caught"—as Berenice says we all are—with "completely extra bounds around all colored people. They done squeezed us off in one corner by ourself." She does not realize that she is participating in the catching.

All through part 2 Frankie resists the social pressures brought to bear on southern, middle-class white girls. She insists that she can be in the world on her own terms. To Berenice's insistence, Frankie adds that "people [are] loose and at the same time caught. Caught and loose. All those people and you don't know what joins them up." She wishes to be free to the world of the law and known sayings and at the same time loose in it. She invents an unknown saying, "the we of me," to describe her imagined place in the wedding and her entry from there into the adult world. In the end she is encapsulated at the level of language indicated by John Henry's simple couplet. When the novel closes, she is caught within the known sayings she shares with Mary Littlejohn, afraid to go beyond. The monkey is not dead; the monkey has taken over the indeterminate creature that was F. Jasmine. She is all imitation, and en route to becoming an adult—a "nice white girl" adult.

AFTER THE NOVEL: McCULLERS' LATER LIFE

Almost immediately after the publication of *The Member of the Wedding* as a novel, McCullers, with the encouragement of her friend Tennessee Williams, started revising it for the stage. During this same year, 1947, she suffered the first of a series of debilitating strokes that would leave her partially paralyzed. *Member* opened in Philadelphia in 1949, then began a string of 501 performances on Broadway. It was awarded the New York Drama Critics Circle Award, among other awards, and profits from it provided McCullers with enough income to support herself for the rest of her life. In analyzing changes involved in the dramatic version, Thadious M. Davis finds that McCullers heightens the drama by falling back on familiar "types," especially where issues of race are concerned. Frankie's father, a teasing, mostly absent source of comfort for his daughter in the novel, has become conclusively racist, railing against "biggety niggers" and insisting that Honey call him "sir." Berenice has become coarser, equating "fun" with sexuality; T. T. has become a servant and handyman instead of a restaurant owner, effectively erasing any trace of a black middle class; and Honey has become a stereotypical

Gish Jen's
Mona in the Promised Land

JEFFREY F. L. PARTRIDGE

MONA IN THE *Promised Land* (1996) is Gish Jen's second novel and her most provocative work to date. The novel takes the reader on a comical excursion through the adolescent world of suburban New York in the late 1960s, at a time when Chinese Americans were emerging as "the New Jews . . . a model minority and Great American Success." Mona and her friends' experiments with cultural identity, epitomized by Mona's conversion to Judaism in the early chapters, are the central narrative interest of the novel. Jen's narrative voice captures the wit and insightfulness of the novel's central consciousness, Mona Chang, while maintaining an ironic distance that lays American racial prejudice and race relations on the surgeon's table. Unlike her first novel, *Typical American* (1991), which is about Mona's parents' and aunt's adjustment to American life after immigrating from China, *Mona in the Promised Land* moves beyond what the Asian American critic Lisa Lowe calls a nativist-assimilationist dichotomy of immigrant fiction by exploring the fault lines between ethnic groups and their relation to the dominant culture. Jen's fictional experiment with fluid ethnic identity is equally successful as a comedy of ethnic errors and a commentary on contemporary American race relations.

Although familiarity with *Typical American* is not necessary to an appreciation of *Mona in the Promised Land,* readers will find that some information about the events of the first novel provides a useful segue into the fictional landscape and narrative concerns of the second. In *Typical American,* Jen tells the immigrant story of Mona's parents, Ralph and Helen, and her aunt Theresa, who initially ridicule the quirky ways of the people around them as "typical American" behavior only to find later that they have become "typical Americans" themselves. Their preconceptions about American behavior (boasting in loud voices, looking out for number one, cheating on one's spouse) highlight by contrast what they superciliously believe defines the Chinese character (filial piety, family and community values over the self, staunch morals). After many years in America, however, Ralph is selfishly absorbed in his restaurant business to the point of neglecting his marriage and family, Helen is fixated on finding her American dream home and stands on the precipice of an adulterous affair, and Theresa sleeps with the husband of their close friend—ironically the man she has an affair with is also Chinese.

Although some reviewers have suggested that *Typical American* shows its immigrant characters assimilating into American society by adopting every negative trait possible, Jen subtly deconstructs an assimilationist view by questioning the Changs' stereotypical notions of both American and Chinese behavior. In his epiphany at the novel's conclusion, Ralph suddenly understands that he is not Chinese and he is not American; that, in short, there is no typical American behavior and by extension there is no typical Chinese behavior. "America is no America," he realizes, suggesting that his idea of America does not match its reality. America, like China, is much larger and far more complex than he had imagined. For this reason one might say that *Typical American* is a novel not about assimilation per se but about the ideal of America—or as it is commonly called, "the American Dream."

In her first two novels Jen proves herself an incisive appraiser of the American Dream. The belief in America as "the land of opportunity" for all of its citizens regardless of birth status, race, and religion has been a hallmark of American idealism since the beginning of American arts and letters. From Benjamin Franklin through Ralph Waldo Emerson and Walt Whitman, early American philosophers and poets saw America as a place where individuals could rise in station by self-reliance and self-determination because of the democratic ideals of the nation. In the early twentieth century, particularly with the rise of modernism and the impact of World War I and the Great Depression, American writers began to write more critically about the bulwark of American idealism. These critical approaches ranged from class-based critiques by authors such as John Steinbeck and Richard Wright to commentaries on the subtle complexities and ironies of American self-invention, the most famous being F. Scott Fitzgerald's *The Great Gatsby.*

CHRONOLOGY

1956(?)	Born Lillian Jen in New York City to Chinese immigrant parents (father, a professor of civil engineering; mother, an elementary school teacher). Grows up in Scarsdale, New York, the source for the fictional Scarshill of *Mona in the Promised Land.*
1977	Graduates with B.A. in English, Harvard University.
1979	Enrolls in Stanford University Business School.
1983	Graduates with M.F.A. from Iowa Writers' Workshop. Marries David O'Connor.
1986	Lectures in fiction writing at Tufts University.
1988	Fellow, National Endowment for the Arts. "The Water Faucet Vision" selected for *Best American Short Stories of 1988.*
1990	Visiting writer at University of Massachusetts.
1991	*Typical American* published by Houghton Mifflin; selected as a New York Times Notable Book and finalist for the National Book Critics Circle Award.
1995	"Birthmates" selected for *Best American Short Stories of 1995.*
1996	*Mona in the Promised Land* published by Knopf; selected as a New York Times Notable Book and named one of the ten best books of 1996 by the *Los Angeles Times.*
1999	*Who's Irish* published by Knopf.
2000	"Birthmates" selected by John Updike for *The Best American Short Stories of the Century.*

Kathryn Hume, in her impressive study of over a hundred novels, *American Dream, American Nightmare: Fiction since 1960,* shows that contemporary American literature has not outgrown its obsession with the American Dream but rather has galvanized around it and intensified the critique begun by modernists. She notes that fiction with an un-ironic and uncomplicated vision of American innocence disappeared from the marketplace of serious literature as the Vietnam War, Watergate, the Kennedy and King assassinations, and other events tainted America's view of itself as a pure and benevolent nation. According to Hume, "the modernist writers tended to analyze social problems in class terms, whereas contemporary writers put more emphasis on race, ethnicity and gender." Gish Jen belongs to this second wave of American Dream critics.

Mona in the Promised Land picks up the Changs' story about ten years after the events of *Typical American* when the family moves to a largely Jewish New York suburb and Mona begins eighth grade. Although the witty narrative voice of *Typical American* is present in the second novel, the narrative voice of *Mona in the Promised Land* is animated by the wry humor and effervescence of its teenage protagonist, Mona Chang. Present too is the examination of the American Dream—this time through a series of adolescent "experiments" with ethnic identity that gain in seriousness and consequence as the novel progresses. The changing notions of ethnic identity in America, as well as the correlation between the Chinese American and Jewish American minority groups, are introduced in the opening paragraph, which describes their drive through "fetching" neighborhoods with their real estate agent. As they drive through the town of Scarshill, the real estate agent comments on its large Jewish population and intimates that she would not wish to live in such a neighborhood. "This is such a nice thing to say, even the Changs know to be offended, they think, on behalf of all three Jewish people they know, even if one of them they're not sure about." This suggests that the Changs may have an innate sense of social justice, but they are hardly aware of the issues facing their own, much less other, minority groups. Much of the novel revolves around the issue of social action, of which Mona believes the Jews have a far better conception than the Chinese.

The "promised land" of the title is both a Jewish reference and an American one. The land of Canaan, "flowing with milk and honey" (Exodus 3:8), was the land God promised to the Jewish nation upon their exodus from Egypt. America, with its wealth of opportunities for the immigrants of the world, stands as the new promised land. According to the legend of the American Dream, anyone can rise above the standard of his or her birth to succeed in the land of opportunity. This is the hope of the Chang family: "For they're the New Jews. . . . They know they belong in the promised land."

"THE COSMOS ITSELF IS FLUX AND MOTION"

Four epigraphs introduce the novel's central themes. Jen selects quotes from the contemporary writers Richard Rodriguez and David Mura to speak to the novel's theme of intercultural hybridity in post–World War II America, but it is the quotes she culls from the ancient Roman and Chinese traditions that get to the heart of the novel's philosophy. Ovid, in the *Metamorphoses,* states the plain fact: "all things change. The cosmos itself is flux and motion." The I Ching, also known as "the book of changes," puts a value on that fact: "dispersion leads in turn to accumulation. This is something that ordinary men do not think of." By quoting from these two ancient meditations upon change, Jen reminds readers that change is not the invention of modern societies characterized by globalization, mass migration, and Internet culture. Rather, change is foundational to all human experience, past or present.

To say, however, that *Mona in the Promised Land* is a novel about change seems to raise a moot point. In a way all novels are about change—or if they are not *about* change, they inevitably *involve* change. Yet change in the story of Mona Chang gains special significance when one considers the issues of multiculturalism in modern America. The multicultural movement has aimed to, among other things, dispel the myth of America as a "melting pot"—a society that assimilates immigrants of various ethnic backgrounds and melts them into one. In place of the melting pot idea, multiculturalism erected what popularly became known as the "salad bowl" metaphor. In multiculturalism, each ethnic group within America retains its distinctiveness; multiculturalism celebrates diversity and resists the idea of ethnic groups assimilating into mainstream culture. Mona's sister Callie epitomizes the anti-assimilationist posture of popular multiculturalism. While their parents, Ralph and Helen Chang, have worked hard to assimilate their family, Callie awakens to ethnic pride in her college years, taking Mandarin classes, practicing tai chi exercises, and cooking authentic Chinese cuisine. Because Ralph and Helen believe their children need English to successfully assimilate, they say that "learning Chinese is basically a waste of time." Ralph, in his nonstandard English, puts it succinctly: "Has no use." But in a flash forward, Jen informs us that "in good time, even Ralph will be affirming his heritage; in good time, even he will be celebrating diversity in this, our country the melting pot—no, mosaic—no, salad bowl." *Mona in the Promised Land* is about changes in America's conception of itself, changes in America's approach to assimilation and cultural diversity, but as this excerpt suggests, the novel also parodies the American urge to reinvent oneself.

Callie learns her nativist approach to cultural heritage from her African American roommate, Naomi. Naomi insists, for instance, that the Changs should not put up a Christmas tree in December because "Christmas trees aren't indigenous to China" and are therefore "a symbol of oppression" to the Chinese. Helen sees nothing wrong with Christmas trees and says that her family always put up Christmas trees when she was a child growing up in China. When Callie argues that the tradition was imposed upon her by the nuns at her Catholic school who were trying to convert her, Helen nonchalantly replies, "we are Buddhist, and Taoist, and Catholic. We do however we want." To Helen, having a Christmas tree was "fun" and "had nothing to do with oppression." The argument over the Christmas tree is a trenchant parody of nativist multiculturalism, the type of multiculturalism that insists upon an ethnic group's adherence to a primordial and organically cohesive cultural practice. Proponents of the nativist approach cannot help but see emigration as a threat to cultural stability and see cultural change as cultural loss. The "dispersion" of ethnic groups into the world inevitably changes those ethnic groups. However, as the I Ching epigraph claims, such "dispersion" also presents the opportunity for growth, for "accumulation." This novel about a Chinese American girl who decides to become Jewish tells a modern fable of dispersion leading to accumulation.

TURNING, BECOMING, INVENTING

Mona in the Promised Land is a bildungsroman, which is to say it is a novel about the dawning self-awareness, growth, and coming of age of its protagonist. Like many such novels, *Mona* is set in the protagonist's adolescent years and follows her to adulthood. The teenage years of any individual are a turbulent time of self-discovery and self-assertion, but several factors intensify the turbulence of Mona's adolescence. First, Mona is the only Chinese girl in a white high school with a large Jewish American population. Second, the novel is set in the late 1960s and early 1970s, a time in America when the civil rights movement, sexual revolution, and drug culture were most intense. Lastly, Mona's parents are immigrants from China who have no firsthand knowledge of teenage life in America and have not considered the ways in which their daughter may differ from them as a result of her "assimilated" upbringing. The three factors outlined here set up the central tensions of the novel's three sections, and running throughout is the motif of metamorphosis, signified variously as "turning," "changing," "becoming," and "inventing."

While *Mona in the Promised Land* is divided into three parts, it may be more fruitful to envision the novel in two parts, with the "Camp Gugelstein" episode of chapter 10 standing as the watershed between the playful experiments of Mona's adolescence and the serious consequences of those experiments that carry Mona into adulthood. Camp Gugelstein tests the authenticity and sincerity of the novel's major themes—individual transformation and religious conversion, the limits of American self-invention, racial equality and the evils of prejudice, social action and the role of the individual in society. Camp Gugelstein measures Mona's commitment to her own conversion to Judaism, her Jewish commitment to social action, and her personal conception of democratic principles. Thus, in order to grasp the significance of Camp Gugelstein, one must first explore the development of Mona's adolescent idealism in the early chapters.

To say that everything before Camp Gugelstein is adolescent idealism is not to suggest that everything before Camp Gugelstein is unimportant. Camp Gugelstein owes its existence to the idealist democratic seeds planted in the first nine chapters. Mona sums up this idealism in her statement, "American means being whatever you want," a sentiment dripping with the sweet honey of the American Dream. Although Mona faces some opposition to her views (particularly from her mother), they are not seriously challenged. Mona's argument with her mother over her conversion to Judaism requires her to make a stand, but in the context of the novel this stand presents little threat to Helen and Ralph's aspirations for their daughter. From the first page of the novel, Chinese Americans and Jewish Americans are grouped together by virtue of their emphasis on success through education. Helen is unhappy with her daughter's conversion to Judaism, but her image of Jewish Americans as hardworking, educated, successful people allows her to overcome the difficulty without putting much strain on their relationship. This Chinese-Jewish affinity is evident when considering, by contrast, Helen's assessment of African Americans. In their argument over Mona's conversion, Helen sarcastically exclaims that next Mona will decide she wants to be black, or a boy, or a tree. This list of imagined transformations charts an exponential multiplication of chaos that extends from one unfilial act: "Children are supposed to listen to their parents," says Helen. "Otherwise, the world becomes crazy." Mona's conversion to Judaism is not total craziness for Helen, but the next step in her imagined chain of events—becoming black—certainly would be.

Ralph's hiring and promotion practices at his pancake house reveal his innate distrust of African Americans, but it is Helen who expresses the most blatant racist attitudes in the novel. Helen resists any kind of solidarity with the African American community and tends to associate class and poverty issues with race, as her refusal to sign the petition to establish a free clinic instantiates. The woman campaigning for the clinic tries to align Chinese and African American social concerns. She tells Helen, *"you people would be welcome."* Helen promptly drives a wedge between them: "We own this restaurant. . . . We live in Scarshill. You should see our tax bracket." Leaving nothing to subtlety, Helen tells Mona, "She want to lump us with black people. . . . She is talking to us as if we are black! . . . We are not Negroes. You hear me? Why should we work so hard—so people can talk to us about birth control for free?" Helen, aware that she belongs to a minority group, wishes to distance herself from what she considers an inferior minority group, and she does so on economic terms. In the process of distancing herself from African Americans, Helen begins to express solidarity with the Jews.

> How similar the Chinese are to the Jews, all of a sudden! What with their cultures so ancient, and so much value placed on education. How are classes at the temple? she asks Mona for a change. . . . and is it true that Jewish mothers are just like

> Chinese mothers, they know how to make their children eat?

In short, Mona's experiment in conversion appears innocuous when measured by Helen's socioeconomic standards.

MANIPULATING CULTURAL IDENTITY

Even before her conversion to Judaism, Mona explores the boundaries of ethnic identity by "turning" Chinese for a brief period. She faces the challenge to selfhood that any young teenager would experience as a newcomer to a new school: making friends, gaining awareness of the social circles, meeting boys, and interacting with teachers. Added to these challenges, however, is the fact that Mona is the only Chinese American in her class. She soon finds that her Chinese identity actually increases her popularity. Her skill at karate, her ability to speak Chinese, her knowledge of Chinese culture and authentic Chinese cuisine become the object of envy of her white classmates. Yet she actually knows nothing about martial arts or Chinese cooking, and the Chinese phrases she shows off for her new friends are bits and snatches in the Shanghainese dialect she has picked up from her mother: "Stop acting crazy. Rice gruel. Soy sauce." While Mona had never identified closely with Chinese culture before, she finds in her new school that she "could probably make a career" of being Chinese. The fact that she knows next to nothing about Chinese culture does not stop her because her Chinese features lend her self-invention authority.

Central to Mona's self-invention is what might be called the invention thesis of Chinese culture. The invention thesis is a strategy for asserting Chinese superiority. The fact that the Chinese invented gunpowder and noodles emphasizes the maturity of ancient Chinese civilization in comparison with other civilizations. In the novel, claims of Chinese "invention" become a way of "fudging" Chinese cultural knowledge and authenticity. Mona learns the invention strategy from her mother. Whenever Helen wants to prove her superiority to her daughters, or the superiority of Chinese culture over American culture, she claims that a particular object or practice was invented by the Chinese. When Mona questions the authenticity of her mother's stir-fried beef and tomatoes, Helen responds, "I'm telling you, tomatoes *invented* in China." To prove that the Chinese were civilized and that she was not in need of "conversion" in her Catholic school in Shanghai, Helen says, "Chinese people invented paper. Chinese people invented ink, and gunpowder. We were wearing silk gowns with embroidery before the barbarians even thought maybe they should take a bath, get rid of their smell." For Mona, the Chinese inventions become a way of "faking" her cultural knowledge in order to impress those who do not know any better. She tells Barbara Gugelstein that she knows how to get pregnant with tea, saying, "That's how they do it in China." Barbara picks up the habit, too. When Andy Kaplan responds incredulously to Mona's assertion that the Chinese use scalpels to cut open monkey skulls to eat live monkey brain, Barbara quips, "Kaplan, don't be dense. . . . The Chinese *invented* scalpels."

The monkey brain story is another instance of Mona's manipulation of Chinese cultural practice to enhance her popularity and further her self-invention as an insider in Chinese culture. Mona decides not to tell her friends that the Chinese eat tomatoes without the skin because it is not "gross enough." However, "the fact that somewhere in China somebody eats or has eaten or once ate living monkey brains—now, that's conversation." Mona's approach to unusual eating practices is typical of an opportunistic attitude toward ethnic foodways described by the Chinese American author Frank Chin as "food pornography." According to Chin, food pornography describes a writer's gratuitous embellishment of unusual cultural eating practices in order to emphasize the mystique and/or barbarity of the ethnic subject and thereby increase the sense of superiority of the writer and his or her audience. The eating practice is put on display for the titillation of the listener much in the way that a pornographic photo displays a person's body for the gratification of the viewer. Mona's description of the monkey brains meal is a classic example of food pornography: the story titillates her listeners and increases her own social standing at the expense of Chinese culture.

Because Jen sets Mona's manipulation of Chinese culture in the realm of growth spurts and raging hormones (eighth grade), one might excuse such disingenuous behavior. However, when these escapades are connected with later events in the novel, it is clear that Jen offers a witty and incisive critique of what Chin calls "faking" culture. Jen treats the manipulation of Chinese cultural practices and the enhancement of the exotic with especial insight in the scene later in the novel when Callie and Naomi return from a meeting with an editor from a New York publishing house. The editor's comment that Callie may "have a book in [her]" because "people are interested in China" is a clear example of the type of racial assumptions Callie and Naomi investigated in their study. Callie has never been to China and has little firsthand experience with authentic Chinese cultural practices. She has no more "natural" ability or authority to write about China than the editor herself. Nonetheless, Callie is so flattered by the thought of publishing a book that she ignores the blatant manipulation of cultural identity suggested by the editor. The irony intensifies when Callie announces that the next time she meets the editor she is going to wear a Chinese dress.

Callie's willingness to manipulate her ethnicity to write a "fake" book on China may be as humorous as Mona's eighth grade antics, but it is more reprehensible because Callie is an adult and because she abandons the principles of her study with Naomi at the mere hint of success and fame. Jen furthermore parodies the publishing marketplace in this passage. Ethnicity, in the eyes of this editor, is a commodity that can enhance the marketability of a book. Callie may "have a book in [her]" because she embodies an exotic quality that will intrigue readers. To the editor it does not matter that Callie has never been to China and is just now learning Mandarin for the first time at the university. The fact that she has a Chinese face is enough to sell books.

Mona's experiments in self-invention through the manipulation of her ethnic identity in the first part of the novel are worth looking at in detail because they set the stage for the action, themes, and character development that follows. These humorous anecdotes underscore Mona's disenfranchisement from the world of her immigrant parents and her desperation to gain popularity among her peers; they also establish Mona as a witty, likable, fast-thinking girl whom the narrator treats with good-natured irony. Mona's manipulation of her identity moreover introduces the important theme of ethnicity as construct. Mona comes to see ethnicity not as an identity that is ascribed by society, history, culture, inheritance, or genes, but as a possibility, a malleable object, a choice. Mona is a study in, to use sociologist Werner Sollors' phrase, "ethnicity as invention." As the novel progresses, Mona finds her freedom to choose and manipulate her ethnic identity restricted by the wishes of her parents and by the prejudices of others. The choice to invent her own identity presents increasingly serious conflicts as she matures. Even experimentation itself becomes a central motif as the novel develops. Mona's experiments with her "inherited" identity here are only the first in a whole series of ethnicity experiments that follow: Mona turning Jewish, Seth turning Japanese and then Chinese, Sherman turning American, Barbara disowning (through a nose job) and then returning to Judaism, Rabbi Horowitz turning secular.

CHOOSING JUDAISM

While Mona's conversion to Judaism sounds like an extreme "experiment," Jen carefully constructs the basis for this transformation not only through the details of the text (moving into a Jewish suburb and gaining Jewish friends) but also through her narrative style. Jen subtly reveals the influence of Judaism on Mona's consciousness through linguistic hybridity. Because Mona is surrounded by Jewish friends and Jewish activities, phrases constructed according to a stylized Yiddish grammar pepper her speech as well as the authorial speech that closely resembles Mona's inner speech. "Also, she knows what is schmaltz" and "if she ever had to say what means Chinese" are examples of this hybrid speech. The reversal of object and verb ("what is schmaltz" rather than "what schmaltz is" and "what means Chinese" rather than "what Chinese means") is typical of Yiddish grammar and marks a subtle change in Mona at the subconscious level. This influence increases when Mona starts hanging out with her friends at the temple and discussing religion and social action with Rabbi Horowitz. Mona's imagined conversation with Sherman Matsumoto highlights the link between conversion and linguistic hybridity:

> *Boy, but that schmuck has got you in the bath,* says he. Says she, *Who asked you, and since when did you start with the Yiddish expressions?* Says he, *Bubbela, about the same time as did you.*

Mona enters into Judaism with a firm belief in American self-invention. In some sense, this conversion seems to promote her popularity in the way that her manipulation of Chinese ethnicity does. Mona Chang becomes a "phenomenon" now called "the Changowitz." It is this maverick quality that first leads Seth to take notice of Mona: "He is interested in Mona, partly because of her superlative grade point average, but mostly because she is a phenomenon. A Chinese Jew!" Mona studies Judaism diligently and takes her conversion seriously. Rabbi Horowitz, Seth, and Barbara respect her for her conversion. However, the attitudes of other characters in the novel toward her Jewish faith range from condescending to dismissive. Eloise Ingle, for instance, hopes Mona "feels welcome" at the temple, even though Mona is a regular member of the group and Eloise is the "newcomer" And Mona's parents believe she is just playing around and trying to get attention—"That's enough Jewish," Helen says after the Camp Gugelstein debacle, "Not funny anymore." Alfred, the African American cook at Ralph's pancake house is the most overtly incredulous about Mona's conversion ("Jewish? . . . You expect me to believe that? Uh uh. Not until you grow your nose, baby"). As she gets to know Alfred and the other African Americans that soon populate the novel, Jen treats her conversion more ironically, as this conversation with Alfred reveals:

> "The whole key to Judaism is to ask, ask, instead of just obey, obey," Mona says. "That's what I learned. Also you've got to know your holidays. You've got to know all the ritual, so you know who you are and don't spend your time trying to be Wasp and acting like you don't have anything to complain about. You've got to realize you're a minority."
>
> "Man, but we're asking, all right," says Alfred. "We're asking and asking, but there ain't nobody answering. And nobody is calling us Wasp, man, and nobody is forgetting we're a minority, and if we don't mind our manners, we're like as not to end up doing time in a concrete hotel. We're black, see. We're *Negroes.*"

In contrast to Alfred's identity as an African American, Mona's embrace of Judaism appears superficial (learn the holidays and rituals; do not forget you are a minority); for Alfred, minority status is written on his skin—it is not something he can opt out of, much less forget. Alfred's awareness that he is trapped in his skin challenges Mona's belief that being American means being whatever you want. American society does not allow him to be whatever he wants to be. Mona's American Dream has its limits.

THE UNDERGROUND RAILROAD

The challenge to Mona's version of the American Dream increases as she and her friends attempt

the dishwashers with an immigrant from Taiwan, Cedric's lesson in Chinese organizational hierarchy is confirmed. "Sure enough, Richard and Edward throw plates at him too. The only difference is that Russell seems to expect this. He doesn't bother to get mad."

The pancake house becomes a microcosm of Chinese society, a society that works when its members know their place. The hierarchy of the pancake house instantiates Mona's observations on Chinese society:

> Mona once went to an exhibit on Chinese portraiture, in which only the faces of monks were depicted in all their idiosyncratic detail. Members of society were depicted in terms of their activities and their clothes, which was to say their rank. For these clothes were not about self-expression; these were closer to uniforms. And that was what mattered—not these people's inner selves, but their place in society. At least to the artists who drew them. But what about to the subjects? Mona was with a friend that day, who thought that if the people portrayed had drawn the pictures, they would have presented themselves very differently. Mona wasn't so sure, though. Mona thought they would have liked to be seen in those beautiful gowns and high-status silks. For she understood what mattered most to the people in the pictures as if it still mattered most to her: not that the world would know them for themselves—they would never dare to dream of any such thing—but only that they might know that they belonged, and where.

Mona's unnamed companion looks through an American lens at the painting and sees a society that suppresses individual expression and ascribes individual identity from birth. Occupation in this society marks one's worth. But Mona looks through a Chinese lens and sees a people who derive their self-worth and sense of identity from their position in society. The novel pits its account of a Chinese understanding of society, manifested in Mona's home and Ralph's pancake house, against its account of an equal-opportunity philosophy of American individualism and American law. Ralph is flabbergasted when Alfred sues him for racial discrimination. Ralph believes he has the right to hire, promote, and fire whomever he pleases. But Theresa tells him, "In China, is one thing. But here in the United States, that's not the way to think. You cannot think all the time about relationship. You have to think about the law."

POST–CAMP GUGELSTEIN AMERICA

Camp Gugelstein dissolves because Mona, Barbara, and Seth still do not trust Alfred and his friends. Despite all the good vibes and shared experiences with their African American friends, Mona, Barbara, and Seth too quickly suspect one of them of stealing the missing flask. One could also argue, however, that Alfred and his friends too quickly denounce Mona, Barbara, and Seth and too quickly abnegate their responsibility to uphold the community through openness and dialog. The suspicions of the three nonblack friends are, to them, immediate proof of racism; black solidarity closes off any hope for forgiveness and reconciliation between the racial groups. However, wherever the blame may lie, it is up to the reader to decide the significance of Camp Gugelstein's demise in the overall scheme of the novel. If Camp Gugelstein represents the ideal of racial integration, what does its failure say about race relations in America?

One possible argument is that Camp Gugelstein was no more than a utopian ideal that could never be attained in the real world. Mona and her friends were naive to believe that American society can get beyond skin color, racial history, stereotypes, and ingrained distrust to live as a community of equals. Mona's claim that "American means being whatever you want" is therefore revealed as the romantic idealism of a young teenager who has yet to experience the real world. However, to read the failure of Camp Gugelstein as such would be to ignore the complex changes that result from it. "Nothing stands still," says Rabbi Horowitz after losing his job and entering secular studies at Harvard.

"All growth involves change, all change involves loss. . . . I'm a richer person for it." Rabbi Horowitz brings together the two epigraphs discussed previously. "Flux and motion" is fundamental to our world (Ovid); and "dispersion," or change, "leads to accumulation" (the I Ching). For Rabbi Horowitz, losing his job was "not fair," but the ultimate result of all the turmoil and change was a richer life.

Camp Gugelstein's demise brings its share of turmoil and change. The failure of the experiment sends shock waves through the lives of the novel's characters that change them forever. Mona and Helen quarrel bitterly and Mona runs away from home; Ralph fires Alfred and Alfred sues Ralph; Seth becomes despondent and spiritually lost (he, of all the characters, takes the Camp Gugelstein breakup most personally); Mona decides to sleep with Seth, and the two eventually move to California to live and bring up their daughter. But through these painful events, the characters of the novel change and mature in ways that would never have been possible without the ruptures caused by Camp Gugelstein's failure. The epilogue to *Mona in the Promised Land* brings all of these rich changes into focus.

In the epilogue, Alfred and Evie represent one significant response to the fallout of the Camp Gugelstein disaster. Besides getting married and devoting themselves to social action ("Mr. and Mrs. Community Organization"), they have also learned to acknowledge their prejudices and racially charged motives as a normal part of their relationship: "they've given up denying that she married him to assuage her own guilt, or that he's a white-bitch-lover who shouldn't have needed her to get him through college." The members of Camp Gugelstein emphasized love and openness, but these ideals were often no more than a camouflage for deep-seated feelings of guilt and fear that they could never openly air. For instance, when Estimator, Benson, and Ray push the conversation on integration and white racism to a point that the others find uncomfortable, Seth calls them into a Yoga circle to "focus the energy." Seth's overt purpose is to channel the energy of the group into a spirit of community; his subconscious purpose is to change the subject. In contrast, Alfred and Evie model a new interracial community, one that has learned from the mistaken notions of Camp Gugelstein that fear, guilt, distrust, and mixed motives are perhaps natural conditions in multicultural America that must be acknowledged rather than hidden for true community spirit to develop.

Ralph's changed attitude toward other ethnic groups represents another significant outcome of Camp Gugelstein. Before Alfred sued him, Ralph was oblivious to his own racial bigotry. As learned in the epilogue, however, Ralph has put a Hispanic American in Cedric's place as manager of the restaurant, and he has hired Moses, an African American, to run his newly opened second restaurant. As with Mona's conversion in the early chapters of the book, Ralph's conversion is represented linguistically. "*Dining room is about make the customers happy,* he shrugs. And then he quotes Moses: *Some things just be's that way.*" While still speaking the nonstandard English of an immigrant, Ralph adopts the words and speech patterns of his African American manager. The linguistic adoption of "be" into his speech represents Ralph's spiritual adoption of his African American employees. Ralph adds his own idiosyncratic linguistic twist to the African American use of the verb "be" by changing it to "be's," which represents his old self with a new attitude.

For Mona, the failure of Camp Gugelstein strengthened her resolve to remain true to her religious conversion. While others jokingly called her "the Changowitz" in her youth, Mona suggests to Theresa that she legally change her name to Changowitz after marrying Seth. She suggests that Seth and their daughter, Io, could change their names too. Changowitz is a name that was once used to make light of her belief that a person could switch ethnicities, but now she suggests adopting the name as a marker for the new community she and Seth have created with their baby daughter. Mona has learned to persist in her belief in American self-invention, but her faith in this American ideal is no longer an innocent or naive one. Camp Gugelstein has taught her that the American Dream is not an impossible dream, although it does have its price.

IMPORTANCE

Judging the importance of a book published as recently as 1996 requires putting it in a particular framework. The question is, to whom is the book important? Book sales may indicate popularity—but that popularity may be here today and gone tomorrow. Critical reviews may praise or condemn a book, but the true significance of that work may not be ascertained until decades later. Awards, like reviews, may judge a book's merits at the time of its publication, but awards do not guarantee a work's lasting importance.

One can begin to appreciate the historical significance of *Mona in the Promised Land* when the novel is placed in the framework of Asian American literary production. Prior to the 1970s there were few Asian American works in English in print. The person who is generally regarded as the first Asian American creative writer in English is Sui Sin Far (1865–1914), the pen name of Chinese Eurasian Edith Maude Eaton. Writers such as Pardee Lowe, Jade Snow Wong, and Lin Yutang published autobiographies and other works; however, some Asian American scholars (Elaine H. Kim, Frank Chin, and others) argue that the writings of these authors were co-opted by mainstream white society to show how unusual and exotic Asians were. Writers such as Luis Chu, Diana Chang, Toshio Mori, Bienvenido Santos, and Carlos Bulosan wrote dynamic works of fiction and autobiography, but their works went out of print soon after their publication. There were also numerous popular works by non-Asian writers that characterized Asians as inscrutable, obsequious, and perilous, the most famous being Sax Rohmer's Fu Man Chu series and Earl Derr Biggers' series of Charlie Chan novels.

In the wake of the civil rights movement of the 1960s, two significant books propelled Asian American literature into the public eye. *Aiiieeee! An Anthology of Asian American Writers,* published in 1974, presented new writing by American writers of Chinese and Japanese ancestry, but more importantly it recovered some of the "lost" writing of the earlier generations (e.g., works by Luis Chu, Diana Chang, and Toshio Mori). In 1976 Maxine Hong Kingston's *The Woman Warrior: Memoirs of a Girlhood among Ghosts* was published to enormous critical acclaim. *The Woman Warrior* brought Asian American literature into the academic mainstream. It was not until Amy Tan's *The Joy Luck Club* was published in 1989 that Asian American literature saw its first blockbuster success in the mainstream market. *The Joy Luck Club* sold 275,000 hardcover copies and was later made into a movie. Large publishing houses were not only willing to take a chance with Asian American authors after *The Joy Luck Club*'s success but were scrambling for their own Amy Tan. Numerous Asian American works of exceptional quality were published in the 1980s (among them Joy Kogawa's *Obasan,* Kingston's *China Men* and *Tripmaster Monkey: His Fake Book,* and Bharati Mukherjee's *Jasmine*), but none gained the popularity of Tan's first novel. The 1990s was a decade of unprecedented Asian American literary output, with works by authors from an array of Asian ethnicities publishing works and garnering awards.

Despite the success of Asian American literature in the years just prior to *Mona in the Promised Land*'s publication, the works published by large commercial presses tended to downplay racial politics, focus on a dichotomy between the "nativism" and the "assimilation," and ignore issues of solidarity with other ethnic groups. Before the 1990s, much Asian American literature was marked by what the critic David Leiwei Li calls "ethnic nationalism." This was a necessary phase in which Asian American writers represented themselves and their characters as belonging to America. "Claiming America" is the term Kingston and others have used for this strategy of writing Asian Americans back into the histories from which they had previously been excluded or undervalued. As a result, the literature was primarily concerned with the American experience of Asian Americans. *Mona in the Promised Land,* with its emphasis on American racial politics and ethnic integration, is one of the first Asian American mainstream successes to usher in a new era of Asian American literature, which Li describes as "an era of energetic heteroglossia that is able to entertain as never before divergent ideological viewpoints and aesthetic expressions."

As discussed, *Mona in the Promised Land* emphasizes a vision of personal and ethnic identity as fluid and constructed. The world of the novel ultimately reinforces a postmodern view of ethnic identity and self-knowledge; in postmodern terminology, the novel portrays contingent ethnic identities, cultural hybridity, cultural fluidity, and what Homi Bhabha calls "the interstices" of culture and "in-between spaces." Mona's transformation from Mona Chang to Mona Changowitz, a transformation which by the end of the novel we are meant to take seriously, requires a redefinition of the self as one who lives between cultures, or perhaps on the cusp of several cultures. Mona Changowitz is a woman who defines herself.

While in her novels and in interviews Jen does not employ the language of postmodern ethnic identity politics, she nonetheless articulates a vision of ethnic identity that is closely aligned with postmodern race theory. For example, in reply to a question about what she hopes readers will learn from *Mona in the Promised Land,* Jen wrote in 1999:

> I hope that they will understand that ethnicity is a very complicated thing, not a stable, unified thing. Right now many people hold the view that if you're a Chinese American, that is far and away the most important fact about you. That is what you were born and will be forever. To try to make yourself something else is being false to your true self. I think that's entirely wrong. I think that all the groups in America have rubbed off on each other, and that no group is pure. There is really no such thing as one who is purely Chinese American or anything else. If you look at what it means to be Chinese American today, for instance, I think you'll find that a lot of our ideas about group identity have been borrowed straight from Jewish and black people. To imagine that being just one thing is the be-all-and-end-all truth about yourself is pretty naïve.

Jen's sense of individual identity as a constructed identity out of the myriad encounters with people, places, and ideas around us is not necessarily a new concept (Ovid says the universe is in flux, the I Ching says dispersion leads to accumulation, and American writers besides Jen have suggested as much—Walt Whitman's "There Was a Child Went Forth" comes to mind). However, when talking about ethnicity in multicultural America, it is hard to let go of nativist assumptions about culture without replacing them with assimilationist ones. Gish Jen's *Mona in the Promised Land* articulates a dynamic view of ethnic identity that successfully situates cultural identity on the cusp.

Select Bibliography

EDITION

Mona in the Promised Land. New York: Knopf, 1996. (The 1997 Vintage paperback is cited in this essay.)

1991	*Harlot's Ghost.* Appointed New York State Author, 1991–1993.
1995	*Oswald's Tale.*
1998	*The Time of Our Time.*
2003	*The Spooky Art: Some Thoughts on Writing.*

and several of the Texans he had known on the Philippine island of Luzon. He saw combat on Luzon and went on a number of patrols, including an ambitious one behind enemy lines that provided a key incident for the novel. But before he transferred into a combat unit, Mailer, a college graduate, served in several headquarters positions. Because he could type and read the coordinates of a military map, he had to volunteer for a reconnaissance platoon in order to escape headquarters duty. He wrote hundreds of letters to his wife and family describing the firefights, the tropical diseases, the men, the jungle landscape, and the ways the army worked and the ways it did not.

The diversity of his assignments, high and low—he was a cook after the Japanese surrender in August 1945—enabled him to study the power structures of the military, what the novel's General Cummings calls the "fear ladder." Power and its permutations, how it is gained, lost, and used, is one of the novel's major themes. It is manifested in the plot and explored in three long, intelligent, but frightening, conversations between Hearn and General Cummings, the latter serving as a prototype for fictional portraits of many autocratic American generals. These dialectical discussions, which foreshadow Mailer's later writing, were added in the final draft and gave the author a great deal of trouble.

The rest of the novel, buttressed by his knowledge of the works of his literary heroes, was much easier to write. In *The Spooky Art* Mailer characterizes his novel as "the solid, agreeable effort of a young carpenter constructing a decent house while full of the practices, techniques and wisdom of those who have built houses before him." Discharged in May 1946, Mailer immediately began work on the novel. He was as ready as he could be: he had written and read a great deal; his Brooklyn upbringing and Harvard education provided contrasting swaths of cultural knowledge about depression-era America; the letters he had written home, crammed with useful incidents and army lore, constituted an on-the-ground report of the Luzon campaign; his wife and family were enthusiastically supportive; and he had been fortunate enough to be assigned to the Pacific. "I was lucky," he recalled in *Vietnam, We've All Been There* (1992), "because the European war would have been too much for me. I realized that when I read *The Young Lions* and saw how much more [the book's author Irwin] Shaw knew about Europe than I did—I knew nothing about Europe." Finally, Norman Mailer was a disciplined, talented, and ambitious young man.

CUMMINGS AND HIS ISLAND

The novel follows a two-month campaign to take a Pacific island. It is divided into four unequal parts. Part one, "Wave," is the forty-page prologue where many of the enlisted men are introduced and the amphibious landing takes place. Part two, "Argil and Mold," is the second and longest part of the novel, almost four hundred pages. It deals with the first six weeks of the campaign leading up to the final battle against the Japanese. Argil is the white clay that the potter molds; General Cummings seeks to mold his forces into the perfect fighting weapon, and Sergeant Croft attempts to do the same at his level. Part three, "Plant and Phantom," is 280 pages long and deals with the culminating event of the novel, a long reconnaissance patrol behind enemy lines. The section title refers to the physical and spiritual aspects of humans and the disharmony in which they exist. This disharmony is one of the novel's fundamental oppositions. The demands of the body and the aspirations of the spirit are starkly contrasted in the novel. The brief concluding section, "Wake," deals with the mopping up after the Japanese are defeated. Except for prewar profiles of ten of the characters, which Mailer calls "The Time Machine," all the novel's action is confined to a Pacific island. This locus gave Mailer tremendous narrative concentration. The reader, with hindsight, knows that the island will be eventually taken. It must, because historically the Japanese were routed from one island after another, and the American forces moved inexorably up to the Philippines and then to Japan itself. This focus also imposes a constrained time scheme; the island campaign will not stretch on endlessly but rather have a beginning, a middle, and an end.

The island where the novel's events take place is Anopopei—a fictional name invented by Mailer. Maj. Gen. Edward Cummings invades the island with a six-thousand-man force sometime, it appears, in early 1944. (Mailer gives no specific dates in order to preserve the archetypal nature of the campaign.) Shaped like an ocarina, Anopopei is 150 miles long by 50 miles wide, tapering at the ends. The ocarina's mouthpiece, a peninsula where Cummings lands his troops after naval and air bombardment, juts out about twenty miles from the northwest quadrant of the island, as depicted on the line drawing included in every edition of the novel. Following the book's title pages, this drawing is the next thing that readers encounter, which is Mailer's way of emphasizing landscape as one of the defining circumstances of the novel.

Cummings meets little initial resistance and quickly moves south on the mouthpiece toward the main part of the island. The Watamai Range runs along the island's east-west axis, anchored in the middle by the rocky Mount Anaka. Except for the mountain peaks, a thin girdle of beach, and a few rolling hills covered with *kunai* grass, the island is all jungle—dense, soggy, nearly impenetrable. The tide of the war is turning in the Pacific, and Cummings, one of Mailer's most deftly drawn characters, must take the island swiftly if he is to gain a position of importance in postwar America. This is especially true after the near fiasco he oversaw on Motome, the previous island (also fictional) his troops invaded, where the other half of Cummings' division is still engaged in cleanup operations. The platoon's veterans on Anopopei several times recall their beach assault at Motome and the antiaircraft guns the Japanese leveled at their rubber boats.

Many of Cummings' troops are sick and demoralized, adding to his problems. Still, he is confident, and for the first weeks of the campaign on Anopopei, his troops "functioned like an extension of his own body." A midwesterner and a West Point graduate, Cummings is renowned for combining "the force, the tenacity, the staying power" of a bulldog with "the intellect and charm and poise of a college professor or a statesman." He is a bold, polished, but ruthless strategist who does not believe that the United States and its allies are fighting to make the world safe for democracy; rather, the purpose of the war "is to translate America's potential into kinetic energy," to become a superpower "extending an imperialist paw." The Soviet Union will have to be engaged and reduced, in Cummings' view, and the United States will then be the only superpower. Anopopei, therefore, is a stepping-stone to the apex of political power in the semi-fascistic state the general envisions the United States becoming. Such a state was (and remains as) Mailer's worst nightmare; like many ex-GIs he worried that World War II would be followed by war with the Soviet Union. "General Cummings," he said in an interview conducted shortly after *The Naked and the Dead* appeared, later published in *Conversations with Norman Mailer,* "articulates a kind of unconscious bent in the thinking of the Army brass and top rank politicians. He's an archetype of the new man, the coming man, the one who's really dangerous." In 1946 and 1947, when he was writing the novel, the Soviets were extending their reach, and Mailer had "the feeling that people in our government were leading us into war again. The last half was written on this nerve right in the pit of my stomach."

After clearing out the weak Japanese force on the peninsula, Cummings' next task is to amass supplies, build a road to carry them, and marshal his tanks and troops to face the main Japanese force led by General Toyaku. Readers never meet Cummings' counterpart, and there is only one significant description of a Japanese soldier in the novel, a prisoner whom Croft murders after giving him food and a cigarette and looking at a photo of his family. It is a shocking episode that prepares readers for later manifestations of Croft's violent nature. About a third of the way into the narrative, Mailer does introduce Lieutenant Wakara, an American officer and Japanese translator, who reads a portion of a captured diary and reflects on Japanese attacks as "mass ecstatic outbursts, communal frenzies," but this is Wakara's only appearance. Like most Americans, Mailer knew little about Japanese culture, and after this tentative probe he hardly tries to understand the psychology of Toyaku's soldiers, nor is there much consideration of the war generally.

The Japanese are entrenched behind a defensive line that runs from the ocean, just east of the peninsula, to the base of the cliffs of the Watamai Range. To bring his troops face-to-face with the Toyaku Line, as it is called, Cummings moves his troops left in a huge arc through the jungle, a complex maneuver requiring artillery support, excellent communications, and transportation. It also requires that his force be eager to fight and responsive to every tactical snap of his fingers. They are, and Cummings easily repulses a Japanese attack that comes across a river parallel to the Toyaku Line. Sergeant Croft, the reconnaissance platoon leader, is instrumental in stopping the river attacks, in one of the finest set pieces of combat in American literature. But after these early successes, the advance stalls. Cummings pauses for a few days—a big mistake—to extend the road and let his soldiers rest. Now the men are unresponsive: "A deep and unshakable lethargy settled over the front-line troops." He has powerful enemies in the high command, and the delay in conquering Anopopei causes him great embarrassment; he could be replaced as commander. A reactionary Prospero who has so far ruled his island with superior knowledge, intellect, and the lash of fear, Cummings is stymied by the inertia of his own forces. At this point in the novel it is becoming clear that the real struggle on Anopopei is not between the Americans and the Japanese but between the American officer class and the enlisted men.

THE PLATOON

Croft's reconnaissance platoon, referred to as "Recon," is representative of the sullen recalcitrance of the division's soldiers, although it is led by a man who is most alive when in battle. It comprises men from all around the country, lower- and middle-class soldiers mainly, who have been beaten down by the Great Depression. Six members of the platoon are veterans of Motome: Croft, a mean, whipcord Texan with a taste for inflicting pain; Private Red Valsen, a Swedish-American miner, leftist sympathizer, and drifter from Montana, who serves as Croft's chief antagonist; Sergeant Martinez, from San Antonio, the outfit's scout and Croft's best friend, also known as "Japbait"; Private Gallagher, a narrow-minded right-winger from Boston whose wife dies in childbirth while he is on Anopopei; Private Wilson, an easygoing southerner with a genius for promoting jungle booze, who is gut-shot late in the novel; and Sergeant Brown, from Oklahoma, a worn-out case who is uneasy with responsibility. A seventh veteran, Private Hennessey, is killed on the beach immediately after the landing.

The other eight are replacements: Private Ridges, a dirt farmer from Arkansas; Private Stanley, Brown's sycophant, who is later promoted to corporal; Corporal Toglio, who gets a "million dollar" elbow wound and is shipped home; Private Roth, an unathletic, college-educated Jew from New York who falls to his death climbing Mount Anaka; Private Goldstein, a welder from Brooklyn; Private Wyman, another midwesterner; Private Minetta, a malingerer from New Jersey; and Private Czienwicz, a criminal from Chicago known to all as "Polack." Mailer was careful in how he allotted space to his characters. The backgrounds of eight of the fourteen enlisted men (Martinez, Croft, Valsen, Gallagher, Wilson, Goldstein, Brown and Polack), and two officers (Cummings and Hearn), are given in the "Time Machine" flashbacks, a device adopted from the biographical interludes in the novels of John Dos Passos. The others are revealed in conversation or via Mailer's omniscient narrator, who presents the thoughts of nearly every named character in the novel. A comment of Mailer's published in *Conversations with Norman Mailer* reveals his scrupulous attention to detail: "I had a file full of notes, and a long dossier on each man. Many of these details never got into the novel, but the added knowledge made me feel more comfortable with each character. Indeed I even had charts to show which characters had not yet had scenes with other characters."

Mailer has been criticized for the Time Machine flashbacks. Critics have argued, with some justice, that a few of the profiles (Brown, Martinez, and Polack) are stereotypical, although he has been praised for others, generally those that his background enabled him to handle more surely (Goldstein, Gallagher, Cummings, and Hearn). Yet most readers agree that the information provided is helpful in understanding the later actions of those profiled. In *The Spooky Art* Mailer explains one of his guiding beliefs when he wrote *The Naked and the Dead:* "One was the product of one's milieu, one's parents, one's food, one's conversations, one's dearest and/or most odious human relations. One was the sum of one's own history as it was cradled in the larger history of one's time." He adds that his "characters had already been conceived and put in file boxes before they were ever on the page." So it is not surprising that some of the characters are predictable, although this is not true of Cummings and Croft, whose heavily worked intellectual conversations show "something of the turn my later writing would take," according to comments Mailer makes in *Conversations with Norman Mailer.* These two and to a certain extent several others (Hearn and Valsen, Ridges and Goldstein, certainly) are dynamic characters who change in unforeseen ways in the crucible of jungle warfare.

The ten Time Machine trips, averaging fourteen pages each, are distributed evenly throughout the novel, which means that the motivational insights into the actions of the soldiers on the island provided by the earlier trips are more useful than those from the later ones. The last profile, of Polack, is anticlimactic, whereas the two preceding, of Goldstein and Brown, are of greater utility in that these two characters perform their most important actions after their profiles appear, something that shows Mailer's careful planning. The other consideration is pace. Mailer's island focus, as noted earlier, allows him to employ the narrative equivalent of Aristotle's dramatic unities of time and space and action, but escaping the island via the Time Machine after some of the protracted horrors of a jungle campaign is a welcome respite. The narrative leaves the island for a full 138 pages, or almost twenty percent of the novel. Thus, Mailer is able to juxtapose scenes of army life and combat with images of the soldiers in their hometowns, including brief glimpses of their wives and families, scenes that they carry with them as cameos of their early, not-always-happy lives during the depression. Mailer has been criticized for highlighting the sexual energies and hang-ups of the men in every Time Machine trip, although this emphasis is a genuine reflection of the anxieties of combat soldiers in the Pacific theater and far from home.

Because Recon is directly under the control of the general and Major Dalleson, his chief of operations (his G-3 in army parlance), this unit has more contact with divisional headquarters than most units do. As the platoon's name denotes, its specialty is going behind enemy lines for intelligence purposes, but it can be given a variety of assignments; it is the headquarters utility outfit. This circumstance gives Mailer the opportunity to provide descriptions of a multitude of miserable tasks—combat takes up only a small percentage of the novel's pages. So readers watch the fourteen men unloading supplies, working on the road from the beach, manning a defensive position on the river, carrying jerricans of water to a hilltop outpost, and moving 37mm antitank guns along a jungle trail. There is also a good deal of waiting around, reading mail, cleaning weapons, digging latrines, erecting pup tents, smoking, goofing off, eating K rations, obtaining and drinking illegal liquor, and hunting for souvenirs. Part of the novel's appeal (especially to World War II veterans) is its merciless rendering of every boring, backbreaking, demeaning activity of the war. Perhaps the best example of this is the early section describing the manhandling of the 37mm guns through the mud, one of the most memorable exertions in a novel. It is an odyssey of fear, exhaustion, and death rendered in meticulous detail.

> They started to move, and the labor continued. Once or twice a flare filtered a wan and delicate bluish light over them, the light almost lost in the dense foliage through which it had to pass. In the brief moment it lasted, they were caught at their guns in classic straining motions that had the form and beauty of a frieze. Their uniforms were twice blackened, by the water and the dark slime of the trail. And for the instant the light shone on them their faces stood out, white and contorted. Even the guns had a slender articulated beauty like an insect reared back on its wire haunches. Then darkness swirled about them again, and they ground the guns forward blindly, a line of ants dragging their burden back to their hole.

Nature seems to resist every effort of the troops. Like other great naturalistic writers—Stephen Crane, Jack London, John Steinbeck, for example—Mailer presents the natural world as uncaring, unyielding, implacable, and occasionally beautiful.

Mailer breaks up the narrative in one other way: "The Chorus," which reveals the men's attitudes and leavens the novel with some much-needed humor, grim though it is. These brief interludes, which are presented like the dialogue of a play, are spaced fairly evenly throughout the novel. Their titles reveal their comic intent: "The Chow Line," "Women," "What Is a Million-Dollar Wound?" "Rotation," and "On What We Do When We Get Out." The opening lines of "The Chow Line" are representative of their wisecracking tone:

> RED: What the fug is that swill?
> COOK: It's owl shit. Wha'd you think it was?
> RED: Okay, I just thought it was somethin' I couldn't eat. (Laughter)
> COOK: (good naturedly) Move on, move on, before I knock-the-crap-out-of-you.

"Rotation" contains a memorable line, again from Red, that points to the military's maddening bureaucratic nature, the catch-22 routine that servicemen and women of all eras remember vividly. The conversation deals with the army's complicated system of rotating soldiers home after their eighteen-month tour, something that seems never to happen.

> MINETTA: I mean what kind of deal is this? Just like the goddam Army, give you something with one hand and take it away with the other, they just make you eat your heart out.
> POLACK: You're getting wise to yourself.
> BROWN: (Sighing) Aah, it makes you sick. (Turning over in his blankets) Good night.
> RED: (Lying on his back, gazing at the pacific stars) That rotation ain't a plan to get men home, it's a plan how not to get them home.

THE GENERAL'S AIDE

The systematic revelation of the nature of the combat army goes on for the length of the novel, and is one of its notable accomplishments. But the chief purpose of this expository material—

which is intrinsically interesting—is to serve as scaffolding for the two central but related plotlines. The first is Cummings' effort to exercise total and exquisite control over his own division and so defeat General Toyaku. The second, a patrol undertaken by Recon at the direction of General Cummings, is the culminating action of the novel. These two actions are linked by Lieutenant Hearn, Cummings' aide and confidante and the novel's linchpin, who is central to both plotlines. Initially, Hearn is attracted to the general: "It was not only his unquestioned brilliance; Hearn had known people whose minds were equal to General Cummings's. . . . What the general had was an almost unique ability to extend his thoughts into immediate and effective action." And Cummings is impressed by Hearn, "the only man on his staff who had the intellect to understand him." The general is "looking for an intellectual equal, or at least the facsimile of an intellectual equal to whom he could expound his nonmilitary theories." These theories, as Hearn later reflects, are based on Cummings' belief that "man is a sonofabitch." If you granted him that, "then everything he said after that followed perfectly. The logic was inexorable."

Cummings believes that the only way to realize one's deepest potential, to accomplish anything of significance in the world, is to first control its nasty, selfish, brutish inhabitants through fear. Therefore, Cummings explains, "the natural role of twentieth-century man is anxiety." This makes the army, with its "fear ladder" on which every man is submissive to those above and oppressive to those below, a forerunner of the near-totalitarian state Cummings believes America's war victory will lead to. Or as he puts it to Hearn, "You can consider the Army, Robert, as a preview of the future." The general sums up his elitist philosophy to Hearn as follows:

> I've been trying to impress you, Robert, that the only morality of the future is a power morality, and a man who cannot find his adjustment to it is doomed. There's one thing about power. It can flow only from the top down. When there are little surges of resistance at the middle levels, it merely calls for more power to be directed downward, to burn it out.

The general's power morality is depicted in several ways. He has many one-way interactions with subordinates—Major Dalleson, for example—always handling them like puppets. But Hearn is more of a challenge, and the general employs all his considerable charm and guile to gain his admiration. He gives the blunt, headstrong Hearn various privileges and gets him out of scrapes. Cummings calls these intercessions "papal dispensations." He is also sexually attracted to Hearn and confides in him about his failed marriage: "The truth is, Robert, my wife is a bitch." At this moment Hearn senses that the general is about to "slowly extend his arm, touch his knee perhaps." Hearn recognizes that his admiration for the general, which is not physical, is based on the fact that on one level they are the same; both are attracted to power and cynical about idealism.

But Hearn, a midwesterner like Cummings, also believes that Cummings is a monster and that there is "a kind of guilt in being an officer." A former Communist sympathizer, Hearn is now a liberal-by-default with a pronounced egalitarian streak that makes him resist Cummings' tutelage. His stubborn individualism ultimately brings their close relationship to a dramatic end. This comes about when the general sets Hearn a number of tasks that will make him contemptuous of enlisted men and, he hopes, become his Pygmalion. Recognizing that the general is corrupting him, Hearn impulsively grinds out a cigarette butt on the clean duckboards of the general's tent. Cummings now sees that Hearn is lost to him and forces him to "crawfish," to pick up the butt or face a court-martial. His resistance burned out by Cummings' superior power, Hearn complies. He then asks for a transfer, which is denied. A few days later Cummings puts Hearn in charge of Recon, replacing Sergeant Croft, and sends the platoon on a mission, initially by boat, to determine if the Toyaku Line can be attacked from the south side of Anopopei.

A LONG PATROL

The initial idea for *The Naked and the Dead* was to center it on a long patrol. "All during the war," Mailer recalls in *Conversations with Norman Mailer,* "I kept thinking about this patrol. I even had the idea before I went overseas." When he started writing the novel, he decided that he should introduce his characters first, but "The next six months and the first 500 pages went into that, and I remember in the early days I was annoyed at how long it was taking me to get to the patrol." Of course, Mailer does a lot more than introduce the characters in the first two-thirds of the book. He creates the island's symbolic atmosphere and landscape and shows the miseries of war in the jungle. He establishes an intellectual and political framework via the Cummings-Hearn conversations, preparing the reader for Hearn's second test, this one by Sergeant Croft and the men of the platoon. By the time they leave on their mission, a few of them are as familiar to readers as their own families, and readers have a good sense of the soldiers' "fear ladder" relationship to Sergeant Croft, Cummings' tyrannical twin.

Finally, Mailer artfully delineates the military deadlock on the island, one that might be broken, Cummings believes, in one of two ways: first, by a daring attack from the south—if Recon can find a pass around or through the mountains; or second, by arranging for the navy to bombard the Toyaku Line from off the northern shore at Botoi Bay while his main force makes a frontal assault. Of the two possibilities, he clearly favors the second; the Recon patrol is a long shot. But the navy is not eager to send a destroyer to help, and for part of the last third of the novel Cummings is away lobbying those above him for more firepower to burn away Japanese resistance.

Hearn's challenge in taking over the platoon is great. It is not that the men love Croft; they do not. But they are comfortable in their subservience because they see no way to resist it. Croft is tougher and meaner than any three of the platoon combined. They also know that he is a fine, fearless soldier who may keep them alive even as he pushes them to the limits of their endurance. They do not know Hearn and distrust his initial attempts to be free and friendly with them. He finds his command to be frustrating at first because of Croft's longtime control of the platoon, but then he begins to enjoy it as he leads the men forward, even when they encounter the Japanese and Wilson is shot.

After an exhausting march, the platoon pushes through the steaming jungle and the foothills to near the base of Mount Anaka. At one point in the march Croft takes a bird that Roth has found and squeezes it to death. Hearn forces him to apologize, to crawfish. But the exercise of power troubles him, and after some reflection he decides to resign his commission after the patrol rather than turn into another Cummings. He realizes that he is "not a phony but a Faust." Shortly after this, Hearn is killed by a Japanese machine gun. His death has been arranged by Croft, who suppresses information about Japanese positions gained by Martinez during a suspenseful nighttime foray behind enemy lines. It is a startling development, and a controversial one. In *The Spooky Art* Mailer admits (many years after he had written the novel) that killing Hearn at this point "may have been too big a price to pay, because the denouement of my novel was sacrificed." He continues:

> Looking back on it, I can give you a good and a bad motive that I had for killing Hearn where I did. The good motive is that it was a powerful way to show what death is like in war. The shoddy motive was that I wasn't altogether sure in my heart that I knew what to do with him or how to bring him off.

War serves up such surprises all the time, of course, but with Hearn, Mailer generates the expectation that he will achieve some sort of a victory, at least a symbolic victory, over Cummings and Croft, even if he dies in doing so. But the general and the sergeant are ultimately checked, if not vanquished, by nature and by chance.

MOUNT ANAKA

Besides the humid jungle, two other things seem ever present on the island: the rumble of heavy artillery and Mount Anaka, symbols, respectively, of technological and natural power. They are touchstones in the novel, and Mailer rubs them regularly. Croft, brave but heartless, stoic yet seething with violence and inchoate passions, is drawn to the weaponry of modern war and the "wise and powerful" mountain. During an earlier fight at the river, Croft "could not have said at that moment where his hands ended and the machine gun began." The Japanese attack is sudden and ferocious, but Croft "fired and fired, switching targets with the quick reflexes of an athlete shifting for a ball. As soon as he saw men falling he would attack another group. The line of Japanese broke into little bunches of men who wavered, began to retreat." Later, when he looks at the mountain through field glasses, "He felt a crude ecstasy. He could not give the reason, but the mountain tormented him, beckoned him, held an answer to something he wanted. It was so pure, so austere."

Not long after *The Naked and the Dead* was published, Mailer revealed in an interview later collected in *Conversations with Norman Mailer* that in addition to Farrell, Wolfe, Dos Passos, and Tolstoy, Herman Melville had been on his mind during the composition of his novel. *Moby-Dick* (1851) was the "biggest influence," he said. "I was sure everyone would know. I had Ahab in it, and I suppose the mountain was Moby Dick." Although Mailer was not specific, it is clear that Cummings is Captain Ahab; they have comparable intellectual attainments and Faustian ambitions. Croft, who actually attempts to conquer the mountain the way Ahab does the white whale, is a visceral extension of Cummings, as virtually every commentator on the novel has noted. It is possible for Croft to be seen as Cummings' demonic underling—what Fedallah is to Ahab—although Croft never interacts with, or even meets, Cummings. Mailer avoids such a meeting to maintain Hearn's singular position as the bridge between the novel's two major parts, and perhaps because it would seem contrived (although Dalleson does mention Croft to Cummings and recommends him for a commission).

This makes Hearn the counterpart to Ahab's first mate, Starbuck, who also argues with his leader, although less effectively. Both are confidantes, and both die as a result of the overreaching and prideful arrogance of their chiefs. But the mountain is the clearest symbolic parallel to *Moby-Dick.* In a comment published in *Norman Mailer: Works and Days* (2000), Mailer says that Anaka "was to serve as an actual mass of stone and as a symbolic base for the book. . . . The mountain was a consciously ambiguous symbol, something too complex, too intangible, to be defined by language." Croft sees the mountain the way Ahab sees Moby Dick: he admires it but hates it; he needs to master it. This challenge engages all of his courage, energy, and sensual intuitions, which are considerable. He has "an instinctive knowledge of land, sensed the stresses and torsions that had first erupted it, the abrasions of wind and water." The platoon follows him without question, confident that he can sense "the nearness of water no matter how foreign the swatch of earth" and that he knows "how a hill would look on the other side."

Before Hearn is killed, he sends four men—Ridges, Goldstein, Brown, and Stanley—back to the beach carrying the wounded Wilson. For the remainder of the novel two physical feats are contrasted: the selfless portage of Wilson and the selfish ascent of the mountain.

During this section of the novel, the narrative shifts back to Cummings only once, when he visits an artillery emplacement and decides personally to pull the lanyard that fires the howitzer. When he does, "an odd ecstasy stirred his limbs for a moment," which recalls Croft's physical pleasure in firing weapons. Writing in his journal that evening, Cummings attempts to link all human striving, even the rise and fall of civilizations, to the parabolic flight of the artillery shell. But he is unable to flesh out his ambitious metaphor in words.

> It had all been too pat, too simple. There was order but he could not reduce it to the form of a single curve. Things eluded him.
>
> He stared about the silent bivouac, looked up at the stars of the Pacific sky, heard the rustle of the coconut trees. Alone, he felt his senses expanding again, lost in the intimate knowledge of the size of his body. A deep boundless ambition leaped in him again, and if his habits had not been so deep, he might have lifted his arms to the sky. Not since he had been a young man had he hungered so for knowledge. It was all there if only he could grasp it. To mold . . . mold the curve.
>
> An artillery piece fired, shattering the loom of the night.
>
> Cummings listened to its echoes and shuddered.

It would never occur to Croft to put his deeper feelings into language, but he burns with the same desire for order and self-knowledge as Cummings. Cummings is aware of his physicality but is dominantly cerebral; Croft is nearly all instinct and lean muscle. Their proportions are exactly opposite; together they make an Ahab. In his Time Machine flashback Croft is described as "efficient and strong and usually empty and his main cast of mind was a superior contempt toward nearly all other men. He hated weakness and he loved practically nothing. There was a crude unformed vision in his soul but he was rarely conscious of it." There is ambiguity here; it is impossible to say how much Croft is being derided and how much he is being admired. The same is true for Cummings. The above description of him under the stars, if not exactly a celebration, does seem to esteem his aspiration.

Much of the critical discussion about *The Naked and the Dead* has centered on who or what is the positive force in the novel, and who or what opposes it. The death of Hearn just as he is preparing to resign his commission and adopt silence and cunning to oppose the corrupt repression of the army, complicates the question. Hearn is a bundle of opposed possibilities, and he dies just as he is beginning to discover his true nature; he is the failed hero. In a 1962 interview later published in *The Presidential Papers* (1963), Mailer complicated matters even further by stating, "Beneath the ideology in *The Naked and the Dead* was an obsession with violence. The characters for whom I had the most secret admiration, like Croft, were violent people." Mailer's novel shows that those who attempt to discover their deepest selves in a combat situation will be more successful in doing so than timid souls like Roth (who might be successful in business or as a scholar), or those who believe in collective action like Red Valsen (who has a career before him as a labor organizer), or decent, hardworking men like Goldstein (a welder) and Ridges (who has the tenacity of a successful farmer), or hoodlums like Polack (who would have thrived in the prewar army).

Each member of the platoon has possibilities ahead; some of them will find their futures enhanced by their military duty, and others will not. A wartime army is a warm place for power seekers and war lovers. Croft and Cummings are able to push themselves, probe themselves, courageously seek the vital core of their natures, often through violent or ungenerous acts. People do not grow merely by being noble, Mailer believes. They learn through the dialectic of winning and by losing, by ignoble acts and those of generosity. The novel does esteem Cummings and Croft, in part, while despising their cruelty. During a 1955 interview, later published in *Conversations with Norman Mailer,* Mailer was asked "Whom do you hate?" He answered, "People who have power and no compassion, that is, no simple human understanding." Mailer sees all humans as disharmonies of good and evil, strength and weakness, phantom and plant. Even those he hates are capable of courage—the cardinal virtue for Mailer—and growth. *The Naked and the Dead* and all of Mailer's subsequent novels and nonfiction narratives are without undeviating, unalloyed heroes and villains. He is much more interested in examining the evil in good people and the good in evil ones and the myriad ways these proportions can shift; this is the stuff of the novel for him. And it helps explain why Cummings and Croft are the most memorable characters in *The Naked and the Dead:* Anopopei is an ideal testing ground for them, perfectly conducive to their talents, their flaws, and their desire for self-realization.

In the novel's conclusion Croft drives the remainder of the platoon up the flank of the mountain. The men, even Croft, are now more severely exhausted than ever before. Rebellion is in the air and Red is the ringleader, but Croft faces him down and they push on. Even when Roth, the weakest, falls to his death after failing to jump across a gap, Croft remorselessly persists. But nature defeats him; he kicks over a hornet's nest, and the angry insects attack the men and drive them back, weapons and gear left behind. The idea, Mailer explains in *The Spooky Art,* "was there before I wrote the first sentence of the book. The incident happened to my reconnaissance platoon on the most ambitious patrol we ever took. They sent out thirty of us to locate and destroy one hundred Japanese marines, but we did get stuck climbing one hell of an enormous hill with a mean, slimy trail."

Alternating with the description of Croft's climb up the mountain is the account of the bleeding, suffering Wilson being lugged through the jungle and hills toward the beach and safety. Brown and Stanley give up, but Ridges and Goldstein, heretofore seen as weak and hapless, continue on resolutely while the dying Wilson raves incoherently about his sexual exploits.

> They did not talk, they were exhausted beyond speech, they only shambled forward like blind men crossing a strange and terrifying street. Their fatigue had cut through so many levels, had blunted finally so many of their senses that they were reduced to the lowest common denominator of their existence. Carrying him was the only reality they knew.

A Brooklyn Jew and an illiterate sharecropper, the novel's odd couple, are tested to the limit and not found wanting. Even when Wilson dies, they do not consider leaving him. They carry on: "Dead, he was as much alive to them as he had ever been." Again, nature intervenes; Wilson's body is swept away by a jungle stream, and Ridges, a devout fundamentalist Christian, swears for the first time since childhood. Bonded by their heroic failure, they stagger to the beach and collapse.

TOTING UP

With General Cummings away trying to "wangle a destroyer or two" from the navy, Major Dalleson is in charge of the situation. In a series of uncertain but effective moves, he first probes, then attacks, then collapses the Toyaku Line, killing General Toyaku and most of his staff. It is later learned that the Japanese were almost out of ammunition and on half rations when the American attack came. In another of war's disproportions, Cummings' inept chief of operations achieves exactly what the general has failed to do. The comic account of his bumbling destruction of Toyaku is one of the novel's finest achievements. Cummings is finally able to obtain a naval bombardment at Botoi Bay, and it is officially credited with turning the tide, but the general knows better. His self-confidence is weakened by his inability to have seen how dispirited the Japanese were: "It was impossible to shake the idea that anyone could have won this campaign, and it consisted of only patience and sandpaper."

Croft has missed "some tantalizing revelation of himself. Of himself and much more. Of life.

Everything," although "deep inside himself, Croft was relieved that he had not been able to climb the mountain." Cummings has taken too long to conquer Anopopei and so will not be promoted to lieutenant general. "When the war with Russia came he would not be important enough, not close enough to the seats of power, to take the big step, the big leap." Cummings is chagrined; Croft has been humbled; Hennessey, Hearn, Roth, and Wilson are dead; Red has backed down. Nature, chance, and Dalleson (whom the general is forced to congratulate) are victorious. On the final page of the novel the exuberant Dalleson comes up with an idea to "jazz up the map-reading class by having a full-size color photograph of Betty Grable in a bathing suit, with a co-ordinate grid system laid over it." He imagines that the idea could catch on all over the army. "*Hot Dog!*" he exclaims.

Dalleson's lucky success and the novel's many defeats have led some to see the novel as excessively pessimistic. But there have been compensations and gains in self-knowledge, certainly for Cummings and Croft. Both are still growing, still in process. So are Ridges and Goldstein, whose dauntless effort balances in part the mendacity and evil of Cummings and Croft. The two privates have become friends and choose adjacent bunks on the boat back. Red has had the satisfaction of seeing the hornets defeat Croft, and now he has the glimmering of an idea that he needs comrades; he begins to see how they might work together for their common good. The others in the platoon have "a startled pride in themselves" for their effort on Anaka: "We did okay to go as far as we did." Every surviving member of the platoon has been deeply affected, perhaps permanently altered, by their struggles and suffering. In response to criticisms that that novel paints a bleak picture of humanity, Mailer offered the following, shortly after publication, later published in *Conversations with Norman Mailer:*

> Actually, it offers a good deal of hope. I intended it to be a parable about the movement of man through history. I tried to explore the outrageous proportions of cause and effect, of effort and recompense, in a sick society. The book finds man corrupted, confused to the point of helplessness, but it also finds that there are limits beyond which he cannot be pushed, and it finds that even in his corruption and sickness there are yearnings for a better world.

At the end the men move off to a new island campaign. Soon they will be in the Philippines, and shortly after that the war will be over. The reader gets the sense that while the campaign (and the novel) has been conclusive, and the men tested in the harshest ways without succumbing, they will now face new opportunities and challenges. The Japanese on Anopopei have been utterly vanquished, and American casualties have been comparatively light, but what lies ahead in the peacetime world is uncertain.

INFLUENCE AND IMPORTANCE

Almost every review of *The Naked and the Dead* was positive. *Time* called it "perhaps the best novel yet about World War II" and compared it to Tolstoy's *War and Peace,* as did John Lardner in *The New Yorker.* The reviewer for *Newsweek* said Mailer was "a writer of unmistakable importance" who made some of the novels of World War I "thin and pale by comparison." Mailer's relentless, exhaustive realism was commented on by almost every reviewer and clearly set a new benchmark for gritty authenticity. There was some division of opinion on the novel's obscene language. The *New York Times* reviewer Orville Prescott said it contained "more explicitly vile speech . . . than I have ever seen printed in a work of serious literature before," but a majority of commentators believed the language to be an accurate reflection of the way World War II soldiers in barracks and in battles had actually spoken. Mailer was seen as a pioneer of free speech, and the book was banned for its language in many places. Despite sharp denials by Mailer, several writers over the years have concluded that he was forced to use "fug" for the book's most common four-letter obscenity. As he put in a 1968 letter to *Newsweek,* "No publisher ever forced me to censor The Naked and the Dead. I decided to use the word fug before the book was even begun. In those days the big brother of fug was simply not ready for public hire."

The most perceptive review of the novel was by the literary critic Maxwell Geismar, in *Saturday Review.* He underlined the significance of the Cummings-Hearn dialogues that permitted Mailer to "build up, often very eloquently, the historical and philosophical connotations of the war." Geismar saw that Mailer had enriched literary naturalism by working in some of the ideas of major thinkers such as the Austrian psychologist Sigmund Freud and the German philosophers Oswald Spengler, Friedrich Nietzsche, and Karl Marx, something that earlier naturalists would have avoided. The chief virtue of the novel, Geismar said, was its critique of "the American Army in war and in peace, as a manifestation of contemporary society, as well as a weapon of conquest and destruction."

Mailer's novel was not merely a story of mud, guns, and death; it also presented an overarching view of the politics of prewar and postwar. On the one hand, it looked back to the Great Depression, and, on the other, it heralded the world-dividing struggle between East and West—the cold war. In Cummings, Mailer achieved a brilliant portrait of a seductive but ruthless philosopher-general who would be the model for figures such as James Jones's General Slater in *From Here to Eternity* (whose philosophy seems to derive from Cummings' fear ladder), and General Dreedle in Joseph Heller's *Catch-22.* Both novels owe debts to *The Naked and the Dead.* Croft, of course, is the prototype for many intense, murderous, military psychopaths, especially in novels of the Vietnam War. Robert Stone (*Dog Soldiers*), Larry Heinemann (*Paco's Story, Close Quarters*), Tim O'Brien (*Going after Cacciato, The Things They Carried*), Michael Herr (*Dispatches*), and Philip Caputo (*A Rumor of War*) could all tip their hats to Mailer, as could the makers of the films *Full Metal Jacket* and *Platoon.*

In *Bright Book of Life,* Alfred Kazin, the dean of American literary critics after the death of Edmund Wilson, said in 1973 that *The Naked and the Dead* "was the first 'important'—and is probably still the best—novel about Americans at war, 1941–1945." In 1984 Anthony Burgess included Mailer's novel in his *99 Novels: The Best in English Since 1939,* saying its implicit antiwar message presented "a heartening vision of hope." Many such accolades could be cited, but one more will suffice: the editorial board of the Modern Library listed the novel as one of the top one hundred English-language novels of the twentieth century.

The most thoughtful evaluation of the novel is that of Donald Pizer in his 1982 study *Twentieth-Century American Literary Naturalism: An Interpretation.* He points out that Mailer's novel is successful because it is a melding of two major types of novel, one that examines power in society (similar to those of Tolstoy and Theodore Dreiser) and another that probes the mysteries of self (similar to those of Melville and Russian novelist Fyodor Mikhaylovich Dostoyevsky). Mailer's novel combines the two types in its exploration of the struggle between humankind's animal, physical roots and its intellectual and spiritual aspirations. Pizer says that Mailer came to a realization:

> Man, in short, was a dualistic creature, and a novel could "straddle" this duality in its effort to dramatize both his inner self and the atavistic sources of his social experience. It is out of this venture in straddling that *The Naked and the Dead* assumes its distinctive shape as well as its power and permanence.

Pizer also notes that many critics have missed the novel's "distinctive and integral quality." He argues that they have missed how well Mailer was able handle both the social and the individual, outer and inner, looking back to the

1930s and forward to the 1950s. "Above all," he says, "Mailer has successfully created a symbolic form to express the naturalistic theme of the hidden recesses of value in man's nature despite his tragic fate in a closely conditioned and controlled world."

Select Bibliography

EDITIONS

The Naked and the Dead. New York: Rinehart, 1948.

The Naked and the Dead. New York: Holt, Rinehart and Winston, 1968. (Paperback edition. Contains Chester E. Eisinger's fine introduction, which notes echoes of Walt Whitman in Mailer's work.)

The Naked and the Dead. Franklin Center, Pa.: Franklin Library, 1979. (Thirtieth anniversary edition, with illustrations by Alan E. Cober and a "special message" from the author.)

The Naked and the Dead. New York: Henry Holt, 1998. (The fiftieth anniversary edition, with a new introduction by the author, is the edition cited in this essay. Also available in paperback.)

OTHER WORKS BY MAILER

Advertisements for Myself. New York: Putnam, 1959. (Contains context on writing *The Naked and the Dead* and Mailer's thoughts on the novel's reception.)

The Presidential Papers. New York: Putnam, 1963. (Contains an interview commenting on *The Naked and the Dead.*)

Letter to the editor. *Newsweek,* December 23, 1968, p. 7.

The Spooky Art: Some Thoughts on Writing. Edited by J. Michael Lennon. New York: Random House, 2003. (Looking back on his career, Mailer puts his first published novel into a cultural context.)

SECONDARY WORKS

Adams, Laura. *Existential Battles: The Growth of Norman Mailer.* Athens: Ohio University Press, 1976. (Comments on Mailer's use of narrators and point of view.)

Aldridge, John W. *After the Lost Generation: A Critical Study of the Writers of Two Wars.* New York: McGraw-Hill, 1951. (First major assessment of *The Naked and the Dead.*)

Braudy, Leo, ed. *Norman Mailer: A Collection of Critical Essays.* Englewood Cliffs, N.J.: Prentice Hall, 1972. (Thirteen essays on Mailer's work, with Braudy's fine introduction.)

Bufithis, Philip. *Norman Mailer.* New York: Ungar, 1978. (Brisk and reliable.)

Burgess, Anthony. *99 Novels: The Best in English Since 1939.* New York: Summit Books, 1984.

DeGrazia, Edward. *Girls Lean Back Everywhere: The Law of Obscenity and the Assault on Genius.* New York: Random House, 1992. (Details Mailer's battles with censors.)

Dickstein, Morris. *Leopards in the Temple: The Transformation of American Fiction, 1945–1970.* Cambridge, Mass.: Harvard University Press, 2002. (Indispensable critique of Mailer and his peers.)

Ehrlich, Robert. *Norman Mailer: The Radical as Hipster.* Metuchen, N.J.: Scarecrow Press, 1978. (How Mailer's later heroes evolved from Sergeant Croft.)

Eisinger, Chester E. *Fiction of the Forties.* Chicago: University of Chicago Press, 1963. (Survey of the emotional temper of the decade.)

Geismar, Maxwell. A Review of *The Naked and the Dead. Saturday Review,* May 8, 1948, pp. 10–11.

———. *American Moderns: From Rebellion to Conformity.* New York: Hill and Wang, 1958. (Among the early major evaluations of the novel.)

Glenday, Michael K. *Norman Mailer.* New York: St. Martin's, 1995. (Excellent examination of Mailer's novels in a sociopolitical context.)

Gordon, Andrew. *An American Dreamer: A Psychoanalytic Study of the Fiction of Norman Mailer.* Rutherford, N.J.: Fairleigh Dickinson University Press, 1980. (Thorough Freudian study.)

Healy, Robert C. "Novelists of the War: A Bunch of Dispossessed." In *Fifty Years of the American Novel: A Christian Appraisal.* Edited by Harold Charles Gardiner. New York: Scribner, 1951. (How conservatives viewed Mailer in the early 1950s.)

Hendin, Josephine. *Vulnerable People: A View of American Fiction Since 1945.* New York: Oxford University Press, 1978. (Intelligent feminist critique.)

Horn, Bernard. "Ahab and Ishmael at War: The Presence of *Moby-Dick* in *The Naked and the Dead.*" *American Quarterly* 34 (fall 1982): 379–395. (Definitive study on the Mailer-Melville connection.)

Jones, Peter G. *War and the Novelist: Appraising the American War Novel.* Columbia: University of Missouri Press, 1976. (Thoughtful study of the novel's structure.)

Kaufmann, Donald L. *Norman Mailer: The Countdown (The First Twenty Years).* Carbondale: Southern Illinois University Press, 1969. (Pioneering discussion of the beast-seer conflict in *The Naked and the Dead.*)

Kazin, Alfred. *Bright Book of Life: American Novelists and Storytellers from Hemingway to Mailer.* Boston: Little, Brown, 1973. (Major study by our finest postwar critic.)

Klein, Holger, ed., with John Flower and Eric Homberger. *The Second World War in Fiction.* London: Macmillan, 1984. ("Uneasy liberalism" of Hearn given careful analysis in Eric Homberger's essay on American novels of World War II.)

Lardner, John. Review of *The Naked and the Dead. The New Yorker,* May 15, 1948, pp. 115–117.

Leeds, Barry H. *The Structured Vision of Norman Mailer.* New York: New York University Press, 1969. (First major study of Mailer's works.)

———. *The Enduring Vision of Norman Mailer.* Bainbridge Island, Wash.: Pleasure Boat Studio, 2002. (Fine consideration of Mailer's evolution.)

Leigh, Nigel. *Radical Fictions and the Novels of Norman Mailer.* New York: St. Martin's, 1990. (An analysis of power in *The Naked and the Dead.*)

Lennon, J. Michael, ed. *Critical Essays on Norman Mailer.* Boston: G. K. Hall, 1986. (Important material on *The Naked and the Dead:* survey of reviews, criticism, and Ihab Hassan's essay.)

———. *Conversations with Norman Mailer.* Jackson: University Press of Mississippi, 1988. (Thirty-four interviews conducted between 1948 and 1987, most of which comment on Mailer's first novel.)

Lennon, J. Michael, and Donna Pedro Lennon. *Norman Mailer: Works and Days.* Preface by Norman Mailer. Shavertown, Pa.: Sligo Press, 2000. (Comprehensive bio-bibliography of 1,100 annotated and cross-referenced entries describing all of Mailer's works in English with annotated secondary bibliography.)

Lucid, Robert F. *Norman Mailer: The Man and His Work.* Boston: Little, Brown, 1971. (First major collection of Mailer essays edited by his authorized biographer.)

Manso, Peter. *Mailer: His Life and Times.* New York: Simon & Schuster, 1985. (Oral biography with many conflicting comments on Mailer's early career.)

Marx, Leo. "'Noble Shit': The Uncivil Response of American Writers to Civil Religion in America." *Massachusetts Review* 14 (autumn 1973): 709–739. (The virtues of the vernacular in Mailer, Ralph Waldo Emerson, Mark Twain, and others.)

Merrill, Robert. *Norman Mailer Revisited.* New York: Twayne, 1992. (One of the best readings of the novel.)

Mills, Hilary. *Mailer: A Biography.* New York: Empire Books, 1982. (Early biography of Mailer that contains an interview with his first wife.)

Muste, John M. "Norman Mailer and John Dos Passos: The Question of Influence." *Modern Fiction Studies* 17 (autumn 1971): 361–374. (Questions the extent of the influence of Dos Passos on *The Naked and the Dead.*)

Pizer, Donald. *Twentieth-Century American Literary Naturalism: An Interpretation.* Carbondale: Southern Illinois University Press, 1982. (Easily the most thoughtful examination of the novel.)

Podhoretz, Norman. *Doings and Undoings: The Fifties and After in American Writing.* New York: Farrar, Straus, 1964. (Contains essay on the roots of Mailer's shifting ideology in *The Naked and the Dead.*)

Poirier, Richard. *Norman Mailer.* New York: Viking, 1972. (The most intelligent overall study of Mailer's works.)

Prescott, Orville. Review of *The Naked and the Dead. New York Times,* May 7, 1948, p. 21.

Review of *The Naked and the Dead. Newsweek,* May 10, 1948, pp. 86–87.

Review of *The Naked and the Dead. Time,* May 10, 1948, pp. 106–109.

Rideout, Walter B. *The Radical Novel in the United States, 1900–1954: Some Interrelations of Literature and Society.* Cambridge, Mass.: Harvard University Press, 1956. (A fine critical survey that includes analyses of Mailer's first two novels.)

Schroeder, Eric James. "Norman Mailer: 'The Hubris of the American Vision.'" In his *Vietnam, We've All Been There: Interviews with American Writers.* Westport, Conn.: Praeger, 1992. (Interview.)

Schwenger, Peter. *Phallic Critiques: Masculinity and Twentieth-Century Literature.* London: Routledge and Kegan Paul, 1984. (The rhetoric of obscenity in Mailer and others.)

Shloss, Carol. *In Visible Light: Photography and the American Writer, 1840–1940.* New York: Oxford University Press, 1987. (Interesting consideration of Mailer as an interpreter of combat intelligence photos.)

Solotaroff, Robert. *Down Mailer's Way.* Urbana: University of Illinois Press, 1974. (Sergeant Croft as existentialist.)

Trilling, Diane. *Claremont Essays.* New York: Harcourt, Brace and World, 1963. (A well-developed examination of Mailer's works through the 1950s.)

Volpe, Edmond L. "James Jones—Norman Mailer." In *Contemporary American Novelists.* Edited by Harry T. Moore. Carbondale: Southern Illinois University Press, 1964. (Useful comparison of the two war novelists.)

Waldron, Randall H. "The Naked, the Dead and the Machine: A New Look at Norman Mailer's First Novel." *PMLA* 87 (March 1972): 271–277. (The U.S. Army as the epitome of technology.)

Weinberg, Helen. *The New Novel in America: The Kafkan Mode in Contemporary Fiction.* Ithaca, N.Y.: Cornell University Press, 1970. (Study of Mailer's activist heroes.)

Wenke, Joseph. *Mailer's America.* Hanover, N.H.: University Press of New England, 1987. (Liberalism and risk in *The Naked and the Dead.*)

William Styron's
Sophie's Choice

JAMES L. W. WEST III

IN THE SPRING of 1973, William Styron found himself at a creative impasse. He had been laboring on a novel that he was calling "The Way of the Warrior," a narrative based on his personal experiences in the U.S. Marine Corps during World War II and the war in Korea. Styron had always meant to write this book: James Jones and Norman Mailer, the other two authors of his generation against whom he measured himself, had both published major novels on the war. Styron believed that he, too, must write such a narrative.

Styron's war experiences, however, were limited. He had enlisted in the marines in 1943, as a college freshman, and had progressed through boot camp and officer training school to earn a commission in July 1945. But the end of the war had found him waiting in the pipeline—stationed in San Diego, scheduled to participate in the planned assault on the Japanese mainland. The nuclear bombs dropped on Hiroshima and Nagasaki in August 1945 brought the war to a quick conclusion; Styron, to his mixed relief and regret, had not seen combat. After the Japanese surrender he had remained in the reserves and had been recalled to active duty for the Korean conflict in the summer of 1951, but a defect in the vision of his shooting eye had resulted in a medical discharge. Thus his fund of experience for writing about warfare was slim.

Styron had nevertheless produced a strong start on "The Way of the Warrior," a ten-thousand-word beginning that had appeared in *Esquire* magazine in September 1971 under the title "Marriott, the Marine." Its central character was Paul Marriott, a career officer whose patriotism and loyalty to the Marine Corps were deep but who was also, improbably, a perceptive reader of literature and a serious student of classical music. Styron meant to embody in Marriott some of the contradictions inherent in military life, which he found mostly repellent but features of which he found seductive. Since the fall of 1972 Styron had been attempting to push forward with "The Way of the Warrior" but had found himself adrift, without inspiration or focus. His failure to advance his manuscript had frustrated him; his friends later remembered that he was touchy and hard to approach during this period.

One morning in June 1973 Styron awoke with a new inspiration. He had been dreaming for the past several nights about a woman named Sophie, a survivor of the death camps at Auschwitz whom he had met at a Brooklyn rooming house in the summer of 1949. Styron was living in Flatbush that summer and had known Sophie only briefly. She lived above him in the rooming house with her lover, a nondescript man whom Styron chatted with a time or two. Sophie, a Polish Catholic, bore a tattoo on her wrist that identified her as a former inmate of Auschwitz, and she told Styron a little about her experiences there. "We took a few walks together," Styron remembered. "One night she gave a party and invited me. I remember going upstairs and seeing her, so beautiful, sitting at a table loaded with everything imaginable: turkeys, hams, sausages, ice cream of various sorts. . . . That's all I remember."

Sophie was young and lovely but weary-looking, as if still recovering from her incarceration. Styron, like most Americans of that period, was only beginning to learn about the horrors of the Nazi death camps. He would have liked to have known Sophie better and to learn more about her past life, but he left the rooming house a few weeks after meeting her, moving to a stone cottage in Nyack, New York, just up the Hudson River from New York City. There he broke through on the manuscript of his first novel, *Lie Down in Darkness* (1951), and brought it near completion before leaving Nyack in the spring of 1950. He never saw Sophie again.

Now, in the summer of 1973, Styron was seized by an internal imperative to set aside "The Way of the Warrior" and to write about Sophie. "Abandoning one novel for another was a strange decision to make," he later told an interviewer. "In a way Sophie imposed herself upon me." Styron began the manuscript almost immediately, choosing a working title, "Sophie's Choice: A Memory," and composing the first few pages of the story. He decided to narrate in the voice of a mature writer called "Stingo." Initially Styron allowed this character to reminisce about his time as a young, bored reader of unsolicited manuscripts in a big New York publishing house during the summer of 1947. The point of view came naturally; Styron

CHRONOLOGY

1925	Born on June 11 in Newport News, Virginia, the only child of William Clark Styron and Pauline Margaret Abraham.
1939	Mother dies on July 20.
1942–1944	Attends Davidson College, enlists in the Marine Corps, and transfers to Duke University. Falls under the tutelage of Professor William Blackburn, who encourages him to become a writer.
1944–1945	Leaves Duke to complete Marine Corps training and is commissioned as a second lieutenant in July 1945. Stationed in San Diego when World War II ends in August.
1946–1947	Returns to finish his degree at Duke and works briefly in New York City at McGraw-Hill. Participates in a writing seminar at the New School under the direction of editor Hiram Haydn.
1951	*Lie Down in Darkness,* his first novel, is published; reviews are laudatory.
1953	*The Long March,* a novella. Marries Rose Burgunder, an American poet from Baltimore.
1960	*Set This House on Fire* is published to mixed reviews; begins work on *The Confessions of Nat Turner.*
1962	The French translation of *Set This House on Fire* establishes Styron's reputation in Europe.
1964	Purchases a summer home on Martha's Vineyard.
1967	*The Confessions of Nat Turner;* initial reviews are enthusiastic, but a backlash from African American critics complicates the reception of the novel.
1973	Unable to finish his manuscript about military life, "The Way of the Warrior"; begins "Sophie's Choice: A Memory."
1979	*Sophie's Choice;* returns to "The Way of the Warrior."
1985	After continued struggle with "The

	Way of the Warrior," suffers acute depression and is hospitalized.
1990	After recovering, publishes *Darkness Visible: A Memoir of Madness* and begins a new novel based on his experiences after World War II.
1993	*A Tidewater Morning,* a trio of long stories.
2000	Suffers a recurrence of depression but recovers and resumes writing, dividing his time between his homes in Connecticut and Martha's Vineyard.

had himself been such a sub-editor at McGraw-Hill in the late 1940s, wading through the slush pile of over-the-transom submissions.

As *Sophie's Choice* (1979) grew under Styron's hand, it became a daring mixture of sexual comedy and high tragedy. On the one hand the novel tells the story of Stingo's search for sexual and artistic initiation; he is a frustrated young would-be author who knows almost nothing about sex and very little about life. On the other hand the novel presents the supremely tragic narrative of Sophie Zawistowska, who has lost everything of her past life—her children, her husband, her parents, her possessions, and even her sense of identity. Stingo learns about Sophie slowly, as she is reluctant to tell him everything about herself. Only later in the narrative, after she has come to trust him, does she reveal the true horror of the camps and of the choices that she had to make there.

Two books influenced Styron strongly in the composition of *Sophie's Choice.* The first was Olga Lengyel's *Five Chimneys* (1947), one of the first narratives published by a survivor of the concentration camps. Styron had read the book in the year it appeared, just after the war, during his last semester in college. In *Five Chimneys,* Lengyel told the harrowing story of her own mistake on the train platform at Auschwitz. She had deliberately understated the ages of her two sons, who were with her, believing that she would save them from the gas chambers if the guards believed that they were very young. In fact she condemned both boys to death, because all young children were judged unfit for work and were immediately executed. Lengyel herself had survived Auschwitz and, just after being liberated from the camp, had written a full account of her experiences, eerily detached and unemotional in tone. The book, translated and published in the United States in 1947, had troubled Styron and kept him from sleeping for several nights after he had first read it. The memory of Olga Lengyel's mistake had stayed in his mind over the intervening years; now he meant to use it as a basis for the central dilemma of his novel.

The other book on which he drew was Hannah Arendt's *Eichmann in Jerusalem* (1964), a controversial account of the trial of Adolf Eichmann in Israel in 1961. In her book Arendt had explored uncomfortable questions of guilt and collaboration at Auschwitz; she had also told the story of a Gypsy woman who had been forced, by Nazi guards on the train platform, to decide which one of her two children would live and which one would die. "That struck me between the eyes," Styron later said in an interview with Stephen Lewis. "This had to be the metaphor for the most horrible, tyrannical despotism in history . . . an evil so total that it could cause a woman to murder one of her own children."

Styron made good initial headway with his manuscript. He also began to read, immersing himself in the literature about the Nazi death camps. He studied a great many books, including volumes by Tadeusz Borowski, Bruno Bettelheim, George Steiner, Simone Weil, Jean-François Steiner, Richard L. Rubenstein, Eugen Kogon, André Schwarz-Bart, Leon Poliakov, Elie Wiesel, and Primo Levi. Styron's fictional alter-ego, Stingo, would later mention and discuss these writings in the novel, allowing Styron to document his own knowledge of the extermination centers, which he had not yet seen.

Styron remedied that deficiency in spring 1974. While on a lecture tour in France, he decided to visit the camp at Auschwitz. He made the trip by train in late March, just as Sophie would have done, and spent a long day in the ruins of Auschwitz—"a horrible visit," he recalled in an interview published in the Paris newspaper *L'Express,* "beyond anything believable." Styron knew, however, that if he were to speak with an authentic voice in his novel, he would have to see the train platform, the gas chambers, and the heartbreaking detritus left behind by the inmates. "I understood to what degree the trip had been necessary," he remembered, "how absolutely necessary it had been to my perception of history to have seen the place, those barbed wires, those fences, those barracks, all those things one cannot believe even when seeing them."

The immediate result of this trip was a short essay titled "Auschwitz's Message," published on the op-ed page of the *New York Times* for June 25, 1974, and later published in *This Quiet Dust* (1982). Styron began the piece on an ironic note:

> Springtime at Auschwitz. The phrase itself has the echo of a bad and tasteless joke, but spring still arrives in the depths of southern Poland, even at Auschwitz. Just beyond the once electrified fences, still standing, the forsythia puts forth its yellow buds in gently rolling pastures where sheep now graze. The early songbirds chatter even here, on the nearly unending grounds of this Godforsaken place in the remote hinterland of the country.

In "Auschwitz's Message" Styron reflected on anti-Semitism and Christian guilt. He also introduced one of the major concerns of *Sophie's Choice:* that the Nazi genocide, while created primarily to exterminate the Jewish people, had also claimed the lives of millions of gentiles. "Of many origins but mainly Slavs—Poles, Russians, Slovaks, other—they came from a despised people who almost certainly were fated to be butchered with the same genocidal ruthlessness as were the Jews had Hitler won the war." Anti-Semitism, for Styron, was only one explanation for Auschwitz. "Its threat to humanity transcended even this," he wrote in the essay. "If it was anti-Semitic, it was also anti-Christian. And it attempted to be more final than that, for its ultimate depravity lay in the fact that it was anti-human. Anti-life."

Styron knew that some critics—George Steiner and Elie Wiesel, for example—had argued that the Nazi final solution was so terrible, so obscene, that it could not be written about. The only possible response was silence. Other critics, historians, and scholars had maintained that only Jews could understand the enormity of the evil perpetrated by the Nazis, and that therefore only Jews could write about it. Styron could not accept either view. As a southerner and a gentile he knew that his qualifications would be questioned, but he believed that the Nazi program to rid the world of the Jews and other "undesirables" was a crime against all human beings and that he must approach the subject from this broad viewpoint. "I knew very well that I was grappling with an enormous subject which could explode in my face at any moment," he later told Michel Braudeau. His position indeed drew criticism after *Sophie's Choice* was published, but he remained steadfast in his conviction that the Holocaust was a subject concerning all of humanity, not just the Jews.

Styron was not simply documenting the unspeakably cruel pogroms in the Jewish ghettos or revealing the ghastly horrors of Auschwitz. These had already been presented, with numbing repetition, in books and magazines and television programs, in movies and lectures and college courses on the Holocaust. Styron's purpose was deeper: to try to understand what, in the human heart, could allow such depravity to flourish. He told interviewer Michael West that he was mystified by the fact "we are all of a species. . . . We came from the same womb, the same source, and we are in effect brothers. But all the horror and suffering, aside from natural disasters which there is no way to explain, are caused by man, by our own species, acting in evil ways toward himself." In *Sophie's Choice,*

Styron set himself the task of investigating this conundrum. A clue to his purpose can be found in one of the epigraphs that he eventually chose for the published book, a sentence from André Malraux's *Lazare:* "I seek that essential region of the soul where absolute evil confronts brotherhood."

Styron continued to move ahead with his manuscript, holding to a daily regimen that brought him to his work table every afternoon at about four o'clock. He wrote slowly, often producing only eight hundred or a thousand words during each writing stint. He revised little. Each day of work, however, produced a section of narrative that went, largely unaltered, into the published book. "I don't write a first draft and then go back and dismantle it," he explained to his friend Hilary Mills. "I write very painstakingly from page one. It's like building a brick wall from the ground up." This had been Styron's working method for many years; he was a methodical writer who needed quiet and the absence of distraction if he was to move ahead. On the doorframe outside his writing studio he had tacked a card on which he had printed an apt quotation from one of Gustave Flaubert's letters: "Be regular and orderly in your life, like a good bourgeois," it read, "so that you may be violent and original in your work."

As he moved further into his story, Styron began to see that Sophie Zawistowska was not telling him the truth. In the peculiar relationship that authors sometimes develop with their fictional creations, Styron had been listening to Sophie during his long afternoons at the writing desk, waiting for her to reveal her story. She had told him that her father, the learned Professor Zbigniew Bieganski, a scholar of the law at the Jagiellonian University of Cracow, had been sympathetic toward the Jews and had been appalled by the establishment of the concentration camps. Sophie had even told Styron that her father had defended the Jews in his writings and speeches and had tried to protect them from the Nazis. Somehow this did not ring true. "This woman is lying to me," Styron later remembered thinking. His task as a writer now became more complex: to persuade Sophie to tell the real truth, to admit that her father had been violently anti-Semitic and had advocated extermination of the Jews even before the Nazis had arrived in Poland—and that she, Sophie, had helped him in his work as his secretary and amanuensis. These things Sophie would eventually confess to her creator—just as she would finally tell Stingo, in the novel, the story of what had actually happened to her and her two children on the platform at Auschwitz.

NARRATION

The narrative technique employed in *Sophie's Choice* is complex and sophisticated, a blending of first-person point of view and third-person omniscience. The dominant voice, the "I" voice, is Stingo's. He tells the story from a mature perspective; he is now a writer in his late forties, experienced and successful, attempting to recapture his early attempts to write a first novel. This older Stingo is relaxed, digressive, and humorous; he is also meditative and engaged, curious about the mysteries of human behavior that he is investigating. Styron created Stingo's voice very carefully. He explained his strategy to an interviewer for the *Saturday Review:* "I had to back off and give the reader, from the very first page, a sense of who was talking. . . . It's at the heart of storytelling and the art of the novel—to establish oneself with great authority as the narrator who's going to tell you a very interesting story, but who has not gotten around to telling you the story yet."

Styron presents most of the novel in Stingo's words, but from time to time he reproduces Sophie's speech and allows her to carry the narrative. Sophie's English has much charm; though broken and ungrammatical, it is vivid and colorful, speckled with words from the other languages that she reads and speaks—French, Polish, and German. Early in the novel, for example, she explains to Stingo about Birkenau, where most of the killing took place:

> I was at Auschwitz for twenty months. When I arrived everyone who was selected to be killed was sent to Birkenau, but very soon later Birkenau become the place where only Jews were killed. It was a place for the mass extermination of the Jews. There was still another place not far away, a vast *usine* where was made artificial—*synthétique—caoutchouc,* rubber. The prisoners at the Auschwitz camp worked there too, but mainly there was one purpose for the Auschwitz prisoners, which was to help in the extermination of *les juifs* at Birkenau. . . . But one must see that the Aryan prisoners was also supposed to die, finally. After their bodies and strength and *santé* was gone and they was *inutiles,* they would be made to die too, by shooting or with the gas at Birkenau.

Styron's rendering of Sophie's talk is a skillful exercise in mimicry. After a few pages, however, her speech becomes distracting, and at these moments Styron performs an act of authorial legerdemain: he switches from Sophie's voice back to Stingo's, but retains Sophie's point of view. Thus readers continue to be privy to Sophie's perceptions and thoughts but hear them in Stingo's voice, which we have learned to trust. The transformation is handled so skillfully that the reader never notices or questions it, never asks, "How does Stingo know this about Sophie?" The two characters have become so close that Stingo seems to be reading Sophie's mind.

Styron made steady progress with *Sophie's Choice* in 1975 and 1976. From the very beginning he had a clear idea of the directions in which he meant to take his narrative; he had filled a long yellow legal-pad sheet with reminders to himself about points he wished to address in his novel, and he had tacked this piece of paper to the wall of his study. (The sheet survives among his papers at Duke University.) These were his only working notes; otherwise he carried the story in his head. Toward the end of the composition period, in 1977 and 1978, he felt confident enough to discuss Sophie's story with friends—an unusual practice for him. On Sunday, December 17, 1978, Styron wrote down the final words of his novel. Then he recorded the time, 1:15 P.M., and penciled words of gratitude in French: "Grâce du Bon Dieu."

The publication of *Sophie's Choice* was a much-anticipated literary event. Random House, Styron's publisher, mounted a strong promotional campaign, and Don Congdon, his literary agent, worked energetically to market book-club, paperback, and film rights. Early activity of this kind is gratifying to a writer: it guarantees that a book will earn money, have many readers, and be seriously discussed. But it can also be daunting because book reviewers will be primed to write about the novel and to home in on any aspect of the story that might be controversial.

Sophie's Choice was formally published by Random House on June 11, 1979, Styron's fifty-fourth birthday. Initial notices were mixed. Many reviewers were respectful but seemed puzzled, unable to come to terms with a work of such length and complexity in limited space and on a short deadline. Some reviews were entirely laudatory. Christopher Lehmann-Haupt called *Sophie's Choice* a "stunning achievement" in the daily *New York Times;* Larzer Ziff, in *Commonweal,* wrote that Styron's "narrative mastery continues to be astounding." Benjamin DeMott praised *Sophie's Choice* in the *Atlantic Monthly:* "The overall scale and tone, the willingness to ask some height of the reader, the quality of the book's ambition to be adequate to a major moral challenge, stand forth, well before the end, as thoroughly admirable." John Gardner, however, writing for the *New York Times Book Review,* judged Styron's novel to be powerful but deeply flawed. "Though I am profoundly moved by *Sophie's Choice* and consider the novel an immensely important work," wrote Gardner, "I am not persuaded by it." Robert Alter, in the *Saturday Review,* was squeamish about sexual elements in the narrative: "I cannot think of a recent novel that is so compromised artistically by exercising the full prerogatives of the new sexual candor," he wrote. Some reviewers complained that *Sophie's Choice* was too long and that Styron's prose was overwrought. Other reviewers found it difficult to distinguish Styron from Stingo—a confusion that the author apparently intended.

Mixed reviews, however, do not doom a novel at the bookshops. Initial clothbound sales of *Sophie's Choice* were quite strong; the novel sold steadily from the first and reached the top spot on the *New York Times* best-seller list in late July. It stayed on the list for some forty weeks, well into 1980. Thousands of additional copies were distributed to readers through Book-of-the-Month Club; a Bantam paperback reached hundreds of thousands more. The novel has since been translated into more than twenty languages, including French, German, Spanish, Italian, Portuguese, Dutch, Swedish, Norwegian, Finnish, Danish, Czech, Polish, and Russian. The original English text has been continuously in print since 1979 and has now, by the reckoning of Styron's publishers, passed the three-million mark in sales, a remarkable record of longevity and popularity.

DISTRACTIONS

Before moving to an interpretation of the characters and themes of *Sophie's Choice,* it is useful to address two concerns that can turn into blind alleys. The first is the "universalizing" of the Holocaust; the second is the broad sexual comedy of the novel, especially the scenes involving masturbation.

When *Sophie's Choice* was published in 1979, Styron feared that an attack on the novel might emerge from part of the American Jewish intelligentsia. Certain Jewish critics, he thought, might object to the fact that Sophie had been portrayed as a gentile and that the Holocaust had been presented as a crime against all of humanity. *The Confessions of Nat Turner,* Styron's 1967 novel about an antebellum slave rebellion in Virginia, had drawn heavy fire from African American critics who accused Styron of falsifying the historical record and making Nat Turner into a weak, vacillating character. These attacks culminated in the publication of a collection of polemical essays, edited by John H. Clark, titled *William Styron's "Nat Turner": Ten Black Writers Respond* (1968). Styron had thought that a similar volume might be published about *Sophie's Choice,* but no such book appeared. No organized campaign against his novel developed in the months just after its publication, and none has emerged in the years since.

Some Jewish writers, however—among them Elie Wiesel and Cynthia Ozick—have criticized Styron in individual essays. They have faulted him for allowing Sophie Zawistowska to remain a Polish Catholic and for trespassing onto intellectual territory not his own. Wiesel and Ozick are representative of a vocal group of intellectuals who see the Holocaust as a rallying point for American Judaism and who wish to interpret it as a phenomenon aimed solely at the Jewish people. An equally vocal group of writers and critics, including Richard L. Rubenstein, Peter Novick, and Emil Fackenheim, maintain that the Nazi extermination camps were a crime against mankind and that Hitler's bureaucracy of death, after disposing of European Jews, would have turned to other races and groups: especially Gypsies, Poles, and Slovaks, as well as homosexuals and people with birth defects.

The dispute, an important one, is unlikely ever to be resolved or shelved. It is certainly a central concern in *Sophie's Choice,* but one must guard against its becoming the only point of discussion. Styron did indeed write his novel in part to redress what he saw as an imbalance in the interpretation of Holocaust history. He wanted to show, through Sophie's story, that many other groups were targets for Hitler's ethnic cleansing and that a great many people who perished in the death camps were not Jews—though Jews were by far the greatest sufferers. Styron made these points in interviews, both before and after the publication of *Sophie's Choice* and in public speeches and essays. But the question can become a red herring, distracting readers from other moral and philosophical questions raised by the book. Sophie Zawistowska's story is indeed about a Polish Catholic caught up in the machinery of the Holocaust, but it is also about any survivor of a historical tragedy who must decide whether to reenter life, beginning again with diminished resources, or to abandon life for the safe haven of death.

The second potential distraction, the comic episodes of masturbation early in the story, can also misdirect a reader's attention from the tragic undercurrents of the novel. Styron had already dealt with masturbation as a serious literary theme in *The Confessions of Nat Turner.* His protagonist in that novel, a rebel slave, was celibate and frustrated, prone to masturbate as a release for his sexual tensions and as a way of calling forth heated fantasies of rape and violence. In *Sophie's Choice* the treatment is much more humorous; Stingo is frustrated artistically and sexually, unable either to write his novel or to persuade any young woman to share his bed. Ergo, he masturbates, spilling his seed to no purpose—a metaphor for his unproductive attempts to write. The novel contains several scenes of sexual comedy, including Stingo's hopeless pursuit of Leslie Lapidus, a Jewish American princess who is a merciless tease, and his heated episodes with Mary Alice Grimball, who will masturbate him but not allow him to touch her. In part Styron is recording what it was like to be young and desirous in the 1940s, a period he later remembered as an erotic ice age; but he is equally keen to juxtapose the low sexual comedy in Stingo's life against the high tragedy of Sophie's story. One finds this technique of mixing tragedy with comedy in other writers of large reach (William Shakespeare, Laurence Sterne, and Herman Melville come to mind). Sophie's story, standing alone, would be unrelievedly painful to read, just as Stingo's story, without Sophie's to counterbalance it, would be merely amusing buffoonery.

But there is another juxtaposition at work here. Stingo, in his masturbatory excess, stands for the forces that Sophie will have to deal with if she chooses to enter life again. Life, like masturbation, is messy. Desire and pursuit, sex and love, birth and childrearing, food, music, literature, art, warmth, laughter, weeping, jealousy, frustration, ecstasy, and pain—all of these are intensely stimulating but also unpredictable and chancy. Can Sophie, who has lost everything to the Nazi death camps, now summon the will to begin again? Can she face and control male sexual desire and all that it brings? Stingo, youthful and feisty, is poised to experience life. His intense desire to learn of sex is intertwined with his longings to produce art; both wishes spring from the same source. Evil, however, can also emerge from these same wellsprings. Surely the Nazi plans for global domination and ethnic purges were also tied in with quasi-sexual desires and fantasies, though of a much darker and more perverted kind.

Can Sophie, who is broken, find a way to mend herself and reenter the disorder of life? Can she once again accept the risks of living? The alternative, of which she is fully aware, is death—and it beckons to her alluringly. Death must seem clean and cool to Sophie, an escape from her guilt and a refuge from the ever-present challenges of daily existence. Sophie does not fear death. She saw it daily at Auschwitz. She knows that death is terrible but can provide a blessed release from suffering and doubt. The clumsy and desirous Stingo represents the potential of life; readers have confidence in him and know that he will live through his early awkwardness, eventually to be fulfilled sexually and artistically. Indeed, the evidence of his success is on the page—his calm voice as a mature, experienced man, narrating the story. Stingo was able to harness his youthful energies and to direct them toward art and sexual fulfillment. Sophie, by contrast, must face life with little emotional capital and with weakened desires; she is by no means as certain of fulfillment as is her young friend.

PRINCIPAL CHARACTERS

Stingo dominates *Sophie's Choice.* He is the most autobiographical character in Styron's fiction; his southern background, his father and mother, his education, his military experience, and his frustrating job at McGraw-Hill are all drawn from Styron's own life. Styron, like Stingo, lived in a boardinghouse in Flatbush in the late 1940s; there, like Stingo, he tried without success to push ahead with a first novel and met a survivor of Auschwitz named Sophie. Many details from Styron's experiences make their way into Stingo's story, though with some heightening for dramatic effect, as with the scurrilous dust-jacket blurbs that Stingo writes for the books published by McGraw-Hill. Stingo's mature voice also seems to be Styron's voice, and the pattern of Stingo's career—early success with a novel called *Inheritance of Night* and later uproar over a book entitled *These Blazing Leaves*—parallels Styron's own successes and controversies with *Lie Down in Darkness* and *The Confessions of Nat Turner.*

But one must be careful not to identify Stingo too closely with Styron. Stingo is both Styron and not Styron. He can best be envisioned as a character from a parallel but independent universe. Stingo's relationship with Sophie and Nathan, for instance, is entirely invented, as are most of his sexual frustrations. Likewise his writer's block is more profound and obdurate than Styron's was, and his experiences as a junior editor are more colorful than Styron's were. These quasi-autobiographical imaginings do allow Styron to ruminate and comment on his own career, and on the Holocaust as it has come to dominate much discourse about World War II. Still, *Sophie's Choice* is fiction, not autobiography.

Young Stingo is attractive and winning. He is lonely and alienated in Brooklyn, but he is also curious and observant, alive to the many sensations and people around him. He desires new experience and wants desperately to have something to write about. He senses, correctly, that some of his artistic problems come from his youth. "I wanted beyond hope or dreaming to be a writer," he says early on, but "I was aware of the large hollowness I carried within me. It was true that I had traveled great distances for one so young, but my spirit had remained landlocked, unacquainted with love and all but a stranger to death."

The mature Stingo, who talks about his former self, is equally charming—self-possessed, ironic, knowing, and affectionate toward the young man he used to be. This older Stingo, however, is also informed about other dimensions of the novel; he knows the details of the extermination camps and is familiar with the historical and moral questions the Holocaust has raised. Was the Holocaust simply a matter of German hatred for the Jews or of Hitler's need for a race of scapegoats? Or was it of deeper and more disturbing origin, caused by man's innate will to dominate his fellow man and to commit atrocities that, finally, are inexplicable?

These questions are addressed in part through Sophie's story. The reader, however, must be patient because Sophie does not entirely understand what has happened to her and how her fate is tied in with larger social and historical events. Sophie reveals herself only gradually to Stingo and probably never admits everything to him. She is mysterious and beautiful but also faintly corrupt. She may even be responsible for some of what happened to her; at least she seems to think so. She was a victim of a broad evil but also, unwittingly, a collaborator in her fate, and perhaps complicit in the deaths of her children. Thus most of her memories come to readers through what Stingo calls "a hideous sense of guilt" and "a filter of self-loathing."

Sophie is fragile emotionally and physically, but she does not shrink from living. We admire her attempts to participate in what life offers—

her relish for food, her love of literature and music, her capacity for friendship with Stingo, and her enjoyment of sex—which for her is "a flight from memory and grief." She is an insignificant bit of flotsam from the war, separated entirely from her earlier existence, and yet she seems determined for a time to make a new life, perhaps even to marry and bear children to replace those she has lost. Finally, though, her past is too heavy a burden, and she is overwhelmed by guilt and self-hatred. The distance she must travel to reconnect with life is simply too great.

Nathan Landau is the most puzzling character in *Sophie's Choice.* His behavior is unpredictable: he can be charming or vicious, sophisticated or ignorant, calm or demented. Obviously he is not the man for Sophie, who needs stability and reassurance, and yet he seems to love her desperately. His powerful sexual jealousies, manifested in wild accusations of unfaithfulness that he levels at Sophie, are the reverse side of Stingo's puppyish desires. Both kinds of behavior, however, come from the same source—a wish to possess Sophie and, in Nathan's case, to dominate and humiliate her.

Though baffling as a character, Nathan is a necessary element in the narrative. He introduces violence and unease and keeps readers (and his fellow characters) off-balance. Nathan acts; Stingo and Sophie then react to his irrationality, arguing with him and placating him. Nathan seems intelligent and well read, passionate and engaged, but he is also the repository of prejudices, especially against southerners, and of powerful sexual and emotional frustrations. Near the end of the book Nathan's brother reveals that Nathan is a paranoid schizophrenic; this provides an explanation for his behavior, but not an especially satisfying one. The diagnosis seems overly pat. Finally it is not enough to account for Nathan's suicidal lunacy.

Nathan is typical of many characters in Styron's novels. Often these characters have complex personalities; many are victims of discrimination and oppression but are not necessarily innocent of prejudice and hatred. In *The Confessions of Nat Turner,* for example, Nat Turner is cruelly mistreated but is himself guilty of prejudice, disdainful of common field hands, for example, whom he considers ignorant and bestial. In similar fashion, Nathan and Stingo in *Sophie's Choice* are unconsciously racist and sexist, and Sophie is likely anti-Semitic. This makes their personalities human and intriguing.

Oppression, in its many varieties, is a major concern of this novel. Sophie has no strong identity because she has become habituated to oppression, first from her father and then from her husband. Thus her incarceration at Auschwitz was an oddly familiar state for her, and she fell readily into the roles of prisoner and servant. After her liberation she has an open chance at freedom but instead falls under Nathan's domination—more damaging in its way than the indifferent cruelty she endured at Auschwitz. "My darling, I think you have absolutely no ego at all," says Nathan as he casually abuses her. Even Stingo's adoration of Sophie is oppressive because it encourages her to let herself be subsumed into a desirous and unquestioning male personality. Sophie never escapes this kind of domination. She tries to flee but is irresistibly drawn back to Nathan, her last executioner, and to the cyanide capsules that will give her final release.

THEMATIC CONCERNS

Many themes resonate through *Sophie's Choice.* Stingo's central mission is to understand the desire that seems to lurk in all men to dominate and enslave other men. Evil flourishes in the world because most people will not oppose it; hatred and apathy coexist because each nourishes the other. Human beings are capable of extraordinary acts of altruism and love but are equally capable of prejudice and hatred. Stingo is finally baffled by these riddles and cannot account either for the Holocaust or for similar incidents in history. At the end of the novel he confesses his defeat: "No one will ever understand Auschwitz," he says. Stingo searches through his own cultural inheritance and finds many correspondences between the American South and Poland, and between American slavery and the Nazi concentration camps, but his meditations, though illuminating, do not finally answer anything. Human oppression, he seems to say, is omnipresent and ultimately inexplicable.

Sophie's Choice is also a penetrating examination of the mentality of the survivor, a subject often treated in discussions of the Holocaust but just as appropriate to the study of any disaster or horror perpetrated by one human being on another. What happens to those caught up in fearful accidents of warfare and violence? Why do some survive and others perish? Is there any answer, or even comfort, in religion? Sophie concludes that there is not; in her farewell letter to Stingo she writes: "FUCK God and all his Hände Werk. And Life too. And even what remain of Love." How deeply does such nihilism extend into everyday life, which seems orderly but which can quickly disintegrate into murderous chaos? How close to the surface do man's worst instincts lurk?

Running alongside these meditations is the question of whether writers can capture such events and deal with them in art. What are the responsibilities of serious authors to the societies in which they live? Can they provide explanations of these frightening riddles or produce works of literature that might influence human behavior? Can they cause human beings to reform themselves and reach toward love instead of hatred? Styron seems to hope so, but he seems also to believe that the artist must stare evil in the face and call it by its name without ultimately understanding it or hoping to defeat it. Finally the artist must recognize evil (and its twin, apathy) in his own soul as well.

The structure of *Sophie's Choice* makes it possible for Styron to address these questions both in the particular and in the general. In Sophie's individual story the effects of the Holocaust on a single human being are evident. Readers come to care for Sophie and to feel her agony and despair. The portions of the narrative dealing with her, however, alternate with sections about the larger implications of the Nazi final solution. This is how historical analysis works, from the particular to the general. Interpretation comes subsequent to the event or tragedy. The historian and the artist both try to account for the forces that have awakened man's murderous hatred for his fellow man. Stingo (and Styron) have listened to the accounts of victims; they have also read the best that has been written about the Holocaust, by both survivors and dispassionate examiners of the phenomenon. What they have read and heard has helped to enlighten them, but stories by victims and analyses by historians are finally incapable of explaining the evil of the death camps, which shattered Sophie's life and the lives of millions of other sufferers. Nor can such accounts—including *Sophie's Choice*—finally penetrate the mystery of man's inevitable and ever-renewable capacity for violence against his fellow human beings.

ADAPTATIONS

Sophie's Choice has been transformed into an award-winning movie and a high-profile opera. These are ways in which a fictional narrative, originally the creation of a single writer, can reach enormous audiences. Successful movies are seen by millions of viewers, many of whom then become readers of the novel. And too, readers already familiar with a novel often go to a film adaptation, curious to see the story put into a visual medium. The same is not quite true of an opera: audiences for serious opera are comparatively small, but they are faithful and committed to the form, and they are usually knowledgeable about literature and music. The commentary generated by a successful opera, through notices and interviews and other publicity, can awaken the curiosity of new generations of readers. Cinema and opera adaptations are themselves independent creations, of course. They begin with the writer's story but render it into images and music. In the case of *Sophie's Choice,* Styron has been fortunate: the movie and opera versions are excellent adaptations that capture and amplify many of his characters and themes.

Plans for a major film of *Sophie's Choice* began before the novel was published. The movie director Alan J. Pakula formed a partnership with a real-estate investor named Keith Barish and acquired the cinema rights in the spring of 1979. Pakula was a director of talent and accomplishment. His movies *To Kill a Mockingbird, The Parallax View, Klute,* and *All the President's Men* had been widely praised and honored, and he had worked with some of the best actors of his time, including Gregory Peck, Jane Fonda, Donald Sutherland, and Dustin Hoffman. Pakula was enthusiastic about filming *Sophie's Choice:* "I was knocked out by the book," he told an interviewer for the *New York Times.* "I have rarely felt this kind of passion for anything in my life."

Pakula cast Meryl Streep for the role of Sophie Zawistowska. His initial instinct was to seek a European actress, perhaps Liv Ullmann, but he finally chose Streep—a fortunate decision. She immersed herself in the role, learning to speak Polish and German so that she could capture the peculiar music of Sophie's speech. The role of Sophie is emotionally intense; the viewer must be made to experience her guilt and pain but also to sense her mystery and elusiveness. Streep played the part with understatement, capturing much of Sophie's character with gestures or through the use of her eyes. Streep's rendering of the scene on the train platform at Auschwitz is difficult to watch and powerfully wrenching to the emotions—much more overwhelming than the comparable moment in the novel. "I read that scene once only for the film," Streep later recalled. "I couldn't read it again. Every time I even thought about it, I had to put it out of my mind, like Sophie. I still can't think about that scene" (quoted in West, ed., *Conversations with William Styron,* 1998). Streep's perfor-mance was widely praised and won her an Academy Award for best actress in the spring of 1983.

Kevin Kline played Nathan with great energy and intensity. Nathan's passion for Sophie is convincing on the screen, as are his humor and unpredictability; Kline was less successful, however, at capturing Nathan's paranoid violence and sexual jealousy. The role of Stingo, who observes the drama between Sophie and Nathan, was played by Peter MacNicol, then a young aspirant in movies. Many viewers found MacNicol to be miscast in the part—too young and boyish, not feisty or sexy enough. Part of this is the fault of the cinema form itself; Stingo loses his mature narrative voice in the movie, except for a few voiceovers, and the audience is not conscious of his dual role as both a young writer and an older man in the way that readers are in the book. The performance of Streep overshadows these flaws, however, and the film is finally memorable and touching—though it avoids the deeper questions of human morality and the omnipresence of evil that dominate the novel.

Styron played little part in the making of the movie. He did receive a copy of the script from Pakula before filming began, and he annotated it thoroughly for the director, trying to think of works of classical music that might be appropriate for various of the scenes. "Allegro 4th mvt. Royal Fireworks," Styron suggests for one sequence early in the movie. "Marriage of Figaro on radio here," he writes in the margin several pages further along. Pakula, however, took almost none of these suggestions, opting instead to have a score composed for the movie. This music is innocuous and forgettable, typical of much movie music that one hears in Hollywood productions. Styron, though generally pleased with the film, was disappointed by its lack of musical dimension. The novel, after all, had been suffused with music; references to works by Bach, Scarlatti, Beethoven, Brahms, Mozart, Haydn, Handel, and Purcell are found throughout the narrative. Sophie desires the presence of music always: "It's my blood, my life's blood," she tells Stingo. Almost none of the music that she loves, however, is heard in the movie.

Thus the opera version of *Sophie's Choice* was welcome. It was composed by Nicholas Maw, one of the leading British composers of his generation, and premiered in London at the Royal Opera House, Covent Garden, in December 2002. Maw first came to Styron's story through Pakula's movie. He watched the film version of *Sophie's Choice* and was seized immediately by the potential of the story for grand opera, a form that demands intense emotion and large themes. Maw read Styron's novel within days of seeing the film. He was struck by the complexity and contemporary relevance of the story and was convinced that he must attempt to render it for the opera stage. He acquired opera rights for *Sophie's Choice* soon thereafter and began work on the libretto.

Again Styron played no part in the production. Maw sent him the libretto, which had been drawn almost entirely from the text of the novel, and Styron was pleased with it, finding the text faithful to his intentions. Maw then began to compose, writing for an orchestra of some eighty musicians and for a large cast and chorus. Maw's most daring innovation was to split the character of Stingo into two roles, one (a tenor part) for the young Stingo in Brooklyn and the second (a baritone) for a character called the Narrator, who is Stingo as an older writer. This Narrator is always present on stage, observing and interpreting, functioning sometimes as an individual and sometimes in the manner of a Greek chorus, offering commentary and perspective. At one point the Narrator and Stingo sing a duet. In this way Maw recaptured the presence and voice of the mature Stingo and the interplay between him and his younger self, elements that had been lost in the movie.

For the premiere performances, the Royal Opera House assembled a talented group. Trevor Nunn, who had experience both in opera and musical theater, was the director of the production; Simon Rattle, the conductor of the Berlin Philharmonic, led the orchestra. The sets, constructed at disturbingly tilted angles, were designed by Rob Howell. The role of Sophie was performed by the Viennese mezzo-soprano Angelika Kirchschlager, Nathan was sung by Rodney Gilfry, young Stingo by Gordon Gietz, the Narrator by Dale Duesing, and Rudolf Höss by Jorma Silvasti. The Royal Opera House at Covent Garden invested over one million pounds in the production. Publicity and journalistic commentary before the premiere were wide, and public curiosity was high. The performance itself, over four hours in length, received mixed reviews, some quite enthusiastic and others decidedly negative. The singing (especially Kirchschlager's) was praised, as was the acting, which is sometimes thought to be superfluous in operas. The gravity and seriousness of the production were also recognized. Some critics, however, found the opera to be long and ponderous, overly literary, and lacking in final resolution.

Nicholas Maw's score for *Sophie's Choice* is the source of some of these criticisms. His music, like Styron's novel, is unsettling. In the earliest bars of the opera he establishes a series of chords, in minor thirds, which underpin the entire score and give a sense of unease to the listener. One longs throughout, and especially toward the end, for an affirming resolution into a major key. One has internalized the minor chords and now desires escape from them, but Maw does not grant it, just as Styron's novel does not provide consoling answers to the questions it raises. Thus Maw's listener (like Styron's reader) is left unsatisfied, pondering the questions that *Sophie's Choice* has raised but cannot resolve.

SUMMATION

Sophie's Choice is the major American novel of the twentieth century to address the Holocaust.

This is odd because William Styron is a gentile and a southerner with no direct experience of the phenomenon. And yet his apprehension of the Holocaust ("Holocaust" is a word he does not use in *Sophie's Choice*) must be the same as that of most Americans, nearly all of whom know what they know about the Nazi genocide from books, magazines, films, lectures, and other second-hand sources. The Holocaust did not occur here, but through the efforts of committed Jewish intellectuals—and of many non-Jews as well—it has become a dominant feature of American life, taught and analyzed in schools, commemorated in monuments and museums, and present constantly in public discourse. The Holocaust and its aftermath have influenced American government and foreign policy profoundly and will continue to do so. And for many older American Jews, especially those who have not wished to give in altogether to assimilation, the Holocaust has become a means of self-definition and a way of educating young Jews about their identities and social responsibilities.

The Holocaust, however, is the property of no single group or race. It belongs to everyone, a point that *Sophie's Choice* clearly makes. Styron's novel is a powerful literary statement that works against any proprietary interpretation and suggests instead that the Holocaust is emblematic of problems that face all of humanity, not just the Jews.

Sophie's Choice is also a story of two of the most memorable and emblematic characters in modern literature—Sophie Zawistowska and her chronicler, Stingo. Sophie's story embodies some of the baffling contradictions of the twentieth century, a period notable for its enormous advances in knowledge and civilized behavior but equally notable for its terrible violence and irrationality. The choice that Sophie is forced to make between her children is impossible to forget; it epitomizes the agony inflicted on individual human beings by the haphazard forces of war and racial hatred.

Stingo (who is really two characters) is the figure who observes, records, analyzes, and transforms these historical happenings into art. Initially he is determined also to explain man's capacity for evil but finds, in the course of the novel, that he cannot. In failing, he becomes the representative artist, attempting to live through dangerous and irrational times and to make enduring literature from what he has seen and experienced. Stingo, like his creator, William Styron, cannot explain man's capacity for evil, but he can identify and deplore it, hoping that someday it will be brought under control and that, finally and improbably, hatred will be overcome by love.

Select Bibliography

EDITION

Sophie's Choice. New York: Random House, 1979. (Reissued: Vintage International, 1992; Modern Library, 1998.)

OTHER WORKS BY STYRON

Lie Down in Darkness. Indianapolis: Bobbs-Merrill, 1951. (Novel.)

The Confessions of Nat Turner. New York: Random House, 1967. (Novel.)

This Quiet Dust and Other Essays. New York: Random House, 1982; expanded edition, Vintage, 1993. (Nonfiction.)

SECONDARY WORKS

Bloom, Harold, ed. *William Styron's* Sophie's Choice. Modern Critical Interpretations Series. Philadelphia: Chelsea House, 2002.

Casciato, Arthur D., and James L. W. West III, eds. *Critical Essays on William Styron.* Boston: G. K. Hall, 1982.

Clarke, John H., ed. *William Styron's* Nat Turner: *Ten Black Writers Respond.* Boston: Beacon Press, 1968.

Cologne-Brookes, Gavin. *The Novels of William Styron: From Harmony to History.* Baton Rouge: Louisiana State University Press, 1995.

Crane, John Kenny. *The Root of All Evil: The Thematic Unity of William Styron's Fiction.* Columbia: University of South Carolina Press, 1984.

Durham, Carolyn A. "William Styron's *Sophie's Choice:* The Structure of Oppression." In *The Critical Response to William Styron.* Edited by Daniel W. Ross. Westport, Conn.: Greenwood, 1995. Pp. 219–234.

Fackenheim, Emil. *To Mend the World: Foundations of Future Jewish Thought.* New York: Schocken Books, 1982. (See especially section IV, pp. 147–331.)

Lang, John. "God's Averted Face: Styron's *Sophie's Choice.*" *American Literature* 55 (May 1983): 215–232.

Lupack, Barbara Tepa. "*Sophie's Choice,* Pakula's Choices." In her *Take Two: Adapting the Contemporary American Novel to Film.* Bowling Green, Ohio: Bowling Green State University Popular Press, 1994. Pp. 91–111.

Maw, Nicholas. *Sophie's Choice: Opera in Four Acts.* London: Faber Music, Ltd., 2002. (Libretto based on the novel by Styron.)

Morrison, Lucy. "Beyond Words and Silence: Classical Music in William Styron's *Sophie's Choice.*" *Southern Quarterly* 36 (fall 1997): 85–97.

Nagel, Gwen L. "Illusion and Identity in *Sophie's Choice.*" *Papers on Language and Literature,* 23 (fall 1987): 498–513. (Part of a special issue on Styron.)

Novick, Peter. *The Holocaust in American Life.* Boston: Houghton Mifflin, 1999.

Ozick, Cynthia. "A Liberal's Auschwitz." *The Pushcart Prize: Best of the Small Presses.* Edited by Bill Henderson. New York: Pushcart Book Press, 1976. Pp. 149–153.

Rubenstein, Richard L. *The Cunning of History: The Holocaust and the American Future.* New York: Harper and Row, 1975. (Reissued in a 1978 Harper Colophon paperback with an introduction by Styron.)

Sirlin, Rhoda. *William Styron's* Sophie's Choice: *Crime and Self-Punishment.* Ann Arbor: UMI Research Press, 1990; reprint, Lanham, Md.: University Press of America, 2002. (Foreword by Styron.)

Steiner, George. "Silence and the Poet." In his *Language and Silence: Essays on Language, Literature, and the Inhuman.* New York: Atheneum, 1967. Pp. 36–54.

West, James L. W., III. *William Styron, A Life.* New York: Random House, 1998.

———, ed. *Conversations with William Styron.* Jackson and London: University Press of Mississippi, 1985. (Includes the interviews from *L'Express,* the *New York Times,* and *Saturday Review* as well as the interviews with Michel Braudeau, Stephen Lewis, Hilary Mills, and Michael West.)

Wiesel, Elie. "Art and the Holocaust: Trivializing Memory." *New York Times,* June 11, 1989, section 2, page 1.

F. Scott Fitzgerald's
Tender Is the Night

PAUL SULLIVAN

TENDER IS THE Night is F. Scott Fitzgerald's most personal and painful novel. His fourth, it is also the one he wanted to be his deepest and most lasting. As he had done with all of his fiction, Fitzgerald relied heavily on his own experiences as the starting point for the story. During the nine years of writing the book, however, his famously glamorous life fell apart, and what started as a trenchant social critique of the upper classes became a dark rumination on the nature of love and loss, on relationships and financial difficulties. Money had always been a problem for Fitzgerald, but during the writing of *Tender Is the Night* (1934), he found himself for the first time struggling artistically as well.

Knowing who the models were for the characters in *Tender Is the Night* offers insight into Fitzgerald's state of mind. Perhaps the best-known models were Gerald and Sara Murphy, who were the inspiration for Dick and Nicole Diver (though as the writing of the novel wore on, Fitzgerald used himself and his wife, Zelda, as the basis for their psychological problems). The Murphys, who were about ten years older than Fitzgerald, were the center of a world in Antibes, France. (The book is dedicated to them for "many fêtes.") Both of them had family money and lived a leisurely life. In Paris in 1924 they met the Fitzgeralds, who were taking a rest from New York, and the two couples continued to spend summers together in Antibes until 1929, just before Zelda had her first breakdown. That event shifted Fitzgerald's characterization of the Divers, but by then he had already set their patrician qualities. Although it became widely known that the Murphys were the model for the Divers, they were not bothered by Fitzgerald's portrayal. "I know now that what you said in *Tender Is the Night* is true," Gerald wrote Fitzgerald in August 1935. "Only the invented part of our life—the unreal part—has had any scheme, any beauty." The Murphys remained friends with Fitzgerald until his death.

Abe North, the frustrated, hard-drinking musician, is based on Ring Lardner, who was Fitzgerald's neighbor on Long Island, in New York, and was a famous sports journalist and short story writer. He and Fitzgerald developed a friendship over long nights of drinking together, and Fitzgerald convinced Maxwell Perkins, his editor at Scribners, to publish Lardner's stories, *How to Write Short Stories,* in 1924. The book was well received, but by then Lardner was drinking so heavily that his best work was behind him. He died in September 1933 as Fitzgerald was struggling to finish his novel. Fitzgerald gave Abe the same melancholic, alcoholic tendencies that Lardner had but saddled him with Fitzgerald's own seven-year curse: seven years was the time that passed between the publication of Fitzgerald's third story collection, *All the Sad Young Men,* and the completion of *Tender Is the Night* in 1933.

Rosemary Hoyt, the young movie star with whom Dick Diver becomes infatuated, is modeled on Lois Moran. In 1927, on Fitzgerald's first trip to Hollywood to be a screenwriter, he met Moran, then eighteen years old. Her background was similar to Rosemary's in that her father, a doctor, had died when she was a child, and her mother had taken her to Paris and enrolled her in acting classes. She even set up a screen test for Fitzgerald—as Rosemary does for Dick—which he failed. However, as Jeffrey Meyers, one of Fitzgerald's later biographers, notes, it is unclear whether Fitzgerald and Moran ever consummated their relationship—though Zelda did suspect it, as Nicole does in the novel.

Tommy Barban, the heroic mercenary, is actually a recycled character. He first appeared in *The Great Gatsby* as Tom Buchanan, the former football star who lives the carefree life of the supremely wealthy. Both Tom and Tommy are based on Tommy Hitchcock, a rich and handsome star on the Long Island polo circuit. Hitchcock was a war hero whose exploits were well-known, and he later became a successful investment banker. Fitzgerald, for all of his literary success, was unusually awed by physical prowess and was particularly impressed by military heroism. The latter stemmed from his feelings of inadequacy for never having been stationed in Europe during the Great War. It is not surprising, then, that Tommy Barban comes across so well in spite of being a mercenary.

Numerous other minor characters are based on people Fitzgerald knew. Nicole's sister, Baby

CHRONOLOGY

1896	Francis Scott Key Fitzgerald born on September 24 in St. Paul, Minnesota.
1911	Enters Newman School in Hackensack, New Jersey.
1913	Enters Princeton University.
1917	Leaves Princeton for the second time and joins the army. Begins novel "The Romantic Egotist," which is the basis for *This Side of Paradise.*
1918	Submits "The Romantic Egotist" to Scribners, which rejects it. Meets Zelda Sayre in Montgomery, Alabama, where he is stationed.
1919	Sells first story to the *Saturday Evening Post,* "Head and Shoulders."
1920	*This Side of Paradise; Flappers and Philosophers* (first story collection). Marries Zelda.
1921	Makes first trip to Europe in the spring. The Fitzgeralds' daughter, Scottie, is born in October.
1922	*The Beautiful and Damned; Tales of the Jazz Age* (second story collection).
1924	Visits Paris and the French Riviera. Meets Gerald and Sara Murphy and stays with them in Antibes.
1925	*The Great Gatsby.* Meets Ernest Hemingway and helps him get published by Scribners.
1926	*All the Sad Young Men* (third story collection).
1927	Goes to Hollywood but returns after failing as a screenwriter.
1930	Zelda has her first breakdown in Paris and is institutionalized at the Prangins clinic in Switzerland, where Fitzgerald moves to be with her.
1932–1933	Rents a home outside Baltimore to finish *Tender Is the Night.*
1934	*Tender Is the Night* published on April 12 after nine years of work.
1935	*Taps at Reveille* (last story collection).
1937	Moves again to Hollywood, deep in debt. Meets Sheilah Graham, his mistress until the end of his life.

1939	Begins to write *The Last Tycoon,* which is published posthumously in 1941 as an unfinished novel.
1940	Dies on December 21 in Hollywood after a series of heart attacks.

Warren, for example, is based on Zelda's sister, Rosalind Sayre, whom he loathed. (Rosalind blamed Fitzgerald for Zelda's breakdown in 1930, and she and Fitzgerald never got along after that.) What all of the characters in the book share is a certain social standing. When he began *Tender Is the Night,* Fitzgerald's lifestyle was on par with the richest people he knew, even though he continually had to write his way out of debt. But through the nine years between his third and fourth novels, Fitzgerald began to decline physically and emotionally as he faced mounting debts for Zelda's psychiatric care, drank more heavily, and sank deeper into despair. By the time *Tender Is the Night* was published in 1934, Fitzgerald, at thirty-seven, was an almost desperate figure. Much of his pain was channeled into the novel's powerful story.

STRUCTURE

The structure of *Tender Is the Night* distinguishes it from Fitzgerald's previous novels. In *This Side of Paradise, The Beautiful and Damned,* and *The Great Gatsby,* Fitzgerald sticks to a linear narrative. The first two are traditional stories—a bildungsroman and a morality tale. *The Great Gatsby* is a stylistic advance for Fitzgerald: Jay Gatsby's story is told through Nick Carraway, a neighbor who knows Gatsby in the last summer of his life. In *Tender Is the Night,* however, Fitzgerald experiments further: a third of the way through the novel, he disrupts the comfortable narrative he has created to unsettling effect.

The novel begins: "On the pleasant shore of the French Riviera, about halfway between Marseilles and the Italian border, stands a large, proud, rose-colored hotel. Deferential palms cool its flushed façade, and before it stretches a short dazzling beach." This is the perfect world of Antibes in 1925. It is sealed off from the rest of France, from the intellectual life of Paris and also from the miles of mazelike trenches still fresh after the Great War. It is not a world of Jazz Age revelry but one of repose and inherited wealth. At the center of the scene are its creators, Dick and Nicole Diver, a wealthy and beautiful American couple. They are surrounded by a group of friends and also by a group that envies their lifestyle. Characters enter and leave this world, but Fitzgerald does not allow them to disrupt it. What should be the most disruptive force is not: When Rosemary Hoyt, fresh from her first Hollywood film, *Daddy's Girl,* and her mother, Mrs. Speers, arrive, they are unsure about Antibes. "Something tells me we're not going to like this place," Mrs. Speers says. But to the contrary, Rosemary is taken in and quickly starts to love it. At the Divers' dinner party, she is enchanted:

> The table seemed to have risen a little toward the sky like a mechanical dancing platform, giving the people around it a sense of being alone with each other in the dark universe, nourished by its only food, warmed by its only lights. . . . the two Divers began suddenly to warm and glow and expand, as if to make up to their guests, already so subtly assured of their importance, so flattered with politeness, for anything they might still miss from that country well left behind.

Even when the group takes a trip to Paris to see off Abe North, the Divers' social scene, with its feeling of inclusivity, moves with them.

Fitzgerald ends book 1 with the drama of Nicole's nervous breakdown and begins book 2 by breaking the narrative: he retreats eight years to 1917, when Dick and Nicole first met. The ostensible purpose of this break is to explain how the Divers came together and how Dick, then a promising psychiatrist, became so loyal to Nicole, one of his patients. Had their history been dealt with at the beginning of the novel, it would have made the creation of the Divers' ideal world impossible. Yet this break has the secondary effect of creating a sense of unease throughout the rest of the novel, even when the action is brought back to 1925 and the linear narrative resumes.

Fitzgerald pulls the narrative back to the present in an unexpected way. In chapter 10 of the second book, Dick and Baby Warren discuss the prospect of his marrying Nicole. Baby is opposed to it, partially on the basis of their family wealth: "It isn't we think you're an adventurer. We don't know who you are," she says. At the end of their conversation Fitzgerald inserts a delirious, erratically punctuated monologue from Nicole that is an obvious allusion to the monologue James Joyce gives Molly Bloom at the end of *Ulysses.* Fitzgerald concludes Nicole's ramblings, which initially focus on the issue of settling her inheritance, with a reference to Rosemary:

> Yes, I'll look. More new people—oh, that girl—yes. Who did you say she looked like. . . . No, I haven't, we don't get much chance to see the new American pictures over here. Rosemary who? Well, we're getting very fashionable for July—seems very peculiar to me. Yes, she's lovely, but there can be too many people.

The next scene shows Dick meeting with Rosemary's mother and attempting to explain what happened in Paris when Nicole had her breakdown. He is the model of decorum and acts as if nothing is amiss. But the reader knows now that Nicole has a history of mental illness and that her breakdown was not an aberration. Moreover, Nicole's mental state will weigh on the narrative to the end, making a resumption of their ideal life impossible.

Another narrative subtlety surfaces toward the middle of book 2 when Dick, who now lives near Nicole at the Zugersee sanatorium, leaves to attend his father's funeral. Since the time Dick began running the sanatorium, the narrative has diverged in parts to follow him. But from the time he leaves for America until his meandering return, which takes him through Rome, the story is Dick's—and Nicole is largely forgotten. Thus Fitzgerald shows Dick growing more estranged from Nicole and more alone by the day: "He dined alone at the hotel, went to bed early." When Dick returns to Zurich in book 3, diminished by his travels, Fitzgerald broadens out the narrative, and that allows him to edge out Dick in favor of other characters. The story shifts to take in Dick's business partner, Franz, and his wife, Kaethe; to focus more on Nicole; and eventually to look at the Riviera without Dick. At the end Fitzgerald seems to forsake his protagonist, as everyone else has done, by exiling him to upstate New York. And there is every indication that summers in Antibes will be no less wonderful without Dick.

By using this structure Fitzgerald exerted his control over time, separating the novel's setting in time from connections with the contemporary events that had occupied his previous novels. However, Fitzgerald was not entirely pleased with this structure after the novel failed to sell. Toward the end of the 1930s, when he was ill and trying to recapture his lost talent, he reordered the novel so that it would read straight through, from Dick and Nicole's first meeting to Dick's exile from Antibes. This version, known as the "author's final version," was published after Fitzgerald's death, but it exists only as a curiosity. The breaks and disruptions in the narrative are too essential to the tragic, fractured lives of Dick and Nicole Diver for a chronological narration to be successful.

EXILE

All of the characters in *Tender Is the Night* are in exile from somewhere or something, and it is this uncertain state that allows them to exist in their own, sealed world. Exile was something Fitzgerald knew firsthand. It was the state that most often defined his Lost Generation of writers. He moved to Paris in 1925 partly to escape the excess of his lifestyle in New York but also partly to try to pay off his debts. Until Zelda's nervous breakdown in 1930 the Fitzgeralds lived a particularly itinerant life, traveling between their rented house in Delaware and their Paris apartment. In one sense this was the normal rhythm of Fitzgerald's life: he had been moving around from the time he left his parents' house in St. Paul, Minnesota. He never owned a home in his life, and he rarely stayed anyplace for more than a year or two. In *Tender Is the Night,* however, Fitzgerald makes the distinction between voluntary and forced exiles. All of the characters share the desire to be in Antibes, so this voluntary exile is their initial point of connection. They enjoy the luxurious life centered around lounging on the beach during the day and socializing at night. For some, such as Mary North, Abe's wife, this luxury is an end in itself, but for others, the physical exile turns into a forced, psychological one.

Dick Diver is the character whose sense of exile shifts the most. Dick created the beach scene at Gausse's Hotel, and he presides over it like an exiled monarch. From the very beginning there is a sense that Dick is finally at home there. As Abe North says of the Divers, "They have to like it. . . . They invented it." Each morning he rakes the beach sand as if it were his own and greets visitors, such as Rosemary and her mother, as if he is glad to have everyone's company. (Nicole is not as welcoming: "Well, I *have* felt there were too many people on the beach this summer. . . . *Our* beach that Dick made out of a pebble pile.") Fitzgerald uses Dick's love of the beach to create an amiable exile. Dick expresses no longing for home, no laments about what the area lacks. Of their trip to Paris to see off Abe North, Fitzgerald writes:

> Although the Divers were honestly apathetic to organized fashion, they were nonetheless too acute to abandon its contemporaneous rhythm and beat—Dick's parties were all concerned with excitement, and a chance breath of fresh night air was the more precious for being experienced in the intervals of excitement.

Dick's exile begins to darken, however, after Nicole's breakdown. With the beach season over and Nicole still convalescing, the Divers go to Gstaad for Christmas. Here Dick is surprised by Franz Gregorovius, an old colleague from the Zugersee sanatorium, who wants Dick to buy Zugersee with him using Warren family money. Dick is of two minds about the proposition: he is stalled on writing his psychological treatise and believes he would benefit from being at Zugersee, yet he does not want to accept money from Nicole's sister, fearing it would leave him indentured. "I wonder how I like the picture of Nicole and me anchored to Zurich," Dick says while he is trying to decide whether to buy the sanatorium. His agreement to the partnership marks the beginning of his decline. After eighteen months of running Zugersee, he is broken: "As he sat on the side of his bed, he felt the room, the house and the night as empty." With only Nicole, their two children, and his mental patients—"Meals with the patients were a chore he approached with apathy"—Dick lacks the kind of social outlet he had in Antibes. His state does not improve even on trips around Europe.

Dick does get a glimpse of his former life, but burdened by the clinic, he cannot regain it. Returning from his father's funeral in Virginia, he stops in Rome, where he runs into Rosemary Hoyt, now far more famous than only a few years earlier. They finally consummate their affair, but Dick pays dearly for it. Wandering the streets of Rome, he gets into a fight with a group of taxi drivers and accidentally strikes a policeman. He has no money and has to send for Baby Warren to bail him out of jail. "Whatever Dick's previous record was, they [the Warrens] now possessed a moral superiority over him for as long as he proved of any use." This is the worst point of Dick's exile: he owes his clinic to the Warrens, and now he owes his freedom to them, too. However, because of his increased drinking, he loses the clinic to Franz within months. This at least allows him to return to Antibes, but his regal manner is gone: he is no longer charming but drunk and boorish. When Nicole tires of his behavior and leaves him for Tommy Barban, Dick is left without his beach as well.

> In the last letter she had from him he told her that he was practising [medicine] in Geneva, New York, and she got the impression that he had settled down with some one to keep house for him . . . his latest note was post-marked from Hornell, New York, which is some distance from Geneva and a very small town; in any case he is almost certainly in that section of the country, in one town or another.

It is his final return to America that is Dick's true exile.

Nicole's exile is from memories of her abusive childhood. The first hint of her instability comes when Violet McKisco returns to the garden at the Divers' party and announces, "Well, upstairs I came upon a scene, my dears—." She is cut off by Tommy Barban, but there is a sense that something is not right. Nicole's breakdown at the end of book 1 confirms this suspicion. But it is not until book 2 that the root of her psychological problems becomes clear. In book 3, her dying father tells Dick, "I've been a bad man. You must know how little right I have to see Nicole again." When Nicole finds out that her father does not have long to live, she rushes to Lausanne to see him, against Dick's advice. Her father manages to leave and avoid a meeting with her, and despite her disappointment, his leaving is the beginning of the end of Nicole's psychological exile. After Dick gives up the clinic and the Divers return to Antibes, Nicole seems far stronger than before. At one point she begins to hum the lyrics to a popular song that begins, "Thank y' father-r / Thank y' mother-r / Thanks for meetingup with one another—." Dick refuses to play it. "'Oh, play it!' she exclaimed. 'Am I going through the rest of life flinching at the word 'father'?'" When she believes that her father is probably dead or else far away in America, she emerges from her clouded existence. The degree of her healing is manifested in her independence in Antibes. Whereas Dick provided her with psychological protection when she was sick, he has little to offer her when she is well. To the healthy Nicole the strong character of Tommy Barban—for whom she leaves Dick—is more appealing. Consequently, Nicole and Dick experience exile inversely, as she becomes the more settled one at the end.

The other characters experience the pain of exile to varying degrees. Rosemary Hoyt attempts to flee Hollywood and her sudden, youthful fame. But instead, when she arrives on the beach, she learns to embrace it as Dick and his circle and the McKiscos' group praise her acting ability. Years later, when Dick finds her in Rome, she has fully accepted her movie-star life: "I can't go out with you to-night, darling, because I promised some people a long time ago," she says to Dick, brushing him off. The film business is her world now, and she is comfortable in it; her period of exile was brief and harmless. For his part, Tommy is most comfortable in battle. He has trouble in the Divers' social world and can only endure it so long before the urge to leave it overtakes him. He is only comfortable in Antibes at the end when he returns and wins Nicole. "Let it be understood that from this moment . . . I stand in the position of Nicole's protector until details can be arranged," Tommy, like a victorious warrior, tells Dick after Nicole suggests they divorce. The case of Abe North is different. His exile is from early success. Once a great musician, Abe has done nothing in seven years and is hiding in Antibes. Having become a heavy drinker, he has lost his confidence and fears returning to America. "I suppose I got bored; and then it was such a long way to go back in order to get anywhere," he tells Nicole at the Paris train station when he is supposed to return to America. Eventually he does go, and he fades from the story until Dick learns he has been beaten to death after leaving a bar in New York City. Exile, in Fitzgerald's calculus, was the fate of his generation: they were cursed to be out of place somewhere.

LOVE

In *Tender Is the Night* love is presented as a bleak emotion associated with obligation and betrayal. This view reflected Fitzgerald's state of mind at the time he was writing. He and Zelda were well past the time when they could love each other naively. They had both had affairs—she with a French aviator named Édouard Jozan in 1924, their first summer in Antibes; he with the actress Lois Moran on his first trip to Hollywood in 1927. Midway through Fitzgerald's writing of *Tender Is the Night,* in 1930, Zelda had her first of several nervous breakdowns and had to be institutionalized. Fitzgerald was still earning a lot of money from his short stories and was able to put her in one of the best sanatoriums in Switzerland. But that meant he could not slow his output of stories to focus on his novel: his expenses were too great. There was also Scottie, their daughter, to worry about. Gone were the carefree times of first love in *This Side of Paradise* and the longing and passion of *The Great Gatsby.* In *Tender Is the Night,* love can be debilitating, and betrayal is common.

Dick and Nicole have a love that seems ideal in book 1. Rosemary is infatuated with them and so, too, are the McKiscos, though their infatuation manifests itself as envy. The couple appears to be perfect: "At that moment the Divers represented externally the exact furthermost evolution of a class, so that most people seemed awkward beside them." Nicole is beautiful and Dick is debonair. When, in Paris, he calls on a friend whose sister has recently shot a man, he leaves a note "signed 'Dicole,' the word with which he and Nicole had signed communications in the first days of love." The fissure in their love becomes apparent when Dick and Rosemary first kiss, but it is not so much the kiss as Dick's comment that reflects a possible problem: "Nicole mustn't suffer—she loves me and I love her—you understand that," Dick says. He may be tempted by Rosemary's youth and beauty, but he will not let it get the best of him. When Nicole collapses into hysteria a few days later, Fitzgerald makes clear the depth of Dick's commitment: he must abandon everything to help her.

When the story retreats eight years, the circumstances of their meeting come to light. They are first doctor and patient and then lovers. From the beginning Dick is caring for Nicole; later her money becomes attractive to support an agreeable lifestyle. "For Doctor Diver to marry a mental patient? How did it happen? Where did it begin?" The marriage, however passionate it is at the beginning, is encumbered by the doctor-patient dynamic. After Nicole's breakdown, Dick contemplates the burden of being with her: "He saw Nicole in the garden. Presently he must encounter her and the prospect gave him a leaden feeling. Before her he must keep up a perfect front, now and tomorrow, next week and next year." Later, Nicole's sister encourages Dick to buy the sanatorium with the Warrens' family money because she believes it will be good for Nicole: "Baby was thinking that if Nicole lived beside a clinic she would always feel quite safe about her." But the clinic does not solve their problems: In the car on their way to the Agiri Fair, "Nicole was silent; Dick was uneasy at her straight hard gaze. Often he felt lonely with her, and frequently she tired him with the short floods of personal revelations that she reserved exclusively for him." Shortly after that Nicole sprints across the fair ground, forcing Dick to leave their children at a booth and chase after her. Ultimately, it is Nicole's dependence on Dick and the unpredictability of her outbursts that break apart their marriage because when Nicole gets well, she no longer needs Dick. She does offer to support him financially, but he cannot allow himself to accept it. "When she said, as she often did, 'I loved Dick and I'll never forget him,' Tommy answered, 'Of course not—why should you?'" Their love lingers as a cliché.

In their individual relations to Dick and Nicole, Rosemary and Tommy play similar roles: they represent passion without obligation. Dick's affair with Rosemary and Nicole's with Tommy commence at opposite ends of the novel because that is when Dick and Nicole are each strongest and most receptive. When Dick kisses

Rosemary, the experience mirrors his first kiss with Nicole. Both women are enamored of him as someone older and more experienced, and with both he is initially wary. Dick appears on the verge of indulging Rosemary further when he travels to a film studio on the outskirts of Paris in the hope of seeing her. In Dick and Nicole's hotel room, "Dick and Rosemary embraced fleetingly. . . . For another half-minute Dick clung to the situation; Rosemary was first to return to reality." Years later, when Dick arrives in Rome and meets up with Rosemary, the dynamic has shifted: he is no longer as strong as he once was, and she is much less naive:

> "You're still beautiful," he said. "A little more beautiful than ever."
>
> "Do you want coffee, youngster?"
>
> "I'm sorry I was so unpresentable this morning."
>
> "You didn't look well—you all right now? Want coffee?"
>
> "No, thanks."
>
> "You're fine again, I was scared this morning."

When Dick and Rosemary do finally consummate their love, he fails to live up to her expectations.

> For three years Dick had been the ideal by which Rosemary measured other men and inevitably his stature had increased to heroic size. She did not want him to be like other men, yet here were the same exigent demands, as if he wanted to take some of herself away, carry it off in his pocket.

Dick is not the confident ruler of the beach he once was; he is in decline, and Rosemary senses it.

Dick and Rosemary's passion starts out strong and weakens over time, but Tommy's involvement with Nicole tracks the opposite way. He has clearly desired her for some time. "You like the Divers," Rosemary says to Tommy in the beginning. "Of course—especially her—but they make me want to go to war." But it is not until Nicole is well—and Dick is in decline—that their affair commences. And when it does, Tommy channels the energy he once put into being a mercenary into their relationship:

> "It's very plain to me that your marriage to Nicole has run its course. She is through. I've waited five years for that to be so."
>
> "What does Nicole say?"
>
> They both looked at her.
>
> "I've gotten very fond of Tommy, Dick."
>
> He nodded.
>
> "You don't care for me any more," she continued. "It's all just habit. Things were never the same after Rosemary."
>
> Unattracted to this angle, Tommy broke in sharply with:
>
> "You don't understand Nicole. You treat her always like a patient because she was once sick."

Dick puts up a minor defense, but in the end Tommy says, "I think Nicole wants a divorce—I suppose you'll make no obstacles?" And with that their marriage ends. Dick, weakened, is no match for Tommy's determination and Nicole's renewed desire.

Fitzgerald's view of romance is not always this stark. Abe and Mary North and Albert and Violet McKisco exist in marriages that are far less passionate. When the two couples are on the beach, both men are presented as frustrated artists: Abe has not produced any music in seven years, and Albert is struggling to finish writing his novel. While they wallow, their wives remain steadfast: Mary relies on her wit, and Violet gossips her way to feeling superior. Hoping to alleviate Abe's artistic troubles, Mary tries to cajole him into returning to America and leaving behind the easy life of Antibes. She confides to Rosemary in Paris, "I've got to get Abe home. His boat train leaves at eleven. It's so important—I feel the whole future depends on his catching it, but whenever I argue with him he does the exact opposite." Theirs is a more traditional love based on her being supportive of him and longing, perhaps, for the way their relationship once was. At the end, with Abe dead, Mary seems happier in Antibes than she was before, dismissing Dick's accusation that she is dull: she says she is one of the "nice people." The McKiscos' marriage moves the other way. In the beginning Violet and Albert are far less in love. "We've been married twelve years, we had a little girl seven years old and she died and after that you know how it is," he confides to Rosemary. "We both played around on the side a little, nothing serious but drifting apart." After he publishes his novel, however, Violet and Albert grow more settled: "Success had improved him and humbled him." For her part, "Violet was very grand now, decked out by the grand couturières. . . . she was happy, though her husband still shushed her when she grew violently naïve." Neither the Norths' nor the McKiscos' marriage is intensely passionate, but they are both steady, something Fitzgerald knew little about: if their marriages feel flat, it is because Fitzgerald had only turbulence to draw upon when thinking about love.

SILENCE VERSUS LOYALTY

Throughout *Tender Is the Night,* Fitzgerald uses silence to signify loyalty. It was something, again, that Fitzgerald knew firsthand. He wanted to keep both his and Zelda's affairs secret and also wanted to maintain his image while Zelda was in the sanatorium. In the novel, silence is used in all of the major relationships to hide something from someone, as well as to trap a person whose secret is being kept. This device is a significant advance in Fitzgerald's writing, and it helps to mark *Tender Is the Night* as a psychological novel, apart from his previous works.

The Divers' relationship is fraught with silences, which their close friends are willing to keep. This is how their image as the perfect couple is maintained. The first time this image is threatened is at the Divers' party in Antibes, where Dick has invited people outside of their immediate circle. When Violet McKisco returns from the bathroom, she is eager to tell everyone what she has seen, but Tommy Barban, suspecting that it involves Nicole, moves to silence her:

> Mrs. McKisco came hurrying down from the house.
>
> She exuded excitement. In the very silence with which she pulled out a chair and sat down, her eyes staring, her mouth working a little, they all recognized a person crop-full of news, and her husband's "What's the matter, Vi?" came naturally, as all eyes turned toward her.
>
> "My dear—" she said at large, and then addressed Rosemary, "my dear—it's nothing. I really can't say a word."
>
> "You're among friends," said Abe.
>
> "Well, upstairs I came upon a scene, my dears—"
>
> Shaking her head cryptically she broke off just in time, for Tommy arose and addressed her politely but sharply:
>
> "It's inadvisable to comment on what goes on in this house."

Tommy maintains her silence at the party, but with everyone drinking, it does not last. In the car trip from the Villa Diana, where the Divers live, to the hotel, Violet cannot contain herself and again begins to reveal the secret; Tommy stops her again, but this time Albert McKisco defends her. The result is a challenge to a duel, the ultimate defense of honor. As Abe tells Rosemary after the car ride, "None of us ever found out anyhow what it was Violet had to say because he kept interrupting her, and then her husband got into it and now, my dear, we have the duel." That the duel ends in both Tommy and Albert shooting past each other does not matter. Tommy has defended Nicole's honor by ensuring Violet does not reveal what she saw. Soon afterward, the McKiscos disappear from the scene.

At the end of book 1 it becomes clear that what was not revealed was Nicole having a mild breakdown. When Nicole has a serious breakdown in Paris, Rosemary realizes what has been kept silent about the Divers. She runs away from seeing Nicole writhing and babbling on the bathroom floor: "Rosemary, back in the salon, heard the bathroom door bang, and stood trembling: now she knew what Violet McKisco had seen in the bathroom at Villa Diana." Even though there is little doubt that Rosemary would have told her mother about Nicole's episode—because she has told her every detail about Dick—Dick refuses to break his silence about Nicole when he meets Mrs. Speers a few months later.

> "I'm sorry Mrs. Diver was upset," she said carefully.
>
> Rosemary had written:
>
> Nicole seemed Out of her Mind. I didn't want to come South with them because I felt Dick had enough on his hands.
>
> "She's all right now." He spoke almost impatiently. "So you're leaving to-morrow. When will you sail?"
>
> "Right away."

Dick deftly parries Mrs. Speers's remark so that she learns nothing else about Nicole's condition. Almost as punishment, he ends the pleasantries of the conversation.

Dick later finds himself the object of a similar marginalizing silence. After his fling with Rosemary in Rome and the realization that there is no longer anything between them, he takes to the streets at night. He wanders in a drunken haze and gets into an argument with a group of taxi drivers that escalates into a fight. He is driven to the police station, where he strikes an undercover detective. For this offense he is beaten by the police and dragged bloody and half-conscious to a cell. He has no choice but to beg a taxi driver to find Baby Warren: "'Go to the Excelsior hotel,' he cried faintly. 'Tell Miss Warren. Two hundred lire! Miss Warren. Due centi lire! Oh, you dirty—you God—.'" Dick is rendered utterly pathetic. He is forced to beg one of the men he has spurned to find his sister-in-law, whom he dislikes, so he can get out of his jail cell. When Baby arrives, she is anything but silent. She screams at the jail guards, who are frightened by her. Then she barges into the American embassy, where the feckless porter and the aloof ambassador try to quiet her. But she is convinced, from Dick's moaning, that something awful has happened to him. She says, "I can't wait until nine [when the consulate opens]. My brother-in-law says they've put his eye out—he's seriously hurt! I have to get to him." She is unflappable, even when the ambassador convinces her to wait. However, once she has freed Dick and learned the real story, her position changes:

> Baby was waiting with a doctor in a taxi-cab. Dick did not want to look at her and he disliked the doctor. . . . It had been a hard night but she had the satisfaction of feeling that, whatever Dick's previous record was, they now possessed a moral superiority over him for as long as he proved of any use.

In return for helping Dick, Baby owns him: she will never reveal to Nicole what has happened, and in keeping this a secret she essentially imprisons Dick with the fear that she may one day break her silence.

> Dick told Nicole an expurgated version of the catastrophe in Rome—in his version he had gone philanthropically to the rescue of a drunken friend. He could trust Baby Warren to hold her tongue, since he had painted the disastrous effect of the truth upon Nicole. All this, however, was a low hurdle compared to the lingering effect of the episode upon him.

This moment is essentially the end of Dick: if Baby were to tell Nicole the truth, Dick may become free, but Nicole would certainly suffer another breakdown.

Rosemary and Tommy demonstrate the extremes of silence in relation to the Divers.

Rosemary is infatuated with Dick when they first meet, but she would not think of revealing this fact to anyone in the Divers' group or to the McKiscos' friends. Instead, she confesses her young love to her mother. "I fell in love on the beach," she tells her mother. But as she is accepted into the Divers' circle, her desire grows, and with it her silence. She is averse to making a scene—despite being an actress—and when she first kisses Dick, she does so in private: "I want you to come into my room a minute while I tell you something. Just a minute," she says. Later, she writes to her mother of the ensuing events, "I'm not even Going to Try to tell you All that's Happened until I see *You!!!* So when you get this letter, *wire, wire, wire!*" In Rome years later she remains silent about her personal life, and this time she excludes even Dick from it:

> "Let me be curious about you again?" he asked.
>
> "What do you want to know?"
>
> "About men. I'm curious, not to say prurient."
>
> "You mean how long after I met you?"
>
> "Or before."
>
> "Oh, no." She was shocked. "There was nothing before. You were the first man I cared about. You're still the only man I really care about." She considered. "It was about a year, I think."
>
> "Who was it?
>
> "Oh, a man."
>
> He closed in on her evasion.

Dick concocts a story about her first lover, but Rosemary dismisses it as "about as wrong as it could be" without providing other details. She has learned to use silence to protect herself.

Tommy's silence is deeper in nature. It stems from his profession as a mercenary, a man trained to keep allegiances to himself. His detachment is established from the outset. Whereas others in the Divers' group are talkative early on, he is described as "the young man of Latin aspect [who] had been turning the pages of *The New York Herald.*" Even in his group of friends he is silent and shut off. He is equally quiet after the duel he fights to defend Nicole's honor; it is the alcoholic Abe North who reveals the reasons behind the pistol match to Dick. So it comes as a surprise to Dick when, years later, he meets Tommy in a Munich bar and he is jovial and boastful: "Tommy was at a table laughing his martial laugh: 'Um-buh—ha-ha! Um-buh—ha-ha!'" But when the talk turns to what Tommy has been doing lately—helping a Russian prince escape his country and killing some guards in the process—Tommy again becomes reticent. His response to a question about fear is terse: "I always get scared when I'm cold. During the war I was always frightened when I was cold." Tommy's silence is unique in the novel because it represents loyalty to himself alone. This helps to explain the extreme reserve he maintains toward Dick when he tells him his marriage is over:

> "Let it be understood that from this moment," he said, "I stand in the position of Nicole's protector until details can be arranged. And I shall hold you strictly accountable for any abuse of the fact that you continue to inhabit the same house."
>
> "I never did go in for making love to dry loins," said Dick.

Dick gets the final word, but Tommy does not care: by staying silent he has finally gotten what he wants in Nicole.

GLAMOUR AND MONEY

Even though Fitzgerald aimed to elevate *Tender Is the Night* to the level of a philosophical novel, he could not get away from the glamorous, wealthy world with which he was associated. By the time he began writing the novel, after *The Great Gatsby* was published in 1925, he and Zelda were as fashionable as any Hollywood couple. Their goings-on were regularly reported in the tabloid newspapers, and they tried hard to live up to their reputation as a high-living, big-drinking couple. But in the novel Fitzgerald wanted to use the glamorous world he knew to give his social commentary a lasting resonance.

Glamour—or the lack of it—is embedded in the settings. In book 1 the characters frolic in Old World splendor. The south of France and Paris became synonymous with the Lost Generation of artists and their bohemian lifestyle after the Great War, but for Fitzgerald, the scene is the set-up for something more. When Nicole suffers her breakdown in a Paris hotel after a summer on the "bright tan prayer rug of a beach" in Antibes, Fitzgerald pokes a hole in this perfect world. As Dick and Nicole's relationship unravels in book 2, the setting reflects their alienation from each other. The Zugersee sanatorium in Zurich is described as "of the modern type—no longer a single dark and sinister building but a small, scattered, yet deceitfully integrated village—Dick and Nicole had added much in the domain of taste, so that the plant was a thing of beauty, visited by every psychologist passing through Zurich." However, this beauty is comparative—relative to other sanatoriums—and constrained, because by definition a sanatorium's grounds have to contain its patients. The trips away from the sanatorium—to Zug, Munich, and Lausanne—are fraught with middle European bleakness. On his return from his father's funeral in Virginia, a "low-forested clayland," Dick stops in Rome. Although a trip to Rome would seem to signify a return to the glamour of Paris, at least compared with Zurich, for Fitzgerald it was not. He finished work on *The Great Gatsby* there and came to hate the city and its residents. In his personal symbolism Fitzgerald tried to imbue the Italian capital with a miasmic feel. Rome is really the end of glamour for Dick, and when the Divers return to Antibes, even the beach's gloss has faded. The final indignity is Dick's exile in upstate New York, "a pleasant place."

Within these settings glamour ebbs and flows through the characters, each of whom represents a different take on it. Dick and Nicole represent the relaxed glamour of leisurely living that comes from inherited wealth. They are beautiful and cordial. Although Nicole can be icy, her aloofness fits her beauty. One sentence at the beginning encapsulates her easy allure: "Nicole Diver, her brown back hanging from her pearls, was looking through a recipe book for chicken Maryland." But if she is sometimes distant, Dick is always attentive to his guests. The first time Rosemary joins them on the beach, she is won over: "He managed the introduction so that her name wasn't mentioned and then let her know easily that everyone knew who she was but were respecting the completeness of her private life—a courtesy that Rosemary had not met with save from professional people since her success." Like exiled nobility, the Divers retain an air of good breeding through their toughest times.

The glamour the other characters possess represents only one facet of their personalities. Rosemary has a new type of glamour, one of which she is not fully aware. In the late 1920s Hollywood was still new and dazzling. In the beginning Rosemary is too innocent to realize the glamour inherent in her profession and is surprised that everyone recognizes her from *Daddy's Girl.* But by the time Dick meets her in Rome, she has become coquettish. Two of Rosemary's lines attest to her new manner: "I was just a little girl when I met you, Dick. Now I'm a woman"; and "Do you realize I've spent the last hour getting ready for you?" She is more confident and glamorous than before, but she has lost that "dewiness" that made her seem attainable. Tommy, in contrast, possesses a grizzled, muscular glamour that Fitzgerald always associated with those who had fought in the Great War. Tommy is silent and strong, almost like a film version of a war hero, and Dick is in awe of him: "Recently an eighth of the area of his [Tommy's] skull had been removed by a Warsaw surgeon and was knitting under his hair, and the weakest person in the café could have killed him with a flip of a knotted napkin." Abe North is the blocked artist who nonetheless is able to captivate a room. His banter with Nicole over cutting a waiter in two with a "musical saw" bemuses Rosemary.

The glamour of the Divers' circle is affirmed by those outside of it. Violet and Albert McKisco's group derisively refer to them as being part of "the plot." "We're not in it. We're the gallery," Mrs. Abrams tells Rosemary. Yet when Dick invites their group to a party, they accept immediately but struggle to fit in, as an exchange between Albert McKisco and Abe North demonstrates:

> "I've met you in Paris," McKisco said to Abe North, who with his wife had arrived on their heels, "in fact I've met you twice."
>
> "Yes, I remember," Abe said.
>
> "Then where was it?" demanded McKisco, not content to let well enough alone.
>
> "Why, I think—" Abe got tired of the game, "I can't remember."

It was this mix of reverence and scorn for glamour that reaffirmed for Fitzgerald its hold over people.

STRENGTH AND DISSIPATION

The various themes of exile, love, silence, and glamour build to the one that obsessed and haunted Fitzgerald throughout the writing of *Tender Is the Night* and that only intensified afterward: dissipation. He believed that a writer has a limited supply of talent from which to draw. Once it is gone, the reserve cannot be replenished. Fitzgerald spent his adult career fixated on this notion and came to believe more and more that his voluminous output of short stories, and later his screenwriting, hastened his decline as a novelist. At the end of his life, after *Tender Is the Night* had failed, he wrote letters claiming to have salvaged enough of his talent for another book, maybe two. In 1931 he encapsulated this feeling in his story "Emotional Bankruptcy." In it the young, party-weary girl at the center of the story loses the love of her life because she cannot feel anything for him: "One cannot both spend and have." Whereas Fitzgerald was a literary star when he began *Tender Is the Night,* he was financially strapped and struggling to finish the book by 1933.

In the novel Abe North is dissipated from the beginning. He is Fitzgerald's proof that once an artist drains his talent, there is no way to replenish it. Abe's problem is that "after a brilliant and precocious start [he] had composed nothing for seven years." He tries to mask his fruitlessness with humorous quips like "A man can't live without a moral code. Mine is that I'm against the burning of witches. Whenever they burn a witch, I get all hot under the collar." But this is the humor of a man uncomfortable with himself, of someone who keeps talking so that no one will have the chance to ask what he is working on. Mary, his wife, knows that he is suffering and wants him to return to America. But at the boat train in Paris, it is Nicole who takes Abe to task for his lethargy.

> [Abe says,] "I'm tired of you both, but it doesn't show because you're even more tired of me—you know what I mean. If I had any enthusiasm, I'd go on to new people."
>
> There was a rough nap on Nicole's velvet gloves as she slapped him back:
>
> "Seems rather foolish to be unpleasant, Abe. Anyhow you don't mean that. I can't see why you've given up about everything."
>
> Abe considered, trying hard not to cough or blow his nose.
>
> "I suppose I got bored; and then it was such a long way to go back in order to get anywhere."

Abe gets on the train, but he doesn't stay on it to the boat. His excuse to a Paris bartender shows his dissipation is so great that even his humor is giving out: "I was reading a serial in Liberty and the next installment was due here in Paris—so if I'd sailed I'd have missed it—then I never would have read it." His fecklessness also causes a race riot when he incorrectly identifies a black man who has robbed him and fails to rectify the situation. After this incident Abe disappears from the story until Dick hears years later that he has been killed. "He's dead. He was beaten to death in a speakeasy in New York. He just managed to crawl home to the Racquet Club to die," Dick is told. This is an ignominious death for two reasons: first, he had so provoked someone in an illegal bar that he got himself beaten, and second, he did not have his own apartment but was renting a room in a social club. However dissipated Abe was in France, he had worsened in the two years since he left Paris and died bereft.

Dick begins dissipating before the book opens, but his loss of strength is slow and not apparent until after Nicole's breakdown, when he buys into the Zugersee sanatorium. In book 2, after he meets Nicole and begins to enjoy their carefree way of life, Dick loses focus. He had been a brilliant young psychiatrist who showed great promise, but living in Antibes he neglects his scholarly work. His disregard first surfaces during a discussion between him and Abe:

> "Something tells me I'll have a new score on Broadway long before you've finished your scientific treatise."
>
> "I hope so," said Dick evenly. "I hope so. I may even abandon what you call my 'scientific treatise.'" . . .
>
> But suddenly Dick laughed again, added to his remark "—abandon it for another one," and got up from the table.

At this point Fitzgerald has not revealed much about Dick's past, and when Rosemary questions Dick about what he does, his life still seems perfect. "There's no mystery. I didn't disgrace myself at the height of my career, and hide away on the Riviera. I'm just not practising. You can't tell, I'll probably practise again some day." This is the essence of Fitzgerald's conception of dissipation: it is not brought on by a single momentous event that breaks a person's spirit but is instead a slow trickling away of ambition and productivity. Dick is not like a politician felled by the release of illicit news. He simply stops caring a little more every day, and soon enough he finds himself in Abe's position, where it is "a long way to go back." His state becomes evident when he and Nicole are settled in the bucolic surroundings of the sanatorium, away from the glamour and distractions of Antibes. He has lost the restless energy of a decade earlier that allowed him to peddle through the streets and conceptualize treatises with titles such as "An Attempt at a Uniform and Pragmatic Classification of the Neuroses and Psychoses, Based on an Examination of Fifteen Hundred Pre-Krapælin and Post-Krapælin Cases as they would be Diagnosed in the Terminology of the Different Contemporary Schools"—a title that "would look monumental in German." Now Dick is consumed by the tasks of attending to his patients and caring for Nicole. Being so wrapped up in his day-to-day work, any time to devote to his research disappears. In Innsbruck, on a trip away from Nicole, he ponders his decline:

> He had lost himself—he could not tell the hour when, or the day or the week, the month or the year. Once he had cut through things, solving the most complicated equations as the simplest problems of his simplest patients. Between the time he found Nicole flowering under a stone on the Zürichsee and the moment of his meeting with Rosemary the spear had been blunted.
>
> Watching his father's struggles in poor parishes had wedded a desire for money to an essentially unacquisitive nature. It was not a healthy necessity for security—he had never felt more sure of himself, more thoroughly his own man, than at the time of his marriage to Nicole. Yet he had been swallowed up like a gigolo, and somehow permitted his arsenal to be locked up in the Warren safety-deposit vaults.
>
> ". . . it isn't over yet. I've wasted eight years teaching the rich the ABC's of human decency, but I'm not done. I've got too many unplayed trumps in my hand."

But he is already done. The cumulative effect of not doing anything for so long has broken his spirit, and as with Abe, it is now too far back for Dick to go to reclaim his vigor.

As important to Fitzgerald's argument of dissipation as Abe and Dick are, there is also their counterweight: those characters who retain their strength or even gain strength as the novel progresses. In Fitzgerald's way of viewing them, they are less sensitive, but that is probably what saves them. Pride of place in this group belongs to Tommy Barban, who loses neither his physical strength nor his confidence. "Tommy Barban was a ruler, Tommy was a hero" is how he is described in the Munich bar where he celebrates the completion of his latest mercenary assignment. In the beginning he looks to the Divers' sodden life as a palliative. "When I'm in a rut I come to see the Divers, because then I know that in a few weeks I'll want to go to war," Tommy tells Rosemary. Rosemary, for her part, seems intent on retaining her strength by closing herself off. As an actress, she is subject to the whims of the audience and the studios, but she uses the money she earns to forge an independence unique for a woman of her time. Her mother tells her early on, "Economically you're a boy, not a girl." Her strength is evident when Dick sees her in Rome: he believes he will woo her again but instead finds she is far more focused. "I can't go out with you to-night, darling, because I promised some people a long time ago. But if you'll get up early I'll take you out to the set to-morrow," she tells him; after their love is consummated the next night she still leaves Dick for "another dinner date, a birthday party for a member of the company."

Nicole and Baby Warren are financially independent as well, but their money comes from their father's wealth, a vast reserve that would be impossible to spend. Baby is strong throughout the book because her father's money gives her brash confidence. When she bails Dick out of jail in Rome, for example, she is not above telling the American consul who she is: "We're people of considerable standing in America." This remark is telling because although it is full of her confidence, in her emotional state she has to stop herself before she says too much: "If it wasn't for the scandal we can—." She still has the wherewithal to keep family secrets to herself in order to maintain her strength. The "scandal"—Warren's father molesting Nicole—is what triggered Nicole's schizophrenia in her youth. And it is not until the end, when her father is near death, that Nicole begins to get better. The guarantee that her father will no longer be around renews Nicole's strength. When they are back on the beach, where Tommy is attentive to her, Nicole begins to grow even stronger. And then there is her money, which Fitzgerald always considered a salve.

CONCLUSION

In many ways *Tender Is the Night* was a very modern novel when it was published, and that contributed to its commercial failure. Fitzgerald had always been fascinated with new technologies and developments. In *The Great Gatsby* he put the automobile, still a luxury in 1925, at the center of the story's defining scene. And in *Tender Is the Night* he does the same with automobiles and commercial air travel. ("In Zurich the next week Dick drove to the airport and took the big plane for Munich.") Film and psychiatry were also relatively new professions at the time Fitzgerald was writing *Tender Is the Night:* the 1920s were the time of great advances by Sigmund Freud and Carl Jung in psychiatry and also the decade in which big Hollywood studios like MGM emerged. Fitzgerald works both into the story. Sexually the book was less progressive, except for his chaste portrayal of Dick's infidelity; Fitzgerald does attempt to deal with homosexuality—by hinting at Campion and Dumphry's relationship—but this is a heavy-handed effort. In the literary realm Fitzgerald pays homage to Joseph Conrad's philosophical realism by addressing the impact of the Great War's disruptive force on all of his characters, and he alludes to James Joyce's stream-of-conscience writing in Nicole's monologue that connects her past and present. For Fitzgerald, *Tender Is the Night* was innovative both stylistically and thematically.

Critically and commercially, however, the novel was a failure. It was discussed seriously by major newspapers, but many critics attacked it for being out of step with the times—something none of his previous novels had been. But the worst blow came from his friend Ernest Hemingway, who was angry that Fitzgerald had created composites of their friends the Murphys. He wrote Fitzgerald on May 28, 1934, "Goddamn it you took liberties with peoples' pasts and futures that produced not people but damned marvelously faked case histories." The novel sold a disappointing thirteen thousand copies, barely enough to cover Fitzgerald's debts, which had grown with expenses for Zelda's psychiatric care. (She had been in and out of sanatoriums since her first breakdown in 1930, but by 1934 she was getting closer to the point where she would be permanently institutionalized.) At the root of the novel's rejection was the fact that the Jazz Age had been replaced by the Great Depression. In April 1934, when the novel was published, Americans were no longer carefree revelers who wanted to know what bon vivants abroad were doing; they were concerned with feeding their families and paying their bills. *Tender Is the Night* could not have had a less receptive audience for its story.

This public rejection probably hastened Fitzgerald's decline. He had planned on the novel not only resurrecting his then-dormant reputation but also bringing him a financial windfall to pay Zelda's medical bills. On March 4, 1934, a month before publication, he wrote Maxwell Perkins, his longtime editor, "I have lived so long within the circle of this book and with these characters that often it seems to me that the real world does not exist but that only these characters exist" (quoted in John Kuehl and Jackson R. Bryer, eds., 1971). When that world was shattered, Fitzgerald, already drinking excessively, descended into debilitating alcoholism. With Zelda away and Scottie in boarding school, Fitzgerald entered the darkest period of his professional life. His story fees fell, his debts continued to grow, and he had trouble writing without Zelda, who for all of their marital problems had been essential to him during his wild ride to success. Living in Hollywood and trading on his reputation to earn amazingly high fees—$1,250 a week from MGM until they canceled his contract—he tried to stage a comeback. But having made a solid start on *The Last Tycoon,* his unfinished novel about Hollywood, he suffered several heart attacks, and on December 21, 1940, he died in his mistress's apartment.

Select Bibliography

EDITION

Tender Is the Night: A Romance. New York: Scribners, 1934. (The 1962 Scribners hardcover edition is cited in this essay.)

OTHER WORKS BY FITZGERALD

This Side of Paradise. New York: A. L. Burt, 1920.

The Beautiful and Damned. New York: Scribners, 1922.

The Great Gatsby. New York: Scribners, 1925.

All the Sad Young Men. New York: Scribners, 1926.

The Last Tycoon: An Unfinished Novel. New York: Scribners, 1941.

The Price Was High: The Last Uncollected Stories of F. Scott Fitzgerald. Edited by Matthew J. Bruccoli. New York: Harcourt Brace Jovanovich, 1979. (Many collections of Fitzgerald's best stories exist, but this one provides some of his worst—and offers great insight into how much and how quickly he was writing to support his lifestyle.)

SECONDARY WORKS

Allen, Joan M. *Candles and Carnival Lights: The Catholic Sensibility of F. Scott Fitzgerald.* New York: New York University Press, 1978.

Bruccoli, Matthew J. *Some Sort of Epic Grandeur: The Life of F. Scott Fitzgerald.* 2d rev. ed. Columbia: University of South Carolina Press, 2002.

Donaldson, Scott. *Fool for Love: F. Scott Fitzgerald.* New York: Congdon & Weed, 1983.

———. *Hemingway vs. Fitzgerald: The Rise and Fall of a Literary Friendship.* Woodstock, N.Y.: Overlook Press, 1999.

Gale, Robert L. *An F. Scott Fitzgerald Encyclopedia.* Westport, Conn.: Greenwood Press, 1998. (A 526-page compendium of all things Fitzgerald.)

Graham, Sheilah. *The Real F. Scott Fitzgerald Thirty-Five Years Later.* New York: Grosset & Dunlap, 1976. (Memoir of Fitzgerald's mistress, who was also a gossip columnist.)

Hook, Andrew. *F. Scott Fitzgerald: A Literary Life.* New York: Palgrave Macmillan, 2002. (Focuses on Fitzgerald's roller-coaster life.)

Kennedy, J. Gerald, and Jackson R. Bryer, eds. *French Connections: Hemingway and Fitzgerald Abroad.* New York: St. Martin's, 1998.

Kuehl, John Richard. *F. Scott Fitzgerald: A Study of the Short Fiction.* Boston: Twayne, 1991.

Kuehl, John, and Jackson R. Bryer, eds. *Dear Scott/Dear Max: The Fitzgerald-Perkins Correspondence.* New York: Scribners, 1971.

Metzger, Charles Reid. *F. Scott Fitzgerald's Psychiatric Novel: Nicole's Case, Dick's Case.* New York: Peter Lang, 1990.

Meyers, Jeffrey. *Scott Fitzgerald: A Biography.* New York: HarperCollins, 1994; Cooper Square Press, 2000. (This is the standard Fitzgerald biography. It is encompassing and authoritative, though occasional debates over previous Fitzgerald biographies will be of little interest to the general reader.)

Milford, Nancy. *Zelda: A Biography.* Rev. ed. New York: Harper Perennial, 2001. (Standard biography of Zelda, though often said by critics to take a feminist-revisionist stance on her marriage.)

Mizener, Arthur. *The Far Side of Paradise: A Biography of F. Scott Fitzgerald.* Boston: Houghton Mifflin, 1951. (The first full-scale biography of Fitzgerald; started the reevaluation of his work.)

O'Meara, Lauraleigh. *Lost City: Fitzgerald's New York.* New York: Routledge, 2002.

Ring, Francis Kroll. *Against the Current: As I Remember F. Scott Fitzgerald.* San Francisco: D. S. Ellis, 1985. (Memoir of his last secretary.)

Roulston, Robert, and Helen H. Roulston. *The Winding Road to West Egg: The Artistic Development of F. Scott Fitzgerald.* Lewisburg, Pa.: Bucknell University Press, 1995.

Schiff, Jonathan. *Ashes to Ashes: Mourning and Social Difference in F. Scott Fitzgerald's Fiction.* Selinsgrove, Pa.: Susquehanna University Press, 2001.

Smith, Scottie Fitzgerald. Foreword to *Bits of Paradise: Twenty-One Uncollected Stories by F. Scott and Zelda Fitzgerald,* by F. Scott Fitzgerald. Selected by Scottie Fitzgerald Smith and Matthew J. Bruccoli. New York: Encore, 1974. (Recollections by the Fitzgeralds' daughter.)

Stewart, Gail. *The Importance of F. Scott Fitzgerald.* New York: Lucent, 1999. (High-school level study of Fitzgerald's life and work.)

Taylor, Kendall. *Sometimes Madness Is Wisdom: Zelda and Scott Fitzgerald: A Marriage.* New York: Ballantine, 2001.

Tomkins, Calvin. *Living Well Is the Best Revenge.* New York: Viking, 1971. (A lively account of the life of Gerald and Sara Murphy, who were among Fitzgerald's most charitable and loyal friends.)

Turnbull, Andrew. *Scott Fitzgerald.* New York: Scribners, 1962; Grove Press, 2001. (As a boy, Turnbull knew Fitzgerald when he was finishing *Tender Is the Night* in a house rented from his parents. A bit hagiographic at times, but a good read.)

Wilson, Edmund, ed. *The Crack-Up.* New York: J. Laughlin, 1945. (Writings by F. Scott Fitzgerald, with other uncollected pieces, notebooks and unpublished letters, together with letters to Fitzgerald from Gertrude Stein, Edith Wharton, T. S. Eliot, Thomas Wolfe, and John Dos Passos, and essays and poems by various other authors.)

Don DeLillo's
White Noise

STEPHEN AMIDON

EARLY IN *WHITE Noise* (1985), a college professor named Murray Jay Siskind announces that it is his overriding academic ambition to immerse himself in "American magic and dread." He might just as easily have been describing what it is like to read Don DeLillo's eighth novel. An intense and at times frightening meditation on death, environmental catastrophe, dehumanizing technology, and Adolf Hitler, *White Noise* is also a deliriously funny satire on our media-soaked world and a very warm portrait of a splintered yet stubbornly coherent American family. That DeLillo was able to mix these seemingly disparate elements into a coherent fictional whole is testament to his status as one of the most acute, intelligent, and sane of America's postwar novelists. *White Noise* stands in the front rank of his body of work.

In many ways *White Noise,* the story of college professor Jack Gladney's attempts to deal with the aftermath of a poison gas leak near his seemingly idyllic home, epitomizes the fictional stance DeLillo has taken since his 1971 debut novel, *Americana.* DeLillo's world is shot through with menace, conspiracy, and paranoia. It is a place where the individual is constantly on the verge of being absorbed by hostile masses and malevolent powers. Dread—whether of rampant pollution, terrorism, political assassination, or nuclear war—is omnipresent in his fiction. This does not mean, however, that DeLillo conceives of a world without structure. His vision is characterized by the strong suggestion that there is an order controlling people's lives. It simply does not happen to be one that is very congenial to the individual.

Can anyone sincerely doubt the accuracy of such a fictional worldview? Although many novels are called "prophetic," in the case of *White Noise* this mantle is accurately, if uneasily, borne. In December 1984, soon after the novel's completion, an accidental leak of chemicals used in manufacturing pesticides at a Union Carbide plant in Bhopal, India, killed at least 8,000 and injured as many as 300,000. This man-made tragedy provided an uncanny echo of the novel's central action, in which a railroad car carrying deadly Nyodene D. gas, used in the production of pesticides, ruptures outside of the fictional midwestern town of Blacksmith. Months after the book's publication, the space shuttle *Challenger* exploded just seconds after takeoff, an event watched over and over on television by millions of people, an incident of mass video voyeurism that brings to mind the novel's central question about why "decent, well-meaning and responsible people find themselves intrigued by catastrophe when they see it on television?" And then, in April 1986, an explosion and radioactive leak at the Chernobyl nuclear power plant in the Soviet Union led to the evacuation of 135,000 people from the surrounding area and caused a still undetermined number of cases of cancer and other radiation-induced diseases. Once again, reality provided an eerie echo of DeLillo's vision, in this case of both the flight of the citizens of Blacksmith from the novel's "airborne toxic event" and the ensuing anxiety of Jack, the novel's narrator, that his exposure to the leak has sown the seeds of his own premature death.

While DeLillo would probably be the first to recoil from suggestions that *White Noise* in any way predicted these episodes, his novel does evoke a type of distinctly modern consciousness that sees Bhopal, *Challenger,* and Chernobyl as the inevitable by-products of dizzying advances in technology. The prospect of man-made catastrophe is the psychic price humans pay for the comfort and convenience of a brave new world. Dread is nothing new to humankind, though its objects have evolved from shooting stars to plummeting spacecraft; from predatory beasts to lethal chemicals. Jack Gladney and his family might have to run for their lives when Nyodene D. drifts toward their house, but they seem no more surprised at its arrival than they are at the sight of the setting sun. Perhaps the greatest irony in this deeply ironic book is its reminder that even though technology might aim for the betterment of human life, it has also managed to bring people much closer to the reality of their impending death.

CHRONOLOGY

1936	Born in Bronx, New York City, on November 20.
1958	Graduates from Fordham University, New York.
1959–1964	Works as copywriter for Ogilvy & Mather advertising agency in New York City.
1963	President Kennedy murdered. Lee Harvey Oswald, who grew up near DeLillo, named assassin.
1971	Publishes first novel, *Americana.*
1972	*End Zone.*
1973	*Great Jones Street.*
1975	Marries Barbara Bennett, a landscape designer.
1976	*Ratner's Star.*
1977	*Players.*
1978	*Running Dog.*
1979	Moves to Greece, where he lives for three years.
1982	*The Names.*
1984	Honored by the American Academy and Institute of Arts and Letters. Finishes *White Noise.*
1985	*White Noise* wins American Book Award.
1988	*Libra,* a fictional portrait of Lee Harvey Oswald, published.
1991	*Mao II.*
1997	*Underworld.*
2001	*The Body Artist.*

THE MEDIA

White Noise is one of the most penetrating examinations ever published of the insidious, overwhelming role of the media in American life. Throughout the novel, reality is distorted by television, radio, and tabloid newspapers, mass media that form a sort of cocoon around phenomena, influencing the way human beings apprehend even the most basic aspects of their everyday life. For most of the novel's characters, if it is not on televsion, then it simply has not happened. After Jack's twelve-year-old daughter Bee realizes that there are no television crews or newspaper reporters at the airport to interview the survivors of a mid-air near-disaster, her reaction is one of telling disappointment: "They went through all that for nothing?" Jack's fellow

"American environments" professor Alfonse Stompanato observes that, in the mind of the typical American, television has gained an equal footing with tactile reality. "For most people there are only two places in the world. Where they live and their TV set. If a thing happens on television, we have every right to find it fascinating, whatever it is."

After the poison gas leak causes the evacuation of the Gladney family and their neighbors, one of the evacuees is outraged to discover that the event is not even being covered by the network news. "Does this kind of thing happen so often that nobody cares anymore? . . . Do they think this is just television? . . . Don't they know it's real?" Jack speaks of television's "narcotic undertow and eerie diseased brain-sucking power," as if it were a drug every bit as addictive as tobacco or heroin. Characters who exist outside of television's seductive aura are considered freakish throwbacks to an era when people were able to experience the world in a truly immediate manner. One notable example of this sort of noble savage is Babette's son Eugene, who is being raised in the Australian Outback. "The boy is growing up without television . . . which may make him worth talking to . . . as a sort of wild child, a savage plucked from the bush, intelligent and literate but deprived of the deeper codes and messages that mark his species as unique."

Television is everywhere. It cannot be switched off. Its static is a permanent white noise that affects nearly all of our perceptions. Even when confronting an undeniably real event, people can act as if they are seeing it on television, as when Jack and his fourteen-year-old son Heinrich witness a fire at a local insane asylum. The people who gather to watch are suitably enthralled, although their rapture is broken when acrid smoke drifts over them, transforming what was a purely visual experience into one that is unpleasantly real. "A sharp and bitter stink filled the air. . . . It changed the mood of the people on the sidewalk. Some put hankies to their faces, others left abruptly in disgust. Whatever caused the odor, I sensed that it made people feel betrayed."

This mastery of the human consciousness by the nonstop babble of television is given stylistic emphasis in Jack's narration itself, which sporadically erupts with bursts of television lingo that have no immediately obvious connection with the ongoing action. Baffling at first, these interludes come to sound like a sort of choral chant. "Dacron, Orlon, Lycra Spandex," he blurts at one point; "CABLE HEALTH, CABLE WEATHER, CABLE NEWS, CABLE NATURE" at another. It is almost as if Jack's subconscious has been completely colonized by television. This is also apparent in his occasional habit of translating reality into the grammar of television commercials, as when he comes upon a crossing guard stopping traffic: "I pictured her in a soup commercial taking off her oilskin hat as she entered the cheerful kitchen where her husband stood over a pot of smoky lobster bisque."

DeLillo at one point planned to call his novel "Panasonic," a term that suggests the all-encompassing nature of the noise emitted by electronic media in our culture. (Given the often unflattering representation of television and radio, it is not surprising that lawyers representing the Japanese electronic giant of the same name denied him permission.) The title he did settle upon is perhaps even more evocative, taken from an invention that mixes together all known aural frequencies to create an ambient hum that is used to keep people who work in atmospherically sealed workplaces from being driven to distraction by utter silence.

DeLillo develops his theme of media omnipresence in a series of characteristically sharp episodes. In one brief but profoundly resonant scene, Jack and his colleague Murray visit "the most photographed barn in America," where they join a seemingly endless stream of other tourists in looking at a building whose only claim to fame is that it is the object of so many gazes and so many lenses. Murray points out that it is now impossible for anyone to see the barn as a thing-in-itself, an assemblage of wood and nails constructed for the purpose of housing animals. The very act of being given a media identity changes the nature of a thing irrevocably. The signs surrounding the barn define it more absolutely than its inherent structure.

> Once you've seen the signs about the barn, it becomes impossible to see the barn. . . . We're not here to capture an image, we're here to maintain one. Every photograph reinforces the aura. Can you feel it, Jack? An accumulation of nameless energies . . . We see only what the others see. The thousands who were here in the past, those who will come in the future. We've agreed to be part of a collective perception. This literally colors our vision.

Media-enhanced identities overwhelm human beings as well. In another scene involving Jack and Murray, the two professors deliver a joint lecture on Adolf Hitler and Elvis Presley, figures who have been utterly transformed by their representations on television and elsewhere in the media. After so many depictions, it is impossible for the average viewer to think about them in any way that separates their original being from all those flickering images. Murray acknowledges this when he guesses that Elvis' mother had a premonition of his decline and early death. "His mother probably saw it all, as on a nineteen-inch screen, years before her own death." There is no need for a crystal ball when there are perfectly good cathode-ray tubes at hand.

The media's ability to define the nature of reality is particularly evident during the "airborne toxic event" that dominates the novel's middle section. At first, Jack and his family are not overly concerned—as long as radio reports are referring to the smoke leaking from the punctured railroad tanker as a "feathery plume." Although there is no precise information about levels of toxicity in this phrase, its benign, almost bucolic overtones are enough to reassure the Gladneys. However, anxiety begins to set in when media reports start speaking about a "black billowing cloud," even though the leak has not actually changed in appearance. Now that the name has taken on a different texture—one of darkness and hard consonants—worry sets in. It is a worry that evolves into panic, at least among the children, who are more finely tuned to the subtleties of media-speak, when the description changes once again, this time to "airborne toxic event." There is no longer an attempt to describe the nature of the cloud. Language has passed over into the realm of concealment and bureaucratic dread, suggesting such other ominously bland phrases as "collateral damage" (dead civilians) and "strategic planning" (nuclear war). Where electronic media were once heralded as a means of forming a more intimate connection between an observer and the thing observed, no matter how great the distance or time separating them, in the world of *White Noise* the media are just as likely to distort or even annihilate the object of observation.

Another sign of the hypnotic power of mediated images and broadcast language comes with the false symptoms the Gladney children display in the hours following the airborne event. After hearing a rumor on the radio that exposure to Nyodene D. can lead to feelings of déjà vu, Jack's daughter Steffie starts showing symptoms of the condition. But then comes an official announcement (which Steffie misses) that déjà vu is no longer considered a side effect of contamination. Jack realizes that Steffie is only experiencing symptoms because she has heard about them. "If Steffie had learned about *déjà vu* on the radio but then missed the subsequent upgrading to more deadly conditions, it could mean she was in a position to be tricked by her own apparatus of suggestibility." In a world where it is difficult to know what to believe, the media are on hand to provide ready answers and absolute authority. And it is not only television that provides simulated meaning for the novels' characters. Babette in particular looks for solace in supermarket tabloids, one of the few remaining modern texts whose authors, with stories such as "Life after Death Guaranteed with Bonus Coupons," are willing to grapple with questions once left to philosophers and churchmen. It is, after all, in a tabloid magazine that Babette finds an advertisement for the death-denying drug Dylar, which comes to dominate the novel's third and final chapter.

In a world so dominated by representation, simulations can often become more real than the objects they are meant to represent. Such is the power of representation in modern life that DeLillo's characters often grant more credence to the facsimile than the tactile reality it denotes. During the evacuation that takes place after the airborne toxic event, an organization known as SIMUVAC arrives on the streets of Gladney's hometown of Blacksmith. Their name stands for "simulated evacuation"—it turns out that they have come not to help people escape the danger but rather to *practice* an evacuation, seeing the poison gas leak as "a chance to use the real event in order to rehearse the simulation." An equally powerful example of the novel's reversal of reality and representation comes when Babette unexpectedly appears on television as the rest of the Gladney family watches. Jack and the children seem momentarily unable to differentiate between the image they are seeing and the woman who left the house just a few hours earlier.

> Confusion, fear, astonishment spilled from our faces. What did it mean? What was she doing there, in black and white, framed in formal borders? Was she dead, missing, disembodied? Was this her spirit, her secret self, some two-dimensional facsimile released by the power of technology, set free to glide though wavebands, through energy levels, pausing to say good-bye to us from the fluorescent screen?

During a family outing to the mall, Jack notices that a "band played live Muzak," another inversion in which the artificial has become the real—the sounds the band are making are a simulacrum, or a copy of a copy. This sense of unreality extends to Jack's own self-image—in order to achieve a more solid sense of self, he starts wearing thick sunglasses and calling himself "J. A. K. Gladney," even though he knows the prestige this gives him is bogus. "I am the false character that follows the name around." This point found a later echo in DeLillo's 1991 novel *Mao II,* in which "a room filled with images of Chairman Mao"—all of them various copies of a copy of a photograph—provide "the deeper meaning of Mao."

This colonization of the imagination by the media leads inevitably to a desensitization, illustrated when the Gladney family gathers for one of their regular sessions in front of the television.

> That night, a Friday, we gathered in front of the set, as was the custom and the rule, with take-out Chinese. There were floods, earthquakes, mud slides, erupting volcanoes. We'd never before been so attentive to our duty . . . Every disaster made us wish for more, for something bigger, grander, more sweeping.

Later, a cozy family moment is interrupted when Heinrich bursts into the room to announce that footage of an air crash is being broadcast. The other children respond with unthinking excitement, racing off to have a look. Stompanato offers a chilling explanation for all of this, saying that the children are suffering from "brain fade" and therefore "need an occasional catastrophe to break up the incessant bombardment of information."

The most extreme example of this swamping of the human mind by the media comes in the person of Willie Mink, the outlaw scientist who has been secretly supplying Babette with Dylar, an experimental drug she hopes will allow her to escape her fear of death. When Jack finally confronts Mink, he finds a creature completely in the thrall of television. His speech is a sort of high gibberish that seamlessly incorporates strands of narration taken directly from the television he watches constantly. Mink's apparatus of suggestibility has become so intense, so internalized, that Jack only needs to describe a particular event for him to behave as if it is actually happening. "I said to him gently, 'Hail of bullets.' . . . He hit the floor, began crawling toward the bathroom, looking back over his shoulder, childlike, miming, using principles of heightened design but showing real terror, brilliant cringing fear."

Although it would be easy to characterize DeLillo's view of television as a radical and even dismissive critique of the medium, the author's stance is considerably more nuanced than simple "Kill Your TV" rhetoric. In a world bereft of traditional communal activities and systems of belief, the television may be the last source of cultural glue holding people together. Murray, perhaps the novel's most acute observer, accepts a media-dominated world as inevitable and seeks to find the magic and the deeper meaning within the waves and radiation bombarding us. Although his students feel ashamed to come from a generation that has been, in effect, reared by the tube, he counsels them to abandon their guilt. "TV is a problem only if you've forgotten how to look and listen. . . . I tell them they have to learn to look as children again. Root out content. Find the codes and messages." Not only does Murray see television as a source of cultural bonding, but he also understands it as a "primal force in the American home. Sealed-off, timeless, self-contained, self-referring. It's like a myth being born right there in our living room, like something we know in a dream-like and preconscious way." Balancing his enthusiasm is the viewpoint of Babette's father Vernon Dickey, who asks simply: "Were people this dumb before television?"

DEATH

In addition to "Panasonic," DeLillo's other working title for the novel was "The American Book of the Dead," an indication of the centrality of the theme of death in the book. Consciousness of mortality infuses nearly every aspect of *White Noise.* It creates a sense of dread and borderline panic from which no character is immune, no matter what his or her age.

After spending four nights trapped in a mall, an elderly woman named Gladys Treadwell dies of "lingering dread." At another point Babette's infant son Wilder wails for seven uninterrupted hours of sourceless terror. Even a scene as seemingly upbeat as the return of college students to campus is filtered through a prism of impending death. "I have trouble imagining death at that income level," Babette remarks when she is told about the hale, wealthy parents dropping off their children. The realization of death's inevitability stands like a black hole at the center of Jack's otherwise healthy relationship with his beloved wife. "Who will die first?" he asks. Awareness of the inevitable end undermines the ability of nearly all of the novel's adult characters to derive any sort of lasting pleasure or satisfaction from their existences. "Once your death is established," Jack realizes, "it becomes impossible to live a satisfying life." A chilling conversation between Jack and Babette paints an unforgettable image of the impending void.

> "What if death is nothing but sound?" [Babette asks.]
>
> "Electrical noise."
>
> "You hear it forever. Sound all around. How awful."
>
> "Uniform, white."

Death looms inescapably, resisting all attempts to reduce it to an abstraction. As Murray remarks: "We're all aware there's no escape from death. How do we deal with this crushing knowledge? We repress, we disguise, we bury, we exclude." Discussing the course Babette teaches to help her mostly elderly students improve their postures, Jack remarks sardonically that people "seem to believe it is possible to ward off death by following the rules of good grooming." A sizable portion of the frenetic activity going on in DeLillo's America seems designed to help the individual overcome the awareness of his own death. "If we could learn not to be afraid," Jack remarks, "we could live forever." When he hears that Heinrich's friend, Orest Mercator, plans to try to break a world record by spending sixty-seven days locked in a cage with deadly snakes, he is outraged that a person so young could be so blind to the very real possibility of his own demise. "These snakes don't know you find death inconceivable. They don't know you're young and strong and you think death applies to everyone but you. They will bite you and you will die." Ironically, despite his righteous indignation at Mercator's denial of death, Jack develops a remarkably elaborate strategy to combat this terminal knowledge. In this he is joined by Babette, whose role as the novel's most optimistic character cannot inoculate her from the terror of death. Both fail in their attempts to deny death, reminding the reader that even though the awesome power of technology might be able to engulf reality, it cannot overcome the simple dictates of mortality.

Babette's battle against death begins when she enrolls in a secret program run by the shady Dr. Grey (Willie Mink) to test Dylar. The drug cannot of course make the patient immortal, but rather promises to help her lose her fear of death. It is illustrative that, in a novel of simulations, it is Babette's attitude toward a troubling reality that is addressed, rather than the reality itself. After all, the fact of our death does not create dread but rather our consciousness of this fact. The experiment's ultimate failure has less to do with Dylar's ineffectiveness than with Babette's refusal to accept the cost to her humanity, both in terms of side effects such as forgetfulness and also in the destruction of a fundamental aspect of her sense of self—her awareness of her own mortality. As the neurobiologist Winnie Richards points out when Jack asks her about Dylar,

> I think it's a mistake to lose one's sense of death, even one's fear of death. Isn't death the boundary we need? Doesn't it give a precious texture to life, a sense of definition? You have to ask yourself whether anything you do in this life would have beauty and meaning without the knowledge you carry of a final line, a border or limit.

The drug is based on a psychological impossibility—that one can remain human without the knowledge of one's end. "I am able to forget many things but I fail when it comes to death," Babette confesses to her husband. People cannot be cured of the fear of death for the simple reason that they would become something other than human, a point Babette reinforces when she tells Jack that the people at Gray Research could not test the drug on animals because animals do not contemplate death. "No animal has this condition. This is a human condition."

In Jack's case, death enters his life in a much more direct and graphic manner than his wife's lingering sense of dread: his brief exposure to the Nyodene D. gas as his family flees the toxic cloud. The nagging fear of death that has tormented the fifty-year-old teacher suddenly blossoms into the realization that the process of his dying has begun. "I'm tentatively scheduled to die. It won't happen tomorrow or the next day. But it is in the works." At first, Jack turns to science for answers and perhaps a cure, though he discovers only frustration and an increasing sense of anxiety. He visits a clinic ominously named Autumn Harvest Farms but only manages to wind up feeling like a prepackaged product on a terminal assembly line. Numbers, symbols, and jargon are thrown at him, none of them offering him any comfort or contradicting the inevitable. In fact, all that his involvement with the world of high-tech medicine manages to accomplish is to provide him with a temporary sense of alienation from himself. "It is when death is rendered graphically, is televised so to speak, that you sense an eerie separation between your condition and yourself. A network of symbols has been introduced, an entire awesome technology wrested from the gods. It makes you feel like a stranger in your own dying."

He eventually looks for release in a more primitive act—a violent confrontation with his wife's lover. After securing a handgun from his father-in-law, whom Jack mistakenly (but perhaps not so mistakenly) takes for a ghostly emissary of death, he decides to kill Willie Mink. His thinking is starkly simple: by becoming a killer, he will no longer be a victim. Murray states it clearly for him: "Think how exciting it is, in theory, to kill a person in direct confrontation. If he dies, you cannot. To kill him is to gain life-credit. The more people you kill, the more credit you store up." When he shoots the renegade doctor, it is not a straightforward act of marital vengeance, but rather a desperate attempt to transcend his sense of mortality. "Great and nameless emotions thudded on my chest. I knew who I was in the network of meanings. . . . I saw things new. . . . I saw beyond words. . . . I tried to see myself from Mink's viewpoint. Looming, dominant, gaining life-power, storing up life-credit." Of course, his project fails. Realizing that killing Mink will do nothing to mitigate his own mortality, Jack abandons his assault and comes to the assistance of the injured man (even though Mink manages to wound him in turn). Like Babette, he recoils from the loss of humanity that would be required to obliterate the knowledge of death. To be human is to know one is going to die. *White Noise* reminds readers that to forget this means they have become something less than human.

HITLER

Perhaps the most troubling aspect of DeLillo's novel is his use of Hitler. Readers and critics have recoiled from the author's seemingly neutral treatment of a figure about whom there can be little debate. Although one might savor DeLillo's playful stances on television, tabloids, and Elvis Presley, there is a sense that he has gone too far in this case. Hitler was undoubtedly a mass murderer and war criminal. How can he be discussed in the bland, unemotional manner employed by Jack and his associates, who often seem to view him as no different from an entertainer or run-of-the-mill politician? Once this initial shock fades, however, it becomes clear that DeLillo's seemingly offhand use of history's worst criminal in fact serves several serious purposes.

The first is satirical. On the most basic level, DeLillo is parodying the overly specialized, value-neutral world of modern academia, the place where Jack's colleagues in the American environments department "make a formal method of the shiny pleasures they'd known in their Europe-shadowed childhoods—an Aristotelianism of bubble gum wrappers and detergent jingles." Jack's choice of the evil dictator as his subject has nothing to do with any incipient fascist tendencies but rather is little more than a shrewd career move. "I invented Hitler studies in North America in March of 1968. . . . When I suggested to the chancellor that we might build a whole department around Hitler's life and work, he was quick to see the possibilities. It was an immediate and electrifying success." Murray is struck by the canniness of Jack's decision to focus on Hitler without even bothering to consider the ethical ramifications of such a project. "I marvel at the effort. It was masterful, shrewd and stunningly preemptive."

When the two men later undertake their joint lecture, in which Hitler's life is contrasted with that of Elvis, it is as if there were a moral equivalence between a pop singer and the man who oversaw the deaths of millions. The Hitler conference Jack organizes at the College-on-the-Hill could have just as easily been focused upon orchids or the Industrial Revolution.

> Delegates to the Hitler conference began arriving. About ninety Hitler scholars would spend the three days of the conference attending lectures, appearing on panels, going to movies. They would wander the campus with their names lettered in gothic type on laminated tags pinned to their lapels. They would exchange Hitler gossip, spread the usual sensational rumors about the last days in the *fuhrerbunker*. . . . They were cheerful and eager, given to spitting when they laughed, given to outdated dress, homeliness, punctuality. . . . They told Hitler jokes and played pinochle.

The joke, of course, is that Jack and his Hitler-obsessed colleagues are gentle, shambling souls who would have fled in terror if confronted by actual Nazis. Only a seriously skewered environment would allow them to treat the topic in such an offhand manner.

In addition to providing some lively satire of contemporary academia, DeLillo's use of Hitler's image also deepens his vision of the overwhelming power of the electronic media. In the novel, Hitler and the media are connected on a fundamental level. There is something distinctly fascistic in the way television dominates the lives of DeLillo's characters, hectoring and overwhelming their imaginations, just as Hitler sought to dominate those who watched his speeches. And television and film have continued to perpetuate Hitler's image in a way the German army or Albert Speer's monumental architecture never could. DeLillo's point here echoes the central action of an earlier novel, *Running Dog,* which took as its premise the alleged existence of a pornographic home movie shot in Hitler's bunker during his last days. Hitler's penetrating eyes, box-like body and bullying voice seem to have been manufactured for the small screen. No presence is better suited to the commanding power of television. They are a perfect fit. "He's always on," Jack claims at one point. "We couldn't have television without him."

Finally, Hitler plays the same role in Jack's troubled imagination as Dylar does in Babette's—he is a seductive but ultimately false means of conquering death. Of all the presences of the twentieth century, Hitler stands out as the character who tried to rise above his own mortality. The people who followed him were not only bent on world domination—they were thirsting to overcome death itself.

> Many of those crowds were assembled in the name of death. . . . Crowds came to form a shield against their own dying. To become a crowd is to keep out death. To break off from the crowd is to risk death as an individual, to face dying alone."

Just as Babette is on some level aware that taking an untested drug to ward off her anxiety is an act of folly, so Jack understands that using a murderous psychopath as a talisman against death borders on madness. But his dread of death is so intense that any reservations he might have are at least temporarily neutralized. As the ever-insightful Murray points out, "Helpless and fearful people are drawn to magical figures, mythic figures, epic men who intimidate and darkly loom. . . . Some people are larger than life. Hitler is larger than death. You thought he would protect you. I understand completely. . . . you wanted to use him to grow in significance and strength." This explains the dark glasses and black robe Jack wears as he teaches; his desire to learn the "heavy metal" language of German.

The desire for immortality becomes horribly enacted in the novel's climactic sequence, when Jack attempts to murder Willie Mink. The language he uses about his own behavior deliberately echoes the words Murray previously used to describe Hitler. "I advanced into the area of flickering light, out of the shadows, seeking to loom." In his confrontation with death, represented by Mink, Jack seeks to become Hitler, the greatest of killers, the world-historical figure who loomed. Just as with Babette and her wonder drug, however, his humanity causes him to pull back at the last moment, taking the wounded Mink to a nearby hospital for treatment by a group of nuns who turn out, with typically jarring irony, to be Germans.

FAMILIES

Until the publication of *White Noise,* DeLillo was generally viewed as a writer uninterested in depicting domestic life. Marital tensions and family dramas were rare in his work. Children were practically nonexistent—when they did appear, they tended to play minor roles or take such stylized forms as Billy in *Ratner's Star* (1976), a boy genius mathematician who wins the Nobel Prize while still in his early teens.

With *White Noise,* however, DeLillo finally took on family life. The results are characteristically original, but also unexpectedly touching. Even those critics who before (and since) have dismissed DeLillo as a hyper-cerebral fabulist were able to take comfort in his vivid, engrossing, and often hilarious depictions of domesticity.

Although the Gladney household at first looks like a "normal" American family—mother, father, two sons, and two daughters—it is in fact a volatile collection of disparate personalities joined together in a complex web of familial ties. Jack has been married three times before his union with Babette, twice to women with ties to the intelligence community, as well as to a woman who is serving as chief financial officer at an ashram in Montana. He has two children who live with him, Heinrich and Steffie, neither of whom is the child of Babette. In addition, he has at least one more daughter, Bee, who lives with her mother. Babette has been married twice before. Like Jack, she has two children who live in the Gladney household, Denise and Wilder. They have different fathers, neither of whom is Jack. Babette, too, has at least one more child, Eugene, who lives with his father in Australia. With typical comic brio and serpentine invention, DeLillo has presented a model for the contemporary American family that can only be termed "nuclear" if the term is meant to apply to the aftermath of an atomic reaction.

This is not to say that the family lacks emotional cohesion. The Gladneys are, in fact, a singularly intimate unit who spend a great deal of time in close and very lively proximity. Their connection is instinctual, almost spiritual. They shop, eat, travel, and harmlessly squabble, infusing these seemingly mundane activities with a sense of wonder and joy. As Jack remarks, "It was these secondary levels of life, these extrasensory flashes and floating nuances of being, these pockets of rapport forming unexpectedly, that made me believe we were a magic act, adults and children together, sharing unaccountable things."

White Noise is a book in which people are spurred to action by their devotion to family. Babette's decision to start taking Dylar results from her fear of widowhood. After his exposure to Nyodene, Jack understands that "she would be devastated to learn that my death would almost surely precede hers." Jack's decision to assault Willie Mink originates in one of the oldest of dramatic urges—feelings of marital jealousy. "Did they make the bed spin with their lovemaking," he wonders as he prepares himself to shoot his wife's lover. The couple derive intense joy and satisfaction from their various offspring. Babette is a beloved and devoted mother who "gathers and tends the children." The place the children hold in Jack's crumbling belief system is made clear as he watches them sleep in the camp where they take shelter from the toxic cloud.

> Watching children sleep makes me feel devout, part of a spiritual system. It is the closest I can come to God. If there is a secular equivalent of standing in a great spired cathedral with marble pillars and streams of mystical light slanting through two-tier Gothic windows, it would be watching children in their little bedrooms fast asleep.

Jack may be a professor of Hitler studies who has been poisoned by a rare chemical compound, but he is also a normal father who is able to take his daughter Steffie's seemingly inane nighttime babble as "a moment of splendid transcendence . . . I depend on my children for that."

The family proves to be perhaps the last bastion of human reality against the encroaching dehumanization represented by mass media and rampant technology. It is a refuge within the nightmarish modern inferno depicted in *White Noise,* a locus of primitive meaning that stubbornly defies the glut of information created by science. Families invent, and then play by, their own rules. While studying the Gladneys, Murray comes to think that their often hilarious discussions are examples of "the other-worldly babble of the American family." For him, they form "a visionary group, open to special forms of consciousness." Jack wonders if his family is in essence a "fragile unit surrounded by hostile facts" that uses "ignorance, prejudice and superstition to protect [itself] from the world." This is an American family that may gather like many others on Friday night to watch television, but they infuse this seemingly mind-numbing activity with such an antic spirit that they are able to resist the medium's crushing effects, to make watching into a "wholesome domestic sport."

Ultimately, it is the Gladney family's tendency toward anarchy, irrationality, and wild banter that makes it the most real thing in a world where so much is simulation. There is no copy of the family; there are no signs pointing the way toward its inner recesses. Within it, everything is spontaneity, incapable of being processed or deciphered. If the technological world is a place of plane crashes, toxic spills, nuclear waste, and carcinogenic radio waves, then Jack and Babette are glad to leave it at least temporarily behind for their household's fuzzy logic.

> The family is the cradle of the world's misinformation. There must be something in family life that generates factual error. . . . Facts threaten our happiness and security. The deeper we delve into the nature of things, the looser our structure may seem to become. The family process works toward sealing off the world.

SHOPPING

White Noise is glutted with consumerism and consumer goods. The novel's characters are acutely conscious of the fact that they live in a society that bombards them with a superabundance of products and the advertising needed to make these often useless objects desirable. It is notable that on the novel's first page the author meticulously notes the litany of belongings that the College-on-the-Hill's students feel they must have in order to undergo the process of higher education.

> As cars slowed to a crawl and stopped, students sprang out and raced to the rear doors to begin removing the objects inside; the stereo sets, radios, personal computers; small refrigerators and table ranges; the cartons of phonograph records and cassettes; the hairdryers and styling irons; the tennis rackets, soccer balls, hockey and lacrosse sticks, bows and arrows; the controlled substances, the birth control pills and devices; the junk food still in shopping bags—onion-and-garlic chips, nacho thins, peanut creme patties, Waffelos and Kabooms, fruit chews and toffee popcorn; the Dum-Dum pops, the Mystic mints.

This sense of commodity-inundation continues throughout the book. Jack's colleagues seem far less interested in talking about such traditional subjects as Plato or Romanticism than in the artifacts of popular consumer culture—the department head, Alfonse Stompanato, is nicknamed "Fast Food," while Murray complains that some of his colleagues are "full professors . . . who read nothing but cereal boxes." This sense of plenitude extends even to pornography—when Babette asks Jack to read her something saucy, he finds himself able to offer her an almost overwhelming range to choose from. "Pick your century. Do you want to read about Etruscan slave girls, Georgian rakes? I think we have some literature on flagellation brothels. What about the Middle Ages? We have incubi and succubi. Nuns galore."

In this product-charged environment, the supermarket and shopping mall become a sort of consumerist Mecca and Medina, places the characters visit to connect with the culture's deepest spiritual currents. Murray is particularly attracted to the supermarket, where he spends hours walking the aisles, sniffing and fondling the produce, trying to read the codes and auras contained within the ripe fruit and packaged goods. He even goes so far as to claim the supermarket is a portal into another dimension of reality, a place of greater meaning and interconnectedness. "This place recharges us spiritually, it prepares us, it's a gateway or pathway. Look how bright. It's full of psychic data. . . . Here we don't die, we shop. But the difference is less marked than you think."

Although DeLillo is clearly exaggerating for comic effect, Murray's point is a serious one. In a world where materialism and consumerism are crowding out religion and other kinds of traditional spiritual communities, it only makes sense that people search for some sort of mystical solace in the place that has the goods. The supermarket plays the same role in a community that the cathedral did in medieval times. Standing near the center of the city, it is the one site least likely to be allowed to fall into ruin by its parishioners.

> Some of the houses in town were showing signs of neglect. The park benches needed repair, the broken streets needed resurfacing. Signs of the times. But the supermarket did not change, except for the better. It was well-stocked, musical and bright. This was the key, it seemed to us. Everything was fine, would continue to be fine, would eventually get even better as long as the supermarket did not slip.

DeLillo, ever ironic, balances this sense of the supermarket as something holy and pristine with the information that the Nyodene Derivative that poisons the town is a byproduct of some of the very pesticides used to keep the shelves so abundantly stocked.

Like Murray, Jack is able to draw redemptive energy from the act of shopping and, indeed, from simply participating in the capitalist system. At one point, he takes quasi-religious solace from checking his balance at the bank's ATM machine. During a trip to the Mid-Village Mall, Jack is insulted by a colleague, who tells him that he looks harmless without his black robe and dark glasses. In order to regain his sense of manhood and autonomy, Jack decides that a quick dose of consumer activity is in order.

> The encounter put me in the mood to shop. . . . I shopped for its own sake, looking and touching, inspecting merchandise I had no intention of buying, then buying it. . . . I began to grow in value and self-regard. I filled myself out, found new aspects of myself, located a person I'd forgotten existed. . . . I traded money for goods. The more money I spent, the less important it seemed. I was bigger than these sums.

Once again, DeLillo uses a comic set piece to illuminate a world in which self-worth and conspicuous consumption are inextricably combined. Shopping has become the new religion, and products on the shelves are the new icons, providing people with the talismanic strength once inherent in statuary, medallions, and rosary beads. Even those items found in the garbage may serve as religious relics. Jack's search of a compacted trash bag for his wife's discarded Dylar tablets takes on the depth and intensity of an archaeological dig.

> Does [garbage] glow at the core with personal heat, with signs of one's deepest nature, clues to secret yearnings, humiliating flaws? What habits, fetishes, addictions, inclinations? . . . Some kind of occult geometry or symbolic festoon of obsessions. I found a banana skin with a tampon inside. Was this the dark underside of consumer consciousness? I came across a horrible clotted mass of hair, soap, ear swabs, crushed roaches, flip-top rings, sterile pads smeared with pus and bacon fat, strands of frayed dental floss, fragments of ballpoint refills, toothpicks still displaying bits of impaled food.

When Jack finally begins to understand that he truly is facing death, one of his first reactions is to throw away some of his possessions. "I was in a vengeful and near savage state. I bore a personal grudge against these things. Somehow they'd put me in this fix. They'd dragged me down, made escape impossible." Although Jack and especially Murray try to gain a sort of tonic sublimity from the abundance and technology surrounding them, their positive attitudes eventually give way to an even more basic feeling—dread. "The greater the scientific advance," Jack realizes, "the more primitive the fear."

Although Jack is temporarily able to prop himself up with the giddy feeling that all of these products (and the technology that produces them) stem from a powerfully ordered system, he eventually realizes that there is no reason to think this order is benign. It is only when he undertakes an act of violence that he truly connects with the ghost in the machine. "I sensed I was part of a network of structures and channels," he claims as he approaches Willie Mink's hotel room. "I knew the precise nature of events. I was moving closer to things in their actual state as I approached a violence, a smashing intensity."

THE AIRBORNE TOXIC EVENT

Another terrible byproduct of rampant technology and consumerist glut is a natural environment that is becoming increasingly, even pervasively, toxic. *White Noise* brims with noxious elements. And it is not just the usual culprits—the nuclear power plants and suppurating chemical factories—that poison the ecosystem; the smoke stacks and sewer pipes and car exhausts are to blame as well. Everything either pollutes or is polluted. Even the most benign aspects of the landscape around the seemingly placid town of Blacksmith ooze toxicity.

Heinrich has no interest in watching the beautiful view out of his sister's window because he feels that "there was something ominous in the modern sunset," its brilliant oranges and intense luminosity created by chemicals released into the atmosphere. His concerns are later reinforced when Jack notices that, after the Nyodene D. leak, "the sunsets had become almost unbearably beautiful." In an earlier conversation with his father, Heinrich's sensitivity to rampant pollution is shown to be so acute that he even doubts that the wet drops splashing on the windshield are what they seem. "You're so sure that's rain," he says to his father. "How do you know it's not sulfuric acid from factories across the river? How do you know it's not fallout from a war in China?" Even when toxins are discovered, their source remains difficult to establish.

> They had to evacuate the grade school on Tuesday. Kids were getting headaches and eye irritations, tasting metal in their mouths. A teacher rolled on the floor and spoke foreign languages. No one knew what was wrong. Investigators said it could be the ventilating system, the paint or varnish, the foam insulation, the electrical insulation, the cafeteria food, the rays emitted by microcomputers, the asbestos fireproofing, the adhesive on shipping containers, the fumes from the chlorinated pool, or perhaps something deeper, finer-grained, more closely woven into the basic state of things.

Of course, the most radical source of pollution in the novel is the "airborne toxic event" that occurs when a railroad tanker car is punctured near Jack's home. Although DeLillo is too agile a novelist to let objects and events stand as straightforward symbols for his themes, there is a sense that the noxious cloud the Gladney clan flees represents a future in which toxicity is no longer localized and abnormal, but instead has become a foundation of the planet's environment. The Gladneys can run, but they cannot hide. The billowing black cloud seems to spring as much from the lingering dread Jack, Babette, and the children have developed in the face of technology as it does from the ruptured skin of a railroad car. The days are long gone when chemical leaks will affect only "people who live in mobile homes out in the scrubby parts of the county, where the fish hatcheries are." From now on, catastrophe will be an event in which every family must participate.

STYLE

The central concerns of *White Noise*—death, pollution, adultery, and dehumanizing technology—might suggest a style that is dour, even oppressive. Despite the urgency and at times deadly seriousness of the novel's central themes, it is still a deeply comic work. From his morbidly funny dialogue to his deadpan descriptions of treacherous events, DeLillo uses a deep, wide-ranging irony to provide a running commentary on the novel's vivid action.

One of the primary locations of humor in the novel is in its dialogue, which at times reaches the giddy vaudevillian absurdity of an Abbott and Costello skit. The discussions among the members of the American environments department are marvelous set-pieces, ranging in topics from where each professor was when James Dean died to which B-movie actor has had the deepest influence on their lives. Hilarious in themselves, these symposiums also illustrate DeLillo's assertion that the American imagination is becoming increasingly colonized by media imagery. The conversation between Jack and Heinrich, in which the father presses his son to tell him if he believes it is raining or not, is also typical of the way the author uses humor to introduce his themes, in this case the vanishing line between illusion and reality.

> "Rain is a noun [Jack says]. Is there rain here, in this precise locality, at whatever time within the next two minutes that you choose to respond to the question?"
>
> "If you want to talk about this precise locality while you're in a vehicle that's obviously moving, then I think that's the trouble with this discussion."
>
> "Just give me an answer, okay, Heinrich?"
>
> "The best I could do is make a guess."
>
> "Either it's raining or it isn't," I said.
>
> "Exactly. That's my whole point. You'd be guessing. Six of one, half dozen of the other."
>
> "But you *see* it's raining."
>
> "You see the sun moving across the sky. But is the sun moving across the sky or is the earth turning?"

Although nearly every character speaks with an ironical tone, the author's primary instrument of irony is his narrator's laconic voice. With Jack Gladney, DeLillo has created a thoroughly modern consciousness. His flat, often affectless commentary on the novel's catalog of death and disaster enables the author to state his themes in language that is direct; it also fits naturally into the novel's narrative flow. Jack is a supremely self-conscious character, able to experience the world with graphic immediacy while simultaneously commenting on these observations. His voice provides a running commentary on the novel while participating in—and occasionally redirecting—the course of events.

Even the most fundamental and intimate of his actions elicit commentary, such as his reaction when he listens to Babette give examples of the sort of dirty talk she does *not* find erotic. "I began to feel an erection stirring. How stupid and out of context." When Babette tells Jack about her adultery, his ironic self-awareness reaches its deepest level. "I felt a sensation of warmth creeping up my back and radiating outward across my shoulders. Babette looked straight up. I was propped on an elbow, facing her, studying her features. When I spoke finally it was in a reasonable and inquiring voice—the voice of a man who seeks genuinely to understand some timeless human riddle." Remarkably, DeLillo has managed in this passage to create a fictional consciousness that is experiencing sexual jealousy, aware that it is experiencing sexual jealousy, and able to comment on how it is expressing both the emotion and the awareness of it. Even when Jack is engaged in the act of attempted murder, he cannot help but provide the reader with a running analysis of his state of mind.

> I continued to advance in consciousness. Things glowed, a secret life rising out of them. Water struck the roof in elongated orbs, splashing drams. I knew for the first time what rain really was. I knew what wet was. I understood the neurochemistry of my brain, the meaning of dreams (the waste material of premonitions). Great stuff everywhere, racing through the room, racing slowly. A richness, a density. I believed everything.

Perhaps nowhere is DeLillo's narration better able to achieve this balancing act of pure descriptive immediacy and framing analysis than in the unforgettable description of the toxic cloud that seems to be literally chasing the Gladney family.

> Through the stark trees we saw it, the immense toxic cloud, lighted now by eighteen choppers—immense almost beyond comprehension, beyond legend and rumor, a roiling bloated slug-shaped mass. It seemed to be generating its own inner storms. There were cracklings and sputterings, flashes of light, long looping streaks of chemical flame. The car horns blared and moaned. The helicopters throbbed like giant appliances. We sat in the car, in the snowy woods, saying nothing. The great cloud, beyond its turbulent core, was silver-tipped in the spotlights. It moved horribly and sluglike through the night, the choppers seeming to putter ineffectually around its edges. In its tremendous size, its dark and bulky menace, its escorting aircraft, the cloud resembled a national promotion for death, a multimillion-dollar campaign backed by radio spots, heavy print and billboard, TV saturation.

Up until that last sentence, the description is immediate in the best tradition of realist fiction, using metaphor ("slug-shaped") and simile ("like giant appliances") to create a verbal picture and appeal to the senses. But then, in the final sentence, DeLillo breaks out of his descriptive narrative to once again have Jack's controlling intelligence point the reader toward a deeper meaning. The standard advice to novice fiction writers is to show and not tell. In this astonishing sequence, and indeed throughout *White Noise,* DeLillo is able to do both.

There are only two occasions in Jack's narrative where his stance of self-conscious irony gives way to something exclusively immediate. The first is when he speaks about his children. Here, the tone becomes gentle, affectionate, startlingly sincere. The second are the eruptions of products' names that emerge from him without context. In both cases, the author is able to heighten the effect of these utterances by having his narrator abandon his normal self-lacerating awareness. Some things—in this case, the love of a parent for a child and the saturation of the mind by mass media—escape the grasp of even the most acute consciousness.

IMPORTANCE AND INFLUENCE

Although there is a strong temptation to read *White Noise* as a devastating satirical critique on American consumerism and mass media, this interpretation, while partially valid, cannot sustain any comprehensive understanding of the novel. The book's importance stems from its insistence that the basic human search for meaning and wonder continues, even though Tintern Abbey has been replaced by Stop & Shop and *The City of God* by the *National Enquirer.* In an interview given in 1988, DeLillo made it clear that White Noise was no simple diatribe against modern culture but rather an attempt to find transcendence in a compromised and hostile environment. It is, he claimed, about "the importance of daily life and of ordinary moments. In *White Noise* . . . I tried to find a kind of radiance in dailiness. Sometimes this radiance can be almost frightening. Other times it can be almost holy or sacred." Novelists working after the book's publication have been put on warning—it is not only the writer's job to report on the dehumanizing absurdity of modern life, but also to chart the progress of the human soul as it searches for meaning among the pollution and the machines.

This point is brought home in the novel's concluding chapter, in which the wry, deadpan narrative of the first thirty-nine chapters evolves into action that is almost reverential. First, young Wilder mounts his plastic tricycle to undertake a "mystically charged journey" across a busy highway in which he miraculously avoids being harmed. Death, it seems, does not always have its day. Next, Jack describes going to the highway's overpass with Babette and Wilder to join the crowds watching the astonishingly beautiful sunsets. Toxicity still imbues the atmosphere, but so does unspeakable beauty. Finally, after telling his doctor that he no longer wants to know about his upcoming death, Jack visits that holiest of places, the supermarket, only to discover that the "shelves have been rearranged. It happened one day without warning. There is agitation and panic in the aisles, dismay in the faces of older shoppers." For a brief moment, before technology can return to provide solace and re-establish order "with holographic scanners, which decode the binary secret of every item, infallibly," the human beings are on their own amid all the merchandise. These three images provide fitting finale for a novel whose importance is as a reminder that "American magic and dread" continue to remain beyond the reach of even the most powerful technologies and dehumanizing myths.

Select Bibliography

EDITIONS

White Noise. New York: Viking, 1985.

White Noise. New York: Penguin Books, 1986. (This is the edition quoted in this essay.)

White Noise: Text and Criticism. Viking Critical Library. Edited by Mark Osteen. New York: Penguin, 1998.

White Noise. Penguin Great Books of the 20th Century. New York: Penguin, 1999.

OTHER WORKS BY DeLILLO

Americana. Boston: Houghton Mifflin, 1971.

Ratner's Star. New York: Knopf, 1976.

Running Dog. New York: Knopf, 1978.

Mao II. New York: Viking, 1991.

The Body Artist. New York: Scribners, 2001.

SECONDARY WORKS

Baker, Stephen. *The Fiction of Postmodernity.* Edinburgh: Edinburgh University Press, 2000. (Contains on excellent chapter on *White Noise.*)

Begley, Adam. "Don DeLillo: The Art of Fiction CXXXV." *Paris Review* 35 (fall 1993): 274–306.

Conroy, Mark. "From Tombstone to Tabloid: Authority Figured in *White Noise.*" *Critique* 35 (winter 1994): 97–110.

Cowart, David. *Don DeLillo: The Physics of Language.* Athens: University of Georgia Press, 2002.

DeCurtis, Anthony. "An Outsider in this Society." *South Atlantic Quarterly* 89 (spring 1990): 280–319. (An unusually revealing interview with DeLillo.)

Duvall, John N. "The (Super)Marketplace of Images: Television as Unmediated Mediation in DeLillo's *White Noise.*" *Arizona Quarterly* 50 (autumn 1994): 127–153.

Hantke, Steffen. *Conspiracy and Paranoia in Contemporary American Fiction: The Works of Don DeLillo and Joseph McElroy.* Frankfurt: Peter Lang, 1994.

Howard, Gerald. "The American Strangeness: An Interview with Don DeLillo." *Hungry Mind Review* 43 (fall 1997): 13–16.

Keesey, Douglas. *Don DeLillo.* New York: Twayne, 1993.

Kerridge, Richard, and Neil Sammels, eds. *Writing the Environment: Ecocriticism and Literature.* London: Zed, 1998. (Contains an illuminating chapter on *White Noise.*)

LeClair, Tom. *In the Loop: Don DeLillo and the Systems Novel.* Urbana: University of Illinois Press, 1987.

Lentricchia, Frank, ed. *Introducing Don DeLillo.* Durham: Duke University Press, 1991. (An essential introduction to the author's work by the leading DeLillo scholar.)

———, ed. *New Essays on* White Noise. New York: Cambridge University Press, 1991.

Osteen, Mark. *American Magic and Dread: Don DeLillo's Dialogue with Culture.* Philadelphia: University of Pennsylvania Press, 2000.

Passaro, Vince. "Dangerous Don DeLillo." *New York Times Magazine,* May 19, 1991, pp. 36–38, 76–77.

Pifer, Ellen. "The Child as Mysterious Agent: Don DeLillo's *White Noise.*" In her *Demon or Doll: Images of the Child in Contemporary Writing and Culture.* Charlottesville: University Press of Virginia, 2000. Pp. 212–232.

Remnick, David. "Exile on Main Street." *The New Yorker,* September 15, 1997, pp. 42–48.

Ruppersburg, Hugh M., and Tim Engles, eds. *Critical Essays on Don DeLillo.* Boston: G. K. Hall, 2000.

Salzman, Arthur M. "The Figure in the Static: *White Noise.*" *Modern Fiction Studies* 40 (1994): 807–826.

Weinstein, Arnold. *Nobody's Home: Speech, Self, and Place in American Fiction from Hawthorne to DeLillo.* New York: Oxford University Press, 1993.

Sherwood Anderson's
Winesburg, Ohio

JASON GRAY

WINESBURG, OHIO (1919), Sherwood Anderson's third book of fiction after two moderate successes, became the foundation for the era of modern literature that was to follow. Hailed by many as a significant influence upon writers such as Ernest Hemingway, William Faulkner, Raymond Carver, and Joyce Carol Oates, the book was exemplary for its artistry of style and for its deviance from the traditional "O. Henry" short story type of the day; that is, a series of building dramatic actions told in sequential order leading to a climax and moral resolution. In ways, the book was the birth of a new form: the novel-in-stories. While described as a book of short tales, *Winesburg* does have a central hero, George Willard. George is the link between many of the stories (he appears in seventeen of the twenty-two). George's eyes are often the eyes of the reader, and he is the character who undergoes the most radical change in the book.

The achievement of *Winesburg* seemed to come out of almost airy nothing. Anderson's first two novels, *Windy McPherson's Son* (1916) and *Marching Men* (1917), while hailed by a few at the time of their initial publication, are considered by many today to be nowhere near the quality of what followed. Anderson did not seem to be stepping up a ladder as he wrote, but rather taking an express elevator to the top. Irving Howe muses, "From Anderson's Elyria work to the achievement that is *Winesburg* there is so abrupt a creative ascent that one wonders what elements in his Chicago experience, whether in reading or personal relations, might have served to release his talents."

Winesburg is the story of a town struggling out of its innocence, out of its pretensions of innocence, into a new century. The industrial revolution is rafting up Wine Creek. Anderson confronts religion, sexuality, psychological abuse, and personal independence all within these slim tales.

THE BOOK OF THE GROTESQUE

Anderson begins his book with a short prologue called "The Book of the Grotesque." The title comes from a fictional book by a fictional and aging author about whom Anderson tells a story. Presumably the narrator of the piece is Anderson. This old author is not necessarily a citizen of Winesburg, so why does Anderson mention him? Anderson is using this device as the filter through which he wants the reader to see his characters. It is a statement of artistic philosophy and the method he has chosen to make the world understand his ideas.

What is a grotesque? The reader must look beyond its contemporary meaning of something merely gross or detestable. The word comes from figures that were once painted on grottoes (hence, grotesque), and the figures were often distorted in some manner, though not necessarily made ugly. Anderson uses distorted figures to represent distorted ideas. The author of the prologue has this theory:

> That in the beginning when the world was young there were a great many thoughts but no such thing as a truth. Man made the truths himself and each truth was a composite of a great many vague thoughts. All about in the world were the truths and they were all beautiful. . . . There was the truth of virginity and the truth of passion, the truth of wealth and of poverty, of thrift and of profligacy, of carelessness and abandon.

The author of "The Book of the Grotesque" goes on to claim that when people started plucking these truths for their own and became obsessed with living according to one particular "truth," they became grotesque; that is, their obsessions distorted them into one particular manner, and they were unable to flex back into a human shape. Perhaps Anderson wrote his book to understand his grotesques. In the preindustrial small town in Ohio where he grew up, Anderson may have observed how some of its citizens tried to cling to certain ideas, while others challenged the status quo. From the vantage point of a writer at middle age, he no doubt understood that other little towns like his own were being pulled forward into the new century at that same time. In *Winesburg, Ohio,* Anderson describes the truths that such towns took as their own even as these truths are bumping into others still floating in the air.

This is a book of loneliness. Anderson presents readers with portrait after portrait of lonely people striving to find what is inside of themselves. They are people who cannot communicate or get out the thing that twists inside of them. As much as they are distorted on the outside—and almost every character who is a subject of these tales is described as malformed in some way—each character is just as misshapen within. For example, Dr. Parcival in "The Philosopher"

> was a large man with a drooping mouth covered by a yellow mustache. . . . His teeth were black and irregular and there was something strange about his eyes. The lid of the left eye twitched; it fell down and snapped up; it was exactly as though the lid of the eye were a window shade and

CHRONOLOGY

1876	Born September 13 in Camden, Ohio, to Irwin M. and Emma Smith Anderson.
1884	Family moves to Clyde, Ohio, the main model for *Winesburg, Ohio.*
1900	Anderson moves to Chicago to become a copywriter for an advertising firm.
1912	Suffers a nervous breakdown and leaves his position as head of a paint company in Elyria, Ohio.
1914	Publishes first short story, "The Rabbit-Pen."
1915	Begins writing the *Winesburg* stories. Returns to Chicago.
1916	*Winesburg* stories begin to appear in magazines. *Windy McPherson's Son* published.
1917	*Marching Men.*
1918	*Mid-American Chants.*
1919	*Winesburg, Ohio.*
1920	*Poor White.*
1921	*The Triumph of the Egg.* Receives the first *Dial* Award for contribution to American writing.
1923	*Many Marriages; Horses and Men.*
1924	*A Story Teller's Story.*
1925	*Dark Laughter.*
1941	Becomes ill on a trip to South America. Dies of peritonitis on March 8 in Colón, Panama.

someone stood inside the doctor's head playing with the cord.

Dr. Parcival is haunted by his failings and feelings of inferiority to his brother, who made money but never shared it and hated the doctor and his mother. Parcival is convinced one needs to despise others to be superior, and he tries to impress this notion upon George. But really he is afraid that he is nothing. He adds nothing to society, refuses to help a dead girl even though he advertises himself as a doctor, and is certain the townsmen will hang him, that he will be "uselessly crucified"—uselessly indeed, for he will be no one's savior.

The people of Anderson's Winesburg are all suffering from their own "truth," meaning their own obsessions, which have a hold over them. Every story pits a character's truth—that is, a character's absolute that has distorted and kept him or her from being a whole person—against a challenge that the character either overcomes or does not. The Reverend Hartman in "The Strength of God," for example, wants nothing more than "to do the work of God quietly and earnestly," but he must confront his desire to view the body of Kate Swift from the safety of his bell tower, as a voyeur.

COMMUNICATION

Communication is also a key theme in the book. The townsfolk are haunted by their failings and are hungry to communicate something of their condition to someone. None of the characters, however, has an easy time saying what he or she really wants to say. But the person to whom many of them do talk, profusely even, is George Willard. He is their true confessor, although he has no power to absolve them.

In addition, *Winesburg, Ohio* is preoccupied with contact, the physical act of communication, as is shown by the numerous occurrences of the word "hands." The people of Winesburg often talk to one another by touch, and it is no surprise, then, that the book's first story is called "Hands." Because of the evenness of tone and style throughout the linked stories (which gives weight to the idea of this book as a novel), one story does not stand out from another, as one might expect in a more assorted collection. However, it is this first story that sets the tone for what follows.

The story of Wing Biddlebaum, "Hands" provides readers with an introduction to the town and to the themes that will soon be discovered. Wing is an outsider; Anderson begins his tales on the outskirts of town and works his way in, almost like a stranger walking into town. Formerly Adolph Myers, a schoolteacher in Pennsylvania, Wing has come to Winesburg to live with his aunt. As a teacher he had been falsely accused of sexually molesting one of his students, a "half-witted" boy who "imagined unspeakable things and in the morning went forth to tell his dreams as facts." What caused the boy to dream such "unspeakable things" was Wing's use of his hands. "In a way the voice and the hands, the stroking of the shoulders and the touching of the hair was a part of the schoolmaster's effort to carry a dream into the young minds."

Wing means no harm to the boys of his school. Yet because of the "half-witted boy," he is nearly hanged by the men of the town who are certain of his guilt. The owner of the saloon beats him with his "fists," and one night a mob forms outside Wing's home. One of the men holds "a rope in his hands."

Wing is both a grotesque and a victim of grotesques. His hands are barely controllable, but they impart dreams and wisdom. In Winesburg he works as a berry picker, and he is an extremely good one. But even though his hands bring him profit, he is looked upon as a freak. What once were the carriers of dreams now are used for common labor.

SEXUALITY

Winesburg is a rural community, a God-fearing community. Despite the onset of modern technology, the town still has the glaze of premodern harmony. Often, though, it is this innocence—"innocence" in a broad sense—that the characters are forced to abandon. Many characters, George included, must confront their sexual innocence, or an intangible innocence that gets confused with sex. But Anderson is also writing about an innocence of knowledge, about one's rightful place in the world, and about the innocent idea that our dreams can be had for nothing.

In "Adventure" poor Alice Hindman, whose "head was large and overshadowed her body," is in love with Ned Currie. Anderson physically distorts Alice only slightly, but the distortion is there. He goes on to write, "She was very quiet but beneath a placid exterior a continual ferment went on." She and Ned become lovers "in the dim light." Ned tells her, "Now we will have to stick to each other." Ned wants to go to Cleveland, and Alice says she will go with him and live with him: "Don't marry me now. We will get along without that and we can be together." Alice here is ahead of her time, but Ned will have none of it and wants to do things the way society dictates. And yet he never comes back.

Alice clings to the hope of his returning for her, putting aside new suitors because she believes she could never marry another man, until one night the loneliness causes her to snap. "Why doesn't something happen? Why am I left here alone?" she asks herself, and her desire to be loved compels her to run naked out into the rain. She has broken the hold Ned has on her and wants to "find some other lonely human and embrace him." But her cries literally fall on deaf ears. The man she stumbles upon cannot hear and does not understand her, and her bid for freedom fails. She runs home, hides beneath her covers, weeps "broken-heartedly," and reproaches herself: "What is the matter with me? I will do something dreadful if I am not careful." This choice of "careful" is a deliberate echo of the prologue and the truth of "carefulness and abandon." Alice, for a brief moment, broke free of her innocence, but the love she ventured upon the world was not returned, and she retreated again, likely for good.

George Willard has a series of sexual adventures throughout the book. Four stories contain moments of intimacy with various girls and women of the town. It is in the first story, "Nobody Knows," that George has sex for the first time, and in the other three stories his attempts are always thwarted. This is a sophisticated move on Anderson's part. Intercourse is not what actually makes George an adult; rather, his unfulfilled desires are what he learns from the most.

When "Nobody Knows" opens, George is understandably nervous: he has been sent a letter from Louise Trunnion saying "I'm yours if you want me," and he is considering having sex for the first time. After "looking cautiously about" all day in the office of the *Winesburg Eagle,* he finally sets himself to the moment. "There had been no decision. He had just jumped to his feet," Anderson writes. "He did not dare think." He goes off to find Louise Trunnion. When he finally coaxes her to join him in the Williams' barn, he thinks, because he only "wanted to touch her with his hand," that he is "not very bold." In his nervousness a "flood of words burst" forth from him. He is, in some ways, still a boy and not ready for sex. But inspired by his recollection of the letter she had sent him earlier, in which she had written "I'm yours if you want me," he "became wholly the male."

George convinces Louise to have sex with him. "There won't be anyone know anything. How can they know?" They sit down on the boards by a berry field (an Anderson nod to the Edenic passing of knowledge) and have sex. In the aftermath George wanders around the town, buys a cigar, and talks to Shorty Crandall. Anderson writes, "He had wanted more than anything else to talk to some man."

The story ends with George repeating to himself the idea he first used to convince Louise it was all right, that nobody would know anything about what happened between them. He is delighted to feel inducted into the world of men, yet at the same time he hopes that no one will find out what he has done. He is on the edge of two truths, of holding on to his innocence like a good boy, and of being a "man"—another truth that is trapping. He is ambivalent toward the truth of the loss of his sexual innocence, unready to make up his mind about which role to play.

In "The Teacher," George becomes entangled with Kate Swift, his former schoolteacher. The day after he goes to get a book from her that she wants him to read, he recalls: "For the fourth or fifth time the woman had talked to him with a great earnestness and he could not make out what she meant by her talk. He began to believe she might be in love with him and the thought was both pleasing and annoying."

Anderson describes Kate Swift as a woman whose "complexion was not good and her face was covered with blotches." However, the night after loaning George the book, Kate is out walking on a cold, snow-filled night, and Anderson adds, "Alone in the night in the winter streets she was lovely." In further description, he makes it clear that her mind is extraordinarily active and that she is a passionate person: "In fact, she was the most eagerly passionate soul among them."

On this snowy night Kate's mind is "ablaze with thoughts of George Willard" because she has recognized a "spark of genius and wanted to blow on the spark." She wants to help her former student become a great writer. The previous summer, she tried to teach him what it means to be a writer, how difficult it is, and warned him that he "must not become a mere peddler of words." Then, on the night he came to borrow the book, something else happened between them:

> As he turned to go she spoke his name softly and with an impulsive movement took hold of his hand. Because the reporter was rapidly becoming a man something of his man's appeal, combined with the winsomeness of the boy, stirred the heart of the lonely woman. A passionate desire to have him understand the import of life, to learn to interpret it truly and honestly, swept over her. Leaning forward, her lips brushed his cheek.

During her walk, she visits George, who is alone in his office at the *Winesburg Eagle.* There, her passion to impart something further of meaning to him takes hold of her, but her needs as a woman come forward. They embrace. She strikes against him and flees. George is left confused. Later, unable to sleep, George thinks, "I have missed something Kate Swift was trying to tell me." In this story the desire to share knowledge and understanding becomes confused with sexuality, and the ability to communicate is lost. Kate cannot make George understand what it is she wants him to know, and George is not quite able to receive the message, though his apprehension that something was trying to be passed to him is a step in the right direction.

"An Awakening" gives George a taste of his own medicine. In his first encounter with Louise Trunnion, he was the user, and now Belle Carpenter will use him. He has been walking about the streets of the town with Belle, who "had a dark skin, grey eyes and thick lips. She was tall and strong. When black thoughts visited her she grew angry and wished she were a man and could fight someone with her fists." Belle is actually in love with a bartender named Ed Handby but has kept it a secret because she does not think he would fit her station. She lets George kiss her to provide relief from her desires for Ed.

George, boasting to the boys in the pool hall, declares "that the fellow who went out with a girl was not responsible for what happened." The reader can almost see the memory of Louise flood George's brain. But one night when George goes looking for Belle, he gets the feeling that he is being used and does not like it.

When he finds her, he tells her, "You've got to take me for a man or let me alone. That's how it is."

As George is about to have his way with Belle, Ed Handby appears from the bushes and "with a quick wide movement of his arm he sent the younger man sprawling away into the bushes and began to bully the woman." George keeps trying to get the man to beat him instead of just pushing him aside, but to no avail. Belle and Ed leave him alone with his humiliation, and he makes his way home, "wanting to get quickly out of the neighborhood that seemed to him utterly squalid and commonplace."

George learns a complex lesson. He can be used by a woman in a sexual capacity, which was once deemed to be a masculine endeavor. He can be bested by another, shattering the privileged position in which he holds himself. Even the place where he lives and in which he seemed so sure of himself—where the lovers walk about in the darkness—can be exposed as "squalid" when the light of understanding breaks through.

It is not until George comes to love Helen White that he starts to understand something about growing up. His first thoughts of her occur in "The Thinker," Seth Richmond's story, when he wants to love her simply to be in love so that he can write a love story. But in "Sophistication" George and Helen have their final and most fruitful encounter. Before this occurs, however, George sees himself for the first time in a larger context:

> From being quite sure of himself and his future he becomes not at all sure. If he can be an imaginative boy, a door is torn open and for the first time he looks out upon the world, seeing, as though they marched in procession before him, the countless figures of men who before his time have come out of nothingness into the world, lived their lives and again disappeared into nothingness. The sadness of sophistication has come to the boy.

George knows that he will die, as his mother has just died, and "with all his heart he wants to come close to some other human, touch someone with his hands. . . . He wants, most of all, understanding." This is the very thing Kate Swift wished for him, and Helen White is the girl he thinks can provide it for him. "He had tried to make her think of him as a man when he knew nothing of manhood and now he wanted to be with her and to try to make her feel the change he believed had taken place in his nature." How different from the earlier George, who already believed himself to be a man and boasted about it. The two walk together into the darkness. Although they kiss and embrace, they do not have sex but wrestle and paw at each other like children. "Mutual respect grew big in them," Anderson writes, and they walk home in "dignified silence. . . . They had for a moment taken hold of the thing that makes the mature life of men and women in the modern world possible."

What George and Helen gain from this moment is that the shift into adulthood is not achieved by anything corporal, but by their knowledge of their places alongside each other in the context of humanity, as two lonely individuals in the same dark place. Without a single positive marriage or male-female relationship in the book, it seems that this is all that is possible to Anderson—the understanding that everyone is lonely. Loneliness is the one thing, ironically, in which no one is alone. George and Helen share their aloneness together, and their recognition of this fact will lead to their individual ability to live in the world without becoming grotesques.

The Reverend Curtis Hartman has a sexual crisis to deal with, too. One night he finds himself preparing his Sunday sermon in the bell tower of the Presbyterian church and discovers, through the window that features a "design showing the Christ laying his hand upon the head of child," Kate Swift lying on her bed across the street, reading. It is only the barest bit of neck and shoulder the minister sees, but still it is enough to shake his faith. It is interesting to note that she is reading here. She is not engaged in some sexual activity, but something intellectual. This is probably what makes it all the more tantalizing for Hartman at first. They are both reading, he from his Bible, she from her choice.

The minister "was not one to arouse keen enthusiasm among the worshippers," and he "sometimes suffered prolonged periods of remorse because he could not go crying the word of God in the highways and byways of the town." This is Hartman's "truth." He believes that to be an effective preacher for the Lord, one must be an evangelical. But it is not in his character to be so effusive. So he suffers doubt yet continues to go about his work quietly; that is, he does so until confronted with the temptation of watching Kate Swift when she is alone in her bedroom.

Hartman's experience with both women and temptation has been limited. Despite his hope to remain free of the desire to watch Kate from his bell tower, he eventually breaks a corner out of the window so he can continue to see her. Then he asks God, "Why now should I be tempted? What have I done that this burden should be laid on me?" As his willpower lessens and God does not come to his aid, he decides that he will not repair the window to avoid temptation but will "sit in the presence of this woman without raising my eyes. I will not be defeated in this thing." When the burden gets the better of him, he decides that because he cannot beat it, he will "utterly give way to sin" and "look at the woman and . . . think of kissing her shoulders." Hartman decides that if he cannot resist sin, he will move to the city.

When Hartman goes up again into the tower to feast his eyes freely for the first time, he does not see Kate as he expects to see her. She is completely naked and *praying.* She looks to him like the Christ in the broken window. He finds now "in the thing that happened what he took to be the way of life for him." Hartman has an epiphany. His soul was not on trial, but rather he was being prepared for "a new and more beautiful fervor of the spirit." Ecstatic, he marches into the office of the *Winesburg Eagle* and declares this to George Willard.

Hartman is able to transmute his sexual desire for Kate Swift into a means of inspiration and thereby overcomes his difficulty. The image of a soul in a desperate situation appealing to God has reminded him of his faith and the reason he has dedicated himself to the ministry, the suffering of his fellow humans. Hartman's struggle with sexual desire is actually a struggle with his intangible faith, and it corresponds to another significant "truth" explored in the book, the truth about religion.

RELIGION

The story of Jesse Bentley and his progeny, the four-part "Godliness," is at odds with the rest of the text. Considered as a whole, it is longer than any of the other stories and relies more closely on chronology. To understand Jesse, Anderson writes, we have to go to a time when "the figure of God was big in the hearts of men." The youngest of a group of sons, Jesse had originally planned to be a Presbyterian minister. Instead, he takes over the family farm and invests all of his energy, and all of the energy of those around him, into making it the premier farm in the area. Jesse is a "fanatic," obsessed, and "he began to think of himself as an extraordinary man, one set apart from his fellows. He wanted terribly to make his life a thing of great importance." Jesse Bentley is possessed, but not with the fervor of God, which is what he wants. He is held by his desire for material gain, for vast tracts of land, which he equates with being a leader of the Israelites. In the amassing of land and wealth, and not in any swelling of the soul, he feels God's munificence. When he wants God to manifest himself, it is not to feel him in his soul, but to see him in a burst of light and a rumble of thunder. He wants to experience the powerful God of the Old Testament, a God whose bigness is not unlike the bigness of the flashy new machines that so fascinate Jesse.

His cry to God at the end of part one to grant him a son, a David to his Jesse, comes from a "fantastic impulse." It is not actually born out of religious fervor or faith but rather out of his dwelling in fantasy and his own megalomania. As one of Anderson's most delightful, smooth, and instructive transitions, the second part of "Godliness" opens, "David Hardy of Winesburg, Ohio was the *grandson* of Jesse Bentley, the owner of Bentley farms" (emphasis added). Immediately the reader knows the answer to Jesse's prayer—that he has been denied a son.

Jesse twice tries to show God to his grandson. The first time, David is a young boy and the grandfather's muttering and crazy eyes frighten him. When David is older, Jesse tries to make manifest the Lord to his grandson by making a sacrifice. He wants this act to open a pathway for the boy, and indeed it does. David is so frightened that he runs off into the woods and never sees Winesburg again. Jesse finds himself Goliath after all these years. The critic Rosemary M. Laughlin, in *The Merrill Studies in "Winesburg, Ohio"* (1971), puts it this way:

> Jesse Bentley . . . has taken for truth the belief that material prosperity and rugged individualism are the formula for God's blessings and for mystical communication with Him . . . By his own admission at the end, his folly alone has brought about the loss of the thing he treasured most, his grandson, David.

He realizes that his greed has kept him from God—not only his material greed, but also his greed for God. "Do not put the Lord your God to the test," Jesus said, and Jesse is doing just that in trying to make God show himself.

Jesse, in all his desire for God, offers little of the comfort to others that one might expect from a man of God. The only moment of true religious comfort actually comes to David from his mother, Louise, when he is brought home after having run away.

> David thought she had suddenly become another woman. He could not believe that so delightful a thing had happened. With her own hands Louise Hardy bathed his tired body and cooked him food. . . . Her habitually dissatisfied face had become, he thought, the most peaceful and lovely thing he had ever seen. . . . He thought that he would have been willing to go through the frightful experience a thousand times to be sure of finding at the end of the long black road a thing so lovely as his mother had suddenly become.

Louise, at least momentarily, is changed from the bitter woman that her father's harsh rule and her unhappy marriage have made of her to a loving, Christlike figure. She bathes her son, feeds him, inspires in him as a light at the end of the tunnel.

Moments like these occur sporadically throughout the book. True religious sensation is rare and usually not direct. Wing Biddlebaum, at the end of his story, kneels and picks up bread crumbs off the floor, resembling "a priest engaged in some service of his church." God, in Anderson's view, is never manifest in the grand old ways but in the redeeming movements of his sympathetic characters.

"Godliness," besides being a tale of religious misunderstanding, is also a story about modernization.

> It will perhaps be somewhat difficult for the men and women of a later day to understand Jesse Bentley. In the last fifty years a vast change has taken place in the lives of our people. A revolution has in fact taken place. The coming of industrialism . . . A farmer standing by the stove in the store in his village has his mind filled to overflowing with the words of other men. . . . Much of the old brutal ignorance that had in it also a kind of beautiful childlike innocence is gone forever.

This passage describes the dichotomy of the town's innocence. The old age where everything was innocent had a lot of terror to it as well. But the approaching modern age is not perfect either.

In Winesburg it is not Nietzsche saying "God is dead" that causes a loss of innocence, but rather a brand-new machine tiller. Anderson's association of modernization with the loss of God is actually quite traditional, and through Jesse's understanding that God abandoned him because of his greed, the author seems to be saying that the new world to come is not the blessing it may appear to be, nor is the loss of God a good thing.

There has been some debate about the appropriateness of Jesse's stories in terms of the collection as a whole because readers lose sight of George Willard for a lengthy period of time, and because Jesse Bentley is nothing like the other denizens of Winesburg. Irving Howe, in his essay "The Book of the Grotesque," opines that "Godliness" is out of sync with the rest of the book and "a failure in any case." But with only two stories directly relating to religion (the other being "The Strength of God") there is the possibility that the two have a bearing on each other.

Joseph Dewey suggests that where religion fails in Jesse Bentley, it succeeds as art in George Willard. Jesse's attempts at communion with God come to naught, but there are other ways to practice this human need for connecting with other souls. "Lovingly," Dewey writes, "George Willard, gradually educated into this power of communion, will come to gather the fragments of Winesburg's shattered souls and will give compassionate expression to that agony. In such a humane gesture there is a wondrous sort of religion.... Winesburg, then, must have its failed prophet to underscore the religious dimension of George Willard's commitment to art."

This idea is supported by the other religious tale, "The Strength of God," and its intersection with "The Teacher," a story that is very important in George's maturation. These two stories are the only two in the book to share time spans and overlapping events. Here art is connected to religion. Although George fails to understand what Kate, his "preacher," has told him, he has learned, at least, that there is something he does not know, and that he must find out what it is.

DREAMS

What the people of Winesburg most often have trouble communicating is their dreams. It is a town full of dreamers, though most of their dreams have been repressed for one reason or another. It is the old author of "The Book of the Grotesque" that is the first dreamer. His dream of the grotesques, and of letting the young thing inside of him out and yet never doing so, launches the book.

Many of the stories about dreaming focus on George, whose dream of becoming a writer and leaving the town dominates the book. Advice about his dream comes first from Wing Biddlebaum, who tells George:

> You are destroying yourself. . . . You have the inclination to be alone and to dream and you are afraid of dreams. You want to be like others in town here. You hear them talk and you try to imitate them. . . .You must begin to dream. From this time on you must shut your ears to the roaring of the voices.

Characters throughout the book expel their secret thoughts to George for their own benefit or for his. He is sometimes the receptacle for unfulfilled desires. This is shown clearly in "Mother." Elizabeth Willard, George's mother, has been physically twisted by her life. Anderson describes her as "tall and gaunt and her face was marked with smallpox scars. Although she was but forty-five, some obscure disease had taken the fire out of her figure." Her dream of love has twisted her internally as well. But she is determined not to let the same fate befall her son.

> If I am dead and see him becoming a meaningless drab figure like myself, I will come back. . . . I ask God now to give me that privilege. I demand it. I will pay for it. God may beat me with his fists. I will take any blow that may befall if but this my boy be allowed to express something for us both.

Elizabeth overhears her husband, Tom, speaking to George one night, telling his son to "wake up" because he is lost too much in his own world. She sees this as a threat to her boy and decides to kill her husband if she must, although she does not go through with that. What quiets her is the appearance of George in her room, assuring her that he is going to leave Winesburg. Her agony is only for a time relieved. In the story titled "Death," she is unable to share with her son something else of importance, the money her father left her.

The story of Wash Williams, "Respectability," is a cautionary tale for George. Wash's "girth was immense, his neck thin, his legs feeble. He was dirty. Everything about him was unclean. Even the whites of his eyes looked soiled," Anderson writes, but, "He took care of his hands." For, after all, Wash is the town telegraph operator, the man who must literally rely on his hands to communicate. George learns Wash's story one night after he has been out walking with Belle Carpenter. Wash tells him, "It is because I saw you kissing the lips of that Belle Carpenter that I tell you my story. . . . I want to put you on your guard. Already you may be having dreams in your head. I want to destroy them."

Wash has been betrayed by his wife, and to him all women are dead. In his hatred for women, and in conjunction, his pity for all men—because "every man let his life be managed by some bitch or another"—he has shut himself off from everyone. He is, it turns out, afraid to be touched because he still loves his wife, even though he knows nothing would be the same if he took her back. He tells George that once he "ached to forgive and forget," and that he went to see her, feeling that if she would only touch him he would "perhaps faint away." Her standing before him naked and apart, yet refusing to touch him, destroyed any thought of reconnection and has buried that dream inside him forever. He does not want George to turn out like him.

Enoch Robinson tells his tale to George for the same reason in "Loneliness." Enoch acts as a foil for George: he is an artist who returned to Winesburg after going to the city to develop his talent and ending up mad. Enoch "never grew up and of course he couldn't understand people and he couldn't make people understand him. The child in him kept bumping against things, against actualities like money and sex and opinions." Although old enough to live in the city, Enoch was too much a child to be able to talk to the artist friends he had over to his room and express to them what his paintings were trying to show. So he invented people that he could talk to when he was alone. He did manage to marry and have children, but eventually he returned to the privacy of his room and to the companions he invented. But a woman who lived in his building kept visiting him. He thought she was too "grown up" for him. He was both attracted to her and afraid of her. When he tried to tell her about his feelings, he said "terrible things" to her, and sent her away. As he confesses to George, "She took all of my people away."

What Enoch's tale reveals to George is that one cannot remain a child and be an artist. Enoch was never able to understand his peers, and his art reflected that. That he thinks George will understand this idea compels him to tell the story to the boy. Although Anderson does not reveal George's reaction, George hears Enoch's chilling sentence, "It was warm and friendly in my room but now I'm all alone," as he leaves the old man, and he must take it to heart.

One of the few times dreams seem to be bad for George is in "The Thinker," where Seth Richmond, his rival for Helen White, is another foil for George. Anderson writes, "The idea that George Willard would some day become a writer had given him a place of distinction in Winesburg, and to Seth Richmond he talked continually of the matter." Seth finds George boring, and he is disgusted with George's idea that because he has been trying to write a love story, he should fall in love. George's target is

Helen White. Seth says to himself, "The busy fool with his love stories . . . why does he never tire of his eternal talking?" George is now the one who blusters about, and Seth becomes the actor, approaching Helen White much the way George will do later and impulsively telling her that he is going to leave town: "Everyone talks and talks. . . . I'm sick of it. I'll do something, get into some kind of work where talk don't count. Maybe I'll just be a mechanic in a shop. I don't care much. I just want to work and keep quiet." How reminiscent this is of Reverend Hartman. However, Seth does nothing of the sort. He broods that Helen and George will turn out like everyone else, foolish and talkative, and he recedes into the background. What George learns here is the importance of action. Dreams will enrich your life and give you something to live for, but you must then make them a reality. Seth does not do this here, and neither does George, although he ultimately will.

"It wasn't Tom I wanted, it was marriage," says Elizabeth Willard in "Death." The people of the town always want something they cannot seem to get and take something in its stead that then destroys their original dream. George, throughout his involvement in the town, has been negotiating with life to keep his dreams intact. He learns that he cannot become one who just explodes uncontrollably ("Perhaps I'd better quit talking," George says in "Sophistication") but must grow up while not growing indifferent to the young thing inside him as the old man of the prologue does. He must live his dreams so that he does not end up clutching at some youngster like himself and, with wild eyes and disheveled hair, torture his mouth with his story over and over. George escapes Winesburg, and on the train he wakes to find the town "had disappeared and his life there had become but a background on which to paint the dreams of his manhood."

CRITICAL INTERPRETATIONS

Since its first publication *Winesburg, Ohio* has brought praise for Anderson, but it has also brought criticism. At its publication, some questioned its quality based on false assumptions. For example, the anonymously written *New York Sun* review of the book ran like this:

> Write the *Spoon River Anthology* in long hand, leave out its subtlety and humor, change its simplicity to crudity, replace inspiration with determination, take from it, in other words, all of those intangible qualities which make it great instead of disgusting, and you will have Sherwood Anderson's *Winesburg, Ohio.*

This and other reviews tried to see the book only as a *Spoon River* knockoff, a poor attempt at realistically portraying midwestern life. Its good reviews, however, included those by Maxwell Anderson and H. L. Mencken.

Overall, criticism of *Winesburg, Ohio* has not focused so much on the book's quality but on what the book is and what it is trying to do. The standard view (and the view taken here) is that Anderson is presenting a series of grotesques set in motion by the old writer in his prologue, and that these characters gather around the figure of George Willard and help him achieve his maturity, both artistically and emotionally. But there are those who argue that the prologue has very little to do with the book. Dale Kramer has said that the initial story "has little bearing on what follows." And Irving Howe, in his thoughtful essay "The Book of the Grotesque," declares:

> The one conspicuous disharmony in the book is that the introductory 'Book of the Grotesque' suggests that the grotesques are victims of their willful fanaticism, while in the stories themselves grotesqueness is the result of an essentially valid resistance to forces external to its victims.

But that is not entirely true. Elizabeth Willard is not resisting anything in her story; in fact, she is giving in. Rather than escaping, she decides to marry Tom, whom she does not really love, because she thinks she wants marriage, the kind the other girls in Winesburg have. Before understanding what it is she truly wants, she entraps herself, and her failed desire becomes the only thing in the world to her. And the not having it eats her until "some obscure disease had taken the fire out of her figure." Nor does Louise Bentley resist. After espying her future sister-in-law making out with her boyfriend, "It seemed to her [Louise] that to be held tightly and kissed was the whole secret of life." But when she engages herself to John Hardy, she realizes, "That was not what she wanted but it was so the young man had interpreted her approach to him, and so anxious was she to achieve something else that she made no resistance." Louise succumbs to the idea of marriage even though it is not what she really wants, and she spends her life bitter at never discovering what it is she does want.

What is perhaps most challenging about the book is its form, and much critical attention has been focused on this issue. The form of the stories is unlike anything seen before its time in America. Anderson comments on his hatred of plot-driven stories in *A Story Teller's Story* (1924):

> There was a notion that ran through all story telling in America, that stories must be built about a plot and that absurd Anglo-Saxon notion that they must point a moral, uplift the people, make better citizens, etc. . . . 'The Poison Plot,' I called it in conversation with my friends as the plot notion did seem to me to poison all story telling. What was wanted I thought was form, not plot, an altogether more elusive and difficult thing to come at.

Indeed, though there is plot in the stories—a few things happen in an order—it is precisely his use, or non-use, of sequential order that displays his feelings on this subject. Anderson's stories rely more on impression than plot, on a combination of detail and psychological probing. They can almost be seen as a series of *tableaux vivant.* The stories are not something one could plot on a Freytag Pyramid to show a clear rising and falling action. Frank Gado, in his introduction to Anderson's *The Teller's Tales* (1983), describes the author's method:

> In his scheme, the story resides not in events or even solely in the relationship between the teller and the thing narrated but in its being told. Although sequentiality is an inescapable quality of narrative, in Anderson the sequence of particulars responds to an urgency quite independent from the usual chronological impulse.

Anderson is fond of shifting time at seemingly strange places. For instance, in "Mother" Anderson begins in the present discussing the state of Elizabeth Willard and her relationship with her son. Readers are privy to a certain conversation of theirs, and then in the next paragraph, they read: "One evening in July . . . Elizabeth Willard had an adventure." After overhearing her husband give her son advice she does not agree with, she plots to kill her husband, whom she has hated for years. But George comes into her room later and stops her by engaging her in a conversation, which turns out to be the same conversation they were having at the beginning of the story. This is an odd circularity that is peculiar to Anderson.

His characters were what mattered to Anderson. Plot would have been a betrayal to these people. Anderson noted in his memoirs:

> What is wanted is a new looseness; and in *Winesburg* I have made my own form. There were individual tales but all about lives in some way connected. By this method I did succeed, I think, in giving the feeling of the life of a boy growing into young manhood in a town. Life is a loose flowing thing. There are no plot stories in life.

The characters in *Winesburg* are real people, and plots don't happen to them; events of a sort happen, but not plots.

"Having abandoned the traditional novel form, Anderson unified the book by using recurring images to function as leitmotivs," writes Robert Allen Papinchak. For example, the characters make their discoveries in the dark or in dim light in all but five of the stories. Papinchak goes on to say, "Just as George Willard collects the separate truths of the people of Winesburg to produce his own worldview, the reader who recognizes how the recurring images work comes away from the book with the same sense of wholeness."

Just as with images, certain key words are repeated: "hands," for instance, appears more often than anything else. As stated earlier, the hands are the way the people of Winesburg communicate with each other. As the critic Walter B. Rideout suggests, "The possibility of physical touch between two human beings always implies, even if by negative counterpart, at least the possibility of a profounder moment of understanding between them." The repetition of images and the repetition of words almost always work together. For instance, Elizabeth Willard reminisces about her days as a young girl, remembering how her suitors, "in the darkness under the trees . . . took hold of her hand and she thought that something unexpressed in herself came forth and became a part of an unexpressed something in them." Each time one of these symbols is used, another layer of gold lacquer is applied, and the weight and shine of the symbol increases. Anderson builds his greater tale out of the many in this way and still maintains the "looseness" he so desired.

Though it is not a novel, it is difficult not to see *Winesburg, Ohio* as a bildungsroman. Not intended as such by Anderson, at least not directly in the manner of *Great Expectations,* it still does work that way. George Willard learns throughout the stories about language, about love, about other people. He, in effect, learns to become a writer. The development of his writerly manner begins with "The Thinker," where he merely fantasizes about the adventurous life, and continues with Kate Swift's scolding of him and her attempt to make him understand how hard a life he has chosen. Another strain of learning for George is his sexual development. The four stories mentioned previously delineate his growth in that area, from the pure physical passage of "Nobody Knows" to the more "sophisticated" learning process he undergoes with Helen White. Both strains of learning are joined in the final story, "Departure," when he succeeds in leaving Helen White and Winesburg behind him and heads to the city to continue his dreaming.

Alongside the question of form, critics have also debated whether *Winesburg* is a product of realism or naturalism. Both were vogue styles of the time, but David D. Anderson suggests:

> The categories of realism or naturalism are unsatisfactory as an examination of Anderson's technique and theme shows clearly. Anderson is not expounding the theory of a universe of mechanistic forces operating on his people as the term naturalism would indicate, but he is showing the essence of their humanity. Neither does he depend for effect upon the constant and careful accumulation of sharply drawn detail in the tradition of realism, but rather he sketches, he implies, he insinuates, and he reveals insights in order to arrive at delineation of character and of situation that is inward rather than external.

Early critics were unsure what to make of this series of sketches of small town life. The book was immediately compared with Edgar Lee Masters' *Spoon River Anthology* and Sinclair Lewis' *Main Street.* Grouped with Masters and Lewis as writers who were "revolt[ing] from the village" (or rejecting the myth of small town America's happiness and harmony), Anderson would seem to be following the method of realism, but as the unusual form of the stories shows, something different is at work in *Winesburg.* Walter B. Rideout states that Anderson was "not a realistic writer in the ordinary sense. With him realism is a means to something else, not an end in itself." He also suggests comparing Anderson's description of the drugstore on Main Street with Sinclair Lewis' Gopher Prairie drugstore: Anderson does not detail each item in the store, but merely names the store and goes on, allowing the reader to fill in the gaps. Reality to Anderson is best sketched in or left abstract so that one can see more easily beneath the surface. "Fidelity to background is after all only a kind of photography and photography is seldom art. It was Anderson's treatment of character, his intuitive perception and sympathy in portraiture, which won him quick recognition and which will ensure him permanent attention," writes John T. Flanagan about the work.

That these two approaches to *Winesburg*, reality and naturalism, have been debated, and continue to be debated, is a mark of distinction for the work. That it defies classification and still elicits attempts to understand it assures the book's position as an American classic.

The stories of *Winesburg* and a handful of others are the only parts of Anderson's work that have received fairly constant praise. Many of his novels and his poetry have for the most part, for better or worse, been discounted. But *Winesburg*'s impact on American writing was and is still very significant. He has been counted as an influence upon the bulk of American authors after him. "Hemingway was regarded as his disciple in 1920," writes Malcolm Cowley in his introduction to the Penguin Twentieth-Century Classics edition of *Winesburg, Ohio*, and Faulkner was "for a time, his inseparable companion." About Anderson, Faulkner had said, "I learned that, to be a writer, one has first got to be what he is, what he was born." Cowley quotes Thomas Wolfe as saying that Anderson was "the only man in America who ever taught me anything."

Sherwood Anderson, in *Winesburg, Ohio*, pushed the boundaries of what a short story could be, of what literature could be, by inserting a lyrical intensity into a prose landscape dominated by realism and by uncovering a view of humanity not seen before. *Winesburg, Ohio* is a beautiful and poignant book. The depth of humanity within it is astounding. Anderson's characters experience dreadful suffering, and some manage visions of joy. In their lonely wanderings in the night, they will continue to exhilarate lovers of good literature and to compel critics to reread.

Select Bibliography

EDITIONS

Winesburg, Ohio. New York: B. W. Huebsch, 1919.

Winesburg, Ohio: Authoritative Text, Backgrounds and Contexts, Criticism. Edited by Charles E. Modlin and Ray Lewis White. New York: W. W. Norton, 1996. (This edition is cited in the text. Several other editions are also available. The Norton edition includes reviews from the *New York Sun,* Maxwell Anderson, and H. L. Mencken.)

Sherwood Anderson's Winesburg, Ohio: *With Variant Readings and Annotations.* Edited by Ray Lewis White. Athens: Ohio University Press, 1997.

OTHER WORKS BY ANDERSON

A Story Teller's Story: The Tale of an American Writer's Journey through His Own Imaginative World and through the World of Facts, with Many of His Experiences and Impressions among Other Writers—Told in Many Notes—in Four Books—and an Epilogue. New York: B. W. Huebsch, 1924.

Sherwood Anderson's Memoirs. New York: Harcourt, Brace, 1942.

The Teller's Tales. Selection and introduction by Frank Gado. Schenectady, N.Y.: Union College Press, 1983.

SECONDARY WORKS

Anderson, David D. *Sherwood Anderson: An Introduction and Interpretation.* New York: Holt, Rinehart and Winston, 1967.

———, ed. *Critical Essays on Sherwood Anderson.* Boston: G. K. Hall, 1981.

Burbank, Rex J. *Sherwood Anderson.* New York: Twayne, 1964.

Cowley, Malcolm. Introduction to *Winesburg, Ohio,* by Sherwood Anderson. New York: Penguin, 1992. Pp. 1–15.

Dewey, Joseph. "No God in the Sky and No God in My Self: 'Godliness' and Anderson's Winesburg." *Modern Fiction Studies* 35 (1989): 251–259. (Reprinted in the 1996 Norton critical edition of *Winesburg, Ohio.*)

Faulkner, William. "A Note on Sherwood Anderson." In Essays, Speeches and Public Letters by William Faulkner. Edited by James B. Merriwether. New York: Random House, 1965.

Howe, Irving. *Sherwood Anderson.* New York: William Sloane, 1951. (See especially his essay titled "The Book of the Grotesques," pp. 91–109.)

Laughlin, Rosemary M. "'Godliness' and the American Dream in *Winesburg, Ohio.*" In *The Merrill Studies in "Winesburg, Ohio,"* compiled by Ray Lewis White. Columbus, Ohio: Charles E. Merrill, 1971. Pp. 52–60.

Papinchak, Robert Allen. *Sherwood Anderson: A Study of the Short Fiction.* New York: Twayne, 1992.

Rideout, Walter B., ed. *Sherwood Anderson: A Collection of Critical Essays.* Princeton, N.J.: Prentice-Hall, 1974.

Small, Judy Jo. *A Reader's Guide to the Short Stories of Sherwood Anderson.* Boston: G. K. Hall, 1994.

Townsend, Kim. *Sherwood Anderson.* Boston: Houghton Mifflin, 1987.

White, Ray Lewis, ed. *The Achievement of Sherwood Anderson: Essays in Criticism.* Chapel Hill: University of North Carolina Press, 1966.

———, comp. *The Merrill Studies in* Winesburg, Ohio. Columbus, Ohio: Charles E. Merrill , 1971.

Index

Roman numbers refer to volumes. Arabic numbers in boldface type refer to subjects of essays.

A Complete Listing of Authors in AMERICAN WRITERS